HARVARD EAST ASIAN SERIES 15

China and the West
1858–1861

THE ORIGINS OF THE TSUNGLI YAMEN

The East Asian Research Center at Harvard University administers research projects designed to further scholarly understanding of China, Korea, Japan, and adjacent areas.

Distributed in Great Britain by Oxford University Press, London

Preparation of this volume was aided by a grant from the Carnegie Corporation. The Corporation is not, however, the author, owner, publisher, or proprietor of this publication and is not to be understood as approvng by virtue of its grant any of the statements made or views expressed therein.

Publication has been aided by a grant from the Ford Foundation

Library of Congress Catalog Card Number 64-13419

Printed in the United States of America

China and the West
1858–1861

THE ORIGINS OF THE TSUNGLI YAMEN

Masataka Banno

HARVARD UNIVERSITY PRESS

Cambridge, Massachusetts

1964

HARVARD EAST ASIAN SERIES

FOR MY PARENTS

Acknowledgments

I should like to express my profound gratitude to Dr. Toshio Ueda, formerly my research supervisor at the University of Tokyo's Tōyō Bunka Kenkyūjo (Institute for Oriental Culture). His warm encouragement pulled me out of the intellectual uncertainty in which I had been groping. He strongly urged me to return to research. This is how, some twelve years ago, I started my study of the origins of the Tsungli Yamen. I am extremely grateful to Professor John King Fairbank, without whose unsparing sympathy and advice I should not have been brave enough to develop my previous articles, in Japanese, into the present book. He was also kind enough to edit an earlier draft of the introduction and the first two chapters. I wish most earnestly to thank Mrs. Elizabeth MacLeod Matheson, a superb editor, for her untiring efforts in improving my whole manuscript.

For scholarly help and inspiration I am particularly indebted to Hsin-pao Chang, Shinkichi Etō, Chao-ying Fang, Jack Gerson, Immanuel C. Y. Hsü, Chūzō Ichiko, Mark Mancall, Masao Maruyama, Jun Matsumura, Ichisada Miyazaki, Po-ch'un Sun, Chūsei Suzuki, the late Sei Wada, Mary C. Wright, Lien-sheng Yang, and Toshihiko Yazawa.

For access to unpublished records I am indebted to the National Archives in Washington, D.C., the British Museum and the Public Record Office in London, the Archives of the French Foreign Office in Paris, and the Institute of Modern History of Academia Sinica in Taipei. Unpublished Crown-copyright material in the Public Record Office has been reproduced by permission of the Controller of H.M. Stationery Office. Grateful acknowledgment is made to Lord Bruce for his kind permission to consult and use transcripts of documents in his family archives in Scotland. The transcripts were originally made by Mr. Jack Gerson. Thanks are also due to Dr. Joseph Lewis Sullivan for permitting me to see and cite his Harvard doctoral thesis on Murav'ev's activities in Siberia.

For all the research facilities extended to me I wish to thank the librarians and staffs of Tōyō Bunka Kenkyūjo and Tōyō Bunko (the Oriental Library) in Tokyo, the Hoover Library at Stanford, the Chinese-Japanese Library of the Harvard-Yenching Institute and Widener Library, both at Harvard University.

For typing assistance I am obliged to the secretarial staff of Harvard University's East Asian Research Center.

For the time to pursue my research abroad I am indebted to Tokyo Metropolitan University, Tōyō Bunko, the Rockefeller Foundation, the Ford Foundation, and the East Asian Research Center.

This book is dedicated to my parents. I hope I partake, if only a bit, of my father's perseverance and my mother's imagination.

Tokyo Metropolitan University
September 26, 1963
on the seventy-seventh birthday
of my father, Shinjiro Banno.

                                     Masataka Banno

Contents

China and the West
1858–1861

Introduction: Ch'ing Management of Foreign Relations Prior to the Arrow War

China's diplomatic history after the Opium War was a complex and long-drawn process of resistance and adaptation to the Western state system, into which she had been forcibly drawn.

As a result of the Arrow War, the Tsungli Yamen or "Office for General Administration" of China's foreign relations was established in Peking early in 1861 to be a central organ for foreign affairs and deal with the Western diplomats who now, for the first time in China's history, were to take up permanent residence in the capital. The establishment of the Yamen was a turning point in China's foreign relations. It made an institutional change in her conduct of foreign affairs, ending the traditional principle of inequality between the Chinese empire and all other states, which had been institutionalized in the tribute system. It did not, however, signify either the end of China's resistance or the completion of her adaptation to the modern state system based on rivalry and coexistence among sovereign and equal states. It was but one step, though certainly a very important step, in a continuing process.

The establishment of the Tsungli Yamen had been made possible by a new and precarious balance of domestic political forces, created by a shift in power distribution in Peking — a shift that itself was directly attributable to an extraordinary circumstance, the intrusion of Anglo-French troops into the metropolitan area; therefore the operation of the Yamen was fated from the outset to be greatly affected by any eventual change in this balance of domestic forces.

This book is a study of diplomatic institutions, ideas, and activities as they intervened between domestic politics and foreign affairs. China's climactic resistance to the West in the late 1850's

and her final submission to *force majeure* in 1860 were accompanied
by an intricate interplay of these domestic and foreign influences,
which led to the eventual establishment of the Tsungli Yamen.[1]
Before going into a detailed treatment of them, we will briefly review the institutional framework of Sino-Western relations prior to
the Arrow War.

BEFORE THE OPIUM WAR

China before the Opium War (1840–1842) would not recognize
any other state as equal to herself. Foreign relations were viewed
as part of an hierarchical order consisting of "China at the center"
(Chung-hua) and "barbarians on the periphery" (*i* or *i-ti*). Foreign
nations were treated as "tributary states" (*ch'ao-kung-kuo*) incorporated into a world order based on this hierarchical distinction.[2]
Consequently China had no institutional organ corresponding to a
foreign office in a modern state, which presupposes the existence of
a state system based on interdependence among equal sovereign
states.

Since 1757 maritime trade by foreign ships in China had been
limited to the single port of Canton. Western powers participating
in this Canton trade were under the jurisdiction of the Reception
Department of the Board of Rites, one of the Six Boards (Liu-pu)
in Peking, and belonged to the same category of tributary states as
Korea, Liu-ch'iu, or Siam.[3] In Canton, foreigners had suffered various kinds of restrictions in trade and in everyday life. They could
communicate with the provincial or local authorities only through
the hong merchants, who were privileged to handle the foreign
trade, and only in the form of a petition (*ping*) symbolizing inequality. This formula of communication became one of the crucial
issues between Britain and China after the abortive effort in 1834
of Lord Napier (the first chief superintendent of trade assigned to
China after the British East India Company's monopoly of the
China trade was abolished) to establish direct communication with

the governor-general of Kwangtung and Kwangsi, who resided at Canton.

Russia was in contact with China through overland trade on China's northwestern frontiers. Russian relations were under the jurisdiction of the Department of Outer Mongols of the Court of Dependencies (Li-fan-yuan) in Peking, which managed the tributary relations with the frontier tribes in the north and west, mainly the Mongols. There were also two imperial agents at Urga (K'u-lun pan-shih ta-ch'en), who were "in charge of frontier affairs concerning Russia." [4] Unlike other Western powers, Russia had an establishment in Peking called the Russian Hostel (E-lo-ssu kuan), assigned to her by the Chinese government. The Russian Ecclesiastical Mission, whose members were limited to four Russian Orthodox priests and six language students, was allowed to be stationed there, and Russian representatives or caravan merchants also used to stay there on their occasional visits to Peking. However, this was a quite different matter from the residence of diplomatic representatives as practiced in the modern state system.[5]

Representatives sent to China by Western powers were expected to adhere to the regulations governing tribute missions, which were set forth in the Collected Statutes (*Ta-Ch'ing hui-tien*): (1) the frequency of tribute was specified for each tributary state — for instance, some states sent missions once every two years; (2) the point of entry and departure in China, and the route to be followed by a tribute envoy between this place and Peking were specified for each tributary state; (3) the size of every tribute mission was specifically determined for each tributary state; (4) the arrival of a tribute envoy at the place of entry was reported by the provincial authorities to the emperor, and the Board of Rites memorialized on his arrival at the capital; (5) upon his arrival at the capital, the envoy presented a memorial (*piao*) through the Board of Rites, performing a full kowtow of three kneelings and nine knockings of the head (*san-kuei chiu-k'ou-li*); (6) tribute was presented (the objects and quantities of tribute were specified for each tributary state); (7) an

audience was given by the emperor, in which the kowtow was performed; (8) imperial gifts were bestowed upon the prince (*kuo-
wang*) of the tributary state and upon the tribute envoy and his
retinue, again to the accompaniment of the kowtow (kinds and
quantities of gifts were specified for each tributary state); (9) the
expenditures incurred during the tribute envoy's stay in China were
paid by the Chinese government; (10) any emergency or accident
occurring to a tribute mission, say the death of the envoy, was taken
care of by the Chinese government; (11) an escort provided by the
Chinese authorities accompanied a tribute envoy on his trip to and
from the capital.

Of this entire procedure the most humiliating element to Westerners was the performance of the kowtow in an imperial audience.
In Western eyes the kowtow was the most striking symbol of the
sinocentric negation of equality, which underlay all Chinese institutions in their dealings with foreigners. Thus the performance of
the kowtow was refused by Western envoys whenever equality was
an issue. In particular, the kowtow became a major diplomatic
issue after its performance was positively rejected by Lord Macartney when he came to China in 1793, incarnating in his person the
national dignity of Britain and representing also British industry's
demand for new markets. The kowtow problem was to play an
important role in the coming protracted conflict between old China
and the modern international order, headed by British military
power and trading interests.[6]

AFTER THE OPIUM WAR

Treaty Stipulations, and the Imperial Commissioner in Canton

The treaties signed in 1842–1844 between China and the Western
powers were "equal treaties" insofar as the treaty-making procedures
and the formulation of treaty texts were concerned. Furthermore,
these treaties prescribed a direct formula of communication between
the Chinese and Western authorities, abolishing the former indirect
formula with the hong merchants as intermediaries. Thus there were

clauses concerning the forms of correspondence on terms of equality between the Chinese and foreign authorities (Article 11 of the British Treaty of Nanking, Article 30 of the American Treaty of Wang-hea, and Article 33 of the French Treaty of Whampoa); concerning interviews and correspondence, on terms of equality, between foreign consular officers and Chinese local authorities in the treaty ports (Article 4 of the Treaty of Wang-hea, and Article 4 of the Treaty of Whampoa); and concerning intercourse on terms of equality between commanders of foreign warships arriving at a Chinese port and the local Chinese authorities (Article 32 of the Treaty of Wang-hea). However, there was no mention in these treaties of a foreign diplomatic representative visiting Peking or of his having an imperial audience or residing permanently in the capital. With respect to contact between foreign authorities and the Peking government, there were stipulations only about the transmission to the court in Peking, through certain specified channels, of communications from a foreign government (Article 31 of the Treaty of Wang-hea and Article 34 of the Treaty of Whampoa), and stipulations about direct correspondence, on terms of equality, between a foreign diplomatic representative and the Chinese high officials at the capital (Article 11 of the Treaty of Nanking, and Article 33 of the Treaty of Whampoa).

There was no indication, in the Treaty of Nanking in 1842 or in the Supplementary Treaty of Hoomun Chai in 1843, as to what kind of organ would be established for managing foreign affairs under this new treaty system or where it would be located. However, direct official intercourse came to be established between foreign diplomatic representatives stationed in Hong Kong or Macao and the governor-general of Kwangtung and Kwangsi, who resided in Canton and was given the status of imperial commissioner (*ch'in-ch'ai ta-ch'en*).

In 1842, after the Treaty of Nanking was signed, I-li-pu, one of the Manchu negotiators in Nanking, was appointed imperial commissioner and Canton Tartar-general and went to Canton to negotiate with the British on the implementation of the new treaty.[7]

When I-li-pu died in Canton in 1843, Ch'i-ying (Kiying), then
governor-general of Kiangnan and Kiangsi residing in Nanking,
who had been the imperial commissioner when the treaty was
signed, was again named imperial commissioner and went to Canton to take over the negotiations.[8] Later in the year, after completing
this mission, Ch'i-ying returned to his post at Nanking and his title
as imperial commissioner was withdrawn.[9] In March 1844 he was
transferred to Canton as governor-general.[10] In April he was made
imperial commissioner in charge of managing "post-war trade affairs in the various provinces" (ko-sheng t'ung-shang shan-hou
shih-i). The immediate reason for this appointment was the impending arrival of Caleb Cushing, American plenipotentiary, for
treaty negotiations.[11] Thereafter, however, the governors-general at
Canton were consecutively in charge of foreign affairs, with the
title of imperial commissioner.[12]

In actuality, from 1844 until the Arrow War (1857–1860) the
Canton imperial commissioner (Kuang-tung ch'in-ch'ai ta-ch'en)
functioned as the officer exclusively in charge of foreign affairs.[13]
In theory this post was to be held only temporarily and concurrently
with the main post of governor-general. In other words, besides
acting as the highest official in two provinces, responsible for their
domestic civil and military administration, the governor-general of
Kwangtung and Kwangsi was supposed to conduct foreign affairs,
which were in fact mainly related to the foreign trade at the five
treaty ports. It was, of course, inevitable that he should be greatly
affected in his thinking and actions by his consideration for local
provincial matters.[14]

The Canton imperial commissioner was under the immediate
control of the emperor. But Canton was the most remote from
Peking of the five new treaty ports. It took at least fifteen days for
one-way communication between Canton and Peking by the official
postal service.[15] Stationed at such a distance the Canton imperial
commissioner thus operated as a "buffer"[16] or "breakwater"[17] to
keep foreign representatives away from the capital.

As a high provincial official, the imperial commissioner was in a very unstable position *vis-à-vis* the central government in Peking; he could be impeached, recalled, disgraced, or punished at any time. This situation could not fail to make the imperial commissioner hyperconscious of the superiority of Peking over Canton. Thus his reports to the emperor tended somewhat to distort facts and conceal truth.[18] This in turn tended to complicate any dealings between China and a foreign nation by creating problems of communication and even misunderstanding.

The actual methods used by the Canton imperial commissioners differed greatly, depending upon the political forces which influenced them. After the Opium War, the office functioned comparatively smoothly as a channel of the conciliatory policy, so long as Ch'i-ying served as commissioner. He was closely connected with Grand Councillor Mu-chang-a, who held the real power in Peking and had led the peace party at the time of the Opium War. The foreign policy of Mu-chang-a and Ch'i-ying, however, was essentially a variation of the "barbarian management" strategy, and its aim was to preserve as far as possible the established regime (*t'ien-ch'ao ting-chih*).[19] In the background there was an antiforeign mood in Peking officialdom and among the literati and officials generally throughout the empire, and in Canton there was a violent antiforeign movement. Consequently the policy of conciliation within the framework of "managing the barbarians" rested on an extremely precarious equilibrium maintained by the influence of Mu-chang-a's clique, by the skillful maneuvering of Ch'i-ying, and by the persisting memory and fear of British military strength.

In 1850, when the Tao-kuang emperor died and the Hsien-feng emperor ascended the throne, a political change occurred in Peking. Mu-chang-a was dismissed, Ch'i-ying was demoted, and Ch'i Chün-tsao's antiforeign clique became influential. The policy of the Peking government thus once again became openly antiforeign.[20] In Canton, after Ch'i-ying was transferred to Peking in 1848, Hsü Kuang-chin became imperial commissioner, to be succeeded by Yeh Ming-ch'en in 1853. These two officials behaved in an openly antiforeign manner and even went so far as to refuse interviews on an equal footing with any foreign diplomatic representative.

Chinese Refusal of Direct Communication
with the Peking Government

As we have seen, the treaties had stipulated that a foreign diplomatic representative could correspond directly with high officials in Peking. When the imperial commissioner at Canton had ceased, from the Western point of view, to operate as a channel of diplomatic negotiation, the foreigners tried repeatedly but in vain to invoke these treaty stipulations.

In 1850 Sir George Bonham, British plenipotentiary, demanded the transmission of a letter of protest to Peking, through the taotai at Shanghai and the governor-general at Nanking. The protest concerned the perennial question of the right of entry to the city of Canton, and was addressed to grand secretaries Mu-chang-a and Ch'i-ying from Lord Palmerston, British foreign secretary. The letter, accompanied by another letter from Bonham to Ch'i-ying, was eventually forwarded to Peking as a result of strong pressure on the part of Bonham. To these letters, however, the Peking government did not reply directly. Its answer took the form of a communication from Mu-chang-a and Ch'i-ying to Lu Chien-ying, governor-general at Nanking, the substance of which was to be conveyed through the latter's subordinate to Bonham. When the message reached Bonham in the form of a dispatch from the taotai of Shanghai to the British consul there, Bonham returned it to the Chinese authorities on the ground that he should get a direct communication from the grand secretaries.[21]

The principle adopted by the Chinese on this occasion was the following: high metropolitan and provincial officials were not to have any relations with foreigners unless specifically "charged with the transaction of foreign affairs concurrently with and in addition to their main duties"; no existing treaty clauses stipulated a correspondence between the high officials in Peking and the British plenipotentiary; hereafter, as heretofore, whenever there was occasion for negotiation, a communication (*chao-hui*) was to be addressed to the imperial commissioner at Canton, and other places were not to be visited at pleasure.[22] In other words, the imperial commissioner in Canton was assumed to be the only proper channel for negotiation, because of the distribution of jurisdictions within the Chinese government, and the treaty clauses concerning correspondence between foreign representatives and high officials in Peking were disregarded. The Chinese authorities may very well not have shared the British assumption that it was a treaty right to communicate with high metropolitan officials; in the Chinese text of Article 11 of the Treaty of Nanking this kind of correspondence was permissive and not mandatory, although from the English text it could be assumed to be mandatory.[23]

In the spring of 1858 and again in 1860, the Peking government, on the basis of the same assumption, replied indirectly through the governor-general at Nanking to communications from foreign representatives which had been transmitted to Peking through that official.[24]

Persistence of the Tribute System in Theory and Practice

The treaties signed after the Opium War forced China to agree to a direct formula for negotiating on equal terms with foreign officials; to that extent, and to that extent only, the tribute system may be said to have been abolished. However, so far as the Chinese legal system was concerned there was no "constitutional change." [25] The principles set forth in the Collected Statutes on the treatment of the Western powers remained intact. We may say that the Canton imperial commissionership was a makeshift, a buffer installed at the point of friction between two diametrically opposite approaches to foreign relations, the Chinese and the Western. In the Chinese official documents which were not to be seen by foreigners, they were still referred to as "barbarians." In official contact with the foreigners, there was a studied and strenuous effort to avoid equality in all matters not specified in treaty clauses.[26]

CHAPTER I

The Arrow War: Western Demands for Diplomatic Representation in Peking

> In one way or another, however we may disguise it, our position in China has been created by force — naked, physical force.
> — *Rutherford Alcock*

THE FOREIGN TREATY DEMANDS OF 1858

Instructions to the Negotiators

The two events of 1856 which touched off the Arrow War — the *Arrow* incident and the murder of the French missionary Father Chapdelaine — were exploited by the British and the French as pretexts for demanding treaty revision.[1] The *Arrow* was a Chinese-owned lorcha which had been registered in Hong Kong, flew the British flag, and was commanded by a British subject. On October 8, 1856, when its registration had been expired for eleven days — a fact not known to the Chinese authorities then — the ship was boarded by Chinese officials and twelve of the Chinese crew were arrested on suspicion of piracy. Also, it was alleged that the British flag was hauled down. This incident furnished the British government with a suitable occasion for forcing their pending issues with China by resorting to war. Lord Elgin, the British plenipotentiary in China during the Arrow War, although he had been made the executor of the gun-boat policy, could not help complaining in private that "nothing could be more contemptible than the origin of our existing quarrel . . . that wretched question of the 'Arrow'" was "a scandal to us."[2] In essence the foreigners were demanding the opening of China as a market for Western manufactures and commerce on the basis of China's incorporation, by force or otherwise, into the modern state system. Among the British, the clash between the Old China Hands and the Foreign Office originated in this period — " a clash between the merchants' folklore which pictures the infinite potentialities of the China trade and official conviction that this vision had been grossly exaggerated." The Mitchell Report of 1852, which exploded the myth of the Chinese market by revealing the self-contained nature of the Chinese economy, was enclosed in Elgin's dispatch of March 31, 1858, with his own support of Mitchell's judgment.[3] In the case of the French government, the primary motivation for its activities in East Asia was "national pride — pride of culture, reputation, prestige, and influence," rather than considerations of immediate trade.[4]

The instructions given by their governments to the British and French plenipotentiaries in China mentioned as one of the most important of their treaty-revision demands the permanent residence of diplomatic representatives in Peking.

Elgin's general instructions of April 20, 1857, from the Earl of Clarendon, British foreign secretary, were to demand, as "the best means of ensuring the due execution of the existing Treaties, and of preventing future misunderstandings," . . . "the assent of the Chinese Government to the residence at Pekin, or to the occasional visit to that capital, at the option of the British Government, of a Minister duly accredited by the Queen to the Emperor of China, and the recognition of the right of the British plenipotentiary and Chief Superintendent of Trade to communicate directly in writing with the high officers at the Chinese Capital, and to send his communications by messengers of his own selection." The other major point in Elgin's instructions was a demand for a "revision of the Treaties with China with a view to obtaining increased facilities for commerce." [5] The instructions of May 9, 1857, to the French plenipotentiary, Baron Gros, from Comte Walewski, French minister of foreign affairs, also called for permanent residence in, or occasional visits to, Peking by a French envoy, along with "revision [of the treaty] with a view to opening as wide as possible the access of the Celestial Empire to trade." [6]

The United States government, although it rejected the British invitation to join in military intervention in China, appointed William B. Reed as plenipotentiary to accompany Elgin and Gros with a view to pressing American claims for reparations and treaty revision.[7] Reed's instructions of May 30, 1857, from Lewis Cass, Secretary of State, enumerated as "the objects which it is understood the allies seek to accomplish by treaty stipulations," firstly, procurement from the Chinese government of a "recognition of the right of other powers to have accredited ministers at the court of Pekin, to be received by the emperor, and to be in communication with the authorities charged with the foreign affairs of the empire," and secondly an extension of commercial intercourse, tariff reduction, and so on. Reed was expected to aid in the accomplishment of these objects insofar as peaceful cooperation would permit.[8]

In response to Anglo-French approaches, the Russian government made it clear in 1857 that it would not join in any coercive measures and would participate only in relation to "the questions of an European interest, such as the protection of the Christians, opening of the Chinese ports to trade and the establishment of permanent legations in Peking." [9] Count Putiatin had already been dispatched to China as Russian plenipotentiary.[10] It may be suspected, however, that the Russian support of the demand for diplomatic representation in Peking was perfunctory. The Russians already held a somewhat privileged, though not quite satisfactory, position in Peking through their maintenance of the Russian Hostel. Furthermore, the Russian government cannot have been very happy at the prospect of having the watching eyes of Western diplomats in Peking while the Russian encroachment on the Amur River area was under way. As a matter of fact, later in 1857 St. Petersburg stated that Russia would support the opening of China to Western contact but not the establishment of resident legations in the capital.[11]

In brief, the demand for permanent residence in Peking of diplomatic representatives was to be made side by side with those demands which were immediately designed to open China more widely as a market, such as the increase in the number of treaty ports, navigation on inland rivers, and travel into the interior.

Motivation for the Demands

The superficially obvious reason behind the Western demand for permanent diplomatic representation in Peking was, of course, that it was a general practice in the modern state system. But the immediate basis for the demand was criticism of the Canton imperial commissioner system.

A representative Western view of that system appeared in a report by Elgin: "I am confident," he said, "that so long as the system of entrusting the conduct of foreign affairs to a Provincial Government endures, there can be no security for the maintenance of pacific relations with this country." After this introductory remark, he made the following two points. In the first place, a governor-general or governor in China was in a position to care for nothing but the interests of his own provincial area. "Nowhere in China, except at Pekin, does any solicitude for the general interests of the Empire, any sentiment which answers to our idea of nationality, exist, even in pretension." Secondly, a governor-general or governor, when charged with the conduct of foreign affairs, was unable to report the true state of affairs to Peking. "His life and fortune are absolutely at the disposal of a jealous Government, which is, in respect to all questions of foreign policy, profoundly ignorant, and which must continue to be so, so long as the Department for Foreign Affairs is established in the provinces. In nine cases out of ten he risks both, if he even ventures to bring to the knowledge of his Sovereign an unwelcome truth . . . In ordinary circumstances, his most prudent course, and therefore the one generally followed, is to allow abuses to pass unnoticed rather than incur the danger of getting into difficulties with foreigners." [12]

In distorted reports to Peking, the behavior of Westerners was usually depicted as servile, as fitted the proper distinction between the Middle Kingdom and the peripheral barbarians. Among other things, such distortions outraged the sensitivity of Westerners. For instance, at the time of the Tientsin negotiations in 1858, the American plenipotentiary, Reed, considered the resident minister clause "anything but desirable," [13] partly because he feared that Peking might be "converted into a new Constantinople and made the seat and scene of diplomatic squabbles and European intrigues" with "a knot of English, French, and Russian diplomatists, exiled at Peking, watching and quarrelling with each other." There was "no little risk to the American representative of being drawn into the vortex of European difficulties with which he has nothing whatever to do." [14] Later in the same year, however, he was astounded by the distortion of facts in the memorials and edicts relating to the treaty-revision negotiations of 1854, in which Robert M. McLane had acted as American plenipotentiary. These documents, of which Elgin gave Reed English translations, were among those that had been confiscated in Canton by the allied forces. "The doubts heretofore expressed," wrote the disillusioned Reed, after reading them, "as to a permanent diplomatic residence at Pekin fade away in the very unpleasant light shed by these intercepted documents . . . and I slowly and almost reluctantly yield to the conviction that, if American interests in China are worth protecting, it can only be done by direct representation at the capital." He also expressed conviction that these documents, in a great measure, justified the coercive policy pursued by the allies in North China.[15]

Elgin, in the report to which we have already referred, also called attention to "a culpable laxity" that he had noticed in the treaty ports, "whereby the worst class of foreigners profit at the cost of the more respectable." This laxity, in his opinion, was ascribable to "the working of the existing system." The same problem had been fully discussed in a memorandum of December 31, 1857, submitted by Rutherford Alcock, British consul at Canton, when he was in London on leave of absence. Among other points he stressed the fact that because of "a wholesale system of smuggling and fraudulent devices for the evasion of duties," foreign trade had degenerated and been converted into "a game of hazard and over-reaching," and that piracy and other kinds of violence committed by foreign outlaws had caused serious antiforeign feelings among the Chinese.[16] These conditions, which were disturbing the development of legitimate trade, Elgin ascribed in part to the present Chinese system for conducting foreign affairs. Direct pressure applied upon the Peking government by resident diplomatic representatives would, it was felt, contribute to the correction of these evils.[17]

A permanent diplomatic establishment was also considered a prerequisite to the effective exercise of the right to travel into the interior, and of the right of trade on the Yangtze, both of which were finally stipulated in the Sino-British Tientsin Treaty (Articles 9 and 10). In his memorandum, Alcock had mentioned the "access to the inner waters and grand inland marts" as "drawing after it, almost of necessity, some direct intercourse of a permanent kind with the Court at Peking." Frederick W. A. Bruce, who accompanied Elgin's mission in 1858 as secretary and in 1859 was sent to China as British minister, sent to London in the spring of 1860 an interesting dispatch analyzing the Chinese system for the conduct of foreign affairs. In this dispatch he remarked: ". . . if the interior of China is to be opened, it [the opening of the interior] will afford little protection to those who wish to avail themselves of the privilege, for the Provincial Governments have no sympathy with or authority over each other. To put pressure, for instance, on the seaboard Province of Che-kiang would have no effect on the authorities of the Province of Hu-peh." Hence the opening of the interior would be useless unless a resident foreign minister could directly influence the Peking government and persuade it to apply pressure on the provincial governments in the interior, where foreign warships had no access.[18]

Just how did the foreign, especially the British, authorities picture to themselves the political structure of imperial China? From the rather fragmentary insights scattered through contemporary reports we may reconstruct a fairly consistent view. Firstly, the Chinese political structure was regarded as something peculiar and incomprehensible. For instance, Laurence Oliphant, Elgin's private secretary in 1858, referred to it as an "anomalous and altogether unique system." [19] Secondly, as our quotation from Bruce's dispatch shows, it was considered a horizontally ill-connected system; any impact on one province would have no effect on another. Thirdly, it was not considered feudal. The power of the emperor was supreme, with the provincial governments operating at the pleasure of the Peking government. Bruce, rejecting the idea that "China be treated as a congeries of separate States" and that all arrangements should be made with the provincial authorities and Peking ignored altogether, summarized his own view as follows: "There are no semi-independent Pashas, nor a feudal nobility like that of Japan, in China. Except in the districts occupied by the rebels, the will of the Emperor is supreme; and were he to change his exclusive and antiforeign policy for a more liberal system, were he to cease to regard increased intercourse with foreigners as an evil, and were he to recommend them to the protection and hospitality of the authorities and population of the provinces, they would enjoy in China the same security as the natives of the country itself." [20] This view was echoed on February 19, 1861, in the House of Lords by Lord Wodehouse, undersecretary for foreign affairs: "The system of China is a highly centralized system; that is to say, although you have local authorities who are in a position of great laxity towards the central government in minor matters, yet you have no great satraps or governors who are independent of the central authority." [21] Fourthly, the emperor's great power was believed to rest on a psychological basis. In Oliphant's view, the emperor was "supported, not by a physical force, but by a moral prestige unrivaled in power and extent." "Backed by no standing army worth the name, depending for the stability of his authority neither upon his military genius nor administrative capacity, he exercises a rule more absolute than any European despot, and is enabled to thrill with his touch the remotest provinces of the empire, deriving his ability to do so from that in-

stinct of cohesion and love of order by which his subjects are super-
eminently characterized." [22]

It was probably because they had this general image in mind that
the Western diplomats expected favorable results from permanent
diplomatic representation at Peking. It is clear, however, that the
foreign authorities entertained at least a partial misconception of
China's political structure. Though they regarded it as something
sui generis, they seem to have been influenced by their concept of
Western absolute monarchy.[23]

Although the primary criticism of the Canton commissioner system was that it hindered the operation of foreign trade, the Western criticisms were also directed at the basic assumptions underlying
the system. The demand for permanent diplomatic representation
at the capital, in other words, was intended also to undermine the
Chinese assumption of superiority. What finally drove Reed to an
approval of Elgin's actions was a revulsion against sinocentrism. In
a report dispatched soon after his arrival at Hong Kong in 1857,
Elgin pointed out that "the obstinate refusal of the Court of Pekin
to place itself on a footing of equality with other Powers lies at the
root of our difficulties with that country," and he advocated direct
negotiations with Peking.[24] In a dispatch at the end of 1860, Bruce
remarked: "Our great difficulty is to substitute for this state of
chronic war, pacific discussion — and the possibility of pacific discussion depends on our being able to induce them to admit those
general principles of mutual fair dealing which form the basis of
international intercourse — I see no means of effecting this change,
short of being alongside the Central Government . . . The first
step is to be up at Peking." [25]

The last but perhaps not the least important reason behind the
demand for diplomatic representation at Peking was probably the
mutual distrust among the British, French, and Russians, with each
fearing the partition of China. In particular, the British had misgiv-
ings over the Russian advance deep into Siberia. In this situation,
what seemed desirable was an arena where the powers could jeal-

ously watch one another, preferably in Peking, the center of China's politics.[26]

THE CHINESE OPPOSITION TO PERMANENT DIPLOMATIC REPRESENTATION

Taku and Tientsin, 1858

From the end of April 1858, negotiations went on at Taku, with T'an T'ing-hsiang, governor-general of Chihli, Ch'ien Hsin-ho, provincial treasurer of Chihli, and the two officials sent from Peking, Ch'ung-lun, superintendent of the government granaries at the capital, and Wu-erh-kun-t'ai, chancellor of the Grand Secretariat, on the Chinese side, until the parleys were broken off and the Taku forts were occupied by the Anglo-French forces on May 20. The plenipotentiaries of the four powers then advanced as far as Tientsin. In June, Kuei-liang, grand secretary, and Hua-sha-na, president of the Board of Civil Appointments, were sent from Peking to continue negotiations, which led to the signing of the four Tientsin treaties. Throughout the negotiations at Taku and Tientsin the Chinese government's strongest opposition was consistently directed against the demand for permanent diplomatic representation in Peking, although it also objected vigorously to the demand for opening the interior to travel and to trade on the Great River. The Chinese opposition was so firm and so intense that the plenipotentiaries of France, Russia, and America withdrew their demand for permanent residence, and settled for occasional visits to Peking by diplomatic representatives.[27] Only the British pressed hard, incurring the most strenuous Chinese resistance, which was countered by ruthless intimidation and threats that refusal of the demand would inevitably be met by a British military intrusion into the capital.[28] Archimandrite Palladii of the Russian Hostel, who was then in Tientsin, reported that Kuei-liang and Hua-sha-na "were in a state of extreme humiliation and trembled at the appearance of Lord Elgin's deputies. Guilian [i.e., Kuei-liang] had entirely broken

talked to Gros, and Gros undertook the delicate mission of bringing the news to Elgin, who was not a little moved. In the end, however, he did not yield, having satisfied himself that "it was at least
doubtful whether any decree to the effect stated had been received
from the Emperor." He agreed only to a minor change, whereby
the Chinese words representing permanent residence were toned
down. He then proceeded to the signing of the treaty.[31]

The British intransigeance on the resident minister clause can
probably be ascribed in part to H. N. Lay's insistence. Lay wrote in
a pamphlet in 1893: "I had urged upon Lord Elgin that the Resident
Minister Clause was in my humble judgment vital, that without it
the treaty would not be worth the paper it was written upon."[32]
Elgin may have had Lay's bullying in mind when he wrote to his
wife on June 12, 1858, in the midst of the negotiations: "Certainly
I have seen more to disgust me with my fellow-countrymen than
I saw during the whole course of my previous life, since I found
them in the East among populations too timid to resist and too
ignorant to complain. I have an instinct in me which loves righteousness and hates iniquity, and all this keeps me in a perpetual boil."[33]
Still he could write to Lady Elgin on June 29, three days after the
treaty was signed: "The resident minister at Pekin I consider far
the most important matter gained by the Treaty; the power to
trade in the interior hardly less so . . . Though I have been forced
to act almost brutally, I am China's friend in all this."[34]

On February 21, 1860, in defense of his actions in China, Elgin
asserted in the House of Lords that he had acted strictly in accordance with instructions: ". . . it was not altogether a matter of
choice to me whether I should make this or that demand upon the
Chinese Government; . . . I should have assumed a serious responsibility if I had abstained from pressing the demand for a resident
Minister at Pekin, in the face of the positive and peremptory instruction from my Government, that if I were forced to have
recourse to coercive measures, I was not to make a permanent
arrangement . . . except after having obtained that concession."[35]

down and Huashana had evidently sought solace in strong li

On June 8 the Chinese delegation was driven to acc
clauses as the free opening of the Great River and acces
interior under passport, but they firmly resisted the resident
clause, maintaining that it was indispensable "to kneel
knees." On June 11, along with other major demands, the
accepted in principle the permanent residence of a British i
expressing the hope, however, that the minister would live ii
sin and his visit to the capital could be postponed, sin
dignity of ours [i.e., of the Chinese government] would per
outraged by (the Minister's) proceeding at once (to Pekin)
the recent collision at Taku with the British war vessels. C
21, however, the Chinese tried to persuade the British to
certain stipulations already agreed to. Concerning the reside
ister clause, they stated: "the north of China, it is to be feared,
be found very cold, and excessively dusty; added to this, the
has many peculiarities, to which (a stranger) could not ac
himself." Again on June 24, the Chinese delegation raised obj
to various points: as for the resident minister, they wished t
his future visits to Peking to occasions of business only, an
objected to his bringing his family.

As early as June 7, Kuei-liang had resorted to a personal ap|
Horatio Nelson Lay, assistant Chinese secretary under Elgin
was the principal negotiator on the British side. He stated tl
was an old man of seventy-four, and if he did not settle the pr
of the resident minister in accordance with the emperor's \
he would inevitably be demoted and punished. He besough
to assist in getting this demand withdrawn, at least for the
being.[30] On June 25, a day before the scheduled signing o
treaty, Kuei-liang and Hua-sha-na asked Reed and Putiatin to i
ate in their behalf, alleging that they had received an edict t
effect that they were forbidden, on pain of death, to accept th
mands for permanent residence of diplomatic representatives
for travel by foreign merchants into the interior. Reed and Put

We would not be justified in saying that Elgin exceeded his instructions. It should not be overlooked, however, that the sudden cooling of Anglo-French relations in Europe early in 1858 had led the Foreign Office to become less and less determined on this demand. Accordingly, when the report of the treaty reached London, the British foreign minister, Malmesbury, was profuse in his praise of Elgin's achievements.[36] To Elgin he wrote: "Her Majesty's Government are fully aware of the difficulties which your Excellency has had to surmount in dealing with a Government such as that of China, and that those difficulties were greatly increased by your position with reference to the Representatives of the other Powers, — but it must be a satisfaction to your Excellency to feel that you have by your firmness and sagacity secured for other nations in common with your own those advantages which the exertions of their Representatives had failed to obtain." [37]

Let us return now to the Chinese reaction to the resident minister demand. While the Chinese negotiators were resisting the demand, they were simultaneously trying to persuade Peking to make a concession. For instance, T'an T'ing-hsiang at Taku repeatedly voiced objections to the foreigners, declaring that the residence or occasional visits of an accredited minister in the capital were inadmissible, indeed could not even be discussed; there was not, and never had been, a law that could permit it, and, in any case, the presence of consuls at the treaty ports made it unnecessary to have ministers in Peking.[38] On May 13 he went so far as to suggest a compromise plan that would allow foreign ministers to go to the capital on specific occasions when important matters needed to be discussed. This proposal was accompanied by a demand for a tacit understanding that the foreigners would not solicit an imperial audience, in order to avoid the kowtow problem.[39]

In a memorial received on May 1, and also in later memorials, T'an and his colleagues had advised rejection of the resident minister demand, although they repeatedly urged Peking to compromise on other issues, pointing to the military strength of the foreigners and the seriousness of the domestic political situation.[40] But in their memorial received on May 15 they dared for the first time to suggest that foreign ministers should be allowed to visit the capital. "We, your officials, also believe," they stated, "that ever since the beginning of the management of barbarian affairs, any requests concerning the trade at the five ports have been referred to Canton, but the officials at Canton, on their part, have been pigeonholing such questions without answering them, or else procrastinating or glossing over the issue, and so have failed to report the real situation to the throne, until at last the foreigners have been infuriated into this [trouble making]." It is clear that the memorialists were here in accord with the foreigners in ascribing the present conflict to the defects of the Canton imperial Commissioner system. "There have been men of the Western ocean like Verbiest," they went on, "who served a lifetime at the Imperial Board of Astronomy. Now they beg to be allowed to proceed to Peking only once in several years or only when they have important business. If the retinue could be limited to a small number of persons and if perhaps an agreement could be made to let them come by land, not allowing them to use the Tientsin sea route . . . this might be one way of mollifying the barbarians." In other words, T'an and his colleagues were apparently advocating the admission of foreign ministers to Peking, using a plausible analogy to the tribute system formula.[41] Peking flatly rejected this proposal.[42] In a memorial received on May 17, T'an and his colleagues vainly repeated their proposal, on the ground that since the barbarians were begging this favor because of the failure of the Canton officials to report the real situation, granting it would not mean "a loss of prestige" to China.[43]

From the outset of the negotiations at Tientsin Kuei-liang and Hua-sha-na consistently advocated peace. Stressing the superiority of foreign military strength and the gravity of the Chinese internal situation, they tried to persuade Peking to meet the foreign treaty demands, as the only way to achieve the withdrawal of the foreign military forces.[44] The signing of the Sino-British treaty on June 26, and of the Sino-French treaty on June 27, was reported in a very long memorial received on June 28. Here the memorialists discussed, point by point, their reasons for believing that the foreign demands should be accepted.[45] They rationalized the resident minister clause thus:

"One reason the barbarians want residence in the capital is that they would like to boast and take pride in it toward other powers. [A projection to the Westerners of the Chinese logic of face. — M.B.] Another reason is that they want to memorialize the throne directly. [A criticism of the Canton imperial commissioner system. — M.B.] There is no far-sighted scheme or wicked design of any kind behind this demand. If we consider that they dare not harm Yeh Ming-ch'en, we realize that they stand in awe of the Celestial Empire. If we consider their willingness to return to Canton and also instantly to evacuate Taku, we can see that they have no territorial ambition. If the visit to Peking were to materialize immediately, there would certainly be a scare in the capital. However, the agreement just arrived at is that they are not to come again until after one year has elapsed, and without soldiers. Therefore, even if a party included two score persons, still it would only be comparable to a mission from Korea. And our state would treat them according to propriety (*li*).

"In calling their envoy an imperial commissioner [a reference to the foreign term 'plenipotentiary'] they have no other intention than to make him equal to our officials of the first rank. Furthermore, the envoy wants to bring his family with him, according to the ancient precedent of bringing hostages. If the precautionary measures are strict, it will be quite easy to keep them in order. As they will number only some two score persons and will be right in the middle of a heavily guarded place, it will not be difficult to control them. . . . When they hire artisans, the arrangements will be made by our officials, so the men hired will be able to spy on their conduct. The barbarians hate most of all to spend money. Therefore we will let them bear their own expenses. Furthermore, they dread the wind and dust. We are quite sure that their residence will turn out to be useless and that they will soon go back voluntarily. These are the reasons why, as an expedient, we may concede permanent residence."

Here again we detect a distortion based on the analogy to the tribute system formula. The full content of the Sino-Russian treaty of June 13 and of the Sino-American treaty of June 18 was only now made known to Peking, copies of them being enclosed in this long memorial. But copies of the Sino-British treaty, the most vital of the Tientsin treaties, and of the Sino-French treaty, were not forwarded to Peking until as late as July 3.[46]

What was the reaction of the Peking court, as reflected in its edicts? During the Taku negotiations, the court had flatly dismissed the resident minister issue, declaring that it was "incompatible with the fundamental principles of the regime (*t'i-chih*)."[47] Even after it had learned of the fall of the Taku forts, the court had stated that sending envoys to Peking and allowing missionaries to travel into the interior would offer "no benefit to the foreigners and would only disturb China," and so it was "really impossible to concede to those demands."[48] A memorandum which must have been prepared for the guidance of Kuei-liang and Hua-sha-ha when they went to Tientsin stated that all the foreign demands were to be rejected except those for an increase in the number of treaty ports in Fukien and Kwangtung and the reduction of the tariff rates. The resident minister idea was again described as "incompatible with, or unprecedented in, the fundamental principles of the regime."[49] As one report after another came from Kuei-liang and Hua-sha-na in Tientsin, the inevitability of submission gradually became clear. By this time the residence or visits of foreign envoys in Peking were now taken for granted, and the issue shifted to the formula under which it should be permitted.

The formula was made clear in an edict of June 20.[50] A diplomatic representative could come to the capital on business but could not reside there; in accordance with the Russian precedent, said the edict, "only students" could be permitted residence. Envoys could not assume for themselves the title of "imperial commissioner."

"They should wear Chinese robes and caps, and submit themselves to Chinese discipline. They should be engaged only in the study of arts and crafts. They should not be permitted to meddle in public affairs." The rules of etiquette were to be arranged only after Canton had been restored to Chinese control. On a visit to Peking, envoys could "come to the north only through the interior, starting from Shanghai and escorted by Chinese officials. All the supplies will be furnished by China; they need not bear the expenses themselves. Hereafter, they may come to the capital once in three years or once in five years. It is not necessary to make the trip every year."

It is clear from this edict that Peking's response was to try to set the new pattern in accordance with the old tribute system formula. This line was reaffirmed in an edict of June 24. If the British insisted upon permanent residence for their "imperial commissioner," the edict instructed, Kuei-liang and Hua-sha-na were to tell them that "this point is absolutely impossible to concede. If we dare to authorize it at our own discretion, the emperor will certainly punish us severely." [51] It was these instructions that drove Kuei-liang and Hua-sha-na to stage the personal appeal of June 25 which so moved and disturbed Lord Elgin. An edict on June 28, issued in reply to the memorial by Kuei-liang and Hua-sha-na reporting the signing of the British and French treaties, still persisted in the same direction. Using as its basis Article 5 of the Sino-American Tientsin Treaty, which was rather near the court's terms, the edict added two or three more terms: protocol should be established with regard to the ceremony of kneeling (kuei-pai) which should be wholly in accordance with the Chinese system (that is, the kowtow was to be performed); an envoy was not to bring his family with him; and in case of permanent residence, Chinese robes and caps were to be adopted.[52]

While negotiations were under way in Tientsin, demands for war were being shouted by the officials in Peking, inspired in large part by objections to permanent diplomatic representation at the capital. When the court received word, on June 20, that Kuei-liang and Hua-sha-na (on June 11) had accepted the principle of a resident minister, the news leaked out and created a sensation. The situation was described thus in a warlike memorial: "Discussions among men on the street, as well as the publicly expressed opinions of officials and gentry, show that there is no one who does not think with trembling and anxiety that the barbarians' residence at the capital would threaten the safety of the imperial ancestral temple and of the altars of the deities of the soil and grain." [53] As a succinct summary of these objections to diplomatic residence we may quote a passage from a memorial by Yin Keng-yun, junior censor overseeing the Hunan and Hupei Circuit, which was received on June 12: "After the [barbarians'] entrance into the capital, I, your official, do not know with what kind of rules of etiquette our Emperor is going to see them. If they should, after all, be unwilling to leave the capital, I, your official, do not know by what means they can be driven out. The metropolis today may be compared with a human body whose stamina has been sapped away. Should we in addition to this permit the entrance of an external evil?" [54]

A typically vehement response to the concessions made on June 11 was a joint memorial by Chou Tsu-p'ei, president of the Board of Civil Appointments, and twenty-two other officials, all of whom were serving on the Commission of Civil Defense in the capital (T'uan-fang-ch'u), an *ad hoc* commission to deal with the current emergency. The memorial, drafted by Yin Keng-yun and Lu Ping-shu, another junior censor, presented eight grounds for objection: (1) if the foreign envoys resided long at Peking, the real Chinese situation would certainly be spied out in detail; (2) from their tall buildings the envoys would look through telescopes at the imperial palace and gardens; (3) as a building site for their legation they would certainly demand a place in the busiest quarters, which would necessitate the removal of government offices or the razing of private houses; (4) the imperial processions would be watched by them either from their high buildings or from the road; (5) a barbarian building (a legation) would be used for the propagation of Christianity; (6) there would be no way of applying judicial procedures in disputes between natives and barbarians, and crafty natives might be lured by much profit and swagger around like asses in lions' skins; also, criminals might take refuge in the barbarian building; (7) taxation and police controls at the capital's gates would be disturbed or interfered with by the barbarians; (8) the tributary states like Korea and Liu-ch'iu, which had been very submissive, would learn to make light of the Celestial Empire.[55]

The keynote of these objections was apprehension as to how the prestige of the weakened dynasty could be maintained at home and abroad, and a barely hidden fear that foreign envoys residing in the capital might intervene in China's domestic politics.[56] The same fears were indicated in an edict of May 8, 1860: "If the barbarians reside at Peking, China will be put under surveillance by the barbarians from afar. From ancient times there has been no precedent of this kind in our institutions. Absolutely impossible to be done!"[57]

The Shanghai Negotiations, 1858–1859

The Sino-British negotiations held in Shanghai in October and November, 1858, in accordance with Article 26 of the Tientsin Treaty, were supposed to be for the revision of the tariff rates. A high official of the Board of Revenue was to be deputed to act on behalf of the Chinese government. Actually, Peking appointed the two very representatives who had been at Tientsin, Kuei-liang and Hua-sha-na, as well as Ming-shan, director of the Imperial Armory, and Tuan Ch'eng-shih, assistant department director of the Board of Punishments, who was serving as a secretary of the Grand Council. Ho Kuei-ch'ing, governor-general of Kiangnan and Kiangsi, was also ordered to join the delegation. The negotiations led to the signing on November 8 of the "Agreement Containing Rules of Trade."

Peking's real motive in appointing these negotiators was to achieve the nullification of the Tientsin treaties in return for total exemption from customs duties. It seems, however, that this idea was never officially submitted to the British. On the contrary, Kuei-liang and his colleagues repeatedly presented to Peking strong objections to this idea, stressing the importance to China of customs revenue and the very slim prospect of getting the treaties nullified. They were thus ordered at least to secure cancellation of the four clauses in the British treaty that Peking regarded as "the most harmful to China": (1) permanent diplomatic residence in Peking (Articles 2, 3, 4, and 5); (2) opening of the Great River to trade (Article 10); (3) travel into the interior (Article 9); (4) indemnification for military expenses, and occupation of Canton until the indemnity had been paid in full (the separate article).[58]

All four, of course, were vital clauses to which the British attached much importance, and so it was almost impossible for Kuei-liang and his colleagues even to broach the subject. In this delicate situation they sent Elgin an elaborate letter stressing the fact that the Tientsin Treaty had been signed under military pressure, and expressing the strong hope that the British government would exercise the option stipulated in Article 3 by directing its minister to visit Peking only occasionally instead of residing there. They proposed an arrangement whereby a grand secretary or a president of a Board would be appointed to reside wherever else the British minister might choose to reside. In the event that China violated any of the provisions of the Tientsin Treaty, the British minister would be free to establish himself permanently in the capital.[59] Elgin rejected this proposal.[60] Kuei-liang and his colleagues repeated their appeal,[61] and this time Elgin promised to suggest to his government that "if Her Majesty's Ambassador be properly received at Pekin when the ratifications are exchanged next year, and full effect given in all other particulars to the Treaty negotiated at Tientsin," it would certainly be expedient not to exercise the right of permanent residence at Peking.[62] In March 1859 Elgin notified Kuei-liang that London had approved this suggestion.[63]

The problem of permanent diplomatic residence in the capital was thus shelved for the time being.

The Taku Incident, June 1859

The Peking government, which actually did not want foreign representatives in Peking on any occasion, could not feel satisfied merely with the foreigners' promise not to exercise the right of permanent residence there. Although both the British and the French Tientsin treaties had stipulated that ratifications were to be exchanged in Peking within a year of signing, an edict was issued on December 20, 1858, ordering that the exchange take place in Shanghai.[64] Another edict, on January 29, 1859, announced the transfer to Shanghai of the imperial commissionership, and ordered Ho Kuei-ch'ing to "manage the affairs concerning various countries" (*pan-li ko-kuo shih-wu*), conferring upon him the status of imperial commissioner.[65] This transfer was intended as an institutional device to prevent the approach of foreign representatives to the capital and to contain them in Shanghai, which was then the center of foreign interests in China.

Consecutive reports from Kuei-liang and his colleagues still remaining in Shanghai, however, gradually persuaded Peking that there was really no prospect of exchanging ratifications in Shanghai. An edict of March 29, 1859, therefore indicated a reluctant readiness to exchange them in Peking, on the following terms: "When [the barbarian representative] enters Peking *via* the sea port, his retinue should not exceed ten persons; they cannot bear weapons; upon arrival at the capital, in conformity with the precedents relating to the visits of foreign envoys to the capital, they cannot ride in chairs or go in a procession; after the ratifications have been exchanged, they should sail back immediately, not being allowed to stay long in Peking." [66] An edict of April 14 then specified Pehtang, some ten miles north of Taku, as the port of entry to Peking from the sea. This decision was reached on the suggestion of Seng-ko-lin-ch'in,[67] who was in charge of the defense of Taku, but it seems not to have been made known to Kuei-liang and his colleagues in Shanghai.

When Frederick Bruce, the British minister, and Alphonse de Bourboulon, the French minister, appeared in Shanghai, Kuei-liang and his colleagues tried to dissuade them from going north, but to no avail. They then advised Bruce that "on his arrival at the mouth of the Tien-tsin river (the Peiho), he should anchor his vessels of war outside the bar, and then, without much baggage and with a moderate retinue, proceed to the capital for the exchange of the Treaties." [68] Meanwhile, the court, though still entertaining a vain hope that ratifications might be exchanged in Shanghai, prepared residences in Peking for the British, French, and American ministers, "in conformity with the precedents of various tribute-bearing barbarians." [69] An edict of June 18 ordered Seng-ko-lin-ch'in at Taku and Heng-fu, governor-general of Chihli, who was to deal with the foreign envoys on their arrival, to delegate officials to meet them off the coast and escort them on Chinese vessels to Pehtang.[70]

Now Bruce was under instructions to go to the mouth of the Peiho with "a sufficient naval force." Furthermore, "unless any unforeseen circumstances should appear to make another arrangement more advisable" (a key qualification which he seems to have forgotten), it was felt desirable that he "should reach Tien-tsin in a British ship of war." He was also to "refuse compliance with any ceremony, or form of reception, which can in any way be construed into an admission of inferiority on the part of Her Majesty in regard to the Emperor of China." [71]

When the foreigners appeared off Taku, they found that the passage into the Peiho had been blocked. On June 21 Bruce and Bourboulon assigned to Admiral Hope, commander of the British squadron, the task of clearing away the obstacles blocking the river. An edict of the twenty-second, on the other hand, ordered Seng-ko-lin-ch'in and Heng-fu to ask the foreigners to anchor and wait off Pehtang harbor. Should the foreigners refuse to wait there, their envoys were to be allowed to proceed to Tientsin *via* Pehtang, with a small retinue and without any weapons.[72] A Chinese message asking Bruce to proceed to Pehtang reached him at 9 a.m. on June 25. It was too late. He was then on a warship nine miles off the coast. Admiral Hope was to start forcing a passage at the mouth of the Peiho at 10 a.m.[73] The operation, which in fact did not begin until 2:30 p.m., was a fiasco. Four gunboats were sunk. A landing party was mowed down. The admiral, himself wounded, lost 432

men and had to abandon the idea of opening the river. Defeated
and frustrated, Bruce and his French colleague left the Gulf of
Peichihli for Shanghai.[74]

The American Tientsin Treaty, in Article 30, had stipulated exchange of ratifications within one year of the signing of the treaty,
without specifying the place. However, John E. Ward, the American minister to China, had taken the stand that under the most-
favored-nation clause in the Treaty of Wang-hea he, like the British
and French ministers, was authorized to go to Peking to exchange
the ratifications.[75] Accordingly, he had gone north along with them,
on an American warship. When the defeated British and French
left for the south, Ward landed at Pehtang and proceeded to Peking.
On his arrival the Peking government demanded that he have an
audience prior to the exchange of ratifications. But the two sides
could not agree on the etiquette of the audience. Ward had to leave
the capital, having succeeded only in transmitting to Kuei-liang
and Hua-sha-na President Buchanan's letter to the emperor. On
August 16 the Sino-American ratifications were exchanged in Pehtang. Throughout their journey to Peking Ward and his retinue
had been treated in a manner reminiscent of the tribute system.[76]

The Russian Tientsin Treaty, on the other hand, had stipulated
in Article 12 that the exchange of ratifications was to take place
in Peking within one year of ratification by the czar. The exchange
was duly performed on April 24, 1859, in Peking between Petr
Perovskii, the Russian representative, and Su-shun, president of the
Board of Revenue, charged with the supervision of affairs at the
Court of Dependencies, and Jui-ch'ang, president of the Board of
Punishments.[77]

The Issue of Audience and Kowtow:
the Final Rupture of September 1860

Following its opportune victory at Taku, Peking took soundings
at Shanghai as to whether the British and the French would be
willing to exchange the ratifications by following the path of the
American minister.[78] As it became clear that the British and French

were not inclined to compromise, the Peking government stiffened. The new Chinese position was revealed in edicts of August 1 and 5, 1859: the Tientsin treaties with the British and the French were to be abrogated, and most-favored-nation treatment was to be given them for the time being in accordance with the American Tientsin Treaty; new treaties should be negotiated with them by Ho Kuei-ch'ing, the Shanghai imperial commissioner, the ratifications to be exchanged in Shanghai, and indemnities should be imposed on Britain and France. By new treaties Peking apparently meant treaties along the lines of the American Tientsin Treaty, which would not include the four clauses that the Chinese found so obnoxious.[79]

During 1860 it became evident that the British and the French were going to demand full execution of the Tientsin treaties, with the support of ample military power — including the exchange of ratifications in Peking and the permanent residence there of ministers, as well as a formal apology for the Taku incident and an additional indemnity. As the Anglo-French pressure increased, Peking retreated step by step. After hearing from the Shanghai authorities that they were assured, through private channels, of the foreigners' resoluteness, the court suggested in an edict of February 27, 1860, that although the negotiation of peace (that is, of new treaties) should take place in Shanghai, the foreign representatives might come to Peking *via* Pehtang for the exchange of ratifications (of the new treaties) "according to the precedents of the American barbarians." [80] Apparently as a reaction to ultimatums from Bruce and Bourboulon, an edict of March 29, 1860, reluctantly suggested that the indemnities stipulated in the Tientsin treaties might be paid.[81] In anticipation of the return to China of Lord Elgin and Baron Gros as plenipotentiaries, an edict of May 8 named as "the most harmful points" in the original Tientsin treaties only the opening of the Great River to foreign vessels and the resident minister clause. With regard to the other clauses, the edict declared, a compromise might be made.[82]

When Elgin and Gros arrived in Shanghai late in June, they refused to negotiate with the imperial commissioner there. Early in

July they left Shanghai for the north, and the allied military forces were concentrated in the Gulf of Peichihli. Seng-ko-lin-ch'in at the Taku forts and Heng-fu, who was then stationed in the Taku area in charge of diplomatic contact with the coming Western representatives, were repeatedly instructed by Peking not to provoke an armed collision and to seize an opportunity for negotiation. Peking was now saying that the foreign plenipotentiaries might be admitted to Peking "according to the American precedent of the preceding year" *via* Pehtang with a small retinue of ten or twenty persons; ostensibly they were to come for the exchange of ratifications of the original Tientsin treaties, but, in fact, the court still hoped to reopen negotiations for reconsideration of the treaties.[83]

The allied forces avoided a frontal approach at the Taku forts, which were heavily fortified, and landed on August 1 at Pehtang, where they found that the defenses, for some reason, had been removed. They advanced toward the rear of the Taku forts, beating down the resistance of the Ch'ing forces. Peking, still eager to make an overture for negotiations,[84] suggested on August 16 that if the British and French representatives insisted on coming to Peking *via* Taku, they might be escorted to Taku on a small Chinese vessel and thus admitted to Peking.[85] After fierce resistance, the Taku forts fell on August 21. On August 25 the advance troops of the allied forces entered Tientsin.

Kuei-liang and Heng-fu were appointed imperial commissioners and sent to Tientsin to negotiate. Kuei-liang asked for instructions, especially on the resident minister issue, and in reply received an edict of August 30 which stated: "If it is really difficult to prevent it by any means, they may be allowed to reside at the capital. But they cannot bring a large retinue. Otherwise the inhabitants would be frightened and disturbed. Even if they only want to come and go occasionally *via* the seaport, they should notify the Chinese authorities in advance so that we can, thereupon, dispatch officials to escort them."[86] On September 4 an edict in response to the report from Kuei-liang and others that they had accepted all the foreign demands took the stand that the withdrawal of the allied military forces from Tientsin, the Peiho, and Taku was a prerequisite to the exchange of ratifications in Peking. The representatives might come to Peking for the exchange only with a small retinue, according to the American precedent; their residences and supplies would be prepared for them by the Chinese government according to Chinese regulations; and in case of permanent residence the sites for their residence must also be selected by the Chinese government.[87]

Because Kuei-liang and his colleagues were not given "full powers" as the foreigners understood them, the negotiations in Tientsin broke down. The allied troops advanced beyond Tientsin. Peking dispatched as imperial commissioners Tsai-yuan (Prince I), and Mu-yin, president of the Board of War and a grand councillor. Prince I was one of the powerful group surrounding the throne;[88] Mu-yin was one of their followers.[89] On September 14, after a parley of some hours at T'ung-chou with Harry Parkes and Thomas Wade, who had been sent there by Elgin, Prince I and Mu-yin at last conceded most of the British demands, approving, among other points, the exchange of ratifications in the capital and the advance of the main body of the British forces to a point five *li* (a mile and a half) south of Chang-chia-wan.[90] They reached a similar understanding with the French on September 17.[91]

In Peking, most of the tents which had been set up, probably for troops, around the Tung-ch'ang-an Gate in front of the Forbidden City and at other places were removed on September 15, and it was reported that peace had been made on the preceding day.[92] The Peking government had been strongly opposed to the foreign request that their representatives be escorted to Peking by their own armed guards, but on September 16 a vermilion endorsement on a joint memorial by Prince I and Mu-yin permitted a foreign military escort, not to exceed 400 persons each for the British and the French.[93]

However, when it was made known on September 17 that the British were demanding an imperial audience in order to deliver their queen's letter personally to the emperor, Prince I and Mu-yin suddenly stiffened and offered strenuous opposition. On the following day military clashes occurred and negotiations were again broken off. Parkes and Henry B. Loch, Elgin's private secretary, were captured, taken to Peking, and thrown into the prison of the Board of Punishments. Twenty-four other Britons and thirteen Frenchmen were also imprisoned. The allied forces advanced quite close to Peking, and on September 22 the emperor fled from the Summer Palace near Peking for the imperial villa in Jehol. An immediate cause of the renewal of hostilities on September 18 was probably that Seng-ko-lin-ch'in, believing that the negotiations had already been broken off because of the audience issue, had sent forward a portion of his troops and had occupied the ground south of Chang-chia-wan, where it had been intended that the allied troops should be encamped.[94]

An edict of September 18, which was issued before receipt of the news of the rupture but with the knowledge that the British were insisting upon an audience, set forth the last stand of the Peking government.[95] It read in part as follows: "If they want to present the state letter [the queen's letter] personally, they can be allowed to do so only if they agree to perform the ceremony of kneeling according to the Chinese rules of etiquette. If they find this impossible, then the only alternative is to follow the American and Russian precedents and bring the state letter to the capital and deliver it to an imperial commissioner who will present it to the throne. Upon receipt of it, a letter stamped with an imperial seal will be given. This would be no different from a personal presentation to the throne. Now peace is just about to be made. The problem of etiquette is not important enough to justify risking a rupture of negotiations. If these barbarians insist on their previous stand, however, and do not repent, then the only thing to do is to fight a decisive battle."

Despite repeated appeals from the officials remaining in Peking, the emperor in Jehol refused to return to the capital from Jehol. A primary reason for his unwillingness to return, as typically stated in an edict of November 13, was the fact that the audience problem had not been resolved.[96] In December, Prince Kung and his colleagues in Peking succeeded in getting written assurance from the British and the French that they would not insist on an audience,[97] thus putting an end to the audience question, at least for the time being. Nevertheless the emperor remained in Jehol, at the imperial villa, where he died the next year.

From this examination of the Chinese reactions to the Western demands it becomes clear that the crux of the Chinese resistance to the resident minister clause was that it implied equality between China and the Western powers. This was a denial of the tribute system formula, of which the final symbol was the kowtow. On the indispensability of the kowtow in an imperial audience the Chinese remained adamant, even after they had been forced step by step to accede to the other Western demands.

RESIDENT MINISTER STIPULATIONS
IN THE TIENTSIN TREATIES

The American Treaty

The Sino-American Tientsin Treaty was signed on June 18, 1858, eight days before the Sino-British treaty. Article 5 stipulated that the American minister in China, "whenever he has business," should have the right to sojourn in Peking, and to confer there with a grand secretary or any other designated high official of equal rank. However, this right was subject to the following qualifications: (1) His visits should not exceed one a year; he was not to make a visit "on trivial occasions"; and he should not stay in Peking any longer than necessary. (2) The Board of Rites should be notified in advance, in writing, of an impending visit, so that it could make the necessary arrangements to facilitate the journey and provide protection (or "escort" [*hu-sung*] according to the Chinese text) en route. (3) The minister could come to Peking either by land or by sea to the mouth of the Peiho; in the latter case he should not bring warships into the Peiho but should inform the local authorities so that boats might be provided for him. (4) His entire suite was not to exceed twenty persons, exclusive of his Chinese attendants.[98] (5) He would be furnished in Peking with a suitable residence, and he would pay his own expenses. (6) None of the members of his mission should be engaged in trade. (The Chinese proposal to bear the expenses of the American legation had been rejected as a tribute system formula; in turn, the Chinese had required the insertion of a clause forbidding members of the legation to engage in trade in Peking, which was permitted to members of tribute missions.)[99]

Pointing to items 1, 2, and 4, the British authorities in China commented on the American treaty: "he [the American minister] will be held . . . by the government and people of China at precisely the same value as a Lewchewan or Siamese Envoy." [100] That they had correctly assessed the Chinese attitude is borne out by an edict of June 28, issued upon receipt of a copy of the American treaty and expressing a favorable view of the arrangements itemized above. Of these arrangements the edict stated that the following should apply also to the British: their minister should visit Peking no oftener than once a year; he should not stay unnecessarily long; he should not enter the Peiho on a warship, or visit Peking on trivial occasions; his retinue should be limited; the Board of Rites should be notified of his visit in advance and his residence should be furnished by the Chinese government. The edict added three more conditions for admission to Peking: the ceremony of kneeling should accord wholly with the Chinese system; the envoy should not bring his family with him; and in case of permanent residence Chinese robes and caps should be worn.[101]

Article 30 of the American treaty outlined a very comprehensive most-favored-nation treatment, which covered "any right, privilege or favour connected either with navigation, commerce, political or other intercourse." In addition to this general clause, there was a special stipulation to the effect that whenever a representative of another nation should be permitted "to reside . . . for a long or short period" in Peking, the American representative in China should have the same privilege "without any further consultation or express permission" (Article 6).[102]

The French Treaty

Although the French, as a mark of courtesy, did not sign their treaty until June 27, one day after the British, the drafting had been completed on June 23.[103] Article 2 stipulated that the French diplomatic representatives in China could proceed to the capital "when important affairs call them there." It then added the following qualifications (unlike the qualifications in the Sino-American treaty, these bore no implications of tribute): The French diplomatic representatives would enjoy the privileges and immunities which "international law grants to them" ("in accordance with human feelings and reason" [an-chao ch'ing-li] according to the Chinese text), "namely, their persons, their families, their houses and their correspondence will be inviolable; they will be able to hire the employees, couriers, interpreters, servants, etc., etc., which may be necessary for them." All the expenses of French diplomatic missions in China would be borne by the French government.

Article 2 further stipulated that if any other treaty power attained the right of permanent residence in Peking for its diplomatic representative, France would immediately enjoy the same right. Finally, if China sent diplomatic representatives to France, they would receive the same treatment as the representatives from other countries.

The British Treaty

Article 2 of the Sino-British Tientsin Treaty, signed on June 26, made it clear that either China or Britain might appoint diplomatic representatives to the court of the other country. Article 3 then stipulated: "the Ambassador, Minister, or other Diplomatic Agent, so appointed by Her Majesty the Queen of Great Britain, may reside . . . permanently at the Capital, or may visit it occasionally at the option of the British Government." Furthermore, the terms incidental to permanent residence or occasional visits were so phrased in

Articles 3 and 4 as to deny explicitly the idea of tribute: (1) The diplomatic representative "shall not be called upon to perform any ceremony derogatory to him as representing the Sovereign of an independent nation, on a footing of equality with that of China. On the other hand, he shall use the same forms of ceremony and respect to His Majesty the Emperor as are employed by the Ambassadors, Ministers, or Diplomatic Agents of Her Majesty towards the sovereigns of independent and equal European nations" (Article 3). (2) He might bring his family and establishment, the size of which was not specifically limited (Article 3). (3) "No obstacle or difficulty" should be put in the way of his free movement, and he and the members of his suite might "come and go, and travel at their pleasure" (Article 4). (4) Any person guilty of "disrespect or violence . . . in deed or words" to him or to any member of his family or establishment should be severely punished (Article 3). (5) The British government might acquire a site for building or hire houses in Peking for the accommodation of its diplomatic mission (Article 3). (6) The representative should be at liberty to choose his own servants and attendants, who were not to be subjected to any kind of molestation (Article 3). (7) He should have full liberty to send and receive his correspondence to and from any point on the sea coast that he might select; his letters and effects should be held sacred and inviolable, and he might employ for their transmission special couriers (Article 4). (8) Generally he should enjoy the same privileges accorded to officers of the same rank by the usage and consent of Western nations (Article 4). (9) All expenses attending the diplomatic mission should be borne by the British government (Article 4).

Article 5 specified that a grand secretary ("one of the Secretaries of State") or "a President of one of the Boards" was to be designated as the high official with whom the British representative should "transact business, either personally or in writing, on a footing of perfect equality." In the Tientsin negotiations, it had first been agreed simply that "one of the Chief Secretaries of State" (a grand secretary) should be appointed for this purpose. The Chinese side, in an effort to broaden the scope of this provision, had then suggested that "an officer of the First Grade" should be appointed instead. The British objected, but accepted the addition to the original stipulation of the words "or one of the Presidents of the Boards." [104] Metropolitan civilian officials of the first rank or grade included not only grand secretaries, assistant grand secretaries, and presidents of the Boards, but also grand preceptors, grand tutors, grand guardians, junior preceptors, junior tutors, junior guardians, grand preceptors of the heir apparent, grand tutors of the heir apparent, grand guardians of the heir apparent, and senior presidents of the Censorate.[105] The addition in the treaty was limited to "a President of one of the Boards," which certainly included the president of the Board of Rites or of the Court (or Board) of Dependencies. As far as the literal interpretation of this clause is concerned, the Chinese government could easily have resorted to trickery — for instance, by naming the president of the Board of Rites, whose jurisdiction included the tributary states, as the high official to deal with Western ministers, thus implying the idea of tribute.[106]

Article 6 of the treaty provided that Chinese diplomatic representatives to Britain should enjoy the same privileges as are described above.

The British agreement not to exercise the right of permanent residence was rescinded after the Taku incident of June 1859.[107] Article 2 of the Sino-British Peking Convention of October 24, 1860, confirmed the cancellation of that agreement and explicitly stated that the British representative would henceforth reside in Peking permanently, or occasionally, "as Her Britannic Majesty shall be pleased to decide."

The Russian Treaty

The Sino-Russian Tientsin Treaty was signed on June 13, 1858, before the treaties with the other three powers. This treaty was epoch-making for the Russians in that it gave them for the first time the right to participate in maritime trade with China. It also departed from the old system in which Sino-Russian relations had come under the jurisdiction of the Court of Dependencies.[108]

Article 2 provided that correspondence between the two governments should no longer be carried on between the Russian Senate and the Court of Dependencies but between the Russian foreign minister and "the senior member of the Grand Council" or the senior grand secretary, on terms of equality.[109] Furthermore, whenever it became necessary to send "a dispatch on a very important affair," a "special official" could be appointed to bring it to Peking.[110] The official might have an interview, and also communicate in writing, with a grand councillor or a grand secretary, on terms of equality. This privilege of sending an envoy to Peking, which was supposed to have been acquired before and to be confirmed anew in this treaty, was subject to the following terms: (1) The dispatch brought by the special official would be transmitted through the Board of Rites to the Grand Council. (2) The envoy might come to Peking via Kiakhta and Urga, through Taku, or through other seaports; this abolished the previous formula, which had specified a single route. (3) Upon receipt of advance notification, the Chinese government was to take immediate steps to insure comfortable travel for the Russian envoy and his suite, arrange for their reception in Peking with due respect, and for their decent accommodation there, and see that they were provided with all necessities. (4) The expenses of the mission were to be borne by the Russian government.

This treaty did not stipulate permanent residence in Peking for Russian diplomatic representatives. It rather anticipated that a plenipotentiary would be stationed in one of the treaty ports (see Article 2).

Article 10 made important changes with regard to the Russian Ecclesiastical Mission, stationed at the Russian Hostel. The expenses of the establishment were now to be borne solely by the Russian government.[111] Secondly, members of the mission might now return to Russia at any time, at the discretion of superior authorities (previously they had been obliged to stay in Peking for a certain fixed period),[112] and other persons might be appointed to Peking in their place.

FOREIGN DETERMINATION TO SUPPORT THE CH'ING DYNASTY

> We might annex the Empire if we were in the humor to take a second India in hand, or we might change the dynasty if we knew where to find a better, but if our object be to impress the existing Dynasty with such a sense of our power as will induce it to accept and faithfully to abide by, the conditions we believe to be essential to the security and extension of our trade, and to the maintenance of pacific relations, without shaking it to its base, handing over the whole Empire to anarchy, we have a work to accomplish which will, I venture humbly to assert, require some delicacy of treatment.
>
> — *Elgin to Russell* [113]

Allied military power had backed up the demand for resident ministers and those other demands which were designed to open China more widely to trade. The result had been two military campaigns in north China and finally the Manchu emperor's flight to Jehol and the destruction of the Summer Palace in the fall of 1860. Yet the allied powers had no intention of overthrowing the existing dynasty and were careful not to deal a fatal blow to the staggering government, which they were becoming determined to support against the Taipings.

Attitude Toward the Taiping Rebellion

In the last analysis, the attitude of the Western maritime powers toward the Taiping Rebellion may be said to have been determined by their calculation as to which of the two sides in China's domestic strife would be more likely to contribute toward the creation of a relatively stable and advantageous market.[114]

After the Taipings took Nanking in 1853 and established their headquarters there, the officials of the maritime powers who were in China contacted the Taipings in order to discover the nature of their situation and their attitude toward foreigners. The northern advance of the Taipings almost to Tientsin was also closely watched. The official attitude of the Western governments in the earlier period of the rebellion had been vaguely friendly toward the Taipings, but it now changed to one of strict neutrality. They continued to maintain the principle of strict neutrality and consistently refused requests for military assistance from Chinese provincial or local authorities, but around 1854 they began gradually to lean rather toward the cause of the dynasty.[115]

The year 1854 can be regarded as the turning point for three reasons. First, the treaty revision negotiations of 1854 were carried on with the Ch'ing government. Second, in order to cope with the confusion caused by the suspension of the Shanghai Customs' operations after the native city fell into the hands of the Triad Society rebels in September 1853, the Foreign Inspectorate of Customs was inaugurated in June 1854. This was achieved through the collaboration of the Chinese government authorities in Shanghai and the local representatives of Britain, France, and America. Third, during the disturbances caused by the Triad Society rebels, Anglo-Franco-American naval forces, as well as the volunteer corps of the foreign community, defended the foreign settlements in Shanghai. Their immediate aim was to protect the foreign interests there. In order to maintain the so-called neutrality of the foreign settlements, the foreigners were ready even to risk an armed clash with the imperial forces, but basically this posture of self-defense was taken against a possible attack by the Taipings. It was anti-Taiping rather than anti-Ch'ing. In particular the French attacked the native city of Shanghai while the imperial forces were also engaged in assaulting it. Though the French action was supposed to be independent, it greatly facilitated the recapture of the native city. In its effect, at least, it was unmistakable military assistance.[116]

This kind of "benevolent neutrality" continued into the Arrow War period. The instructions concerning the civil contest in China which were given to Bruce by Malmesbury, the British foreign secretary, on March 1, 1859, stated that if the rebellion was so locally limited as to be easily suppressible by foreign naval forces, Great Britain could assist the imperial government, with the previous understanding that her allies would collaborate. "In the present state of our knowledge," Malmesbury went on to say, "it would not be proper for you to encourage any expectation of material assistance on our part." He was cautious enough, however, to leave to the discretion of Bruce, as the man on the spot with superior local knowledge, the conduct of all matters with which he might be called upon to deal.[117] Reed's instructions from Cass, the American secretary of state, on May 30, 1857, though drafted on the assumption that the treaty revision negotiations were to be with the Ch'ing government, indicated an opportunistic and almost cynical indifference to the development of the insurrection: "We have no other concern as to its progress or result than to take care that our rights are preserved inviolate. We have no reason to believe that one of the contending parties is more favourably disposed towards foreigners than the other, or more ready to extend commercial intercourse with them, while both are bound by treaty stipulations to us and to other powers, and will be held to their faithful observance; but in all that relates to these internal disturbances you must be guided by your own discretion, applied to the circumstances in which you may find yourself placed." [118]

How did the Chinese authorities view these trends in the attitude of the foreign authorities? At the time of the Shanghai negotiations in the fall of 1858, a memorial received in Peking on November 14 from Ho Kuei-ch'ing dealt at length with the historical background of the treaty revision problem, as well as with the current situation. It suggested that it was in all probability impossible to secure the cancellation of the four points to which Peking so objected. Ho pointed out, in a passage reviewing the treaty revision negotiations of 1854, that the foreign authorities had at that time shifted their policy toward favoring the imperial government, and that this shift had not been unconnected with their demands for treaty revision. Although Ho Kuei-ch'ing here mentioned only the American representative, McLane, with no reference to the British and the French, and although he distorted the picture by saying that McLane had suggested offering military assistance in return for treaty revision, it may safely be said that he saw the drift of affairs in its proper perspective.[119]

With the knowledge of Kuei-liang and others, Elgin left Shanghai on November 8, 1858, to sail up the Great River on a British warship. He went as far as Hankow and on the way contacted some important figures among the Taipings. At Nanking and An-ch'ing fire was exchanged with the Taiping forces. He returned to Shanghai on January 1, 1859. This observation tour by Elgin annoyed the Peking government considerably.[120] Kuei-liang and his colleagues repeatedly assured Peking that the British were not in collusion with the rebels.[121] After the Taku incident of June 1859, Peking worried about the possibility of collusion between the Taipings and the British and French, and ordered the imperial commissioner Ho-ch'un, one of the field commanders besieging Nanking, to be on the alert.[122] In a memorial received on July 23, 1859, Ho Kuei-ch'ing, citing information from foreign papers in Shanghai, indicated his suspicion that the British might join with Taipings to get revenge for their defeat at Taku.[123] In response, Peking again ordered Ho-ch'un to be on the watch and to take precautions.[124] Seng-ko-lin-ch'in too was worried by this information.[125] In brief, although the Chinese authorities were aware that the Western maritime powers were rather leaning in the direction of the dynasty, they were not free from a suspicion that there might be collusion between the Taipings and the Western authorities.

In May 1860 the Taiping forces broke a stalemate and proceeded down the Great River. Tanyang fell on May 19, Ch'ang-chou on May 21. Ho Kuei-ch'ing, who was stationed at Ch'ang-chou, fled without trying to meet the attack. Wusih fell on May 30. On June 2 Soochow fell, and Hsü Yu-jen, governor of Kiangsu, died in battle. The Chinese authorities and influential people in and around Shanghai were alarmed by the course of events. From the moment when the attack on Soochow was felt to be imminent, they repeatedly begged for military assistance from the British and French. The British and French officials in Shanghai took the stand that they would continue to maintain strict neutrality, although they would use their military forces to defend Shanghai itself. In August the Taiping forces finally approached Shanghai and were driven back by Anglo-French troops. The Chinese urged the dispatch of Anglo-French forces to Soochow, but at this stage the foreign authorities dared not consent to send their troops beyond the Shanghai area. The group of foreign mercenaries who later came to be known under the name of the "Ever Victorious Army" originated in the organization by the American Frederick T. Ward of a troop of 100 Filipinos, with the sponsorship of Wu Hsü, taotai of Shanghai, and Yang Fang, an influential Shanghai merchant known among foreigners as Taki or Takee.[126]

With these developments in 1860, Chinese officials in troubled areas now began to write openly in their memorials to Peking about the need for foreign military assistance. In 1853 and 1854 also officials on the scene had repeatedly requested military assistance from the foreign authorities, but in reporting to Peking they had given the impression that the foreigners had reverently offered their assistance.[127] In contrast, a memorial received on June 18, 1860, from Ch'iao Sung-nien, Lianghuai salt controller,[128] and a joint memorial received on June 26 from Ho Kuei-ch'ing and Wang Yu-ling, acting governor of Chekiang,[129] both advocated peace with Britain and France, and argued that China should ask for Anglo-French military assistance against the Taipings in return for acceptance of the Anglo-French demands on the Peking government.

The memorial by Ho Kuei-ch'ing and Wang Yu-ling was an especially detailed one. After stating that Bruce had refused a request by the Chinese authorities and people for assistance and was determined to go north with military support in order to secure the British demands, the memorial went on in the following vein: "Now the strategic points in the southeastern region [of the empire] are all occupied by the rebels. In Kiangsu there is now not one soldier or officer. The whole area is deserted and there is no means at all to take any step. Even if reinforcements were sent from every direction, how could they be fed and paid? Where could the munitions for them be procured? Just at this time when the flames of rebellion are raging so madly, if the rebels happen to discover that our war with the barbarians is not yet ended they will necessarily bribe the barbarians generously and enter into collusion with them, taking advantage of the opportunity." In this desperate tone the memorial continued its argument, stressing heavily the possibility of collaboration between the rebels and the profit-seeking barbarians. The memorialists earnestly recommended, as a lesser evil, that China swallow all the demands of the British and the French and in return secure their military intervention against the Taipings. In a vermilion endorsement on the memorial from Ch'iao Sung-nien[130] and in the edict responding to the joint memorial by Ho and Wang,[131] Peking rejected this proposal on the ground that if China accepted barbarian assistance, "the aftermath might be beyond description." The group of foreign mercenaries was reported to the throne by saying that 100 Filipinos had been hired and made "barbarian braves"; the name of Frederick T. Ward was not mentioned to Peking at this stage. In response, Peking was rather inclined to suggest that the corps should be disbanded.[132]

The crisis at Shanghai cannot have failed to affect the attitude of the Peking government, however. The gravity of the domestic situation, with the government threatened by the Taipings and the Nien Army, was already recognized in the edicts and memorials of the Arrow War period. But it was probably the crisis at Shanghai in the summer of 1860, against the background of the anticipated northern expedition of the allied forces, that forced the government to consider the situation in concrete and immediate terms. Although the edicts strongly opposed foreign assistance, it may safely be suspected that its desirability began to be seriously considered in the inner core of the government. On September 14, 1860, at the negotiations in T'ung-chou, after having complied with most of the British demands, Prince I tried to sound out Parkes on the possibility of British cooperation against the Taipings.[133]

Concern for the Stability of the Dynasty

In 1858 the Western representatives in China were more or less of the opinion that excessive demands on the Manchu government might incur consequences disadvantageous to the Western powers. In a report drafted off Taku before the opening of negotiations, Elgin remarked that the rural population around Shanghai was in distress because of the decreased demand for cotton fabrics manufactured by the cottagers in their leisure hours, a decrease that was ascribed largely to the consequences of the rebellion. "I infer from this circumstance," he went on, "that nations which desire to trade with China are deeply interested in the preservation of order in the Empire, and that privileges acquired by a process which enfeebles the Government, and destroys its moral influence, may sometimes be purchased at too great a cost." [134] Putiatin warned Elgin and Gros, in identical notes notifying them of the signing of the Russian treaty: "It is for your Excellency now to decide on the future fate of the present Government . . . The too great concessions which might be exacted from a Government so roughly shaken would but precipitate its fall, which would only produce new and much graver difficulties." [135] In their replies, both Elgin and Gros indicated that they shared Putiatin's apprehension.[136]

Separate articles attached to the British and French Tientsin treaties stipulated that the authorities in Kwangtung were to pay an indemnity of four million taels to Great Britain and two million taels to France. Elgin and Gros purposely avoided trying to "exact money directly from the Imperial Government in the north," because, being aware of its penury, they felt that "it would be unwise to drive it [the Chinese government] to despair, and perhaps, to extreme measures of resistance, by putting forward pecuniary claims which it could satisfy only by resorting to measures that would increase its unpopularity and extend the area of rebellion in the Empire." [137]

After the Taku incident, in the fall of 1859, when the British and French began to consider the demands to be placed before the Chinese government in the coming retaliatory joint expedition, Elgin was reported to have strongly opposed the demanding of additional indemnities, on the ground that it might "compromise the Chinese government in the eyes of their people, by giving the appearance of paying tribute to the foreigners and thus creating a political difficulty much more considerable than a simple question of money." [138] The Peking conventions of 1860 stipulated that Great Britain and France were each to receive a total of eight million taels as indemnity, including the original sums designated in the Tientsin treaties (Article 3 of the British Peking Convention and Article 4 of the French convention). Except for the half million taels each to be paid to the British and French governments soon at Tientsin, the greater part of these indemnities was to be paid in installments out of the customs revenues at the treaty ports. In 1860, in addition, as indemnities to the families of deceased prisoners and to the survivors of atrocities, 300,000 taels were paid in Peking by the Chinese government to the British and 200,000 taels to the French.[139] When the measures to be taken as revenge for the atrocities had been considered, Elgin had hypothetically considered demanding an additional sum of money not as a compensation for the sufferers but as "a penalty" to be inflicted on the Chinese government; however, it was dismissed on the following grounds: ". . . in the present disorganized state of the Chinese government, to obtain large pecuniary indemnities from it is simply impossible, and . . . all that can be done practically in the matter is, to appropriate such a portion of the Customs' revenue as will still leave to it a sufficient interest in that revenue to induce it to allow the natives to continue to trade with foreigners." [140]

On dispatching expeditionary forces to China for the second time, both the British and the French governments were worried about the possibility that the march of the allied forces might force the emperor to flee from the capital and eventually cause the collapse of the dynasty. Elgin's instructions, dated April 17, 1860, from Lord Russell, the British foreign secretary, read in part: "It may happen that, after taking the forts at the mouth of the Peiho, after the capture of Tientsin, and even in contemplation of the capture of Peking itself, the Emperor of China may refuse the terms of peace demanded. He may retire from his capital, and await in retirement in Tartary the future measures of the allies. Such a course might expose to danger the authority of the Emperor of China . . . the Emperor would suffer greatly in reputation. The rebels would take heart; the great officers of the Empire might find it difficult to maintain the central authority; the Governors of Provinces might hardly be able to quell insurrection. In short, the whole Empire might run the risk of dissolution." [141] The French government's instructions to Gros, dated April 21, 1860, indicated a similar fear.[142] The Russian government, expressing its fear that the forcible occupation of Peking might lead to the downfall of the reigning dynasty, hoped that the British and French would exercise prudence in the coming expedition.[143]

Before landing in north China, Gros conveyed to Elgin his hope that they might stop at Tientsin and threaten Peking from there, rather than attack the capital directly.[144] While in Tientsin Gros wrote to the French commander and admiral that he hoped there would not be too strong a demonstration against Peking.[145] The British, on their part, were watchful lest the French, who had no serious stake in the China trade, become reckless in their military operations.[146]

When revenge for the atrocities committed on allied prisoners was discussed in the suburb of Peking, there was much difference of opinion between the British and the French. Among the measures suggested by the British, the French objected to the destruction of the Summer Palace, to the Peking officials accompanying the remains of the victims to Tientsin, and to the erection there of an expiatory monument. They only agreed to the imposition of indemnities for the families of the deceased and for the survivors.[147]

Major-General Nikolai Ignat'ev, who had succeeded Petr Perovskii as the Russian representative and who had followed the allied representatives north from Shanghai, disputed the advisability of all of these measures, including the indemnities.[148] Elgin apparently also proposed to Gros the immediate destruction or seizure of the imperial palace, but Gros wanted to reserve this action as a final card.[149] In the end, the Summer Palace was destroyed on October 18 by the British alone. Elgin decided upon this action in order "to make the blow fall on the Emperor, who was clearly responsible for the crime committed; without, however, so terrifying his brother [Prince Kung] whom he had left behind him to represent him, as to drive him from the field." [150]

Around October 16 Ignat'ev had entered Peking. Establishing himself at the Russian Hostel, he kept in touch with the high officials remaining within the city, and through them with Prince Kung himself, who was still staying outside the city.[151] Gros wrote confidentially to Ignat'ev, urging him to make the Chinese understand that, in order to save the dynasty, they must indicate compliance with all the allied demands before 10:00 a.m. on October 20. At 2:00 a.m. on that day Gros received a letter from Ignat'ev announcing Prince Kung's submission.[152] The subsequent negotiations proceeded smoothly, and on October 24, in the principal hall of the Board of Rites, ratifications of the British Tientsin Treaty were exchanged and the British Peking Convention was signed. On the next day, the exchange of ratifications and the signing of the convention were similarly performed by the Sino-French representatives.

The resident minister issue was also weighed by the allies as to its possible effect on the dynasty. One reason why France, Russia, and America did not persist in their demands for a resident minister was their fear that so extreme a demand might weaken the Manchu regime. The British, on the other hand, expected permanent diplomatic residence to be instrumental in strengthening the Chinese government. "I have no doubt," Reed wrote to Cass, in explaining Elgin's stand, "that such a reconstruction or invigoration of the central authority of this disorganized empire is hoped for as England thinks she has effected in Turkey . . . The imperial power is to be sustained, and among the means of doing so is that which this treaty provides — a sort of diplomatic protectorate at the capital." [153]

Nevertheless, the British too came to fear that the immediate effectuation of permanent residence might weaken the Manchu regime. One of Elgin's reasons for agreeing, at Shanghai, not to exercise the right of permanent residence was his appreciation of the argument presented by Kuei-liang and others that, "in the present critical and troublous state of our country, this incident would generate, we fear, a loss of respect for their government in the eyes of her people." [154]

In a report on June 10, 1860, Bruce, then the British minister residing in Shanghai, discussed in detail the reasons for not acceding to the requests of provincial Chinese authorities for military assistance against the rebels. Here again the matter of permanent residence in Peking is discussed in terms of its utility for a pro-Manchu policy. Military assistance given directly to the provincial authorities would not only be reported to Peking in distorted form, but would also incur the following consequences: "The Imperial authority would be entirely discredited in the eyes of the people. The Chinese officials, pressed for money, and relying on foreign support, would become more than ever cruel, corrupt, and oppressive; and the Chinese, deprived of popular insurrection, their rude but efficacious remedy against local oppressors, would with justice throw on the foreigner the odium of excesses which his presence alone would render possible. The consequence would be, popular hostility, reprisals, and that train of events which would render it necessary to appropriate permanently the province occupied, or to retire from it, leaving behind a bitter ill-will among the people. No course would be so well calculated to lower our national reputation, as to lend our material support to a Government the corruption of whose authorities is only checked by its weakness." Bruce worried about the possibility that China might thus eventually become partitioned. Obtaining "an undisputed footing" in Peking he held to be "an indispensable condition if intervention is not to end in a partition of the Chinese Empire." He thus tried to persuade Ho Kuei-ch'ing that "the true policy of the Chinese Government was to put an end to its differences with foreign Powers, and apply their resources to the restoration of internal tranquility." [155]

On October 12, 1860, Elgin wrote to Bruce asking him to join him in Peking as quickly as possible. Elgin wanted to confer with him personally before coming to a final decision on the question of permanent residence, taking into consideration such factors as the emperor's flight, the ill-treatment of the allied prisoners, and the prospects of the existing dynasty. In this letter he asked: "Is it advisable to take a step which will identify Great Britain more closely with the Dynasty at a time when it seems to be tottering to its fall?" [156] In other words, the permanent residence of a minister was regarded as an integral part of the policy of supporting the Ch'ing dynasty. Here in an atmosphere of desperation, with negotiations with Prince Kung proceeding very slowly, Elgin seems to have felt some doubts about the advisability of the policy itself.

CHAPTER II

The Arrow War: the Domestic Political Scene

During my absence, the Prince had been in conversation with Mr. Parkes, who . . . had remarked that an increase of intercourse would doubtless make us better friends, and that he rejoiced in the prospect of an acquaintance between the Representatives of foreign Governments and the three Princes. Your Excellency will bear in mind that, from all we have ever been given to understand, the actual Government of the country is in the hands of Prince Hwui, the Prince of Ching, and the Prince of I, to whom Mr. Parkes was speaking. He started at the words "the three Princes"; by whom, added Mr. Parkes, we have been much misunderstood: and he immediately rejoined, Not by them alone, but also by (writing the character with his forefinger in the air, *à la Chinoise*) the "Han" (Chinese). He then rose, went round the table, and again whispered the word "Han." They then became very friendly . . .

— *A dialogue at T'ung-chou between Prince I and Parkes,
September 14, 1860*

The purpose of this chapter is to investigate the changes in the balance of domestic political forces in China during the Arrow War period. The following analysis is, of course, documented as far as possible, but since the sources now available are not quite adequate for complete documentation it has been necessary to hypothesize to some degree.

THE POWER CONFIGURATION IN PEKING

In theory the seat of power in the Peking government was the Grand Council, where the edicts of the emperor were drafted and the more important memorials dealt with. In the late 1850's, however, power in Peking was said actually to be in the hands of Tsai-yuan (Prince I),[1] Tuan-hua (Prince Cheng),[2] and Su-shun,[3] Tuan-hua's younger brother and the real manipulator of the group. As favorites of the Hsien-feng emperor, these three wielded enormous power. Their position is understandable in the context of the shift in the power structure of the Ch'ing government which had been taking place under the impact of the Taiping Rebellion, and of the repercussions of this shift in Peking.

As is widely known, the banner forces and the Army of the Green Standard, which together formed the military foundations of the Ch'ing dynasty, were hopelessly ineffective against the Taiping army. The Manchu government had to rely for survival upon the newly emerging military power of personally led regional armies organized in their native places by Chinese scholar-officials like Tseng Kuo-fan. This formation of a new kind of military power contributed to changes in the Ch'ing power structure in three ways: (1) The balance between the Manchus and the Chinese began to shift in favor of the Chinese. (2) Chinese officials of a new type emerged. They still had a scholarly background, but their power was based on personally led regional forces, and they were undesirable and suspect in the eyes of Chinese senior officials of the traditional type. (3) A tendency toward regionalism developed as a result of the gradual monopolization in the provinces, by the officials of the new type, of both military and financial power and patronage. This tendency became clearly evident when Tseng Kuo-fan, in 1860, was appointed governor-general of Kiangnan and Kiangsi.[4]

Amid the general mood of suspicion and jealousy in Peking,[5] Wen-ch'ing, Manchu grand councillor, was quick to see that a shift in the balance of domestic political forces was unavoidable, and to save the dynasty he took the initiative in adapting to the inevitable. He supported Tseng Kuo-fan and restrained the antagonism of Ch'i Chün-tsao, Chinese grand secretary and grand councillor, who as a representative senior official of the traditional type resented Tseng's growing reputation. Wen-ch'ing also supported other Chinese scholar-officials who were fighting the Taipings, such as Hu Lin-i, Yuan Chia-san, and Lo Ping-chang. By thus patronizing Chinese officials, he rendered "distinguished service by mediating in the promotion of the trend" (*wo-hsuan ch'i-yun chih kung*).[6] It must be remembered that at this time the Manchus still occupied a much higher position in the political hierarchy than the indigenous Chinese (leaving Chinese bannermen out of account). The voice of Chinese officials like Tseng Kuo-fan could probably have been heard in Peking only through the mediation of Manchu officials of high prestige.[7] For this situation the government military forces were at least partially responsible. Their garrisons were heavily concentrated in the metropolitan area, and although they were impotent against foreign invasion or large-scale insurrection, they were still powerful enough to maintain the Manchu hegemony at least in the political arena of Peking.

After Wen-ch'ing died in 1856, his policy of adaptation and mediation was taken over by Prince I and his clique. Prince I and Prince Cheng were among those princes who enjoyed the right of perpetual inheritance of the status of prince of the first or second degree.[8] When the Tao-kuang emperor died in 1850, these two princes of the first degree were adjutants-general. They were among the courtiers who were enjoined by the emperor's so-called "testamentary decree" (*ku-ming*) to assist the succeeding emperor.[9] They were thus in a position to have an influential voice in the court. Su-shun got close to the Hsien-feng emperor through Prince Cheng, his elder brother. He was promoted gradually and in the course of time became a high official.[10] He seems to have been a domineering person with an intense drive to power, who often behaved licentiously. As a resourceful and aggressive politician, he manipulated Prince I and Prince Cheng, who had indecisive personalities, and through them influenced the emperor. Like Wen-ch'ing, he patronized Chinese officials of the new type and supported in various ways Tseng Kuo-fan, Hu Lin-i, and Tso Tsung-t'ang.[11] He was fond of receiving notable Chinese scholars or officials as guests and used to seek their advice. Among these guests were such friends or followers of Tseng as Yin Keng-yun, Kuo Sung-tao, and Wang K'ai-yun.[12] Chinese officials of the old type, like Ch'i Chün-tsao and P'eng Yun-chang, who had both climbed the bureaucratic ladder to the uppermost step of grand councillor and grand secretary, were not on good terms with Su-shun, and they also resented the rise of Tseng Kuo-fan.[13]

THE COUNCIL OF PRINCES

Throughout the edicts and memorials of the Arrow War period collected in *Ch'ou-pan i-wu shih-mo* (a complete account of the management of barbarian affairs), we encounter many instances in which the emperor sought the advice of "Prince Hui and others" (Hui-ch'in-wang *teng*) on important military or foreign affairs, or in which he received memorials from them. There are also numerous similar instances in which Prince Hui's name is mentioned together with the specific names of some other princes. From this evidence, which will be examined presently, I infer that there was in operation in Peking at the time of the Arrow War a *de facto* organ which consisted of several princes with Prince Hui as the senior member or chairman, and that this organ, which I should like to call here the Council of Princes, acted as an advisory body to the emperor, either independently or jointly with the Grand Council, affecting to a great extent the decisions reached by the government.[14]

Mien-yü (Prince Hui) (1814–1865) was the fifth son of the Chia-ch'ing emperor, and so a younger brother of the Tao-kuang emperor and an uncle of the Hsien-feng emperor.[15] As the emperor's uncle he enjoyed special privileges; for example he was permitted to dispense with the kowtow except on certain particularly solemn occasions. When the Taiping army entered Chihli in 1853–1854, he served as commander-in-chief of all the forces defending Tientsin and Peking, with the title of *feng-ming ta-chiang-chün;* he was stationed in Peking, while Seng-ko-lin-ch'in, as his assistant, fought in the field and drove back the Taipings. (Charles Gützlaff tells of a report — probably hearsay — that the Chia-ch'ing emperor wanted in his last moments to designate Mien-yü, then still a boy, as his successor but was dissuaded by the young prince's mother. Also according to Gützlaff, Prince Hui was active as an advisor to the Tao-kuang emperor. He was supposed to be a wise, moderate and statesmanlike courtier. He is said to have been involved more than once in power struggles as a potential pretender to the throne, when the Tao-kuang emperor fell seriously ill.[16])

It is not entirely clear who were the members of the Council of Princes, but from those cases in which Prince Hui's name is mentioned together with those of other princes, we may reconstruct the membership and perhaps safely infer that the same group or groups were meant by "Prince Hui and others." I shall cite a number of these cases to support my conclusions in the following discussion.

There seem to have been three groupings, always with Prince Hui as the senior member. The first combination was Prince Hui, Prince I, and Prince Cheng.

Case 1: Early in June 1858 these three princes, together with two grand councillors, were put in charge of the Commission of Defense (Hsun-fang-ch'u), a temporary emergency organ for the defense of the capital; they were given the title of *hsun-fang wang-ta-ch'en*.[17] (This is the earliest mention of Prince Hui in the *Ch'ou-pan i-wu shih-mo* volumes covering the Arrow War period.) It was probably in this connection that an advisory body of princes was first constituted, and it seems actually to have continued in existence after the Commission of Defense had been discontinued.

Case 2: On June 23, 1858, a large assembly of courtiers was called to discuss the problem of war or peace. Before the session opened, "the grand councillors, and the Princes Hui and I and Cheng of the Commission of Defense" had had an audience with the emperor.[18]

Case 3: At the time of the Tientsin negotiations in 1858, these three princes, probably jointly with the grand councillors, recommended Ch'i-ying to the emperor as an additional negotiator to be sent to Tientsin, there to join Kuei-liang and Hua-sha-na, who were already dealing with the Western representatives. Later, when Ch'i-ying was insulted by the British and left Tientsin for Peking at his own discretion, it was these princes, in the capacity of *hsun-fang wang-ta-ch'en,* who impeached him and urged that he be summarily executed.[19]

Case 4: Jointly with the Board of Punishments, these three princes, as *hsun-fang wang-ta-ch'en,* in 1858 tried the officials responsible for the fall of the Taku forts.[20]

Case 5: On July 15, 1858, Chi-p'u, senior vice-president of the Board of Revenue, who had once been a Hoppo (superintendent of customs) in Canton, was appointed a member of the delegation headed by Kuei-liang and Hua-sha-na to negotiate with Western representatives on the tariff rates. According to Chi-p'u's autobiography, at an audience two days later the emperor told him to discuss the problem with Prince Hui, Prince I, and Prince Cheng, as well as with Kuei-liang and Hua-sha-na. Consequently he drafted a memorandum on his views and explained it to the three princes. A fortnight later, they summoned him and conveyed the emperor's orders that it was unnecessary for Chi-p'u to proceed to Shanghai.[21]

Case 6: Around July 27, 1859, the three princes, jointly with the grand councillors, sent a letter to some high official in the Taku and Pehtang area (probably Heng-fu, governor-general of Chihli), relating to the dispatching of two officers from the coast to Peking to serve Kuei-liang and Hua-sha-na when they received the American minister, John Ward.[22]

Case 7: On August 5, 1859, when John Ward was staying in Peking, the three princes jointly memorialized in opposition to the idea of granting him an imperial audience with American etiquette, stating that they had consulted on the matter with Kuei-liang and Hua-sha-na.[23]

Case 8: According to a memorial of August 9, 1859, from the grand councillors, the three princes had made a suggestion about how to return a British war prisoner, and the grand councillors had drafted an edict accordingly.[24]

Case 9: On February 1, 1860, a banquet was given in the presence of the emperor for these three princes, the grand councillors, and Seng-ko-lin-ch'in.[25]

Case 10: Late in August 1860 these three princes were sent to T'ung-chou to consult with Seng-ko-lin-ch'in on matters of defense.[26]

Case 11: In September 1860, Thomas Wade reported: ". . . from all we have ever been given to understand, the actual Government of the country is in the hands of Prince Hwui, the Prince of Ching [Prince Cheng] and the Prince of I . . ." [27]

Case 12: On September 25, 1860, Prince Kung wrote to these three princes, who were then on the way to Jehol with the emperor, responding to a letter from them inquiring about certain European prisoners and giving them a brief account of the general confusion following the emperor's departure. He also promised to write again at the first opportunity.[28]

The second combination was Prince Hui, Prince Kung, and Prince Tun.

Case 13: In response to a question from the emperor, Prince Hui in June 1858 presented a memorial on foreign affairs jointly with I-hsin (Prince Kung)[29] and I-tsung (Prince Tun), two younger brothers of the emperor.[30]

Cases 14, 15, 16: During the ten days or so just prior to his departure for Jehol the emperor repeatedly gave audiences to princes. On three occasions during this period, Prince Hui, Prince Kung, and Prince Tun gathered in the presence of the emperor.[31]

There was a third grouping which amalgamated the two preceding combinations, still with Prince Hui as the senior member.

Case 17: On September 9 or 10, 1860, the emperor ordered Princes Hui, Tun, Kung, and Cheng to discuss the advisability of his planned trip to Jehol (Prince I was then at T'ung-chou).[32]

Case 18: On the occasion of Ch'i-ying's impeachment in 1858, the emperor first ordered the three impeachers (Princes Hui, I, and Cheng) and Prince Kung, Prince Tun, and the grand councillors, to discuss the case jointly. He then ordered a joint examination of Ch'i-ying by Princes Hui, I, and Cheng, and also by the grand councillors, the Imperial Clan Court, and the Board of Punishments. Finally, he ordered Prince Kung and Prince Tun, the grand secretaries, and the Six Boards and the Nine Ministries (Chiuch'ing), to draft a sentence.[33]

Case 19: On September 9, 1860, the emperor gave audience to the grand councillors, Prince Hui, Prince Tun, Prince Kung, Prince I, and Su-shun.[34]

Case 20: On September 19, 1860, the emperor summoned to his presence Princes Hui, Tun, Kung, Ch'un (another younger brother of the emperor), and I.[35]

Case 21: Early in the morning of the day he left for Jehol, the emperor summoned to his presence Princes Hui, Kung, Tun, I, and Cheng, and the grand councillors.[36]

Case 22: In January 1859 the British seized at Shektsing near Canton a letter to someone in the entourage of Huang Tsung-han, the antiforeign governor-general of Kwangtung and Kwangsi; the letter was from a minor official sent by Huang to Shanghai to watch the course of events.[37] It reported on inside facts in Peking and Shanghai around the time of the Shanghai negotiations in 1858, stating: "The Administrators-in-chief of barbarian business in the capital are the three Princes, Hwui, Kung, and Ching [Cheng]." If we can rely on this information, we may assume that Prince Kung was then an important member of the Council of Princes.

It would seem from this documentation that the Council of Princes consisted of Princes Hui, I, Cheng, Kung, and Tun.[38] The combination of the first three was apparently the most frequent and regular grouping. They formed the inner core of the council, and in June and July of 1858 they acted mostly in the capacity of *hsun-fang wang-ta-ch'en.*

The Council of Princes functioned not only independently but also in conjunction with other bodies. *Firstly,* as in cases 2, 18, 21, and perhaps also in 6, we have evidence of joint conferences between the Council of Princes and the Grand Council.

Case 23: In a memorial presented late in May 1859, the grand councillors stated that they had not yet consulted with "Prince Hui and others" about a communication to be sent to Perovskii, who was then in Peking. A draft would be prepared after a consultation with them on the following day and would then be presented to the throne.[39]

Case 24: A memorial of September 21, 1859, from the grand councillors stated that, as a result of consultation with "Prince Hui and others," they proposed sending to the military governors of Heilungkiang and Kirin copies of five communications from the Grand Council or from Su-shun and Jui-ch'ang to Ignat'ev in Peking relating to the Sino-Russian boundary question.[40]

Case 25: In a memorial received on November 14, 1858, Ho Kuei-ch'ing discussed fully the current situation, advocated submission to the foreign demands, and criticized an antiforeign and uncompromising stand as unrealistic. The vermilion endorsement to this memorial reads in part: "Read this with Prince Hui and others. This memorial is very important. Order a thorough deliberation." The phrase "read this with Prince Hui and others" (*Yü Hui-ch'in-wang teng t'ung-k'an*) in all probability meant that the Grand Council and the Council of Princes were to hold a joint session to discuss the matter.[41] In the following seven instances the expression, "Read this with Prince Hui and others," and one variation of it, was used in a vermilion endorsement or rescript and can be interpreted as ordering a joint session of these two groups:

Case 26: On June 23, 1858 (the day of the assembly of courtiers mentioned in Case 2), concerning six memorials on the problem of war or peace, all of which had been received on that day.[42]

Case 27: In February 1859, concerning a Russian representation on the alleged murder of an Indian by Chinese soldiers.[43]

Cases 28, 29, 30: In May, June, and August 1859, concerning the Russian penetrations into the Amur River area and beyond.[44]

Case 31: In September 1859, concerning the removal by Seng-ko-lin-ch'in of defenses at Pehtang.[45]

Case 32: In January 1860, concerning a defense program proposed by the junior censor Lin Shou-t'u. In this case the vermilion endorsement read: "Read this with Prince Hui and others. Also fully deliberate upon it with Seng-ko-lin-ch'in." [46]

Case 33: On December 17, 1858, Su-shun and Jui-ch'ang were appointed to negotiate with Perovskii. The implications of this appointment were explained in a vermilion rescript of the same day.[47] At the end of the rescript was written: "Read this with Tsai-yüan [Prince I] and others. Tell Prince Hui about it tomorrow." [48] This must mean that if Prince Hui had also been at court on that day, the rescript would have been perused with him. In other words, we can regard this as a variation of "Read this with Prince Hui and others."

Possibly we should assume that the Council of Princes functioned principally in joint session with the Grand Council. Certainly the two councils must have been closely related. It may be well to recall in this connection that the Council of Princes originally evolved from within the 1858 Commission of Defense, in which two grand councillors took part.

Secondly, there were joint conferences of the two councils in which Su-shun participated (see Case 19).

Case 34: On September 7, 1860, the emperor issued a vermilion rescript giving a detailed program for a strong policy of resistance, and on this asked the advice of Princes Hui, I, and Cheng, Su-shun, and the grand councillors.[49] Probably the audience of these persons and Princes Tun and Kung on September 9 (Case 19) was held in order to receive their report and discuss their opinions. This consultation took place in the tense and critical days of the rupture of the Tientsin negotiations. It may be worth noting that the manipulator Su-shun was on this occasion openly on stage and participating in the discussion.

Thirdly, in at least one case there was joint management by the Council of Princes, adjutants-general, and grand councillors.

Case 35: On September 13, 1860, the emperor, who had canceled for the moment his plan to go to Jehol, decided to give 200,000 silver taels out of the privy purse for distribution among soldiers, in an effort to raise their morale. He ordered Prince Hui, Prince

Cheng, adjutants-general, and grand councillors to handle the matter (Prince I was then at T'ung-chou).[50]

Fourthly, there were consultations between the Council of Princes and Seng-ko-lin-ch'in (see Case 10).

Case 36: During the Tientsin negotiations of 1858, Prince Hui was sent to Seng-ko-lin-ch'in's camp at T'ung-chou, apparently for consultation.[51]

Case 37: In April 1859 Prince I was sent to Taku to inspect the maritime defenses there under Seng-ko-lin-ch'in.[52]

Fifthly, we know of at least one identifiable instance of consultation (in August 1859) between the Council of Princes and Kuei-liang and Hua-sha-na (see Case 7). One may infer also from case 5 that in July 1858 consultations took place between the same persons, relating to the coming negotiations in Shanghai.

Sixthly, Chi-p'u's account of his own experiences with the three princes (see Case 5) shows that there could also be personal consultation on public affairs between the Council of Princes and a high official on the level of a vice-president of a Board.

Seventhly, Cases 4 and 18 indicate that the Council of Princes sometimes handled judicial matters jointly with other bodies.

The main function of the Council of Princes seems to have been to act as an advisory body to the emperor on important matters concerning foreign affairs and defense.[53] One thing to be noted here is that high officials occasionally sent letters to the Council of Princes, which in turn presented them to the throne either directly or through grand councillors. In other words, besides memorializing the throne directly, high officials did try to exert influence through the Council of Princes; at least they kept in contact with it, which would seem to be another indication that the council had great influence in policy decisions. Following are several such instances referred to in edicts or memorials in *Ch'ou-pan i-wu shih-mo.* (1) Communications to "Prince Hui and others" from Kuei-liang and his colleagues who were negotiating directly with the foreign authorities. During the Shanghai negotiations in 1858, Kuei-liang and his colleagues sent a letter to "Prince Hui and others" in Peking, reporting the prospects of the negotiations and opposing Peking's idea of granting the foreigners total exemption from customs duties.[54] Again, during the Tientsin negotiations in 1860, Kuei-liang and his colleagues wrote to "Prince Hui and others," reporting the course of events.[55] (2) Communications from Seng-ko-lin-ch'in while stationed at Taku, one in 1859, and three in 1860. Three of these communications concerned the appearance off Taku of foreign vessels; the subject of the remaining one cannot be determined.[56] (3) In September 1860 Chiao Yu-ying, subdirector of the Banqueting Court, and two other metropolitan officials, all three of whom had been sent to Tientsin from Peking to organize local militia, wrote to "Prince Hui and others" reporting the firm attitude of the British negotiators.[57]

Case 6 gives evidence of an exchange of letters in July 1859 between Princes Hui, I, and Cheng, and the grand councillors on the one side and probably Heng-fu on the other. In this case one end of the correspondence was not the Council of Princes alone, but a joint body of the Council of Princes and the Grand Council. From this it may be permissible to infer that in some of the above cases references in an edict or memorial to "Prince Hui and others" as recipients of letters may likewise be to the two councils combined.

The weight of all this evidence makes it reasonable to assume that the clique of Prince I, the real power-holders in this period, participated in and influenced policy decisions through a *de facto* Council of Princes.[58]

THE WAR PARTY AND THE PEACE PARTY

When the Arrow War began, the atmosphere in Peking was predominantly antiforeign. This antiforeign mood was a natural response to the external pressures that had been felt more or less constantly since the Opium War, and it had been still further strengthened by the retrogressive orientation of Chinese foreign policy after the Hsien-feng emperor ascended the throne in 1850. What, then, was the reaction in Peking when external pressure was intensified, in the form of demands, backed by overwhelming military power in North China, for permanent residence in Peking, the opening of the interior, navigation on the Great River, and so on?

Probably the reaction assumed the following pattern. To the suddenly intensified pressure, the initial reaction, after some indecision, was a pretty general advocacy of war. When the pressure increased, there was a split into a war party and a peace party.[59] The latter was a minority group whose influence in Peking was small, but as foreign pressure continued to increase, the peace party gained strength, supported by the sheer logic of expediency. When the pressure reached its limit, the war party, or at least its members at the decision-making level, could not do otherwise than align themselves for the moment with the peace party, although the war advocates at the lower level did not readily follow the lead of the men at the top and severely criticized them. As soon as external pressure began to diminish, however, the alignment with the peace party dissolved and the war party regained strength.

The word "party" in this context means simply a group of war or peace advocates — a rather amorphous group which may at any given moment have been no more than the product of a temporary alignment. "Party" in this sense was used in the Blue Books and other contemporary Western reports, and I should like to retain it here.

The War Party

It is probable that metropolitan officialdom in general, or at least those members of it who could be vocal enough to exert influence, more or less favored war. With varying nuances, depending upon the memorialist and upon the immediate state of affairs, almost all the memorials of this period in *Ch'ou-pan i-wu shih-mo* which were written by officials in Peking were fundamentally warlike in tone. Generally speaking the memorials in 1858 and 1859 quite unrestrainedly advocated war. To be more precise, the fall of the Taku forts on May 20, 1858, at first brought on a temporizing mood, but it was soon superseded by a growing clamor for war.[60] In 1860, after the second fall of the Taku forts, on August 21, the uproar suddenly gave way to counsels of prudence, but with the rupture of negotiations in Tientsin intense war advocacy re-emerged.

Among the many officials in Peking who memorialized against compromise or submission, there appears to have been a nucleus of violent war advocates. This was a relatively small group of indigenous Chinese officials who were not at the top level; they were serving especially in such government organs as the Censorate or the National Academy, and were thus in an excellent position to remonstrate loudly without assuming any responsibility for making decisions. As a representative figure we may mention Yin Keng-yun, junior censor, or Yin Chao-yung,[61] chief supervisor of instruction, or Hsü P'eng-shou,[62] subexpositor of the Academy. Yin Keng-yun, for example, presented some eight warlike memorials of his own, and also drafted at least two important joint memorials, each of which was signed by more than twenty officials and which recommended an uncompromising policy.[63]

Behind this war advocacy by officials in Peking, there was a latent but potent antiforeignism among the literati throughout the empire, which had persisted since the Opium War. There was also an antiforeign movement in Kwangtung, which was led by three high officials who were then home on leave and were certainly maintaining contact with the Peking government.[64]

Although we cannot here enter into a detailed analysis of the way of thought revealed in the warlike memorials, such an analysis would be worth undertaking since these memorials reveal Chinese traditional cultural values on the defensive in the actual process of political resistance to the Western impact. In brief, the war advocates were against the formula of intercourse adopted by the modern Western state system and favored the old, hierarchical tribute system. They were also extremely sensitive and hostile to any possible undermining of the existing domestic political and social structure, which was also hierarchical. Their concern was not only to preserve the political and social status quo, but also to defend a sacrosanct cultural tradition which was assumed to be superior to any other. This basic attitude was intensified by resentment against the repeated use of force by Western powers from the time of the Opium War, and the result was often fanatical outbursts.[65]

Certainly one reason for the frenzied advocacy of war was the prevailing ignorance of the military strength of the allied forces, coupled with undue optimism as to the effectiveness of the popular militia (*t'uan-lien*). Many warlike memorials indulged in discussions of military strategy.[66]

One common feature of these discussions was an ignorance of the might of Western firearms: rattan shields or curtains of old wet cotton wool were recommended as protection against gunfire; approaching the enemy with troops dispersed in lines of battle, and seeking hand-to-hand encounters were supposed to be effective tactics.[67] Another common feature was a repeated demand that the popular militia be aroused to act in cooperation with government troops.[68] Much was expected of this method because the local militia at Tientsin had once been effective in repulsing the Taipings and also because the antiforeignism of the militia in Kwangtung in 1858 had led to the harassment of the allied troops there. Elgin later admitted in Parliament that as soon as the Tientsin Treaty was signed, the British were obliged to abandon his intention of proceeding directly to Peking because they had to send their troops back to Canton.[69]

The Peace Party

While the mood in Peking was overwhelmingly warlike, counsels of peace were strenuously put forward by the treaty negotiators themselves, who were compelled to realize the might of the foreign troops and had to deal directly with the determined foreign negotiators who were backed by this military power. T'an T'ing-hsiang and his colleagues at Taku in 1858, Kuei-liang and others at Tientsin in 1858, Heng-fu at Taku in 1860, Kuei-liang and his associates at Tientsin in 1860 — all of them consistently and repeatedly sent in memorials favoring peace.[70] Among them it was certainly the experienced Manchu politician Kuei-liang who was at the center of the peace moves in 1858–1860.[71]

These men did not advocate peace as a matter of principle, nor did they favor the opening of China. In point of fact, they came to advocate peace only because they had been obliged personally to face the situation and found that the relative strength of the two sides made war impossible. In 1854 Kuei-liang, as the governor-general of Chihli, had supervised from his post at Paoting the treaty revision negotiations at Taku with the British, American, and French representatives. On that occasion he had recommended to Peking the rejection of the foreign demands. He did this, no doubt, because the foreign demands were not then supported by sufficient military power.[72] T'an T'ing-hsiang, a peace advocate in 1858, presented late in 1860 a memorial favoring a firm foreign policy from his current post as the acting governor of Shensi, this he did jointly with Lo-pin, governor-general of Shensi and Kansu.[73] Chiao Yu-ying, subdirector of the Banqueting Court, and Chang Chih-wan, compiler of the first class (expositor in 1860) of the Academy, who were both war advocates in 1858,[74] in 1860 repeatedly urged peace after they had been sent to Tientsin.[75] They were apparently influenced also by the counsel of peace and prudence offered by leading Tientsin merchants like Chang Chin-wen.[76] During the 1858 Tientsin negotiations Pien Pao-shu, department magistrate of Ts'ang-chou, was probably the most active and conspicuous figure among the Ch'ing negotiators. He participated in all of the four separate series of negotiations that were going on. In the eyes of the Western negotiators he was shrewd, tricky, unscrupulous, and obtrusive. He behaved quite brazenly, acting as a sort of spokesman or prompter for his superiors, opposing the foreign demands most strongly, and not hesitating to interrupt or correct remarks by his superiors or to speak without regard for them.[77] He must have been an agent of the war party in Peking, who had been charged to keep an eye on and check the actions of Kuei-liang and Hua-sha-na. Probably Kuei-liang sought to mollify the war party by purposely putting Pien in the forefront of the negotiations.[78]

The stand taken by Kuei-liang in North China was strongly supported by official circles in Shanghai, represented by Ho Kuei-ch'ing,
governor-general of Kiangnan and Kiangsi. When Huang Tsung-
han, imperial commissioner and governor-general of Kwangtung
and Kwangsi (newly appointed in January 1858 to replace Yeh
Ming-ch'en, who had been taken prisoner by the British), traveled
to his new post, he visited Ho Kuei-ch'ing en route. Ho tried to
"detain him with bitter tears," vainly urging him to negotiate at
Shanghai with the representatives of the four powers.[79] Twice before the Taku negotiations in 1858 Ho Kuei-ch'ing presented memorials advising prudence, to the second of which he added a long
confidential memorial. In this confidential memorial Ho rejected
the warlike opinions of Huang Tsung-han and recommended peace,
analyzing in detail the current situation at home and abroad.[80]
During the Tientsin negotiations, he sent a confidential letter to
Ch'ien Hsin-ho, provincial treasurer of Chihli, in which, apparently
in reply to an inquiry by Kuei-liang, he discussed diplomatic tactics and urged peace.[81] Ch'ien Hsin-ho had had some experience in
foreign contact, having participated in negotiations at Taku in 1850,
1854, 1857, and 1858.[82] He and Ho were both from K'un-ming-
hsien in Yunnan, and they were *chin-shih* of the same year.[83] It may
be worth noting that Ho Kuei-ch'ing exerted pressure upon Kuei-
liang through the channel of this close relationship.

Later in 1858 Ho Kuei-ch'ing was appointed a member of the
Ch'ing delegation in the Shanghai negotiations. His views greatly
affected Kuei-liang and his associates, who had been sent to Shanghai with the most positive instructions to annul the Tientsin treaties.[84] Ho also submitted a memorial of his own, favoring peace.[85]
As we have already mentioned, after the fall of Soochow in 1860
he presented a joint memorial with Wang Yu-ling outspokenly
urging that the government ask for foreign military assistance
against the Taipings, in return for China's unqualified submission
to the foreign demands.

The diplomatic machinery under Ho Kuei-ch'ing when he served
as Shanghai imperial commissioner from January 1859 consisted

of Wang Yu-ling, provincial treasurer, who was a financial expert,[86] and people experienced in foreign affairs in Shanghai, like the provincial judge Hsueh Huan,[87] the taotai Wu Hsü,[88] the ex-taotai Wu Chien-chang,[89] and the former acting taotai Lan Wei-wen.[90] Most of these men had entered officialdom through the purchase of rank or office. These diplomatic officials were surrounded by the Shanghai merchants engaged in foreign trade, for example, Yang Fang (Taki or Takee).[91] Shanghai had developed rapidly as a trade center since its opening as a treaty port under the Nanking Treaty. The city was thriving through the export of silk and tea and the import of opium. In the 1850's the foreign trade at Shanghai amounted to roughly one half of the total foreign trade of the country.[92] Shanghai merchants were thus very much interested in the peaceful continuation of trade. On the one hand they had intimate connections with the Shanghai authorities; on the other they were close to foreign firms like Jardine, Matheson and Co.[93] Thus the Chinese engaged in foreign trade in Shanghai constituted a latent but not negligible influence for peace.[94] They functioned as unofficial channels for negotiation between Chinese and Western authorities in Shanghai, and occasionally Peking actually ordered that this channel be used.[95] When the Taipings approached Shanghai in 1860, these merchants along with the Shanghai officials sought military assistance from the foreign authorities, and, as we know, Yang Fang and Wu Hsü sponsored the organization of a corps of foreign mercenaries.[96]

The merchants in Shanghai were perhaps all the more pacifist because they were also connected with the extensive junk trade between the ports of Shanghai and Ningpo and those in the north like Chefoo and Newchang. Roughly 3,000 junks with crews totaling some 100,000 men were believed by contemporary foreign observers to be engaged in this native coastal trade. These junks carried native goods and foreign produce like opium to the north, and brought back peas, beans, and oil cakes to the south. About one-third of the junks were freighted in season on government account for the transport of tribute rice to Tientsin. The capital invested in this shipping and trade was estimated at £7,500,000 sterling and was held in shares by Shanghai and Ningpo merchants.[97] Because British warships had given assistance against pirates, the junk proprietors were well disposed toward the British and were ready to inform them of the situation in North China.[98] In April 1860 the British and French authorities in China planned a naval blockade to intercept the tribute grain transport with a view to harassing the Peking government. At the suggestion of the Shanghai authorities the Chinese merchants in Shanghai appear to have brought some kind of pressure on the British merchants. Apparently as a result, the idea of a blockade was given up.[99] Just after the fall of the Taku forts in May 1858, junk supercargoes from Ningpo or Shanghai, who were then around Taku, petitioned the allied authorities for permission to discharge their cargoes. They were used, by T'an T'ing-hsiang and his colleagues, as go-betweens for negotiating with the foreigners, though with no effect.[100]

In Canton, the former hong merchant Wu Ch'ung-yueh (Howqua IV) and other merchants engaged in foreign trade were acting as middlemen between the Chinese and foreign authorities there. On the local level, their aim was peace.[101] But there is no visible sign that they positively sought to influence the peace party on the national level, as did the Shanghai merchants, probably because Canton under the allied occupation was surrounded by the antiforeign movement and the channels for diplomatic contact had been transferred by the foreign diplomats from there to Shanghai.[102] In July 1858 Peking ordered that Wu Ch'ung-yueh and P'an Shih-ch'eng, a wealthy man who had once been an advisor on foreign affairs to Ch'i-ying, be sent from Canton to Shanghai to be at the service of Kuei-liang and his associates in the coming negotiations.[103] Wu, obviously the more important of the two, was tied down in Canton, involved in public affairs; P'an Shih-ch'eng went to Shanghai, but arrived there too late for the negotiations. He remained there, however, and worked for some time for the Shanghai authorities.[104] The activities in Shanghai of P'an Shih-ch'eng and of the ever-present Wu Chien-chang may be taken as an indication that the commercial interests in Canton were influencing Ch'ing diplomacy to some extent through Shanghai channels.

Generally speaking, the population on the coast — the commercial classes especially — which could share in the prosperity brought by the foreign trade, whether or not at the treaty ports, was inclined to be favorable toward the foreigners. The local officials also rather encouraged, though tacitly, the visits of foreigners to ports which were officially not opened, insofar as they could profit indirectly from the trade.[105]

War and Peace Advocates in the Council of Princes

How was the opposition between the war and peace parties reflected in the Council of Princes, which was presumably the arena for an ultimate policy decision on war or peace?

First, we must consider the rivalries that existed among the princes of the Council, which were to overlap with their differences in foreign policy. As we have said, the clique of Prince I and Prince Cheng, with Su-shun as manipulator, constituted the most influential group in the Council, partly on the strength of imperial favor. Prince Kung was opposed to this clique; he was not on good terms with the emperor, his elder brother,[106] and he and Prince I were hostile to each other.[107] Prince Hui, senior member of the Council, must have been a sort of elder statesman and mediator. (The position of Prince Tun at this time cannot be determined. Though he was presumably a member of the Council, he does not seem ever to have played a noticeable role in it.)

During the period 1858–1860 it was Prince I's clique that represented the war advocates in the Council of Princes. *Ch'ou-pan i-wu shih-mo* contains no document that positively and directly shows their counsel of war, but the following two instances implicitly indicate that this was their position. A memorandum which was attached to a joint memorial by "Tsai-yuan (Prince I) and others," presented before the opening of the 1858 Tientsin negotiations, proposed an over-all rejection of the major foreign demands.[108] On the question of how to punish Ch'i-ying, Prince I and Prince

Cheng, along with Prince Hui, urged summary execution for the aged diplomat and, in opposition to a recommendation of commutation by Prince Kung and others, Shu-shun presented a memorial urging summary execution and implicitly striking at the weak-kneed diplomacy of Kuei-liang.[109] As haughty Manchu princes, who were at the apex of their power and were manipulated by that domineering politician Su-shun, it was probably natural for Princes I and Cheng to be aggressive and warlike. Furthermore, since their power rested in part upon their policy of patronizing Chinese officials like Tseng Kuo-fang who were fighting the Taipings, they must have been affected by the warlike mood in Peking officialdom in general and especially among certain intransigeant Chinese officials. The furious war advocate Yin Keng-yun, who was rather close to Tseng, was certainly one of those officials under the patronage of Su-shun.[110] Huang Tsung-han, who was supervising the antiforeign hostility around Canton, was also a follower of Prince I's clique.[111] According to the contemporary information that reached the foreign authorities, the nucleus of war advocates in the emperor's entourage was also identified with this clique.[112]

The ultimate responsibility for policy decisions rested, of course, with the emperor. The Hsien-feng emperor was antiforeign in disposition.[113] Furthermore, he was a young and mediocre despot, who sought relief in personal indulgences from the great strain of dealing with one crisis after another. During the period 1858–1860, he was reported to be a sickly man in consequence of sensual excesses and opium smoking. He had difficulty in walking because of a leg ailment.[114] In making political decisions, he was influenced by his entourage, especially by the favorite clique of Prince I, and it may be assumed that the persistent warlike tone of the edicts of this period was attributable to the direct pressure of Prince I's clique.

It was Prince Kung who, in the Council of Princes, was forced into the position of supporting Kuei-liang's counsel of peace. It is true that a directly opposite inference can also be drawn from the available sources. During the 1858 Tientsin negotiations, Prince

Kung presented three rather vehemently warlike memorials, one
jointly with Prince Hui and Prince Tun, the other two by himself.[115] A common view, based on these memorials, is that *in 1858*
Prince Kung was a war advocate.[116] Our assumption here, however, is that he was a peace advocate *from 1858,* an assumption based
on the following reasoning.[117]

If we recall that he was an unloved younger brother of the emperor and was on bad terms with Prince I and his clique, and
that he was a son-in-law of none other than Kuei-liang,[118] we may
assume that, if there was any person in the Council of Princes
likely to be privately influenced and kept informed by Kuei-liang,
it must have been Prince Kung. If there had been no one in the
Council working, even if in secret, for eventual peace, Kuei-liang
and other peace negotiators could not have been so vocal in advising peace, and it would hardly have been possible, when the foreign
pressure reached its limit, to turn the Council toward peace, even for
a moment. His warlike memorials may thus be taken as *"ballons
d'essai* released in order to find out how the wind was blowing at
the court." [119]

What was the position of Prince Hui? As we have seen, he, with
Princes I and Cheng, formed the nucleus of the Council, and in
many cases he acted with them. But there were also instances in
which he acted with Princes Kung and Tun. There was also the
third grouping with Prince Hui, which amalgamated the preceding
two combinations. His role in the Council must have been that of
a mediator. Though he played for time in the midst of the generally
warlike mood, he must have been in a position eventually to undertake the task of hastening the adaptation to reality.[120] Incidentally, he too was a son-in-law of Kuei-liang.[121]

Internalization of the Foreign Pressure

A temporary alignment of the war and peace parties could be
brought about only by the penetration into the domestic political
arena of the pressures exerted by the foreigners. The factors responsible for this penetration were the realistic judgment of the

military situation by Seng-ko-lin-ch'in and the acute awareness in Peking of the intensity of domestic unrest.

Seng-ko-lin-ch'in was a member of the Borjigit clan and the Korchin tribe of Inner Mongolia.[122] The Korchin tribe had been favored by successive Ch'ing emperors. So-t'e na-mu to-pu-chi, a prince of the second degree and the chieftain of one of the banners of the tribe, had married a daughter of the Chia-ch'ing emperor, but he had no son of his own. Seng-ko-lin-ch'in, a relative, was appointed his heir at the personal choice of the Tao-kuang emperor. Seng-ko-lin-ch'in thus inherited a princedom of the second degree and became chieftain of the banner. He was generously patronized by the Tao-kuang emperor, and as an adjutant general he was among the group of courtiers who received the emperor's "testamentary decree." [123] In 1853–1854 he drove back the Taiping forces that had penetrated into North China, which won him resounding fame and elevation to a princedom of the first degree. At a time when most of the government's military forces were impotent, Seng-ko-lin-ch'in with his well-trained troops was certainly a most important military figure to the Ch'ing dynasty.[124] As a favorite courtier from the days of the late emperor, his prestige at the inner court in Peking was very high.[125] During the Tientsin negotiations he was stationed as a field commander at T'ung-chou, and after the treaties had been signed he made efforts to strengthen the Taku forts. He repelled the Anglo-French warships in 1859, and continued his untiring efforts to reinforce the defenses.

Contemporary Western authorities in China believed him to be a tough war advocate and a prominent leader of the war party,[126] for the following reasons. First, the fact that he was seriously engaged in extensive fortifications at Taku quite understandably gave this impression. Second, most of the reports given to Western officials by Chinese informants gave the same impression.[127] Third, the memorials, copies or originals, which fell into the hands of the foreigners and were believed, correctly or not, to have been written in the name of Seng-ko-lin-ch'in, were aggressive in tone. This last point must be examined in some detail.

In August 1860 the British seized at Hsin-ho near Taku copies of two memorials by Seng-ko-lin-ch'in.[128] One of them concerned some technical problems of fortification. The other was a memorial presented in April of the same year jointly with Heng-fu, which assumed that the British were simply bluffing and had no real intention of waging a war. The memorialists therefore recommended a firm attitude in negotiating with the British.[129] This document is probably the most firm and the most self-confident among his memorials on war and diplomacy during this period. The original of another memorial by Seng-ko-lin-ch'in dated August 26, 1860, which besought the emperor "to proceed on a hunting tour" (flee to the imperial villa in Jehol), was seized at the Summer Palace; this memorial is also aggressive.[130] After the Taku incident of June 25, 1859, the foreigners secured privately circulated copies of two other joint memorials by Seng-ko-lin-ch'in and Heng-fu, reporting the Taku victory. As reports of victory, these memorials are inevitably exalted in mood.[131]

In addition to the documents mentioned, there are at least three more intensely warlike memorials which were believed to be by Seng-ko-lin-ch'in and of which English or French translations were published. Henri Cordier, in his book on the 1860 allied expedition to China, regards the Mongol prince as a representative of the war party and quotes a contemporary French translation by Baron de Méritens, interpreter for the French legation in China, of two memorials allegedly presented jointly by Seng-ko-lin-ch'in and Heng-fu.[132] These memorials, which are doctrinaire in tone, read like memorials on military affairs by an aggressive civilian official. They were, in fact, presented not by Seng-ko-lin-ch'in and Heng-fu but by Ch'üan-ch'ing, president of the Board of War, and Lien Chao-lun, superintendent of the government granaries in the capital.[133]

The *North China Herald* (September 10, 1859) carried an English translation of an undated memorial which was supposed to be Seng-ko-lin-ch'in's. To judge from its content (which was a request for the recall of Kuei-liang and Hua-sha-na), if it was really a memorial from some official, it must have been drafted during the 1858 Tientsin negotiations, when Seng-ko-lin-ch'in, as we shall see, was pessimistic about the military prospects. In its manner of presentation and its tone it is quite different from Seng-ko-lin-ch'in's memorials, which were usually rather factual and realistic. It reads like a warlike memorial from a Chinese civilian official. While S. Wells Williams in his journal quotes in full this same English translation with the same footnotes, without mentioning the source or disputing Seng-ko-lin-ch'in's authorship,[134] the *North China Herald*, on the other hand, seems to have harbored some doubt about the authenticity of the document, pointing out that it and a memorial by Yin Chao-yung are "in perfect accord" in their "sentiments."[135] Perhaps we can draw one of the following conclusions: (1) the disputed document was a forgery manufactured for foreign consumption; (2) it was a memorial by another official, which had been put into circulation mistakenly as Seng-ko-lin-ch'in's; (3) a copy of a memorial by some other official was sold to the foreigners as Seng-ko-lin-ch'in's, with the memorialist's name changed in the text.

In any event, there is no doubt that most of the documents which reached the foreigners and were identified, correctly or not, as Seng-ko-lin-ch'in's, were warlike or defiant.[136] However, a perusal of the many memorials by Seng-ko-lin-ch'in which are included in *Ch'ou-pan i-wu shih-mo,* and a comparison of them with the belligerent memorials from other officials, lead to the conclusion that he was by no means a war advocate.[137] Two memorials on military affairs, which he presented during the Tientsin negotiations, discussed in detail and in an unmistakably pessimistic vein, the current state of defenses between Tientsin and Peking, painstakingly describing the inadequacies, complaining of the low morale of the soldiers and of the unreliability of the Tientsin populace, and stressing the difficulty of procuring supplies because of the high prices.[138] A memorial presented about one month after the Taku victory in 1859 was full of self-confidence, but discussed diplomatic measures to stabilize the situation following this military success.[139]

A memorial received on April 4, 1860, was, as we have mentioned, probably the most resolute. Citing a report that extensive preparations were openly under way in Shanghai for an allied military expedition to the north, he asserted that this was nothing but a bluff; the allies lacked the will to fight. He suggested allowing the Shanghai imperial commissioner to negotiate a settlement with the allied diplomats, offering them some minor concessions to save their faces.[140] A memorial presented soon after the landing of the allied troops at Pehtang showed a marked change of attitude. He now openly sounded a warning, reporting the enemy's willingness to fight.[141] Thereafter, he reported frankly and in detail one defeat of the Ch'ing forces after another, emphasizing among other things the formidable firepower of the allied troops and their high morale.[142] Just before negotiations opened at Tientsin he advocated peace.[143] While Kuei-liang was negotiating at Tientsin, Seng-ko-lin-ch'in presented a memorial supporting his desire for peace.[144] After Prince Kung took charge of negotiations, Seng-ko-lin-ch'in reported on the demoralization and dispersal of his troops[145] and urged haste in making peace;[146] indeed he repeatedly pressed Prince Kung to the rapid conclusion of a peace.[147]

These views of Seng-ko-lin-ch'in's must have had a decisive influence upon the inner core of the Peking government. He not only presented suggestions in memorials, but on important occasions he was asked personally for his views by the Council of Princes.[148] On such occasions, Seng-ko-lin-ch'in must have spoken even more frankly.

We may safely conclude that he was not a doctrinaire war advocate, though he may not have been a peace advocate in line with Prince Kung or Kuei-liang. Perhaps we should say that his position was that of a rather hard-headed military expert. According to a report given to the allied authorities in Shanghai in June 1860 by Ignat'ev, who had then been in Peking for almost a year, the civilians in power at Peking were "determined to wage war to the last extremity," while Seng-ko-lin-ch'in and military mandarins were inclined toward peace.[149]

The overwhelming allied military power must have impressed the Ch'ing government all the more acutely in view of its difficulties in meeting the vigorous activities of the Taipings and the Nien army. The counselors of peace unanimously stressed the gravity of the domestic crisis. As we have seen, even Prince I, a leader of the war party, when he took charge of negotiations and went in person to T'ung-chou, sought to sound out the British about the possibility of military assistance against the rebels.[150] Furthermore, in North China, where the allied military campaign took place, the sympathies of the populace were far from reliable so far as the Ch'ing government was concerned.

The general response of the commoners in North China to the allied forces was fear, indifference, or curiosity.[151] If not molested by the foreign troops, they were ready to cooperate with them, and, if paid, they would furnish supplies in abundance.[152] When Parkes and Loch were confined in the prison of the Board of Punishments in Peking, officials treated them brutally, while native fellow-prisoners showed them much kindness and respect.[153] Just the reverse of their attitude toward foreigners was the antipathy that the common people harbored toward their own authorities. In 1858 the people around Taku expressed no sympathy or concern for Governor-General T'an T'ing-hsiang, who was then stationed there, and who had extorted everything he wanted from the local populace.[154] In the spring of 1860, when Seng-ko-lin-ch'in was busy strengthening the Taku fortifications and concentrating many troops, reports reaching Bruce through Roman Catholic missionaries described the people of Chihli as "heartily tired of the presence of their defenders." [155] When the allied troops landed at Pehtang later in the year, the people there were ready to give them whatever information they could. A Manchu field commander in that area, named Hsi-ling-a, was particularly unpopular with them because of his cruelty and extortions. They also hated the Mongol soldiers, whose bodies smelt offensive because they ate raw mutton.[156] After the Taku forts fell, an aged native resident expressed to a British interpreter his burning resentment against the Manchus:

"What need was there of squeezing the people to build forts for the purpose of driving you away? . . ."[157]

An edict of September 5, 1860, deplored the fact that while "the worthies among the gentry" (*shen-shih chung chih hsien-che*) were eager "to preserve their native villages" (*pao-ch'üan hsiang-li*), "the merchants or small peddlers" were "ignorant enough to be apt to work for the benefit of the barbarians," and "the unemployed vagrants" might be enticed into collusion with the barbarians.[158]

In the background there was a ferment of social unrest in Chihli. Shen Chao-lin, president of the Board of War, wrote in a memorial late in 1860: "While the capital was on guard (*chieh-yen*), bandits were active everywhere in the southern part of Chihli. The people everywhere dared to postpone the payment of their taxes for the latter half of the year. It is said that in spite of stern requests they are still refusing to pay."[159] Even in the city of Peking, there was, during the period 1858–1860, a disquieting air of discontent, because of the rise in prices.[160] According to Ignat'ev, Peking in 1860 was "on the eve of revolution."[161]

In such a situation, the organizing of local militia, of which great hopes were entertained by the war advocates, could not be effective against foreign troops. It was admitted by the foreign authorities in China that the allied forces would have been greatly harassed and perhaps stopped altogether if partisan warfare had been waged against them.[162] In point of fact, however, the militia could be efficacious only in keeping off bandits.[163] A major purpose in organizing militia was really to bring the unemployed under government control and to feed them as militiamen, in order to prevent their cooperation with the enemy.[164]

DISSENSION WITHIN THE WAR PARTY

When the external pressure reached its limit, the conflict between the war and peace parties was suspended and peace was agreed upon. However, the war advocates did not all adapt themselves at the same tempo. When the war advocates in the Council of Princes executed a *volte face,* thus making possible the top-level decision for peace, the war advocates at the lower level criticized them severely. Typical illustrations were the head-on clashes of Prince I's clique with Yin Keng-yun and with Yin Chao-yung, in 1858.

Yin Keng-yun, as we know, was one of those scholar-officials patronized by Su-shun; he was also close to Tseng Kuo-fan. In a warlike memorial received on June 11, he criticized the men at the top, saying: "What the high officials in the entourage of the emperor are saying consists of either bold words of bluff or the sweet talk of flattery. [The information on the negotiations] is kept positively secret, not to be shared with the people in the outer court. The more concealment there is, the more false stories circulate." [165] On June 23, he untiringly advocated war at a large assembly of courtiers.[166] Earlier on the same day, Prince Hui, Prince I, Prince Cheng, and the grand councillors were summoned together in the presence of the emperor. Perhaps it was before this audience that the same people were ordered to peruse together six memorials on the problem of war and peace (including the joint memorial cited below from the Commission of Civil Defense), all of which had been presented to the throne on that day.[167] After this audience there was another joint audience, this time with Chou Tsu-p'ei, president of the Board of Civil Appointments, Chao Kuang, president of the Board of Punishments, and Hsü Nai-p'u, president of the Board of Works — the three top officials on the Commission of Civil Defense (T'uan-fang-ch'u). They and other officials of the commission, many of whom were on the commission in their capacity as censors assigned to duty as police censors (*wu-ch'eng yü-shih*), had presented that day a joint memorial.

This warlike memorial, drafted by two members of the commission, Yin Keng-yun and Lu Ping-shu, strongly opposed the resident minister clause, enumerating eight anticipated evil consequences.[168] In the joint audience, the emperor ordered Chou Tsu-p'ei and his two colleagues to convene "the princes and the officials down to the level of censors" (*wang i-hsia chih k'o-tao*).[169] He also gave them a vermilion rescript which ordered the Hsun-fang wang-ta-ch'en (Prince Hui, Prince I, Prince Cheng, and perhaps also three other high officials of the Commission of Defense, two of whom were grand councillors[170]), the grand councillors, Chou Tsu-p'ei and other cosigners of the joint memorial, as well as Sung Chin, who had opposed the foreign demand for free navigation of rivers,[171] and Wan Ch'ing-li, who had opposed the resident minister clause,[172] all to discuss thoroughly the problem of war or peace. Prince Kung was also ordered to join the consultation. The rescript stressed the need for careful appraisal of the possible consequences of the alternative courses and implied a preference for peace on the part of the emperor at least for the moment.[173]

From this sequence of events, which led to the convocation of an assembly of courtiers, we may infer the following: In the audience with Prince Hui, Prince I, Prince Cheng, and the grand councillors, the decision for peace was made. The placating of the diehard war advocates was now in order. First Chou Tsu-p'ei and his two colleagues on the Commission of Civil Defense, which was obviously a center of vehement war advocacy, were summoned and won over. The emperor then gave them the rescript, which must have been drafted during the preceding audience with Prince Hui and others. The emperor also ordered a meeting of courtiers.

First the princes and high officials (*wang-ta-ch'en*) gathered and Chou Tsu-p'ei showed them the vermilion rescript. They kept silent. Then Prince Hui called in the censors. After the rescript had been read aloud, Yin Keng-yun rose from his prostration, ahead even of the princes, who then all stood up. Prince Cheng angrily asked Yin whether he had any opinion to express. Yin replied that he was loath simply to look on with folded arms at the handing over to the barbarians of the imperial ancestral temple and the altars of the deities of soil and grain. A stormy argument was thus touched off between Prince Cheng and Yin in which Yin urged war. Prince Hui intervened and sought to mollify Yin. Wang Mao-yin, senior vice-president of the Board of War and cosigner of the joint memorial from the Commission of Civil Defense, Wang Ch'ing-li, and Ch'ien Pao-ch'ing, presiding controller of the Imperial Clan Court, sided with Yin. Finally, Yin withdrew from the assembly. Looking back at the palace, he "made lamentation and wept bitter tears."

Recalling this meeting, Lu Ping-shu stated in a memorial received on September 1, 1860: "On that occasion the court was crowded with the people gathered for the debate. Many of them advocated war. But the session ended in a decision for peace."[174]

Sometime after the assembly of courtiers, Yin Keng-yun remonstrated with Su-shun at a drinking party.[175] His outspoken argument with Prince Cheng gained him a reputation for straightforwardness, but later he was involved in a scandal concerning the Shun-t'ien (Peking) provincial examination and in September 1859 he was demoted in rank by five grades and relieved of his post. This rather severe punishment was attributed by some people to resentment against him on the part of Prince Cheng and Su-shun. Nonetheless, Su-shun remained on good terms with him.[176]

In a warlike memorial presented on June 26, 1858, Yin Chao-yung, then subdirector of the Court of Judicature and Revision,[177] criticized the princes. "The ignorant and mediocre high officials," he dared to write, "are eager only to settle the situation by a hasty peace agreement. If the state can indulge in relaxation for one more day, then they can remain for one day longer princes of the first degree or chief ministers of state. They have, however, no time to worry about the real sorrows of the country . . . The opinions of the princes in the imperial entourage are not always right. Measures suggested by the officials, major or minor, are not always fantastic."[178] Prince I and Prince Cheng saw this memorial. They threw it on the floor in a rage and openly talked of a reprisal. To those who feared for him, Yin Chao-yung replied: "They are hastening the coming of a curse upon themselves. I believe in the intellect of His Majesty, who knows. Why should I fear?"[179]

The contrast between the comparative flexibility of the Council of Princes and the intransigeance of Chinese war advocates like Yin Keng-yun and Yin Chao-yung can be ascribed, first of all, to the difference in their positions in the government. The Manchu princes were at the top level, had the actual responsibility of making decisions, and also had direct access to confidential field reports. The Chinese scholar-officials, on the other hand, were on a lower level in the bureaucracy, had no direct responsibility for making decisions, and had relatively scanty information on the realities of the situation.

Not all the Chinese scholar-officials favored war, of course. Apart from the commercially minded barbarian experts at the treaty ports, there were Chinese scholar-officials who had to meet the real situation squarely and so advocated peace. T'an T'ing-hsiang at Taku and Tientsin in 1858, and Ho Kuei-ch'ing in the Shanghai area were cases in point. Nonetheless, we may suggest that there was a fundamental difference in attitude toward the foreign demands between the Manchus and the Chinese. The position of the Chinese officials was that of defenders of the deeply rooted cultural, political, and social traditions of Chinese society. Their culture-centered traditionalism in particular retarded their adaptation to the changing situation. The position of the Council of Princes, on the other hand, was that of the Manchu élite, whose primary concern was the survival of the tottering alien dynasty. Held less in check by traditionalism than the Chinese scholar-officials, the Manchu élite were more sensitive to any change in power relations and more ready to adapt. In the last analysis, they were above all political, in an opportunistic sense. Kuei-liang, the central figure among the peace advocates, was a politician *par excellence* in this sense. Spurred by Kuei-liang, the Council of Princes thus chose peace, despite the vociferous opposition of the Chinese officials. In the long run, the Manchu and the Chinese élites had a common aim: the preservation of the social and political status quo. But at a given critical moment they could be at odds because of differences in motivation and in their adaptability.

When the external pressures began to lessen, the Council of Princes again split in two. Prince I and his clique, reverting to war advocacy, harassed the peace advocates, until Kuei-liang and his associates were instructed to have the Tientsin treaties annulled at the coming Shanghai conference.

In July 1858, some two weeks after the signing of the Tientsin treaties, the senior vice-president of the Board of War, Wang Mao-yin, a war advocate, presented a long memorial containing a critical discussion of the Ch'ing conduct of foreign affairs.[180] First, deploring the incompetence of the officials involved, who had been compelled to make peace without offering any effective countermeasure, he urged the emperor to read Wei Yuan's *Hai-kuo t'u-chih*, which gave a detailed description of the political and human geography of overseas countries and treated fully the "methods of defense, attack, and negotiation" for China. Wang also suggested that the book be reprinted and copies distributed to "princes of the first degree and high officials" and to "imperial clansmen and bannermen," so that they might study it.

Second, he discussed the matter of the recruitment of officials. There was a tendency, he pointed out, to believe that "other persons than the princes cannot necessarily be trusted." He also noted the current stress in the state examinations on such purely technical aspects as skill in writing "eight-legged essays." He suggested two corrective measures. One was to change the examination subjects. Following the proposal made in the twenty-second year of Tao-kuang (roughly 1842) by Ch'i Kung, governor-general of Kwangtung and Kwangsi,[181] the new subjects should be history, military science, "engineering and mathematics" (*chih-ch'i t'ung-suan*), astronomy or astrology (*yin-yang chan-hou*), and geography, with considerable emphasis on "practical learning" (*shih-hsueh*). The other measure was to make good use of the system of recommendation (*pao-chü*). The various officials should recommend talented candidates who, in turn, should be screened personally by Tseng Kuo-fan, who had "incomparable discrimination in reading a person's talent." He called attention to his own memorials presented in 1851 and 1852, which had discussed the same matter of reforming the examination and recommendation systems and also the necessity for serious training in military affairs for the imperial clansmen and bannermen.

Finally, he frankly urged upon the emperor the necessity for self-cultivation. He dared to attack sinocentric complacency, writing: "Nowadays, overseas countries are becoming increasingly powerful and are struggling for ascendancy. From the human point of view, there is a distinction between the Middle Kingdom and outer nations (*Chung-wai chih fen*). But in the eyes of Heaven, there can hardly be any difference. It is stated in the Book of History that 'Great Heaven has no affections; — it helps only the virtuous.' " [182] He went on to point out that if the emperor, "who had received the important trust from the preceding emperors and had become the sovereign of China," wanted "the barbarians to come [to China] from every direction for submission (*pin-fu*)," it was imperative for him to cultivate his own virtues.

This memorial was an incisive criticism by a Chinese scholar-official of the deterioration in vigor and competence of the Manchu élite, not excluding the emperor and princes. It also indicated that the center of power among the Chinese officials had rather shifted to Tseng Kuo-fan and other builders of the new-style military forces. Supporting this shift, and also definitely committed to Confucian ideology, Wang Mao-yin wanted to see the Ch'ing government revitalized. In particular, he requested that the emperor should fully perform his function as the topmost figure in the hierarchy. We have in this memorial a reflection of the power situation behind the division within the war party.

It seems clear that in 1860 there was again conflict in Peking between the war and peace parties after the same pattern as in 1858, and that there was also a similar split among the war advocates and again a *volte face* on the part of Prince I's clique. On his arrival in Shanghai from Peking in June 1860 Ignat'ev stated that Kuei-liang definitely had no real influence but that "the party of the war to the knife" led by Su-shun and his company would disappear very quickly if an effective blow were struck at Taku. [183]

As a matter of fact, the second fall of Taku must have been a critical turning point. In a memorial reporting the fall on August 14 of T'ang-erh-ku near Taku, Seng-ko-lin-ch'in made it clear that he had no real confidence in his ability to defend the Taku forts. [184]

In response to this report, the Peking government took measures for reinforcement, but a cordially phrased vermilion rescript was also sent to Seng-ko-lin-ch'in ordering him, if the fall of Taku became imminent, to retreat to Tientsin.[185] On August 21 Taku fell and on August 26, in a memorial, Seng-ko-lin-ch'in besought the emperor to retreat to Jehol.[186] This development must have been shocking enough to precipitate the second about-face of Prince I's clique.

During the T'ung-chou negotiations, it was Prince I who personally assumed the task of dealing with the British and French. On September 14, after an agreement had been reached between the Prince and Parkes, Parkes remarked that the British had been much misunderstood by "the three Princes" (Prince Hui, Prince I, and Prince Cheng). Prince I immediately rejoined that they had been misunderstood not by the princes alone, but also by the "Han" (Chinese), writing the character with his forefinger in the air. "He then rose, went round the table, and again whispered the word 'Han.'" Prince I and Parkes then became "very friendly," and it was then that the prince sought to sound out Parkes on the question of cooperation against the Taipings. He also asked Parkes to supply the capital with grain at a reasonable price.[187] This dialogue again indicates the division among the war advocates. Incidentally, Prince I on September 16 sent in a memorial advocating peace, claiming that Seng-ko-lin-ch'in had no chance at all against the enemy.[188]

The T'ung-chou negotiations broke down on September 18, and on September 22 the emperor left for Jehol. Prior to his departure Prince I's clique and Peking officialdom were in sharp disagreement on the advisability of his flight.

On September 9 an assembly of courtiers was held to discuss the problem of peace or war, to which the princes and the high officials of the inner and outer court were summoned. Seng-ko-lin-ch'in's suggestion that the emperor go to Jehol was referred to the assembly for discussion, as a result of which a memorial against the proposal was submitted jointly by Chia Chen, grand secretary, and twenty-five other officials, including all the grand councillors then in the court.[189] Many Manchu and Chinese officials, either jointly or individually, presented memorials opposing the flight.[190] These memorials were in essence an earnest remonstrance, declaring that the walled city of Peking should be the last line of defense and that the imperial villa at Jehol was more exposed to danger, that the emperor's flight would cause a panic among the populace, and that the emperor should not be so irresponsible as to desert, leaving behind him the imperial ancestral temple and the altars of the deities of soil and grain. The vehemence of these remonstrances startled the allied personnel, who seized some of these memorials at the Summer Palace.[191] General Montauban went so far as to write that he saw in "the more imperious than respectful tone" of the mandarins toward the emperor "the coming fall" of the dynasty.[192]

The prime movers in forcing the flight to Jehol were Prince Cheng and Su-shun.[193] In this matter again Yin Keng-yun argued passionately with them. In a joint memorial of September 13 from Ch'üan-ch'ing, president of the Board of Civil Appointments, and twenty-three other high officials, which was drafted by Yin Keng-yun, he hinted that there might be "some about your Majesty's person" who would support the idea of the flight. He also wrote bluntly: "Your Majesty is well familiar with the maxim that the Prince is bound to sacrifice himself for his country." [194] In another memorial presented by him alone, Yin urged that Prince Cheng be punished.[195] Furthermore, he sent a letter to Su-shun, trying to dissuade him from supporting the emperor's flight.[196]

As we shall see in Chapter V, the emperor was accompanied to Jehol by Prince Hui, Prince I, Prince Cheng and many other princes, Su-shun, most of the grand councillors, and by the harem. Of those left behind, Prince Kung, Kuei-liang, and Grand Councillor Wen-hsiang formed the nucleus of the peace negotiators. Prince K'o-ch'in (Ch'ing-hui), Prince Yü (I-tao), and other high officials were in charge of defense, the preservation of order, and other public affairs in the city of Peking. Dealing with the allied authorities, who were restraining themselves from dealing a fatal blow, and simultaneously placating the frustrated war advocates in Jehol and in Peking,

Prince Kung and his associates finally succeeded in making peace. The emperor's flight, which the foreign powers had feared would lead to the collapse of the dynasty, in actual effect helped to maintain the new precarious political equilibrium which had been created by external pressure and in which the peace party could now have a decisive voice. The diplomatic machinery headed by Prince Kung, which was considerably expanded in the course of the protracted muddling-through of the peace negotiations, was later to be formally institutionalized as the Tsungli Yamen.

ANGLO-FRENCH SUPPORT OF THE PEACE PARTY

The allied powers took certain specific steps intended to strengthen, or at least not to weaken, the unpopular peace party. When the aged Ch'i-ying was recalled from obscurity in 1858, perhaps as a tool of Prince I's clique, and sent to Tientsin as an additional representative, the foreign negotiators and Kuei-liang were both embarrassed by his obstructive tendencies. The British wanted him removed. As "the most effective and certain way" of accomplishing this result, Thomas Wade and Horatio Lay unexpectedly produced in the presence of Ch'i-ying, Kuei-liang, and Hua-sha-na, Ch'i-ying's own memorial on the management of barbarians, which was drafted when he was imperial commissioner at Canton and which had been seized there by the British at the yamen of the governor-general. This cynical act was so effective that it opened the way to Ch'i-ying's tragic end by suicide on order of the emperor.[197] Kuei-liang and Hua-sha-na thanked Lay for his bold step and presented him with a saddled and bridled horse.[198] (Though this British action must have strengthened the position of the peace advocates, it seems that at this stage the British did not yet distinguish between the peace party and the war party. The distinction became clear to them probably around October 1858.)[199]

One reason why Elgin, in the Shanghai negotiations, agreed not to exercise the right of permanent diplomatic representation in Peking was his fear that Kuei-liang and his colleagues would be demoted and punished if consideration were not given to the representations of these officials, whose hands were tied by the rigid instructions of the court.[200]

In order to strengthen the position of Kuei-liang and his group *vis-à-vis* the war party in Peking, Elgin sent to Kuei-liang and his colleagues on January 20, 1859, a very strong letter of protest against the antiforeign movement around Canton. This letter repeated Elgin's earlier demand for the removal of Huang Tsung-han and for the removal of all authority from the three leaders of the committee of gentry employed in organizing braves and directing antiforeign operations. This time the demand was accompanied by the threat of a punitive military operation by the British forces in Kwangtung. This missive had the desired effect. Kuei-liang and his colleagues immediately reported the British protest to Peking. The original of Elgin's letter was also transmitted to Peking. Kuei-liang and his colleagues also enclosed a copy received from Elgin some time before of an alleged secret edict to the three gentry leaders. (This edict had been seized by the British near Canton.) Peking reacted instantaneously, issuing on January 29 an edict announcing the transfer of the imperial commissionership from Canton to Shanghai and appointing Ho Kuei-ch'ing to this office.[201] The official diplomatic channel was thus transferred from the center of the antiforeign movement into the hands of the pacifist Shanghai authorities.

In February 1860, Yang Fang, on behalf of the Shanghai authorities, contacted the Shanghai manager of Jardine, Matheson and Co., in an effort to learn the British intentions. Taking advantage of this approach, Bruce allowed the manager to tell Yang Fang about the very firm attitude of the British. This step was taken with a view to "strengthening the hands of the peace party," [202] and it resulted in the Peking government retreating a step or two.[203]

In April 1860, when the allied authorities canceled their plan for a naval blockade, one factor influencing them was their fear that the pacifist junk traders might thus be alienated. "It [a blockade] will inflict a serious blow on commerce for years to come," commented Bruce, "and on the interests of a class of men who are the best friends we have in this country, and have given their whole weight in support of those who sought to make pacifist counsels prevail at Peking." If thrown out of work as a result of the blockade, the junk crews (estimated at 100,000 men) might cause social unrest or become antiforeign.[204]

In November 1860 the allied diplomats evacuated Peking, postponing until spring the establishment of legations there. This decision grew out of Gros's belief that the immediate establishment of legations might cause the overthrow of Prince Kung at the hands of the emperor's entourage.[205] However, certain Anglo-French forces were stationed in Tientsin as a guarantee against the full payment of the indemnities demanded by the allies, in accordance with stipulations in the Peking conventions (Article 9 of the British Convention and Article 9 of the French Convention). The presence of these forces in Tientsin also served to support Prince Kung. Elgin expected thus to strengthen Prince Kung's position sufficiently to avoid his being overwhelmed by the reaction that would occur if the emperor and his "bad advisors" chose to return to Peking. "Kung will claim credit," wrote Elgin, "for having induced us to remove from Pekin to Tientsin, while the fact that we are still as near as Tientsin will be an *in terrorem* argument in support of his policy of conciliation." [206]

CHAPTER III

The Conduct of Foreign Affairs Following the Tientsin Treaties

If the said barbarian chiefs want to reside at Peking, Hsueh Huan must be kept at the capital as managing secretary.
— *Vermilion endorsement of June 6, 1859*

. . . and he [Hsueh Huan] seemed particularly struck with my suggestion, that henceforward they would have to have a foreign office or board specially for foreign affairs at Pekin, composed of men who had had some experience of foreigners. He evidently arranged for himself a place at this board, observing, "Yes, with you by our side we should get along capitally. With you as go-between on your side, and me on ours, what great things we would accomplish."
— *A dialogue at Shanghai between Hsueh Huan and H. N. Lay,*
April 1860

TRANSFER OF THE IMPERIAL COMMISSIONERSHIP TO SHANGHAI

Steps Leading to the Transfer

In the Shanghai negotiations of 1858 the Ch'ing delegation succeeded finally in obtaining from Elgin an agreement not to exercise the right of permanent diplomatic residence in Peking. Kuei-liang and his colleagues had suggested to the British as an alternative having a grand secretary or a president of a Board stationed in the provinces wherever the British representative might see fit to reside. When Nanking was retaken from the Taipings, he might, if it suited him, reside there.[1] However, in a joint memorial received

in Peking on November 4, 1858, Kuei-liang and his colleagues gave
a distorted report on the proposal they had made to the British.
They stated that they had proposed that "a change would be made
and the affairs concerning various countries (*ko-kuo shih-wu*)
would be managed in future at Shanghai." "As they had asked
before to have an imperial commissioner dispatched for a tour of
the various ports, we told them: 'If an imperially commissioned
high official [stationed at Shanghai] makes a representation or request [to Peking in behalf of the foreign authorities] whenever
there occurs a matter to be discussed, communications to and from
Peking will be transmitted in a very short time. Affairs can thus
be handled more conveniently and swiftly than if a high official
were dispatched from Peking [each time to handle a specific case].
It may also become unnecessary to make a long trip [to Peking]
for the exchange of ratifications in the next year.' " [2]

In brief, when they requested Elgin not to exercise the right of
permanent diplomatic representation at the capital, Kuei-liang and
his associates proposed to Peking the alternative course of making
Shanghai a formal channel for foreign affairs. In making this
proposal, it should be noted, they did not forget to hint that this
might be a means of preventing the exchange of ratifications in
Peking.

In a joint memorial received on November 7, three days after
the preceding one, Kuei-liang and his colleagues repeated this suggestion. In reply, an edict of the same day censured them for not
having followed instructions. The edict uttered not a word about
the memorialists' proposal. They were again sternly ordered to obtain at least the cancellation of the four objectionable points in the
British treaty.[3]

In a memorial received on November 14, Ho Kuei-ch'ing, who
was a member of the delegation at Shanghai, declared it impossible
to secure nullification of the Tientsin treaties. In the course of his
discussion, he criticized the operation of the Canton imperial commissionership. As the latest cause for complaint, he regretted that
Huang Tsung-han, the newly appointed imperial commissioner and

governor-general at Canton, when en route to his new post, had refused Ho's earnest request to negotiate in Shanghai with the representatives of the four Western powers. Ho asserted that this refusal was the immediate cause of the Western demand for permanent residence. The foreigners thought, he wrote, that "if everything could be settled personally with Your Majesty, there would be no room for the machinations of metropolitan and provincial officials." [4]

This memorial seems to have shocked the emperor. It was referred to a joint session of the Grand Council with "Prince Hui and others." [5] An edict of the same day, which must have been drafted in the light of the discussion in this joint session, for the first time took up the idea of transferring the imperial commissionership to Shanghai, although at the same time it stated that it was still imperative to secure cancellation of the four points. "As to the intentions of these barbarians, they originally wanted to have the imperial commissioner transferred to Shanghai." Thus treating the idea as if it had first been raised by the British, the edict went on to state that, in the event of success in the repudiation of the four points, "Kuei-liang and his colleagues may agree to the *transfer* to Shanghai of the imperial commissioner in sole charge of *trade* affairs (*chuan-pan t'ung-shang shih-wu*)." [6] One thing to be noted here is that, while Kuei-liang and his colleagues had simply suggested sending to Shanghai an imperial commissioner for foreign affairs and had not necessarily implied the transfer to Shanghai of the existing commissionership at Canton, the Peking government took the matter up as "the transfer to Shanghai" of this office.

Then, in a joint memorial received on November 24 which dealt with the results of the Shanghai negotiations, Kuei-liang and his colleagues reported that they had barely succeeded in obtaining from the British an agreement not to exercise the right of permanent residence in the capital — or, to be more exact, Elgin's promise to suggest to his government the advisability of not exercising this right.[7] In answer, an edict of the same day stated that the transfer to Shanghai of the imperial commissioner should make it possible to persuade the British to drop their demand for permanent residence. The edict went a step further, suggesting that even an occasional visit to Peking should be prevented, which implied that the ratifications should not be exchanged at Peking. The edict even instructed the negotiators to declare to the British that if they came to Tientsin the Ch'ing forces would "immediately open fire." [8]

In response, a memorial from Kuei-liang and his colleagues received on December 20 affirmed that it was their desire to block the British from coming to the capital that had inspired their request to "establish at Shanghai an imperial commissioner." Notice that they did not say "transfer." They expressed their determination to do everything possible to secure the exchange of ratifications in Shanghai. They also pointed out that the British were firmly resolved to go north for the exchange, and they did not forget to note the intensity of Anglo-French resentment against Huang Tsung-han: "Their hatred of Huang Tsung-han is even stronger than [their hatred] of Yeh Ming-ch'en, which is most incomprehensible." [9]

Still insisting upon the repudiation of the four points, an edict of the same day explicitly ordered Kuei-liang and his colleagues to exchange the ratifications in Shanghai. "It was in fact with a view to preventing their coming to the capital and to the Tientsin area that we have allowed the *transfer* to Shanghai of the imperial commissionership. If we permit their occasional visits to the capital, how shall we drive them out once they have arrived? [If we cannot drive them out] there will be no difference from residence in the capital. There would be no need either to transfer to Shanghai the imperial commissionership . . . In short, it is absolutely impossible to admit them to the capital." [10]

The idea of Kuei-liang and his colleagues had been to appoint an imperial commissioner soon, in consideration of a British agreement on nonexercise of the right of permanent residence. Now, in a joint memorial received on January 9, 1859, they retreated, in deference to Peking's firm attitude, to the position that the appointment of a

Shanghai commissioner might be made after both the repudiation of the four points and the exchange of ratifications at Shanghai.[11] An edict of the same day confirmed this line and added: "To sum up, as it has already been proposed that the imperial commissioner be transferred to Shanghai, not only is it impossible to permit permanent residence at the capital but even occasional visits are uncalled for. The distance from Shanghai [to Peking] cannot be compared with that from Kwangtung. So what matter could not be presented [to the throne from there]?"[12]

It may be said that Kuei-liang's original proposal had had two aims: to humor the foreign authorities by establishing the main channel for negotiations in Shanghai, then the center of foreign interests in China, and, at the same time, to block the approach of Western diplomats to Peking. The Peking government, dominated by the war party, must have agreed to a Shanghai commissionership because it saw in it a countermeasure with which to meet British pressure. On the other hand, transferring the main channel of diplomacy from antiforeign Kwangtung to pacifist Shanghai would certainly mean strengthening the peace party, and this is probably why Peking did not agree to immediate actualization of the idea, but conditioned it upon the cancellation of the four points. Kuei-liang and his colleagues thus were obliged to retreat from their initial position.

Difference in opinion between Peking and Kuei-liang and his colleagues was also evident in the curious matter of the "transfer" of the commissionership from Canton to Shanghai. As we have already stated, Kuei-liang and his colleagues proposed simply the establishment of a commissioner at Shanghai; they never used any expression in connection with their proposals that meant "transfer." Yet Peking consistently treated the matter as one of "transfer (*i-chu* or *kai-chu*) to Shanghai" of the commissionership then at Canton. If we consider this discrepancy in approach in connection with the later controversy aroused by Ho Kuei-ch'ing's proposal for a fulltime imperial commissioner at Shanghai, we see that there were probably from the beginning between Peking and Shanghai two points of controversy with regard to a Shanghai commissionership.[13] The first concerned the advisability of establishing a commissioner at Shanghai and the preconditions to such a step; the second concerned the institutional form that such a commissionership should assume.

The actual establishment of the Shanghai commissionership took place suddenly as a result of a jolt delivered from outside. As we have seen, on January 20, 1859, Elgin sent a threatening letter to Kuei-liang and his colleagues, stating that a punitive military operation by the British forces would be started in Kwangtung if the Chinese government did not comply with his earlier demand for the removal of Huang Tsung-han and the removal of authority from the three gentry leaders of the Kwangtung antiforeign movement. In an instantaneous response to the report from Shanghai on this matter, an edict of January 29 (which did not use the word "barbarian") announced the transfer of the imperial commissionership from Kwangtung to Shanghai, and appointed Ho Kuei-ch'ing, to this post, to manage "the affairs concerning various countries" (ko-kuo shih-wu). The reason given in the edict for this transfer was that Shanghai, where "trade affairs" were now handled, was far from Kwangtung. The edict declared that the alleged secret edict to the antiforeign gentry leaders that had been seized near Canton by the British was a forgery. Huang Tsung-han was ordered to find, arrest, and punish the author of the document. A full copy of this edict was transmitted to Elgin through Kuei-liang and his colleagues.[14] The edict was also published in the Peking Gazette.[15]

Ho Kuei-ch'ing's Proposal for a Full-time Commissioner

Like the Canton imperial commissioner, the Shanghai commissioner was a provincial governor-general and had to manage foreign affairs in addition to his principal duties. The commissionership, in short, was a part-time and concurrent post. In a memorial received on March 15, 1859,[16] the same day as another memorial from him[17] acknowledging with thanks his appointment as imperial commissioner at Shanghai, Ho Kuei-ch'ing criticized this system. As the result of "a previous friendly and thorough consultation at Shanghai with Kuei-liang and Hua-sha-na," he suggested that after the peace negotiations had been definitely concluded, a metropolitan high official should be appointed to the office of "imperial commissioner for trade affairs" at Shanghai on a full-time basis, with an official residence in Shanghai and an extra stipend. This memorial discussed extensively the current Ch'ing machinery for foreign affairs with special attention to the Shanghai commissionership, on which Ho's ideas may be summarized as follows: The imperial commissioner for foreign affairs should be a high metropolitan official, and he should be appointed to the post on a full-time basis for the following reasons. The governors-general or governors whose territorial jurisdiction incorporated the treaty ports were unfamiliar with the foreigners and quite ignorant of the content of the treaties. A full-time imperial commissioner charged with the direction of foreign management could give them advice or instruction. In any Sino-foreign dispute he should go to the scene of trouble, and deal with the matter personally. A governor-general who was concurrently imperial commissioner tended to be concerned only with those treaty ports within his own territorial jurisdiction. "The governor-general of Kwangtung and Kwangsi has been called the imperial commissioner supervising trade at the five ports. In actuality, the official in this post has taken notice only of the Canton port. Whenever the governors-general or governors in whose territorial jurisdiction the other four ports are located have sent communications to Kwangtung for consideration, the letters have simply been pigeonholed or answered several months later. The result is that each [treaty port] has come to manage its affairs independently. The imperial commissioner has thus become merely nominal." Furthermore, the foreign authorities recently had tended to be contemptuous of the high provincial officials. Hence if their demands were not complied with by the imperial commissioner, who was governor-general of Kiangnan and Kiangsi, and they thus wanted to come to the capital for personal consultation with a grand secretary or a president of a Board (as stipulated in Article 5 of the British Tientsin Treaty), the governor (of Kiangsu) would not be able to dissuade them from going north by offering mediation.

Ho suggested also that such a full-time imperial commissioner should be resident in the city of Shanghai. The governor-general of Kiangnan and Kiangsi, in whom the commissionership was now vested, was temporarily resident in Ch'ang-chou, and he would have to return to Nanking when it was recovered by the imperial forces. Shanghai, however, was the place where foreigners from various countries were gathering, and where issues to be dealt with were most likely to arise. With the commissioner stationed so far from Shanghai, correspondence with the foreign officials would take time, and the foreigners were impatient. If the imperial commissioner could observe the situation personally in Shanghai, it would facilitate matters. Another point to be considered was that after the return to Nanking, if the commissionership continued to be vested in the governor-general, the foreign officials would often dare to go to Nanking.

The Peking government rejected Ho's proposal on the following grounds. The imperial commissionership had been transferred to the Shanghai area because it had been noted that Kwangtung was too remote from Peking for prompt communication. There was no reason to worry about foreign contempt for the provincial officials: "When the governor-general of Kwangtung and Kwangsi held the concurrent office of imperial commissioner, the foreign officials did not on every occasion have a personal discussion with the governor-general. Whenever an occurrence demanded discussion with any country, the governor-general used first to dispatch his subordinate officials to receive the foreign officials. Yeh Min-ch'en, however, would never dispatch officials for their reception, and there was a great deal of mutual contempt. Moreover, he failed to build up defenses. The disaster of this time [the Arrow War] has thus finally been brought about. If the management [of barbarians] is done properly, governors-general or governors will not be made light of." Furthermore, "as a high official with territorial jurisdiction, a governor-general has adequate means with which to keep order. If we separately appoint a high metropolitan official to the office of imperial commissioner, we fear the mutual response [between the governor-general and the imperial commissioner] may not be effective enough when some incident occurs." [18]

What did this difference in views mean? What was Ho Kuei-ch'ing's aim in making his proposal, and why did Peking not accept his suggestions? Ho may have been motivated partly by a desire to evade the responsibility of the hazardous office for reasons of personal safety. Aside from such personal considerations, we may assume two motives. Firstly, Ho Kuei-ch'ing intended his proposal to be a suggestion for an institutional innovation. In making it, he was rather boldly critical and aligned himself to some extent with Western criticism of the imperial commissioner system. Within the framework of that system, it was most radical to call for the appointment of a full-time imperial commissioner who, independent of provincial involvements, would directly represent the Peking government.[19] Peking's response, after a careful re-examination of the existing system, was to reconfirm the present system. Ho's second aim was to strengthen the position of the peace party. The dispatching of a high metropolitan official as imperial commissioner would be one step away from the existing system toward the formula stipulated in Article 5 of the British treaty (nomination of a grand secretary or a president of a Board to transact business with a Western diplomat). It also corresponded roughly with Kuei-liang's proposal to Elgin that a grand secretary or a president of a Board might be stationed wherever the British chose. Furthermore, the machinery for foreign affairs that was then in actual operation at Shanghai consisted of the pacifist Shanghai authorities plus the imperial commissioners from Peking, among whom Kuei-liang was a grand secretary and Hua-shu-na was president of the Board of Civil Appointments. Kuei-liang had been the central figure of the peace party from the days of the Tientsin negotiations. Thus Ho Kuei-ch'ing's intentions may have been to perpetuate this pacifist machinery for foreign affairs at Shanghai with Kuei-liang at the top. At least the Peking government may have suspected that this was his intent.

Foreign Objections to the Shanghai Commissionership

As a result of the British agreement not to exercise the right of permanent residence in Peking, Britain and France took steps to station their ministers to China temporarily in Shanghai. On March 1, 1859, in a letter of instruction to Frederick Bruce, newly appointed minister to China, the British government stated that the minister, who was now also chief superintendent of British trade (a post heretofore invested in the governor of Hong Kong), would carry on in Shanghai "the general direction of British affairs in China" until such time as circumstances should admit of his mission being permanently established in Peking.[20] The French government in January 1859 decided to transfer their legation in China from Macao to Shanghai, temporarily.[21] In March 1859 the American minister, John Ward, on his way to China, reported from Paris that the French government had abandoned "all idea of a residence at Pekin." Bruce informed him in London, wrote Ward, "that he had abandoned all idea of residing at Peking, but that he hoped to go there for a short time."[22] All this did not mean, however, that the Western powers would recognize the Shanghai commissionership as the regular channel for foreign affairs.

In reply to a complimentary address from the representatives of the British and Indian firms in Shanghai, Elgin stated on January 17, 1859, just before the unexpected transfer of the imperial commissionership to Shanghai: "I have long held the opinion that Shanghai was the place where, if anywhere, it might be hoped that peaceful negotiations for extension and development of commercial relations with China might be conducted with success, for the obvious reason, that the benefits accruing to the Empire from foreign commerce and intercourse, are more manifest at Shanghai than elsewhere."[23] When the transfer had been effected, thanks to his own diplomatic exertions, he appraised the event by saying: "It is clear that the vigorous measures . . . have, for the present at least, restored the influence of Ho, the liberal Governor-General of the Two Kiang, which the antiforeign party at Peking and Canton had previously shaken"; he also commented that the language of the edict which announced the transfer was "studiously conciliatory, and indicative of a desire to maintain peaceful relations." [24] The *North China Herald* in Shanghai commented: "The transfer of the Office of Imperial Commissioner for Foreign Affairs, from Kwantung to this province will materially lessen the influence of the Cantonese, and raise in a corresponding degree the political importance of Shanghai." [25]

Thus the transfer was welcomed by the Westerners in China insofar as it meant a certain increase in the strength of the peace party. However, as an institution for the conduct of foreign affairs the Shanghai commissionership was in essence nothing more than a continuation of the Canton commissionership, and this meant that the Western criticisms of the Canton commissioner system could also be applied to the new arrangement. Hence, while the Western authorities decided to refrain for the time being from residing in the capital, they explicitly reserved the right to make occasional visits to Peking. Furthermore, they never did admit that the Shanghai commissionership could be a standing substitute for the arrangement stipulated in Article 5 of the British treaty.

In reply to the communication from Kuei-liang and his colleagues informing him of the transfer of the commissionership to Shanghai, Elgin stated that, as a precondition to the nonexercise of the right of permanent residence in Peking the British minister (Bruce), then on his way to China with the ratification of the Tientsin Treaty, was to be "properly received" in Peking, where the ratifications were to be exchanged; also, full effect should be given in all other particulars to the Tientsin Treaty. If these conditions were fulfilled, the British minister would choose a place of residence other than the capital and he might "make his visits there [to Peking] either periodical or as frequent as the exigencies of the public service may require." [26] Similarly, Gros, when notified of the transfer, expressed dissatisfaction that the Ch'ing authorities had unilaterally chosen the new location for the imperial commissioner. He asserted that this was a matter to be decided by France and Britain after the exchange of ratifications in Peking.[27]

Bruce arrived in Hong Kong in April 1859. In June he stopped at Shanghai on his way to Peking for the exchange of ratifications. There was some correspondence between him and Kuei-liang and his colleagues, who had been waiting in Shanghai in order to exchange the ratifications there. On this occasion communications from Bruce were addressed to "the Chief Secretary of State [grand secretary], Kweiliang." According to Thomas Wade, this was done "in accordance with the spirit of Article V" of the Tientsin Treaty. In other words, it meant that the British would not recognize the Shanghai imperial commissioner as the channel for foreign affairs stipulated in that article.[28] In a letter of May 28 to Bruce, Kuei-liang and his colleagues wrote concerning the transfer of the commissionership and the appointment of Ho Kuei-ch'ing to this office: ". . . it is felt consultation on business between China and foreign nations will be much facilitated." [29] The British considered this passage "a feeler regarding the extent to which our former relations are modified," and thought that "the Chinese would prefer continually to regard them as merely commercial; the Chinese Superintendent of Trade [imperial commissioner at Canton or Shanghai] as Foreign Minister." [30]

As we know, the British and French representatives proceeded north by boat, and suffered humiliating defeat at Taku on June 25. After the Taku incident, in a memorandum analyzing current Sino-British relations, Thomas Wade stated in retrospect: ". . . and the Commissioners were, I make no doubt, to detain us at Shanghae under one pretext or another, until the year was so far spent that we might be induced, in our greed for commercial advantages, to accept an exchange of ratifications at Shanghae. Foreign relations, which in Chinese are simply synonymous with a Superintendence of Trade, would then have been handed over to Ho, whose 'soothing and bridling' [*fu-yü*] we are evidently assumed to prefer, and the great gain of the Treaty, the one means of preventing local misunderstandings, viz., the right of appeal to the Central Government against the acts of its subordinates, would, in default of precedent, have been as much in abeyance as though it had never been concluded." [31]

On August 1, 1859, Ho Kuei-ch'ing wrote to Bruce asking whether, since Ward had already gone up to Peking to exchange the ratifications, Bruce would consider proceeding north with Bourboulon.[32] In his reply on August 9 Bruce made it clear that he would communicate with Ho on matters of trade but not on diplomatic affairs. Referring to Ho's title of "Imperial Commissioner for the General Superintendence of Trade at the Ports" (*ch'in-ch'ai ta-ch'en tsung-li k̯o-k̯'ou t'ung-shang shih-wu*), which he had used in writing to Bruce, Bruce argued: "From his Excellency's official title it would appear that his function as Imperial Commissioner is the superintendence of trade at the ports; and upon questions of trade the Undersigned can have no difficulty in corresponding with his Excellency . . . The question the Imperial Commissioner Ho, in his letter, has addressed to the Undersigned, does not relate to trade, nor does the Undersigned conceive himself at liberty to correspond with his Excellency upon any matter connected with the late proceedings of the Chinese Government in the North." [33] To this Ho retorted by saying, "It is for trade that the Treaties are exchanged," and he asserted that he was certainly competent to handle the matter of the exchange of ratifications.[34] Upon Ho's retort Wade commented: "I believe the passage to be a simple declaration of the view of foreign relations to which China desires to adhere . . . the provision of Article V of the new Treaty is, I think purposely, ignored. There is to be no such thing as diplomatic intercourse." [35]

In March 1860 Bruce and Bourboulon sent ultimatums to P'eng

Yun-chang, senior grand councillor and grand secretary.[36] The Peking government replied to these missives indirectly: the Grand
Council sent communications addressed to "Ho Kuei-ch'ing, imperial commissioner and governor-general of Kiangnan and Kiangsi," copies of which were to be sent to both Bruce and Bourboulon, enclosed in a communication to each of them from Ho.[37]
From the Anglo-French viewpoint, this indirect formula of answering disregarded the right of the foreign diplomats to communicate
directly with the high metropolitan officials, as stipulated in Article
11 of the Treaty of Nanking and Article 33 of the Treaty of
Whampoa. From the Chinese viewpoint, however, "trade" was not
under the jurisdiction of the Grand Council; the Grand Council
was simply following the precedent established in 1850 when they
disregarded the direct communication.[38] Ho Kuei-ch'ing was the
imperial commissioner "who manages the trade affairs of various
countries" (that is; who was in sole charge of foreign affairs).[39]

In a dispatch of April 7 ,1860, Bruce gave the following analysis
of the actual operation of the Shanghai commissionership.[40] "The
Imperial Commissioner, Ho, is the Governor-General of the Two
Kiang Provinces (of which Nanking is the capital), as well as Superintendent of Commercial Affairs. He resides at Chang-chow-fu,
about 130 miles from Shanghae. The distance makes it impossible
to establish and keep up the constant personal intercourse with
him which is so essential to a speedy and amicable solution of important questions, while his duties as Governor-General afford an
excuse for not meeting a foreign Minister whenever the subject
of discussion is one he wishes to avoid. Thus Mr. Ward was unable
to obtain an interview for the purpose of conferring on the best
mode of suppressing the abuses connected with emigration. It is
also remarkable that when Ho consented to meet him and fix a
time for opening the ports of Swatow and Tai-wan, he followed
the precedent established at Canton for the reception of a foreign
Minister, and instead of receiving Mr. Ward at his official residence,
he selected an out-of-the-way place by the river-side for the interview.[41] The visit itself was of short duration, Ho being called away

the same afternoon, as he alleged, to attend to important provincial affairs."

CHINA'S INITIAL ARRANGEMENTS FOR FOREIGN CONTACT IN PEKING

When communications from Kuei-liang and his associates had finally persuaded the Chinese government that the exchange of ratifications in Peking was probably inevitable, Peking began to make preparations for the reception and housing of the foreign envoys. It also began to prepare for the possible permanent residence of foreign ministers, should this too prove unavoidable. These preparations give us an indication of the arrangements which Peking had in mind for conducting foreign affairs at the capital in the event that it became necessary to do so.

Preparations for the Exchange of Ratifications

An edict of March 29, 1859, prescribed the conditions under which the envoys might come to the capital for the exchange of ratifications,[42] and ordered Kuei-liang to ask the Western diplomats not to come to the Tientsin area until Kuei-liang and his party had returned to Peking. The edict further instructed Ho Kuei-ch'ing to send to Peking two of the following officials: Wang Yu-ling, provincial treasurer, Hsueh Huan, provincial judge, and Wu Hsü, acting taotai of Shanghai. These two men were to proceed to Peking posthaste, along with "Kuei-liang and others." From this edict we gather that in case of an exchange of ratifications in the capital, Grand Secretary Kuei-liang and Hua-sha-na, president of the Board of Civil Appointments, who together had been principally responsible for the handling of diplomatic negotiations from the time of Tientsin, were to be in charge of the reception of the foreign envoys. As assistants they would have two officials from the inner core of the Shanghai diplomatic authorities, men who were experienced in foreign contact. The treatment of the foreign envoys while in Peking was to be based on tribute system.

A memorial from Kuei-liang and his colleagues, received on June 6, 1859, made it clear that the northern journey of the British and French ministers was now imminent.[43] Enclosed with the memorial was a copy of a communication from Bruce (then at Hong Kong) announcing his arrival in China as envoy extraordinary and minister plenipotentiary and his desire to present his credentials to the emperor in person, and also stating that he was prepared to exchange the ratifications in Peking. (The original of Bruce's communication was to be transmitted to the Grand Council.) In an appended memorial, the memorialists stated that Wang Yu-ling, who was engaged in raising money for the military campaign against the Taipings, and Wu Hsü, who was busy dealing with foreign affairs in Shanghai, were both irreplaceable and so unable to proceed north; hence they wanted to bring with them to Peking, in addition to Hsueh Huan, Li Huan-wen, expectant prefect and former acting subprefect at Shanghai. Li Huan-wen, a mature man, was not only familiar with foreigners, but was also, as a native of T'ung-chou, well acquainted with the local situation in the Tientsin area.[44] This proposal was approved in the vermilion endorsement to the appended memorial.[45] A vermilion endorsement appended to the main memorial also stated that, if the foreign ministers insisted upon residing in Peking, Hsueh Huan would be kept in Peking as "managing secretary" (*pan-li chih ch'ang-jen*).[46]

As of June 18, the Peking government was taking steps to have the authorities of the Metropolitan Prefecture prepare, "in conformity with the precedents of various tribute-bearing barbarians," for the accommodation of the British, American, and French ministers.[47]

Kuei-liang and his party, including Hsueh Huan, left Shanghai for Peking on June 13.[48] In the party was also a certain Huang Chung-yü, expectant district magistrate, who had been active from the time of the Tientsin negotiations as an informal channel of communication between the British and Ch'ing delegations.[49] After the allied defeat at Taku on June 25, the British and French turned back to Shanghai, but John Ward, the American minister, remained in the Gulf of Peichihli and later proceeded to Peking. Ward's visit to Peking will be examined below in considerable detail. A full analysis of the event, based on both Chinese and Western sources, has not previously been presented, and it will serve to throw light on aspects of the Peking government's actual conduct of foreign affairs in the context of the conflicts behind its façade.

The vermilion endorsement statement that Hsueh Huan would be kept at the capital as "managing secretary" should the foreign ministers insist upon permanent residence in Peking may be taken as an indication of a new plan for the conduct of foreign affairs, drawn up in preparation for the worst possibility. Perhaps Peking's plan in its entirety was to appoint, in accordance with Article 5 of the British treaty, a grand secretary or a president of a Board to be responsible for foreign affairs, and to assign under this high official one of lower rank but sufficiently experienced in foreign affairs to work in daily contact with the officials of the foreign legations. Hsueh Huan, who had a long experience of foreign contact in Shanghai, was then, as a provincial judge, an official of the principal class of the third rank.[50]

During Ward's stay in Peking, from July 27 to August 11, it was Hsueh Huan who acted as principal intermediary between Ward and Kuei-liang and Hua-sha-na. After the Ward mission had left the capital, Hsueh Huan was kept on in Peking. On November 27, 1859, he was promoted to provincial treasurer of Kiangsu at Nanking (Chiang-ning *pu-cheng-shih*),[51] to which post he was ordered to proceed on December 9, having no further business in Peking. At the same time Ho Kuei-ch'ing was instructed that Hsueh Huan was to stay between Soochow and Ch'ang-chou to assist in the conduct of "barbarian affairs." [52] The British saw in this step a possibly conciliatory move on the part of the Peking government.[53] On March 10, 1860, the honorary title of governor was conferred upon Hsueh Huan and he was also formally ordered to "assist the management of trade at the five ports." [54] On the ground that Ho Kuei-ch'ing was now too much involved in suppressing the rebels to attend to foreign affairs, an edict of April 28 ordered Hsueh

Huan to memorialize individually whenever an urgent situation arose in foreign affairs.[55] On May 16 he was transferred to the office of provincial treasurer of Kiangsu at Soochow (Chiang-su *pu-cheng-shih*).[56]

Meanwhile, under the increasing threat of an Anglo-French retaliatory expedition, the Peking government retreated step by step from the aggressive stand it had taken after the Taku repulse. Once again it turned to the idea of having Hsueh Huan in Peking if the allied forces came north. An edict of February 27, 1860, suggested that, although treaty negotiations with the British and the French should take place in Shanghai, they might come to Peking *via* Pehtang for the exchange of ratifications, "according to the precedents of American barbarians." The edict ordered Hsueh Huan to hasten to the capital if the foreign officials refused to negotiate in Shanghai and the allied ships sailed for the north.[57] An edict of March 29 repeated these instructions to Hsueh Huan.[58] On June 8, Hsueh Huan was made acting imperial commissioner at Shanghai, Ho Kuei-ch'ing having been relieved of office as a result of the accusation that he was responsible for the fall of Soochow and Ch'ang-chou to the Taipings.[59] On June 18 Hsueh Huan was made acting governor-general of Kiangnan and Kiangsi, though still to be stationed in the Shanghai area.[60] On the next day he was appointed governor of Kiangsu.[61] On August 10 Tseng Kuo-fan was appointed governor-general of Kiangnan and Kiangsi,[62] thus relieving Hsueh Huan of the acting governor-generalship, though he still continued to be governor of Kiangsu and acting Shanghai imperial commissioner. Probably because he thus became involved in important duties in the Shanghai area, Hsueh Huan did not, after all, go north to join the diplomatic parleys of 1860.

The Ward Mission to Peking

The Journey to Peking

Ward's departure from Pehtang for Peking[63] was timed to suit the convenience of the Ch'ing authorities. Ward wanted to go to

the capital at once and await there the arrival of Kuei-liang and
his party, but Heng-fu and other Ch'ing officials, who were dealing
with Ward in Pehtang, took the stand that Ward should postpone
his departure until Kuei-liang and his party had reached Peking.
At one time the Peking authorities suggested that Ward might
come at once to the capital, but they later changed their minds and
sided with Heng-fu. Thus, when the expected date of Kuei-liang's
arrival became known, Ward was notified that he might start any
time after July 19. To this, Ward replied that he would set out on
July 21.[64] In accordance with the spirit of Article 5 of the American
treaty, it was agreed by the two sides that Ward's party was to con-
sist of twenty Americans and ten Chinese (scribes and other assistants).[65]

The party was escorted by Ch'ing officials. The Peking government put in charge of the escort Ch'ung-hou, taotai of Paoting
(*Ch'ing-ho-tao*) with the honorary title of salt controller, and
Chang Ping-to, major of the central battalion of the brigade of
Süanhwa, expectant lieutenant-colonel with the honorary title of
colonel. When notified of these appointments, Ward replied that
he was "satisfied with the officers appointed to be his escort." The
Americans thought that "These men bear a rank quite high enow
for the dignity of the United States embassy." [66]

The route was set by the Ch'ing authorities. The party traveled
overland from Pehtang to Pei-ts'ang *via* Chunliangcheng, then by
ship on the Peiho from Pei-ts'ang to T'ung-chou, from which they
proceeded by land to Peking. One reason for choosing this route
was that it avoided approaching the city of Tientsin, where the authorities feared a collision with the inhabitants. The Americans
thought that the route had been chosen to prevent their seeing the
defenses in the Peiho above Taku. The Peking government had
ordered the officials dealing with Ward not to force their choice of
route on the Americans, who as a matter of fact offered no objections.[67]

When Ward and his party traveled overland, they rode in carts
or carriages pulled by mules or horses. The Americans had brought

two sedan chairs with them for Ward and the senior naval officer, but the Ch'ing officials at Pehtang were so opposed to their use that the Americans did not insist on it. The Peking government had given instructions that, although sedan chairs absolutely must not be used in the city of Peking, the American envoy might ride in one en route between Pehtang and the point of embarkation on the Peiho; after landing at T'ung-chou he was to ride in a cart or a mule chair.[68] Between T'ung-chou and Peking, the springless carts jolted so unbearably that the Americans were forced to get out and walk. The escorting mandarins offered some horses. The Americans got into the carts again near Peking, and on July 27 entered the city in a procession through the Ch'ao-yang Gate.[69] On the Peiho between Pei-ts'ang and T'ung-chou Ward and his party were on board "a kind of three-decker" which was drawn by sixteen men. Its masthead bore an American flag.[70]

The Americans repeatedly asserted that they should themselves bear the expense of their journeys between Pehtang and Peking and of their stay in Peking. The Ch'ing authorities did not concede this, however, and the Chinese government paid all the expenses.[71] This was one step backward toward the tribute system, since Article 5 of the American treaty stipulated that the expenses of the American legation in Peking should be defrayed by the American minister.

The Stay in Peking

It was Kuei-liang and Hua-sha-na, both still holding the status of imperial commissioner, who received Ward and negotiated with him. As their assistant or secretary Hsueh Huan actually conducted most of the negotiations, going constantly to and fro between the two sides.[72] A temple in the imperial city called Chia-hsing-ssu was used as the office where Kuei-liang and Hua-sha-na received Ward.[73]

In Peking, Ward and his party were lodged in Shih-san-t'iao, in the neighborhood of Lao-chün-t'ang, a Taoist temple, about one and a half miles from the Ch'ao-yang Gate of the imperial city. This place had formerly belonged to Sai-shang-a, a Mongol, former grand councillor, and had been confiscated by the government upon his disgrace.[74]

The party was lavishly entertained but drastically restricted in its freedom of action. W. A. P. Martin, who accompanied Ward as interpreter, wrote: "We were lodged in a well-furnished house and luxuriously fed, but we were guarded like criminals." [75]

Although Ward's boat on the Peiho carried an American flag, the Americans could not hoist a flag on the compound of their Peking lodgings. At one point the Ch'ing authorities promised to erect a flagstaff, and its position and height were determined, but the plan was then canceled on the grounds that the Russians then in Peking had no flagstaff. The Americans therefore contented themselves with hanging their flag in the reception room over the seat used by visitors.[76]

A body of policemen was stationed at the lodgings, and contact between the Americans and the populace was cut off.[77] Ward ordered his party to remain in the lodgings until the first interview with Kuei-liang and Hua-sha-na had taken place; this he considered a mark of respect toward the Chinese government.[78] At the interview with Kuei-liang and Hua-sha-na at Chia-hsing-ssu on July 30, Ward asked that four or five horses be sent to the American residence so that the gentlemen in his suite might ride about the city. Kuei-liang replied that he would be happy to show the Americans everything of interest after they had seen the emperor and exchanged the ratifications.[79] When the imperial commissioners returned Ward's visit on August 2, Ward asked them why soldiers were quartered about his lodgings. They assured him that the soldiers were there only to maintain order and to keep off the Chinese crowd, which would otherwise gather about the Americans and be very annoying; any of Ward's suite could leave the grounds and return as they pleased. At the same time, however, they requested that the gentlemen go out as little as possible until after the official business had been transacted.[80] Probably on August 3, some Americans went "a few rods away" from the house, accompanied by one or two of their custodians and followed by a large crowd, but they found nothing to see in that region of the city and so returned.[81] On August 10 the chaplain in the party went out. Though his walk was interfered with by the police, he forced his way to the foot of the city wall, from which he turned back because the police were evidently averse to his ascending it.[82] The Cantonese servants of the legation left the compound from time to time. The Ch'ing authorities objected to this, and one of the officials appointed to oversee the Americans was punished because he had allowed some of the Cantonese to go out.[83]

One reason for the confinement of Ward and his party was that the Peking government wanted to prevent any intercourse between the American legation and Ignat'ev, who was also in the city.[84]

The American lodgings and the Russian residence were far apart,[85] and the members of the two missions were not permitted to meet directly. Written communications could be exchanged between Ward and Ignat'ev, but the letters were conveyed solely by the Chinese authorities, and delivery was often delayed.

A letter of July 6 from Ward to Perovskii (Ignat'ev's predecessor), notifying him of Ward's coming visit to Peking, was handed over to the Ch'ing authorities in Pehtang on July 8, for transmittal. Heng-fu assured Ward that the letter would be sent on immediately.[86] However, Heng-fu reported to Peking that he had accepted the letter to allay American suspicion, but that he would return it to the Americans and tell them that they might bring it to Peking themselves.[87] In reply, Peking stated that there was no need to reject the American request, and ordered that the letter be sent to the capital where it could be transmitted to the Russians.[88] The next move came from Seng-ko-lin-ch'in. Believing that the Russian maneuvers should be guarded against, he favored not permitting the Americans and the Russians to communicate in any way. He thus asked for instructions as to whether or not the letter, still retained by Heng-fu, should be delivered by the Americans themselves on their arrival in the capital.[89] This was perhaps a mild way of indicating his opposition to communication between the Americans and the Russians. In response, the Peking government, though stating that Seng-ko-lin-ch'in's concern was justified, ordered Heng-fu to send the letter to the Grand Council, which would turn it over to the Court of Dependencies for transmission to the Russians: "This letter will eventually have to be delivered to the Russian barbarians, so it is better to let the government be the medium and thus prevent the evil of their personal communication." This was on July 14.[90] This letter finally reached Ignat'ev on July 18, ten days after Ward had left it with Heng-fu.[91] A return letter of July 19 from Ignat'ev was delivered to Ward while he was on his way to Peking.[92] On July 28, the day after his arrival in Peking, Ward sent a letter to Ignat'ev. For some reason, this letter was delivered promptly; a note of acknowledgment from a member of the Russian delegation reached the American residence the same day.[93]

At an interview between Ignat'ev and Su-shun and Jui-ch'ang at the Russian Hostel on July 22, the Ch'ing officials announced that interviews between the Russians and the Americans would not be allowed until after the American treaty ratifications had been exchanged. Furthermore, Ignat'ev might not delegate officials to send compliments upon Ward's arrival, and correspondence between the Russians and the Americans would be transmitted through the Ch'ing authorities.[94]

Two letters from Ignat'ev, one dated July 26 and the other July 28, reached Ward as late as August 3.[95] A letter from Ward of August 3, written in reply to these two, reached Ignat'ev on August 6.[96] A letter of August 7 from Ignat'ev was delivered to the Americans on August 10.[97] This indicates that the delivery of letters was deliberately delayed. Of these four letters, the last two were delivered comparatively quickly, probably because Ignat'ev sent a strong letter of protest to the Grand Council on July 30.[98] It is most likely that the Peking government initiated delivery of the first two letters only after they had received this protest.

On at least one or two occasions Ignat'ev delegated some of his officials to go to the American residence. They were repelled by the guards, however, and made no personal contact with the Americans.[99]

While in Peking, Ward went twice to Chia-hsing-ssu, the office of Kuei-liang and Hua-sha-na: on July 30 for the first interview with the two commissioners, and on August 10 for the transmission of the American president's letter. On July 30, at the request of the Ch'ing authorities, Ward was accompanied by only three of his suite: his brother W. W. Ward, secretary of the legation; S. W. Williams, secretary and interpreter; and W. A. P. Martin, interpreter.[100] On August 10 Ward was accompanied by the same three persons. (The Americans had favored the idea of the whole American company's going in parade to bring the president's letter, with an orderly carrying the American flag before the letter, but this idea had finally been dropped, since refusal by the Ch'ing authorities was almost certain.)[101] On July 30 the four men went their way to and from Chia-hsing-ssu on horseback through a curious crowd.[102] On August 10, they were carried in carts or carriages; they were thus sheltered from the sun's heat, although they could see almost nothing.[103]

At Ward's interview with Kuei-liang and Hua-sha-na on July 30, and on their return visit to him on August 2, Hsueh Huan was present and spoke very often. He also came to the American lodgings on July 29, August 2 (prior to the arrival of Kuei-liang and Hua-sha-na), 4, 5, and 8, principally to negotiate with the secretaries and interpreters of the legation.[104] There was also an exchange of correspondence between Ward and Kuei-liang and Hua-sha-na.[105] The central issue in all these contacts was the etiquette to be adopted in case of an imperial audience,[106] which the Ch'ing officials insisted was an absolutely essential prerequisite to the transaction of any other business in the capital. The Americans firmly rejected the performance of the kowtow; the Ch'ing officials asserted that it was indispensable. Ward proposed the following alternative: "I would enter the presence of His Majesty with head uncovered and bowing low; I would stand and not sit; I would not speak unless addressed and retire by walking backwards, never turning my back until out of his presence." [107] At one point, the Ch'ing authorities ventured to suggest that just one kneeling and three knockings of the head might be enough, because the United States was equal with China; envoys from Burma, Liu-ch'iu, Korea, Annam, Siam, and other tributary states, of course, must perform the full kowtow of three kneelings and nine knockings.[108]

In the end, the Ch'ing negotiators gave way, and on August 4 a compromise plan was suggested to the Americans through Hsueh Huan, who also told them that an audience would probably be held on August 8. S. W. Williams recorded this compromise plan: "The Minister was to come into Court, bearing the letter (or his Secretary for him), and approach the Throne, bowing as low as he had shown the commissioners, when two chamberlains would come up to him and say, 'don't kneel,' raising him up at the same time, or pretending to do so. He would then take the letter and deposit it on the table (covered with long curtains) standing between him and majesty [sic], from whence an officer would take it and, kneeling, hand it to Hsienfung [i.e., the Hsien-feng emperor] himself. The cunning design of this table with an apron on it was to hide the republican knees of the Envoy from the Emperor, who might think he went to the ground if he liked." [109] On August 5, however, Hsueh Huan returned to the American legation dispirited and weary, apparently having been overpowered by the opposition at the court. He retracted his proposal of the day before and asked whether the American minister would not bow so low as to touch one knee, or the ends of his fingers, to the ground. The Americans refused, and it was thus that the discussion of an audience ended.[110]

Once the matter of an audience had definitely been settled in the negative, Kuei-liang and Hua-sha-na refused, in a communication to Ward dated August 6, to exchange the ratifications in Peking, on the ground that it was not required in the treaty. They also rejected Ward's proposition to present President Buchanan's letter to the emperor through Kuei-liang.[111] In a reply of August 8 from Ward, the following passage was inserted at the last moment at

the request of Hsueh Huan: ". . . the undersigned has only to observe in the most explicit manner that it has been from no want
of respect to his Majesty, and with sincere regret, that he has found
himself unable to comply with the ceremonies of an audience at
his court. He not only entertains for the Emperor of China the
highest respect, but if he should fail of rendering him every mark
of respect not wholly inconsistent with the laws and usages of his
own country, he would be sternly rebuked by the President, who he
is well assured, entertains the greatest respect likewise for his
Majesty." [112]

In response an edict of August 9 announced: "Today Kuei-liang
and Hua-sha-na presented for our perusal the communication from
the American envoy (Mi-kuo *shih-ch'en*) John Ward. We see that
its expressions and spirit are very respectful and derive from utmost
sincerity." The edict ordered that Kuei-liang and Hua-sha-na should
receive the letter from the American President, and that the ratifications should be exchanged at Pehtang with Heng-fu. A copy of
the edict was transmitted to Ward, enclosed in a communication of
August 9 from Kuei-liang and Hua-sha-na which stated that the
presidential letter would be received on August 10 at Chia-hsing-ssu,
and that Ward's departure from Peking was scheduled for August
11. [113]

On August 10 the president's letter was transmitted according to
schedule. Ward respectfully took from his brother the box containing the letter and, holding it as high as his head, handed it to
Kuei-liang. Elevating the box above his eyes, Kuei-liang delivered
it to an attendant who placed it on a table under a guard of
honor. [114]

On this same occasion, Kuei-liang announced that the special
commission granted to him and Hua-sha-na in the preceding year
ended with this interview. Their seal was to be returned to the
emperor on the next day, and Ho Kuei-ch'ing would thenceforth
handle the details of foreign commerce. [115] A communication of
August 9 from Kuei-liang and Hua-sha-na (a different one from

the one of the same date cited above), which notified Ward of the exchange of ratifications to be performed at Pehtang, had already stated that they desired Ward to confer with "Ho, the commissioner of foreign commerce" on the implementation of the new treaty.[116] In other words, the Ch'ing government was adhering to its assumption that the Shanghai imperial commissioner was the standing official channel of diplomacy.

On August 11, Ward and his party left Peking. They traveled in the same manner as on their journey to the capital and arrived at Pehtang on August 16. On the same day, the ratifications were exchanged with Heng-fu at a "temple" in Pehtang.[117] The Americans weighed anchor on August 18 off Pehtang and arrived in Shanghai on August 22.[118]

The Domestic Political Context

On August 11 S. W. Williams wrote in his journal, "the proceedings of Chinese politicians are usually without reference to any principle of policy when foreigners are concerned." The Ch'ing government's sudden reversal on the etiquette of an audience Williams regarded as "one of the instances of fickleness which render dealing with them so doubtful, and furnishes melancholy proof of their ignorance of their best interests." [119] What Williams interpreted as an act of "fickleness," however, was more likely an indication of the indecision of, and the disunity within, the Peking government in the face of a difficult situation. The behavior of the mandarins, as described in Williams' journal, supports such an assumption.

Although Peking's predominantly warlike mood must have been intensified by the Chinese victory at Taku on June 25, 1859, nonetheless, just after Taku the Peking government was rather cautious in its actual handling of foreign affairs. A similar cautiousness was visible in its rather conciliatory attitude toward Ward's journey to Peking. Peking stated that Ward might use a sedan chair on the first part of the journey, and the choice of itinerary was not to be forced upon him. Furthermore, Peking repeatedly ordered the transmission of Ward's letter to Ignat'ev, which the officials at Pehtang were holding up.

In Seng-ko-lin-ch'in's memorial received on July 23, which was a discussion of the post-Taku situation, Seng-ko-lin-ch'in discussed Ward's impending visit to Peking. Pointing out that Ward at Pehtang had sent a letter to Ignat'ev in Peking and that Russian officials were also going from Pehtang to Peking at roughly the same time as the Americans, the Mongol prince voiced his suspicion of Russo-American collusion, and warned against the possibility of their making use of threatening bluffs on behalf of the British and the French. He then criticized the conciliatory attitude of Kuei-liang and his colleagues and proposed the appointment of a high official of courage and discernment to collaborate with them in handling the foreigners with dignity and righteousness.[120] An edict of the same day stated in reply that there was no need to appoint another high official, commenting that the Americans were submissive and more manageable than the British and the French.[121]

In the aggressive atmosphere of Peking, Kuei-liang must have felt more constrained in negotiating with the foreigners than he had in Tientsin or Shanghai. Seng-ko-lin-ch'in's criticism may also have influenced him. The Americans were struck by the change in Kuei-liang's attitude back in Peking. Writing about the five-day controversy over the etiquette of an audience, Williams specifically stated that the Chinese commissioners never once trespassed the bounds of strict politeness, and that they never dropped a word of menace (a reminder of the helplessness of the Americans, with only twenty of their people in the capital).[122] On the other hand, Williams records his surprise that at the July 30 interview at Chia-hsing-ssu, after exchanging compliments with Ward, Kuei-liang abruptly broke out "in a tone of unusual asperity for the mild old man" fully expressing his feelings at what had happened on June 25 at Taku and at his having been refused an interview in Shanghai by the British and French ministers. Williams ascribed this behavior to the circumstance that Kuei-liang was then in the presence of his fellow courtiers (most likely including high officials and princes, all incognito), many of whom were opposed to his policies and waiting for his fall.[123]

This change of manner, seen even in such a high-ranking person as Kuei-liang, was most strikingly evident in Hsueh Huan, who was nothing more than a provincial judge, and who was regarded as an undesirable person by the scholar-officials, especially the war advocates, because his experience in foreign contact in Shanghai had made him a useful figure to the foreigners. Williams referred to Hsueh Huan in Peking as "the sly fox," or "a slippery man" who "can't be trusted." [124] At dinner during the interview of July 30, Hsueh Huan, who seemed to have been elated by the unexpected victory at Taku, "got rather free in some of his remarks after drinking four or five glasses of samshoo and intimated that China was quite able to take care of herself against all her enemies." [125] As the meeting was breaking up, he approached W. A. P. Martin "and said to him in a most insolent manner, 'I want you to know that I know when you are lying and when you are telling the truth!' " (At Ward's insistence Hsueh Huan apologized to Martin early the next morning.)[126] After this interview, Williams was inclined to think that Hsueh Huan was "the evil genius of the convention." [127] On August 8 he even wrote that the Americans would have seen the emperor if Hsueh Huan had been kept in Shanghai.[128] It is probable that Hsueh Huan's behavior in Peking was calculated to secure his own safety. In Shanghai in April 1860, in reply to Lay's criticism of Ward's reception in Peking, Hsueh Huan acknowledged: "The fact was, you see, I did not dare to show them the slightest good will; if I had, I should have been denounced as a traitor. I was obliged to snub them. I could not help myself." [129]

Pien Pao-shu, who had been the most active and aggressive member of the Ch'ing delegation at the Tientsin negotiations, was among Ward's escorting personnel to and from Peking. He also came to see the Americans at their lodgings in Peking. Williams watched for Pien. He referred to him as "the ever present Pien," "the mercurial Pien," and stated that Pien was "as sharp and scornful as ever," "as bustling as ever." On August 10 he wrote: ". . . he [Pien Pao-shu] and Sieh [Hsueh Huan] are our evil geniuses, I am convinced, though I should be puzzled for proofs." [130] Pien Pao-shu's ubiquitousness may be taken as a further indication that watchful eyes were kept on the officials who escorted or received Ward and his party.

On the subject of how Ward was to be received and treated, there seem to have been two opposing views among the officials at the top level in Peking, between which the government vacillated. Eventually the more conciliatory view was overruled. Li T'ung-wen, department magistrate of I-chou, who was also a member of the escort, told Williams on August 18 on the latter's boat that neither he nor Ch'ung-hou had been permitted to visit the Americans in Peking. He also said that both Kuei-liang and the emperor had wished to see Ward on his own terms, but that Hsueh Huan had opposed this and had been upheld in his determination to get the Americans to kneel "by the princes and others who were of Seng-ko-lin-ch'in's party." [131]

In a secret and confidential dispatch of January 21, 1860, Bruce reported an account given by a certain English-speaking Chinese named "Hwang" (Huang Hui-lien), who had been sent to Shanghai by Seng-ko-lin-ch'in to gather information about the foreigners' intentions and the strength of the anticipated allied expeditionary force. Among other things, Huang's account stated that Seng-ko-lin-ch'in had favored a courteous reception to Ward and had disapproved of his being sent back to Pehtang to exchange the ratifications with an inferior officer, but he had been overruled, thanks to the influence of Prince Hui, two other princes of the first degree (most likely Prince I and Prince Cheng), and "the Senior Chinese Secretary of State Pen Wen Chang" (P'eng Yun-chang, who was also the senior grand councillor), "who all cling to the antiquated Chinese prejudices with more tenacity than even the Emperor himself." [132]

These two accounts disagree on the attitude of Seng-ko-lin-ch'in.

According to Li T'ung-wen, the Mongol prince was one of the leading war advocates. This view is at variance with the conclusion which was reached in Chapter II and with which Huang Hui-lien's account coincides in substance. Perhaps we should discount Huang's presentation to some extent, since he had been sent to Shanghai by Seng-ko-lin-ch'in to gather information about the foreigners. Huang's statement that the general favored receiving Ward courteously seems rather at variance with the stern line advocated by Seng-ko-lin-ch'in in his memorial of July 23. But the accounts of Li and Huang agree with regard to the emperor, who, probably because the ultimate responsibility was his, appears to have been rather cautious. They also agree in indicating that there was in all probability at one point an articulate difference of opinion as to Ward's treatment, and the more aggressive view finally prevailed.

The sudden Ch'ing reversal between August 4 and 5 on the subject of an audience, which so surprised the Americans, presumably occurred because the compromise plan, which had probably originally been worked out by Kuei-liang and Hsueh Huan with perhaps the implicit approval of the emperor or some officials at the top level, and which had been accepted by Ward, had finally been overruled in a top-level policy-decision meeting. And if we can rely upon Li T'ung-wen's account, Hsueh Huan, in a dilemma, had probably played a double role: he probably cooperated in drafting the compromise plan and then, reversing himself, advocated a firm line at the top-level meeting.[133]

There is some fragmentary evidence available which throws a dim light on the mysterious process of how and where the compromise plan was overruled.

On August 4, when the compromise plan was discussed, Hsueh Huan and the Americans also drafted two letters to be exchanged between Ward and Kuei-liang and Hua-sha-na on the problem of audience etiquette. The drafts were taken by Hsueh Huan "to be submitted to the Privy Council [the Grand Council]." One of the drafts, which was intended to be a reply from Ward, read in part: "I . . . would render [to His Majesty] every mark of respect and deference which I render to the President, without addition or diminution." [134]

On October 7, 1860, the British found at the Summer Palace a "Draft of an Imperial Rescript in Vermilion." This paper, though undated, seems to have been composed upon perusal by the emperor of this very draft reply from Ward. It read in part as follows (in its English translation in the Blue Book): "Besides, these barbarians, by their averment that their respect for His Majesty the Emperor is the same as that they feel for their Pih-li-si-tien-teh (President), just place China on a par with the barbarians of the South and East, an arrogation of greatness which is simply ridiculous." [135]

On August 5, 1859, Princes I, Hui, and Cheng jointly presented a memorial which opened as follows: "We, your officials, have just read the vermilion rescript. We were filled with a great admiration for Your Majesty's penetrating insight and profound concern." Evidently it was the above rescript to which they referred, for the princes proceeded: "Thereupon we, your officials, consulted with Kuei-liang and Hua-sha-na. And we have already ordered Hsueh Huan to visit the residence of the American barbarian chieftain and to state that, if they want to have an audience only in accordance with the etiquette of their country, there can never be any audience at all." The memorialists also suggested that, if there was to be no audience, the president's letter might be received by Kuei-liang and Hua-sha-na at Chia-hsing-ssu and the ratifications exchanged, not in Peking, but either in the Tientsin area or in Shanghai, whichever the Americans chose. In the vermilion endorsement on the memorial the emperor approved the proposals, adding that, to avoid further complications, the Tientsin area was rather preferable to Shanghai.[136]

From these documents we infer that the influence of Princes Hui, I, and Cheng was visible in the reversal of decision over the audience. Apparently the wording in the draft of Ward's reply touched off a serious reconsideration of the compromise plan. Perhaps the emperor was really angered by the assumption in writing of America's equality with the Celestial Empire. Or perhaps the draft was used by some people as an excuse to tip the delicate balance between the opposing views on the problem of etiquette and the emperor was thus induced to issue such an uncompromising rescript.

Whatever may actually have occurred inside the Peking government, we may say in brief that Ward was treated pretty much in accordance with the stipulations of the Sino-American Tientsin Treaty, except that his expenses were defrayed by the Ch'ing government. The fact that Ch'ing officials raised the question of audience etiquette, which is not mentioned in the treaty, reminds us of an edict of June 28, 1858, issued just after the signing of the Tientsin treaties. This edict, while viewing rather favorably the newly signed American treaty's provisions on the American minister's visit to Peking, added, among other things, that the protocol concerning the ceremony of kneeling should be wholly in accordance with the Chinese system.[137] In short, Peking sought to adopt toward the Ward mission the same attitude that it had taken at the time of the Tientsin negotiations.

Anglo-French Appraisals of the Mission

In concluding a paper read before the Royal Asiatic Society in Shanghai on October 25, 1859, S. W. Williams stated that "the reception of the Embassy was courteous, rather than cordial or open." Summing up the manner in which Ward had been treated, Williams commented that "they designed to carry out that part of the treaty of Tientsin which related to the visit to their capital."[138] Secretary of State Lewis Cass assured Ward that "your proceedings in China in the difficult circumstances in which you have been placed meet the approbation of the President, and I have no doubt will be equally approved by the country."[139]

On the other hand, the British and French officials in China were bitter in their appraisal of Ward's visit to Peking for the obvious reason that they had to justify their recent failure at Taku.

Copies of the communications in Peking between Ward and the imperial commissioners were obtained through a secret channel by the British officials in Shanghai. On the basis of these documents and what he had learned from the Americans, Bruce, in a dispatch of September 3, 1859, gave a thorough analysis of the treatment accorded to Ward. As a general comment Bruce stated that "whatever they [the Ch'ing authorities] may have apparently conceded on paper, they practically refuse to admit diplomatic intercourse on a footing of national equality." He pointed out that in spite of "the expediency of a friendly and honorable reception being accorded to the American mission," the Ch'ing government did not take such a course. And thus, he asserted, in comparison with what had taken place on the occasion of the previous British embassies to China, the position of the American envoy was "markedly inferior." Moreover, according to Bruce, Ward informed him that he had returned from the north "more convinced than ever of the soundness of the British determination to proceed to Tien-tsin under their own flags." [140]

In a dispatch of September 1, Bourboulon also discussed Ward's visit in detail. In a conclusion based on a personal account by Ward, the French minister stated: "In short, to judge only from what we have already learned from the accounts of the Americans themselves, the visit of Mr. Ward to Peking does not signalize any progress in the relations of the Western powers with the Chinese empire." "What this Minister did," he continued sarcastically, "may have been in conformity with the intentions and the instructions of his Government. In this respect, Mr. Ward may find for himself a consolation and a justification in the consciousness of an accomplished duty. But as a man of courage (which I believe he is) and a representative of a nation of which an excessive national self-respect is the distinctive characteristic, he must have, I am convinced, profoundly resented all the humiliations which they made him go through. This feeling is at least general among his countrymen. It has been shown especially, without any disguise, we may say, in the words of the American naval officers who joined the expedition." [141]

CHAPTER IV

Sino-Russian Contact in Peking (1859–1860)

Su-shun . . . dared to fling upon the table the text shown him of
the Treaty of Aigun, remarking sharply that this document had
no significance at all. Ignat'ev immediately rose and announced
loudly that he broke off the conference since Su-shun could not
behave properly and forgot himself to the extent of daring to treat
international documents disrespectfully in the presence of a Russian plenipotentiary. Then and there he added that he would ask
the Grand Council to appoint other plenipotentiaries who would
be able to behave decently.

— *Baron A. Buksgevden*

The Russian Tientsin Treaty, unlike the other Tientsin treaties,
became effective without much dispute. The Chinese and the Russians came into conflict in this period not over permanent diplomatic
residence and related institutional matters, but over a territorial problem. In the course of negotiations dealing primarily with this territorial problem, the matter of a formula for communication between
the two governments also became an issue. A formula had been
agreed upon in the Tientsin Treaty, but the persistent efforts of two
successive Russian negotiators — Perovskii and then Ignat'ev — failed
to bring the Chinese to its full implementation.[1]

The territorial dispute concerned the Sino-Russian eastern frontier.
In 1689 after years of intermittent frontier war, it had been agreed
in the Treaty of Nerchinsk that the boundary between the two
countries would be demarked by the Kerbechi and Argun rivers and
the Yablonoi Mountains. China, then at the height of her military
strength, had thus retained and extended her sovereignty over the

Amur valley. A century and a half later, with the appointment in 1847 of Nikolai Nikolaevich Murav'ev as governor-general of eastern Siberia, renewed Russian interest in this area became conspicuous. Between 1854 and 1858, Murav'ev sent three major expeditions down the Amur River and established garrisons at strategic points on its left (north) bank. By 1858 the whole vast area north of the Amur was actually under Russian control. In 1858 Murav'ev led a fourth expedition down the Amur and succeeded in bringing the Chinese into a conference at Aigun, a Chinese garrison town on the Amur. Evidently under strong Russian pressure, the Treaty of Aigun had been signed on May 28, 1858, by Murav'ev and Petr Perovskii, councillor of state of Russia's Foreign Office, and by I-shan, military governor of Heilungkiang, and Chi-la-ming-a, military deputy lieutenant governor of Heilungkiang. The treaty provided, among other things, for the cession to Russia of the left (north) bank of the Amur River and Sino-Russian joint control over the land lying between the Ussuri River and the sea. The Peking government at first approved the Aigun Treaty, but later inclined toward its repudiation.[2]

PEROVSKII'S NEGOTIATIONS
(DECEMBER 1858–JUNE 1859)

Article 12 of the Russian Tientsin Treaty called for the exchange of ratifications in Peking within a year of ratification by the tsar. Putiatin, who had signed the treaty, suggested that a representative be sent to Peking as soon as possible to resolve the boundary question before the arrival there of diplomats from other powers. The Russian government decided not to send a new envoy from St. Petersburg; instead, the ratification and a commission of full powers were sent to Peking to Perovskii. Perovskii had been sent to China as conductor (*pristav*) of a new ecclesiastical mission to Peking, headed by Archimandrite Gurii, which was to relieve the preceding mission there. On his way Perovskii had been temporarily detached to participate with Murav'ev in the Aigun negotiations and had subsequently proceeded to Peking with Gurii's mission.[3] In addition to exchanging the ratifications, Perovskii was charged by the Russian Foreign Office to secure confirmation from the Peking government on the Sino-Russian frontier. He was further to acquire the cession to Russia of the coastal area between the Ussuri River and the sea, and to exact a number of rights for Russian trade.[4]

In a communication of December 15, 1858, Perovskii notified the Grand Council that he had received full powers to exchange the ratifications and to conduct negotiations on any matter, and he requested the appointment of a Chinese plenipotentiary to deal with him.[5] In response an edict of December 17 announced the appointment as negotiators of Su-shun, president of the Board of Rites, charged with the supervision of affairs at the Court of Dependencies, and Jui-ch'ang, president of the Court of Dependencies.[6] The appointment implied what was made clear in a vermilion rescript of the same day — that the management of Russian affairs should remain, as heretofore, under the jurisdiction of the Court of Dependencies. The same rescript also revealed expectations of a firm attitude on the part of Su-shun, whose extreme aggressiveness Jui-ch'ang was expected to counterbalance.[7] The emperor ordered the grand councillors to read the rescript with "Tsai-yuan [Prince I] and others" and to inform Prince Hui on the matter the following day. This indicates that the Council of Princes was also consulted on Russian affairs.[8]

Perovskii and his party seem to have enjoyed considerable freedom while in the city of Peking. A Russian courier who returned to Irkutsk from Peking early in March 1859 reported that members of the new mission walked about Peking in European dress and that he himself had gone about freely in the city without meeting the slightest hindrance.[9]

In a dispatch from Shanghai on March 27, 1859, Baron Gros quoted from a report of February 19 from Father Mouly, apostolic vicar of Chihli. According to the report, which was allegedly based on eye-witness accounts by Chinese priests living in the capital, the Russian mission had been officially installed at Peking, "the Ambassador" had hoisted a Russian flag, the embassy personnel were rambling freely through the streets in European costume, the Russians were behaving very well, were very charitable to the poor, and were much liked by the people. There had occurred only one conflict over etiquette, according to Mouly's report: the Chinese authorities had asked the Russian ambassador not to use a chair with eight bearers, since this privilege was reserved exclusively for the emperor; the Russian agent had complied by using only four bearers.[10] In May 1859 Robert Hart, interpreter at the British Consulate in Canton, reported an account given by a native informant who had just returned to Canton from Peking to the effect that "a Russian Ambassador" had visited Peking on March 2 (*sic*), the Russians in the capital, more than 100 (*sic*) in number, roamed about just as they pleased much to the grief of the emperor and the antiforeign party, the Russians had bought up large quantities of grain, and the emperor in alarm had forbidden the traffic.[11]

Against this kind of Russian behavior bitter complaints were heard from scholar-officials. According to a memorial from Yin Keng-yun which must have been drafted after Perovskii's arrival in Peking, the newly arrived Russian barbarians were far more numerous than the Russian priests and students on previous occasions. There were among them barbarians from another country (or countries) too. At first they only wandered through the streets. Then there was a report that they climbed up on the city walls to look around, and that they made weapons and privately bought horses. Yin recalled that at the court assembly of June 23, 1858, in reply to his objections to the resident minister clause, Prince Hui had sought to mollify him by stating that a foreign minister residing in the capital would be something like the Westerners of the Imperial Board of Astronomy in the K'ang-hsi era or the students at the Russian Hostel; he and his suite would number only a few persons, with tonsured heads and in Chinese costume. The presence of the Russians in Peking might be used as an irrefutable argument by the British, with whom Kuei-liang and Hua-sha-na were then negotiating in Shanghai in an effort to prevent their coming to the capital. If the barbarian vessels should sail north in the coming spring, the Chinese military operations would be closely watched by the Russians. Though the presence of powerful bannerman forces would be sufficient to restrain the barbarians in the Russian Hostel, which was located so near the imperial palace, if any trouble occurred it would disturb the imperial ancestral temple and the altars of the deities of the soil and grain. Yin therefore suggested that the Court of Dependencies and the Office of the Gendarmerie be ordered to keep the barbarians under control. Russians who were in excess of the allowed number of priests and students should be ordered back to their country. If they did not obey, their misdemeanors should be made known to their king and a competent high official should be sent to oblige them to leave, using military force.[12]

Bitter resentment was also expressed in an intensely warlike joint memorial received on February 21, 1859, from Sheng-pao, imperial commissioner and lieutenant-general of the Mongolian Bordered Yellow Banner, and Weng T'ung-shu, governor of Anhwei, both then actively engaged in suppressing the Taipings. The memorialists suggested that the Russians in the capital should be allowed nothing more than to stay in the Russian Hostel for scholarly purposes, as theretofore. If they did not obey, their chieftain should be seized and killed, or at least they should be arrested and sent back in custody, while a letter of censure should be sent to their king from the Court of Dependencies.[13]

Late in the afternoon on May 29, 1859, when Perovskii was riding through the Ch'ung-wen Gate, the easternmost of the three southern gates of the Imperial City, he was stoned by some persons, probably soldiers, who were standing on the city wall, and several of the stones hit his horse. The next day he addressed a letter of protest to the general commandant of the Gendarmerie, Prince Cheng, in which he asked that copies of a proclamation be posted throughout the city, prohibiting the molestation of Russians in Peking. He also stated that since his arrival in Peking Russians had often been noisily pointed out in the street by local inhabitants. The Court of Dependencies refused to transmit the letter, so Perovskii sent it to the Grand

Council with a covering letter dated May 31. The Grand Council referred the matter to the General Headquarters of the Banners for an inquiry as to whether the persons charged with the stoning were soldiers on duty or idlers. In an indirect communication through the Board of Rites the Grand Council informed Perovskii of the steps taken, adding that the Russians would not be insulted in the streets in future if they behaved with propriety.[14] The incident may have been purely accidental, or it may possibly have been an indication of latent but increasing anti-Russian feeling. It may even be imagined that it was secretly instigated.

The Content of the Negotiations

The Exchange of Ratifications

Before the Tientsin Treaty ratifications were exchanged, the matter of discrepancies between the various texts and versions of the treaty became an issue. The treaty had been drafted in Russian, Manchu, and Chinese. Article 12 stipulated that the Manchu text should be considered the authentic one. However, there were two versions of the Manchu text, both of which had been signed by the plenipotentiaries of both countries. One of these was evidently a translation by a Russian interpreter from the Russian text; the other one was made by the Chinese, but how this version, as well as the Chinese text, had been drafted is not quite clear. This second Manchu version and the Chinese text seem to have been in close agreement, but there were some discrepancies between the two Manchu versions and apparently also between the Manchu version made by the Russians and the Chinese text. It took several months to resolve these discrepancies. Meanwhile, inquiries were made of Kuei-liang and his colleagues, who were then in Shanghai, and the four original copies kept by the Chinese government (one in Chinese, two in Manchu, and one in Russian), which had been brought to Shanghai, were sent back to Peking. It seems that in the end the version of the Manchu text made by the Chinese was replaced by a new version, to which the emperor's ratification was given and his seal affixed; and that the Chinese text was replaced by a new definitive version. This was a translation from the new Manchu version, which is substantially the same as the Manchu version made by the Russians.[15]

The ratifications were exchanged on April 24, 1859, between Perovskii and Su-shun and Jui-ch'ang.[16] Perovskii's negotiations leading to the exchange seem to have been kept secret from the officials of the other powers who were then in China. Bruce reported from Shanghai in August 1859, not quite accurately: "It appears that the Russian Minister, General Ignatieff, succeeded in reaching Pekin, and in exchanging the ratifications of the Russian Treaty towards the end of May." [17]

Article 2 of the Sino-Russian Treaty, which now became effective, laid down a new formula for correspondence and negotiation, replacing the old system whereby the relations between the two countries had been under the jurisdiction of the Court of Dependencies. Correspondence between the two governments was now to be carried on not through the Russian Senate and the Court of Dependencies but through the Russian foreign minister and "the senior member of the Grand Council" or the senior grand secretary, on a footing of perfect equality. When it was necessary to send "a dispatch on a very important affair," a "special official" was to be appointed to bring it to Peking, where it would be transmitted to the Grand Council through the president of the Board of Rites. This Russian official might have an interview with a grand councillor or a grand secretary. The original Chinese text provided for communication in writing in Peking between the Russian official and a grand councillor or a grand secretary, without mentioning an interview. The Manchu version translated from the Russian text provided also for an interview.[18] The definitive Chinese text also provided for an interview.

The Supplementary Agreement of April 25, 1859

Article 2 also stipulated that a Russian official might come to Peking through Kiakhta and Urga, through Taku, or through other seaports. This abolished the previous system, in which the single route through Kiakhta and Urga has been specified. Among the other routes now opened, however, the one that could become a subject of dispute was the route through Taku, where the allied forces had landed in 1858, escorting the representatives from the four powers. The Taku area was now being heavily fortified by Seng-ko-lin-ch'in, on whose suggestion an edict of April 14, 1859, had specified Pehtang, some ten miles north of Taku, as the port of entry for representatives of Britain, France, and the United States.[19] Evidently in the light of these developments, a supplementary agreement concerning the passage of a Russian official to Peking via the sea coast was signed on April 25, 1859, by Perovskii, Su-shun, and Jui-ch'ang.[20]

The terms of the agreement were as follows: (1) When the Russian government wanted to send an official on very important business to Peking via "Tientsin seaports," a written request for permission would be sent to Peking through Urga. (A communication to the Russian Senate from the Court of Dependencies, giving notice of the exchange of ratifications,[21] specified that such a request should be made in the form of a communication to the imperial agent at Urga.) (2) Written permission would be granted only if the seaports were at peace (*ju hai-k'ou wu-shih*) — a qualification that was often to cause dispute. (3) The port of entry would be Pehtang (not Taku). (4) The Russian vessel would anchor off the bar, and the Russian official would be escorted in to Pehtang by Chinese officials, on a Chinese vessel.

There is in *Ssu-kuo hsin-tang* a document which looks like an original or an alternative draft of this agreement. According to this document, a Russian official coming to Peking, despite the new arrangement in the Tientsin Treaty, was "not to be allowed to proceed through Taku or any other seaport, but to come and go through Kiakhta as before."[22] It may be assumed that this was the original proposal of Su-shun and Jui-ch'ang, to which Perovskii was of course not in a position to consent, and that a compromise was reached in the Supplementary Agreement by which the Chinese negotiators at least succeeded in putting restrictive qualifications to the passage to Peking via the sea coast.

Further Russian Proposals

Probably early in April 1859 Perovskii presented to the Peking government an eight-article draft for another treaty, which proposed the following: (1) the cession to Russia of the coastal area between the Ussuri River and the sea (Article 1); (2) a conference to be held within a year at Kiakhta or elsewhere (Article 2), to negotiate regulations on: redefinition of the western frontier (Article 3), reciprocal expansion of facilities for overland trade (Article 4), the appointment of consuls to Urga, Kalgan, Kashgar, Tsitsihar and some other Chinese cities, and to St. Petersburg and some other Russian cities (Article 5), postal service between Peking and Kiakhta (Article 6), and re-examination of the existing treaties between the two countries (Article 7); (3) appointment of a Chinese envoy to Russia (Article 8).[23]

The debate on the draft continued until June, with Peking consistently rejecting the Russian proposals both verbally through Su-shun and Jui-ch'ang and in three written communications from the Grand Council.[24] The second of these communications, which was a reply to one of May 28 from Perovskii, was drafted after a consultation with "Prince Hui and others," [25] another indication that the Council of Princes was behind the scenes in the Sino-Russian negotiations.

The Pattern of the Negotiations

Perovskii conferred with Su-shun and Jui-ch'ang at least four times. Their first meeting probably took place soon after the appointment of the Chinese negotiators on December 17, 1858;[26] the second one on April 24, 1859, for the exchange of the ratifications; the third on the following day for the signing of the Supplementary Agreement; and the fourth probably on May 19, 1859.[27] Another meeting may also have occurred some days before April 24, 1859, after the originals of the Tientsin Treaty had been brought back to Peking from Shanghai.[28]

Su-shun and Jui-ch'ang seem to have shown persistent reluctance to confer with Perovskii. In his communications to the Grand Council Perovskii repeatedly emphasized the necessity for personal meetings and complained of the Chinese negotiators' inaccessibility.[29] Indeed the conference of May 19 was apparently arranged because Perovskii had hinted that he hoped some high official other than Su-shun and Jui-ch'ang would be appointed to meet him.[30]

The conferences presumably took place at the Russian Hostel, or to be more precise, at the Russian Southern Hostel (E-lo-ssu nan-kuan).[31] On one occasion — probably early in January 1859 — Su-shun and Jui-ch'ang refused Perovskii's request for an interview on the ground that they were too busy to visit him.[32] This would indicate that the Russian Hostel was their customary meeting place.

Let us now examine the manner in which Perovskii conducted official correspondence with the Peking government. *Ch'ou-pan i-wu shih-mo* reproduces only five communications to Perovskii from the Grand Council.[33] Five more appear in *Ssu-kuo hsin-tang,* which also contains thirteen communications from Perovskii to the Grand Council, three to Su-shun and Jui-ch'ang, and one to the general commandant of the Gendarmerie, Prince Cheng.[34]

Perovskii's announcement of December 15, 1858, that he had received full powers from St. Petersburg, was addressed to the Grand Council.[35] After the appointment of Su-shun and Jui-ch'ang as negotiators, Perovskii corresponded not with the Grand Council but with these two high officials. In January 1859, there were three exchanges of correspondence, all of them concerned with the discrepancies between the various texts of the Tientsin Treaty.[36]

On January 28 Perovskii appealed to the Grand Council, claiming that Su-shun and Jui-ch'ang were evasive and insincere.[37] The Grand Council replied promptly, refuting Perovskii's argument.[38] Thereafter, on the problem of the treaty text discrepancies, Perovskii corresponded only with the Grand Council. When he asked Su-shun

and Jui-ch'ang to discuss his eight-point treaty draft he complained
that they told him they had been appointed only to exchange the
ratifications; on any other matter he should write to the Grand
Council.[39] Accordingly correspondence relating to the new treaty
proposals was also conducted solely with the Grand Council. Perovskii thus discontinued correspondence with Su-shun and Jui-ch'ang
on substantial matters of dispute, but he sent them at least three
further communications relating to other rather technical matters.
One of them concerned the return of a courier to Russia. Another,
which will be discussed below, was a protest against the dispatch by
the Court of Dependencies of a communication to the Russian
Senate. The third concerned the sending of a Russian official to
Kalgan to meet Ignat'ev, who was coming to Peking to replace
Perovskii.[40]

A change took place in the Grand Council's method of communicating with Perovskii. Until the ratifications were exchanged, his
communications were transmitted to the Grand Council through the
Court of Dependencies; the Grand Council replied indirectly in a
communication to the Court of Dependencies, which was to convey
its substance to Perovskii. This procedure must have implied inequality.[41]

Soon after the exchange of ratifications, the Court of Dependencies
sent to the Russian Senate a letter which is reproduced in *Ch'ou-pan
i-wu shih-mo* in the entry for April 25. It gave notice of the exchange
of ratifications and also dealt with a specific detail in connection
with the Supplementary Agreement.[42] On May 4 Perovskii wrote to
Su-shun and Jui-ch'ang, stating that he had heard about this letter,
which had been sent in violation of the Chinese promise not to send
any communication to Russia without notifying him. He asserted
that this was a breach of international etiquette, and asked for a copy
of the letter. He also pointed out that according to Article 2 of the
Tientsin Treaty communications should be sent no longer from
the Court of Dependencies to the Russian Senate, but from the
senior grand councillor or senior grand secretary to the Russian
foreign minister.[43] Evidently as a result of Perovskii's protest, a

second notification of the exchange of ratifications was issued, this time by the Grand Council, and addressed to the Russian foreign minister.[44]

Around May 8 the Grand Council notified the Board of Rites of a new regulation approved by the emperor, according to which thenceforward any document delivered by "Russia" (or the Russian representative) to the Board of Rites was to be received and transmitted to the Grand Council; communications from the Grand Council to "Russia" (or the Russian representative) were to be transmitted through the same board.[45] This arrangement was apparently intended to be in accordance with Article 2 of the Tientsin Treaty.

In communicating with Perovskii, the Grand Council now followed two different procedures. A letter of May 16 was sent to the Board of Rites, which conveyed its substance to Perovskii. The letter acknowledged receipt of the silver returned by him, which had originally been earmarked to meet the expenses for the first three months of 1859 of the Russians in Peking. It also set the date for Perovskii's fourth interview with Su-shun and Jui-ch'ang.[46] This indirect approach was chosen deliberately after the grand councillors had consulted with Su-shun.[47] However, the Grand Council's reply to a letter of May 21 from Perovskii, which, among other things, rejected point by point all of his treaty proposals, was addressed to him directly. (This reply is reproduced in *Ch'ou-pan i-wu shih-mo* under May 25.)[48] Two subsequent communications were addressed directly to Perovskii, both of them concerned with the Russian treaty proposals.[49] On the other hand, the indirect approach through the Board of Rites was also used on at least two further occasions. The first was the Grand Council's reply to Perovskii's complaint about having been stoned in the street. (Perovskii had first written a letter of protest dated May 30 to the general commandant of the Gendarmerie, Prince Cheng, but when the Court of Dependencies refused to transmit it, he sent it to the Grand Council through the Board of Rites with a covering letter dated May 31.)[50] The second occasion was the Grand Council's reply to

Perovskii's inquiry of June 6 as to the expected date of Ignat'ev's arrival in Peking.[51]

In brief, after the exchange of ratifications, the Grand Council wrote directly to Perovskii on the subject of the eight-point Russian treaty draft; on less substantial matters it addressed him indirectly — no longer through the Court of Dependencies, but through the Board of Rites. The Grand Council probably thus meant to preserve, though in a limited form, its assumption of superiority. It cannot be ascertained from the documents consulted whether Perovskii took exception to the Grand Council's using different correspondence procedures according to the subject under discussion.

The Grand Council's communication which is in *Ch'ou-pan i-wu shih-mo* under May 25 and to which we referred above spoke of the Russian penetrations beyond the Amur River into the right-bank area of the Ussuri River, penetrations for which Murav'ev was chiefly responsible. Earlier in the year the Court of Dependencies had sent a protest against Murav'ev's activities to the Russian Senate. Murav'ev had intercepted the letter, which had been sent from Peking without Perovskii's knowledge, and sent it back to Perovskii.[52] The latter enclosed it in his communication of May 21 to the Grand Council. In this missive he recalled that upon his receipt of full powers from the tsar he had made it clear to Su-shun and Jui-ch'ang that any matter for discussion between the two countries was to be referred to the Russian plenipotentiary in Peking and that Su-shun and Jui-ch'ang had agreed to this. Since then, however, the Chinese government had sent several communications to Russia without notifying Perovskii. As to the letter intercepted and sent back by Murav'ev, Perovskii stated that Su-shun and Jui-ch'ang had assured him that they had no knowledge of it. "Hereafter, no matter what is the case," he proceeded, "no missive should be sent to my country without giving prior notice to the high officials specially appointed by the emperor of your country to negotiate with the Russian plenipotentiary." [53]

The Grand Council asserted in its reply that since the ratifications had not yet been exchanged, there had been nothing improper in sending the letter from the Court of Dependencies to the Senate. Since the letter concerned an important matter on which the Chinese government wanted again to write to the Russian government, the Grand Council asked what government office in Russia should be the addressee of a new letter to be sent through Perovskii. However, to Perovskii's request that the high officials appointed to deal with the Russian plenipotentiary be informed in advance of any future communication to Russia, the Grand Council firmly replied: "Our country has its own settled rules. Only what should be made known can be made known. It is impossible to notify them of what should not be made known." [54] The Grand Council probably meant to retain freedom to contact St. Petersburg directly, if necessary, without using Perovskii as the medium, because he was suspected of being under Murav'ev's influence.[55] In fact, an edict of May 28 ordered the imperial agent at Urga to find out in secret the whereabouts of the Russian foreign minister, to whom Perovskii said a communication from Peking should now be addressed, according to the new treaty.[56] Later in 1859, the Peking government repeatedly ordered the imperial agent at Urga to communicate with the Russian Foreign Office about the murder in San-hsing, Kirin, of a Russian who had allegedly attempted to rape a native woman. (The case was referred to a joint conference of the Grand Council and "Prince Hui and others.")[57] This may have been another instance in which Peking tried to contact St. Petersburg over the head of the Russian representative in Peking (then Ignat'ev).

Late in May 1859 the Court of Dependencies sent to Perovskii a reply to a petition (*ch'eng*) from Archimandrite Palladii, head of the old ecclesiastical mission (which had been relieved by Archimandrite Gurii's mission), concerning the anticipated departure for Russia of the "high official in Peking" (that is, Perovskii — perhaps in his capacity as conductor), priests, students and others. The Grand Council had drafted the reply and submitted it for the emperor's inspection, after having checked on "the precedent of always sending a communication [from the Court of Dependencies] to the [Russian]

Senate on the return home of relieved Russian priests and students." [58] The event probably indicates that even after the exchange of ratifications the Court of Dependencies was still considered by both sides to retain some authority in the management of Russian affairs. There is certainly other evidence which shows that the Court continued to function as a secretariat, so to speak, in such matters as the maintenance of the Russian Hostel or the escort of a Russian representative traveling between Kiakhta and Peking.[59]

IGNAT'EV'S NEGOTIATIONS (JUNE 1859–MAY 1860)

In January 1859 the Russian government appointed Major-General Nikolai Ignat'ev political agent at Peking.[60] His duties were twofold: he was to lead a group of Russian military instructors to China and deliver firearms to the Taku forts;[61] he was also to settle the question of the boundary on the Ussuri River.[62] The origin of this military assistance was a Russian promise given in 1858. With a view to establishing Russian influence in China, Putiatin had proposed to Kuei-liang and Hua-sha-na after the Tientsin treaty was signed that Russia provide the Chinese government the following year with military instructors and also with fifty cannons and ten thousand rifles for the Taku forts. Peking's response had been rather cool, but it had finally accepted the offer.[63]

Ignat'ev left St. Petersburg on March 18, 1859. On April 16 he reached Irkutsk, where he joined Murav'ev. A week later they left Irkutsk together, arriving in Kiakhta on April 29. On May 2 Karpov, frontier commissar, who had been to Urga on Murav'ev's orders, returned with the news that the Chinese imperial agent at Urga refused to allow the Russian representative to proceed to Peking; he was to wait in Kiakhta for permission from the Peking government to travel further.[64] (In March [Julian calendar] the Russian Foreign Minister, Prince Gorchakov, had written to the senior grand councillor, informing him of Ignat'ev's appointment as Perovskii's successor, in accordance with Article 2 of the Tientsin

Treaty. Also in March, the Chinese imperial agent at Urga had notified the Russian governor of Kiakhta that travel to Peking by any important persons other than priests was forbidden by the emperor; accordingly Ignat'ev could not proceed without permission from the Court of Dependencies.)[65]

On May 12 Khitrovo, Murav'ev's adjutant and the bearer of the exchanged ratification of the Tientsin Treaty, arrived in Kiakhta en route from Peking to St. Petersburg. He brought a report from Perovskii which, among other things, made it known that the Chinese officials (apparently Su-shun and Jui-ch'ang), once they became aware of Perovskii's intention of connecting the Russian military assistance with demands for concluding an additional treaty, had formally refused both firearms and military instructors. They had also expressed astonishment that a new Russian representative was coming; in their opinion this was utterly useless. In view of this information, Ignat'ev decided on his own responsibility not to follow his instructions concerning the military assistance. The firearms, which had already reached Verkhneudinsk, he ordered diverted to the use of Russian troops in Siberia. Of the military instructors, he kept only Captain Balliuzek with him; the others were placed under Murav'ev's command. The half-million rubles originally intended to cover the cost of organizing Chinese troops were deposited in the treasury at Irkutsk.[66] On May 14 Murav'ev left for the Amur River area, leaving Ignat'ev in Kiakhta.[67]

The unexpected Chinese refusal of military assistance and the resultant change of his mission to one of a purely diplomatic nature placed Ignat'ev in an awkward position, for he had not been given any diplomatic title. He thus demanded instructions as to what official title he should now assume. (The instructions from the Russian Foreign Office conferring on him the title of minister did not reach him until a year later, on May 19, 1860.)[68]

A memorial received on May 14 from the Urga imperial agent reported that a certain Russian major had brought a notification that Ignat'ev was coming as successor to Perovskii. To this he had replied that Ignat'ev should wait at Kiakhta until instructions arrived from the Court of Dependencies.[69] An edict of the same date gave permission for Ignat'ev to come to Peking, stating that since the treaty ratifications had already been exchanged it was difficult to prevent his coming.[70]

According to the same memorial and edict as well as another edict of the same day giving orders to Seng-ko-lin-ch'in and Heng-fu,[71] the Russians had also expressed their intention to deliver the firearms by sea, which elicited instructions from the emperor that the Russians should anchor outside the sand bar off Taku and transship the firearms in Chinese vessels. This means that the Chinese government showed in edicts its intention to accept Russian military assistance, although a formal refusal had been given to Perovskii by his Chinese counterparts. This discrepancy suggests that there was difference of opinion within the Peking government as to whether the military assistance should be accepted — a point to which we shall return.[72]

Permission for Ignat'ev to proceed to the capital was conveyed to the governor of Kiakhta on May 27. On June 6 Ignat'ev left Kiakhta, accompanied by Balliuzek, three other officials, and five Cossacks as escort. On June 8 they reached Urga, where they stayed for two days. They arrived in Peking on June 27. At the Russian cemetery outside the city they were met by Perovskii, Archimandrite Gurii, and all the other people staying at the Russian Hostel. Ignat'ev entered the city in a chair, surrounded by his suite and the escorting Cossacks, all on horseback. He used a chair despite the Chinese authorities' warning that it might arouse antagonism among the people. The party approached the Russian Hostel in state and met with no trouble.[73] On June 30 Perovskii left Peking to return to Russia by overland route.[74]

Like Perovskii and his party, Ignat'ev and his group seem to have enjoyed considerable freedom in Peking. According to Buksgevden, all the Russian officials and even the servants were completely free to stroll about undisturbed.[75] A Russian topographer made a map of the city (which, incidentally, was made available in the fall of 1860 to the Anglo-French military authorities in China). The data for the map had been obtained by traversing the streets in a cart from which angles were taken, while an indicator fixed to the wheel marked the distances covered.[76]

On the other hand, there is at least one indication that the Ch'ing authorities tried insofar as possible to prevent contact between the Russians and the native inhabitants. Soon after his arrival Ignat'ev wrote: "In Kovalevskii's time native inhabitants could still often be seen at our Hostel. But at present not a single respectable Chinese would drop in at our place, nor would any Russian visit someone in the city. In spite of all their inborn greediness Chinese shop-keepers even refuse to sell to Russian customers. We are compelled to make all our purchases through our Chinese servants. We have no agent, or spy. We know only what is known to everyone from the *Gazette*." [77] However, Ignat'ev seems later in his sojourn in Peking to have secured various bits of information, veracious or not, about behind-the-scenes actions of the Ch'ing authorities. Probably this kind of information was obtained from the Chinese liaison officials who used to come to the Russian Hostel.[78]

According to a memorial received on November 1, 1859, from Fu-chia, censor overseeing the Kiangnan circuit, the Russians who had come to the capital this time occasionally invited poor people to their hostels and distributed among them cloth and coins. The Court of Dependencies had already issued a proclamation prohibiting the Russians from leaving their hostels. It was rumored also that under the pretext of offering relief, the Russians of the Northern Hostel were trying to lure the needy into Christianity by giving alms and by having native children work at the hostel on one-week shifts. The memorialist suggested that a secret and thorough investigation be made and the necessary action taken.[79]

In brief, although the Russians could stroll about in the city freely, they were in effect isolated from the natives. As we know, during John Ward's stay in Peking personal contact between the Americans and the Russians was physically blocked and only correspondence between Ward and Ignat'ev was permitted, letters being transmitted through the Ch'ing authorities.

The Course and the Pattern of the Negotiations

The Pattern at the Outset

Apparently at Perovskii's insistence Su-shun and Jui-ch'ang sent two officials to congratulate Ignat'ev on his arrival.[80] On the following day, June 28, Ignat'ev wrote to the Grand Council, notifying them of his arrival as Perovskii's successor with a view to continuing negotiations for the benefit of both countries, and requesting the appointment of reliable high officials as negotiators. On July 1 four officials came to the Russian Hostel and orally stated that Su-shun and Jui-ch'ang had again been appointed to negotiate with the Russian plenipotentiary. Ignat'ev insisted upon written confirmation of their appointment, declaring that the fulfillment of this point was basic to negotiations. He took this step in order to deprive the Chinese authorities of any opportunity later to refuse to negotiate and also to give the negotiations an official character. Later on the same day the Grand Council wrote him that Su-shun and Jui-ch'ang were to be sent for an interview. An edict of July 9 announced that Su-shun and Jui-ch'ang were to make an appointment for an interview with the Russian representative. What should be noted here is that Ignat'ev asked simply for the appointment of negotiators, without specifying that they should be grand councillors or grand secretaries. Furthermore, he did not take exception to the appointment of Su-shun and Jui-ch'ang, neither of whom was a grand councillor or a grand secretary.[81]

Ignat'ev's first interview with Sh-shun and Jui-ch'ang took place on July 10 at the Russian Hostel. The Chinese negotiators had wanted to meet at the Court of Dependencies, but Ignat'ev had insisted that a plenipotentiary of the Great Russian Tsar could not accept the arrangements that applied to the envoys from small countries like Korea; he did not want to confer elsewhere than in his own residence.[82] At this first interview it was decided that discussions preparatory to further meetings would be held at the Russian Hostel between the Russian interpreters and Su-shun's deputies. Su-shun and Jui-ch'ang would come to the Russian Hostel only on especially important occasions and only on Ignat'ev's invitation.[83] Ignat'ev's second interview with them took place on July 22, and the third on August 31.[84]

At the first interview of July 10, Ignat'ev presented to Su-shun and Jui-ch'ang a draft of a supplementary treaty in six clauses, along with a brief memorandum and a detailed explanatory note.[85] A reply in the form of a four-point memorandum was brought from the Chinese plenipotentiaries to Ignat'ev on July 12.[86] Thereafter correspondence was carried on mainly between Ignat'ev and Su-shun and Jui-ch'ang, until the third interview.[87] Their communications seem to have been transmitted through the Court of Dependencies.[88]

A letter of July 27 to Ignat'ev from the Court of Dependencies complained that a Russian named P'ing had forced his way into the residence of the American minister, who was then in Peking. In a letter to the Grand Council Ignat'ev refuted this charge, stating that there was no one named P'ing in his suite or among the priests and students. He also voiced his objections to the fact that personal contact between the Russians and the Americans in Peking was prohibited and that the delivery of his letters to the Americans was retarded. Moreover, he made an issue of the fact that the Court of Dependencies had communicated with him; this, in his opinion, was not in accordance with the formula stipulated in Article 2 of the Tientsin Treaty. The Grand Council replied that P'ing's case was just "an ordinary sort of affair concerning the Hostel" (*hsun-ch'ang kuan-wu*), and so the communication had been sent from the Court of Dependencies as theretofore; on an important or urgent matter, a communication would be sent either from the Grand Council through the Board of Rites in accordance with the treaty, or from "the imperially commissioned high officials" (*ch'in-p'ai ta-ch'en*) (Su-shun and Jui-ch'ang in this case).[89]

In brief, Ignat'ev initiated formal contact with the Peking government by corresponding with the Grand Council, but he carried on the actual negotiations with Su-shun and Jui-ch'ang either through interviews or by correspondence. In other words, he found it expedient to adopt a formula of communication that was a compromise between the old system and the new one stipulated in Article 2 of the Tientsin Treaty. His formula was roughly the same as the one Perovskii had resorted to. On the other hand, when the Court of Dependencies communicated with him, he addressed an explicit protest to the Grand Council, thus making it clear that he would admit to no regression to the old system.

The Territorial Controversy

Ignat'ev's negotiations with Su-shun and Jui-ch'ang were stormy from the beginning. At the outset of the first interview on July 10, the Ch'ing negotiators communicated to Ignat'ev, in a most unceremonious manner, the emperor's astonishment on hearing of the new Russian representative's arrival. They stated further that through some misunderstanding the representative must not have heard from Perovskii that the Tientsin Treaty ratifications had been exchanged, that the matter of Russian military assistance had been settled in the negative, and that most explicit answers had been given to all the new Russian treaty proposals. They concluded that since there were no unsolved Russian problems the emperor assumed that the newly arrived representative would soon return to his own country.[90]

The draft of a six-clause supplementary treaty which Ignat'ev sent to Su-shun and Jui-ch'ang was roughly the same in substance as Perovskii's eight-point draft.[91] As for the eastern frontier between China and Russia, Ignat'ev demanded, as had Perovskii, cession of the coastal area between the Ussuri River and the sea.

On July 24 Lieutenant-Colonel Budogovskii, Murav'ev's quartermaster-general, came to Peking *via* Pehtang, bearing a map of the Sino-Russian eastern frontier that he had made during an extensive survey of the Ussuri area. He had come by sea to the Gulf of Peichihli in Murav'ev's suite. (Murav'ev had gone from the Amur area to Nikolaievsk, and then to De Castrie. He had then visited

Hakodate, Hokkaido, and had proceeded to the Possiet Bay, where he had met Budogovskii. Murav'ev had brought Budogovskii to the Gulf of Peichihli to send him to Ignat'ev with the map.)[92]

Ignat'ev's treaty demands met the same fate as Perovskii's: the Ch'ing government would yield to none of them. The negotiators clashed most sharply over the problem of delimiting the eastern frontier. On June 14, 1858, about two weeks after the signing of the Treaty of Aigun, an edict had been issued approving this treaty. In a state of panic over the ever-increasing diplomatic and military pressures being exerted by the allied powers, and especially the British, the Ch'ing government had probably taken this step in the expectation that Putiatin would mediate with the allies on China's behalf. Putiatin, then in Tientsin, had certainly been informed of this edict — a fact that Ignat'ev repeatedly referred to in the course of his negotiations.[93] Later, however, the Peking government gradually inclined toward repudiation of the treaty.[94] In May 1859 the Grand Council had informed Perovskii that it considered effective the boundaries as delimited by the 1689 Treaty of Nerchinsk, and it implicitly denied the validity of the Aigun Treaty by stating that the Russians in "Marinsk (K'uo-t'un-t'un) and other coastal places on the Amur river" were only "temporarily allowed to live in wastelands." [95] A subsequent edict of June 16 had announced the punishment of I-shan and Chi-la-ming-a, both of whom had been responsible for the signing of the Aigun Treaty.[96]

Ignat'ev arrived in Peking on June 27, only two days after the Ch'ing success at Taku, which was scarcely the moment to expect a conciliatory attitude from the Peking government on the frontier question.[97] As a matter of fact, Su-shun and Jui-ch'ang assumed a very firm attitude at their first interview with Ignat'ev. They agreed that the frontier should be defined and suggested that the matter should be discussed not in Peking but on the border, with the military governor of Kirin (perhaps a polite form of evasion), but they categorically denied the validity of the Aigun Treaty by asserting that I-shan had not had full powers, an authorized seal, or authority to cede the left (north) bank of the Amur. They also declared that their government would never countenance any territorial seizure in Manchuria, for which region they were ready to fight. Ignat'ev stressed the inviolability of treaties and referred to the emperor's edict approving the Aigun Treaty. He also resorted to bluff, asserting that "being contiguous to China to the extent of 7000 versts, it is easier for Russia than for any other maritime power to strike a severe and painful blow at China any time and anywhere." [98]

The four-point memorandum of July 12 from Su-shun and Jui-ch'ang in answer to Ignat'ev's Treaty proposals also considered still effective the border defined by the Treaty of Nerchinsk. At the same time the memorandum stated: "As for the border of the province of Heilungkiang (Hei-lung-chiang *chiao-chieh* [the border on the Amur], negotiations should be held between the military governor of Heilungkiang and your representative, Murav'ev. Those places in question in Kirin are really not contiguous to Russia. So it is not necessary to discuss delimitation or trade in them." [99]

Though they toned down their assertions and qualified their arguments with such ambiguities, the Ch'ing negotiators stood firm on the frontier problem, both at the five-hour conference on July 22 [100] and in their subsequent correspondence with Ignat'ev.[101] At one point in the exchange of bluffs, Su-shun and Jui-ch'ang declared that Sino-Russian trade might be suspended.[102]

Ignat'ev's Efforts to Change the Chinese Negotiators

An opportunity fell to Ignat'ev to try to break the stalemate by invoking Article 2 of the Tientsin Treaty. At the third interview on August 31, Su-shun went so far as to fling upon the table the text shown him of the Aigun Treaty, declaring that the document had no significance at all. Ignat'ev immediately shouted that he broke off the conference since Su-shun dared to treat international documents disrespectfully in the presence of a Russian plenipotentiary. He also declared that he would ask the Grand Council to appoint other plenipotentiaries who would be able to behave decently.[103]

The next day Ignat'ev sent a letter to the Grand Council which reviewed the negotiations at length and bitterly criticized the arguments and attitudes of the Ch'ing negotiators, especially of Su-shun; apparently in order to save Su-shun's face, he did not mention the third interview. Ignat'ev asked the Council either to persuade Su-shun to be more conciliatory or to ask the emperor to appoint a grand secretary or a grand councillor to negotiate with him, in accordance with the Tientsin Treaty. He also did not forget to draw attention to China's existing conflict with Britain and France and the possibility that Russia might become either China's friend or enemy, depending upon her response to Russia's treaty proposals.[104]

The Grand Council replied four days later, refusing to change negotiators: "The imperially commissioned high officials, Su and Jui, are both trusted dignitaries of Our Great Emperor. They have already been managing affairs with Your Excellency. There is absolutely no reason why they should not deal [with Your Excellency] with sincerity. We, this Council, are already fully aware that the statements made in their correspondence or in their interviews with Your Excellency are plain speaking based on reason . . . When your representative, Perovskii, arrived in the capital, Our Great Emperor dispatched the high officials Su and Jui to exchange the treaty ratifications. No objection at all was raised to this." [105]

After this particular exchange, correspondence was carried on mainly between Ignat'ev and the Grand Council, transmitted through the Board of Rites.[106] (There were a couple of exchanges of further correspondence with Su-shun and Jui-ch'ang over the transmission of Russian letters between Peking and Pehtang.)[107] Though two further interviews were held with Su-shun and Jui-ch'ang, Ignat'ev continued to demand personal contact with a grand councillor or a grand secretary.

In a letter of September 10, which also ignored the third interview, Ignat'ev informed the Grand Council that Su-shun and Jui-ch'ang had asked him through their deputies whether he wanted another interview; he had replied in the affirmative and had asked them to set a date at their convenience, but they had kept silence since.[108] The Grand Council's reply of September 13 did not touch upon this complaint.[109] In a letter to the Council of September 17 Ignat'ev did not ask for another interview with Su-shun and Jui-ch'ang but simply requested an interview with a grand councillor or a grand secretary.[110]

Apparently as a consequence of Ignat'ev's insistence, Ch'ing officials came to the Russian Hostel on September 18 to arrange for another interview[111] with Su-shun and Jui-ch'ang, which took place on September 22. Su-shun and Jui-ch'ang were extremely courteous and assured Ignat'ev that they were acting with the knowledge and consent of the emperor, whom they were keeping informed on the progress of the negotiations. They also chided Ignat'ev for having affronted them by complaining needlessly to the Grand Council.[112] As to the border problem, Su-shun asked Ignat'ev to report to the tsar that the emperor absolutely could not comply with the Russian demands, and he proposed that negotiations be postponed until a reply had been received from St. Petersburg.[113] (As the result of a consultation with "Prince Hui and others," the grand councillors on September 21 proposed sending to the military governors of Heilungkiang and Kirin copies of five communications to Ignat'ev from the Grand Council and from Su-shun and Jui-ch'ang concerning the boundary question. This proposal was approved by the emperor.)[114]

After two further vain complaints to the Grand Council about the obduracy of Su-shun and Jui-ch'ang, Ignat'ev broke off correspondence with the Grand Council for some three months.[115]

On December 23, asserting that he had received an edict from the tsar the previous day, Ignat'ev requested the Council, "in accordance with Article 2 of the Treaty of Tientsin," to appoint "a grand secretary" to "negotiate on matters of importance to the two countries."[116] (Note that here he specified simply a grand secretary, not as before "a grand councillor or a grand secretary.") The Council in reply flatly dismissed his request: "Upon the arrival last year of your representative, Perovskii, Our Great Emperor especially deputed

President Su and President Jui to hold interviews. All matters under negotiation with your country have been reported to the throne on your behalf. Under the Chinese institutions, each grand secretary has some specific business which is his exclusive province. [Furthermore,] whenever something happens, an edict ought to be requested, according to which the affair is to be dealt with. [In other words, a grand secretary] really can neither take part in everything nor discharge his duties at his own discretion. President Su and President Jui are both high officials of the first rank and are the persons who have been deputed by an imperial order to conduct the negotiations. Please tell them whatever your country wants to discuss. They are certainly in a position to report about it to the throne on your behalf." [117]

On December 28 Ignat'ev repeated his request to the Council and drew attention to two precedents: a grand secretary had been sent to Tientsin in 1858 to negotiate with the representatives of Russia and other powers, and the American representative while in Peking had interviewed a grand secretary. He also pointed out that Perovskii's meetings with Su-shun and Jui-ch'ang had preceded the exchange of ratifications. [118] The Grand Council retorted in a reply delivered on January 1, 1860, that although Ignat'ev had arrived in Peking after the exchange of ratifications, he had already met several times with Su-shun and Jui-ch'ang. "How, then, can it be permissible to request the appointment of another person?" [119]

In response to this rebuff, the tireless Ignat'ev sent to the Council a carefully worded letter dated January 5, challenging it to a showdown. He recalled that upon his arrival in Peking the government had appointed as negotiators Su-shun and Jui-ch'ang, although the Tientsin Treaty had already become effective. He had not objected because, in view of the long-established peace between the two countries, he had not wanted to waste time in argument. Also, he had expected that Su-shun and Jui-ch'ang would act with sincerity and that, as imperially commissioned high officials, they would be cognizant of the existing treaties between the two countries. Deceived in this expectation, he had demanded appointment of "a grand secretary," as called for in the Tientsin Treaty (notice that he did not say "a grand councillor or a grand secretary" here either). "If affairs are not to be arranged in accordance with treaties, what need was there to make this treaty?" After a brief review of the past negotiations on the border problem and other pending issues, Ignat'ev then proceeded to make it quite clear, resorting to cajolery and bluff, that it was quite possible that Russia might join Britain and France in their war with China; on the other hand, she would mediate with the allies on China's behalf if China complied with her demands. He concluded: "To sum up, I look forward to hearing from Your Excellencies as to whether Your Excellencies want to handle affairs in accordance with Article 2 of the Treaty of Tientsin." [120]

Peking's response to this clever presentation was delicate and somewhat mysterious. On January 8 Ignat'ev received a brief note from the Grand Council stating that its reply to his letter of January 5 had already been handed over to Su-shun and Jui-ch'ang for personal transmission to him, and that he might arrange with them the time of their next meeting.[121] In this brief note Su-shun and Jui-ch'ang were not entitled "plenipotentiaries" (ch'in-p'ai ta-ch'en) as theretofore but simply "presidents" (shang-shu).[122] No deputy from Su-shun came to the Russian Hostel to arrange an interview, however, so Ignat'ev again wrote to the Council on January 13. He expressed his surprise at the Council's procedure in this matter: "Why should the communication not be transmitted directly through the Board of Rites? The note mentions personal transmission. Really I cannot understand why." After complaining that he had vainly waited for five days for Su-shun and Jui-ch'ang, he suggested that the communication be transmitted in the ordinary fashion or that another high official be appointed to confer with him personally. He then reiterated his previous points on the border question with the renewed proposal that, in return for China's concessions, Russia would persuade Britain not to carry out her anticipated expedition. In closing, Ignat'ev again stated his expectation that a grand secretary would be appointed to discuss these problems personally.[123]

In response came officials sent by Su-shun to arrange for an interview. Ignat'ev informed them through his interpreter that he would receive Su-shun and Jui-ch'ang not as negotiators but only as bearers of the Grand Council's communication, or, if desirable, as personal acquaintances of his.[124]

The fifth interview with Su-shun and Jui-ch'ang was held on January 16 at the Russian Hostel. Ignat'ev received them politely, but his manner was cold and grave. Su-shun was exquisitely courteous and friendly, but restrained. He solemnly transmitted the Grand Council's communication (dated January 8), and the interview lasted for some two hours. Besides some inevitable discussion of the border question, the conversation circled around a variety of random topics.[125]

Now, as to the Grand Council's communication, there is a noticeable difference between the version reproduced in the entry for January 8, 1860, in *Ch'ou-pan i-wu shih-mo* (and also in *Ssu-kuo hsin-tang*) and the one quoted in Buksgevden, which is the one that was actually delivered to Ignat'ev on January 16. The latter contains a very important passage that is not included in the former.

The version in *Ch'ou-pan i-wu shih-mo* denies Sino-Russian joint jurisdiction over the area between the Ussuri River and the sea, referring among other things to the punishment of I-shan and Chi-la-ming-a. It also asserts that a petition was presented jointly by the military men and the people of Kirin, protesting that I-shan had exceeded his authority in "granting a lease" of the aforementioned area to Russia ("the popular wrath is difficult to control"). On the other hand, it makes no mention of the Amur River, Marinsk, or Kizi Lake, to which locations previous communications from the Grand Council or from Su-shun and Jui-ch'ang had referred. On the whole, this document could be taken as a tacit admission that Russia's possession of the left (north) bank of the Amur River was at least an indisputable *fait accompli*.[126] However, Buksgevden's version contains the following passage which flatly disavows the Aigun Treaty: "It is positively known to us that Your Plenipotentiary, Count Murav'ev, compelled I-shan to sign this treaty out of fear. Forced to satisfy his demands, our high official did this with the secret expectation that without the authorized seal his signature would have no value and thus he could justify his conduct to the emperor." [127] It will be remembered that Su-shun used a similar argument in the first interview with Ignat'ev. The addition of this passage certainly changed the tone of the Grand Council's communication, nullifying the conciliatory nuance in the *Ch'ou-pan i-wu shih-mo* version.

How are we to explain the discrepancy between the two versions? A natural assumption would be that after the communication had been drafted, under date of January 8, its very content again became an issue within the government and, as a result of renewed deliberations, a neutralizing passage was added to the original version. In other words, the assumption here is that there were conflicting views in Peking as to how to deal with the Russian demands and vacillation among the decision-makers.

There is some circumstantial evidence that seems to support this inference. First, it will be recalled that Su-shun and Jui-ch'ang, once Perovskii was suspected of linking Russian military assistance to his treaty demands, formally refused both Russian firearms and military instructors, while edicts issued on Ignat'ev's arrival in Kiakhta indicated the readiness (unknown to the Russians) of the Ch'ing government to accept military assistance. Back in January 1859, the Court of Dependencies had informed the Russian Senate as to where the Chinese would receive the expected firearms.[128] This probably means that at this stage Su-shun, who was then president of the Board of Rites, charged with the supervision of affairs at the Court of Dependencies,[129] must not have been opposed to Russian assistance, and that he later changed his mind. As we know, at his interview with Ignat'ev on July 10, 1859, he reiterated the Chinese rejection of military assistance. On the other hand, an edict of June 11, 1859, and an edict of March 27, 1860, indicate that the arrival of firearms was still expected.[130] All this would indicate that there was a difference of opinion, with Su-shun on the negative side, as to whether the military assistance should be accepted — at least after the Russians in Peking gave the impression that they were using it to bargain for territorial concessions.

Secondly, according to Buksgevden the Russians in Peking later learned that Chinese high officials had gathered for consultation prior to the January 16 interview: as a result of their deliberations the following course had been decided upon, with the emperor's full approval: "To avoid a rupture with Ignat'ev, not to allow Russia to ally herself with European powers, and not to comply with a single one of her demands." [131] If we can rely upon this account, whose source is not indicated, we may assume that the Grand Council's communication was re-examined at this gathering and the addition made to it.

Furthermore, there is another matter that may have to be taken into account here, and that is the mysterious circumstances surrounding Hua-sha-na's death. An edict of December 30, 1859,[132] announced and mourned the death of Hua-sha-na, president of the Board of Civil Appointments, who had been cosigner with Kuei-liang of the four Tientsin treaties and had continued until August 1859 as Kuei-liang's colleague in dealing with foreign diplomats in Shanghai and then in Peking. The edict was a commonplace obituary edict, except that it ordered an extra grant of 300 taels in silver for funeral expenses in addition to the customary bestowal of funds in accordance with the regulations governing the death of a president of a Board (*chao shang-shu li tz'u-hsü*).[133] While none of the Chinese sources I have consulted gives an adequate explanation of Hua-sha-na's death,[134] there are several Western reports that suggest in one way or another that there was something mysterious about it. The *North China Herald* reported on December 31, 1859, that in the last few days a rumor had been prevalent that Hua-sha-na had been put to death. The *Herald* questioned the authenticity of the story, citing the *Peking Gazette* to the effect that he had been at court on November 27. On February 4, 1860, the *Herald* reported his death, quoting in full from the *Peking Gazette* the above edict, but making no reference to the cause of death. Again on February 11, the *Herald* stated that Hua-sha-na's death appeared to have been a subject of discussion among local Chinese officials. It quoted them as saying that he had concurred in the policy recommended by Ho Kuei-ch'ing in his secret memorial of the preceding year, a policy of faithful adherence to the terms of Lord Elgin's treaty, and that his disappointment on finding that the emperor was slow to perceive the importance of amicable settlement with the allies had caused his death.

On the other hand, Buksgevden and Shumakher, whose accounts must have been based on Ignat'ev's dispatches, assert that Hua-sha-na committed suicide. The two accounts differ, however, as to the cause of his suicide. According to Buksgevden, the Peking government, in response to Ignat'ev's demand that a grand secretary be appointed as a negotiator, decided to appoint Hua-sha-na as a third negotiator along with Su-shun and Jui-ch'ang. Hua-sha-na killed himself by poison before the formal appointment was made. "Knowing that the angered emperor intended to entrust him, as one of the persons blamable for the conflicts which had occurred [with the Western powers], with the task of resolving the situation, entering into negotiations with the foreigners, he decided to commit suicide, because he saw no way out of his difficult situation." [135] According to Shumakher, the story was as follows: Kuei-liang and Hua-sha-na had misrepresented to the emperor their negotiations with foreign diplomats in 1858 and 1859, and several clauses in the British and French Tientsin treaties they had not made known to him as they were expressed in their European texts. The emperor summoned them both to his presence and questioned them on the past negotiations and on the British and French treaties. It was not known what had happened at the audience, but when he came home from the court Hua-sha-na took poison, Kuei-liang requested retirement (or leave) because of his advanced age, but the emperor dismissed his request.[136] This version coincides roughly with what Ignat'ev told Western diplomats in Shanghai in June 1860.[137]

We cannot ascertain the authenticity of these two Russian accounts, as the sources of their information are not known. But taken in conjunction with the rumors reported in the *North China*

Herald, they lead to the conclusion that there is more than a mere possibility that Hua-sha-na committed suicide for some reason. Perhaps only one of the Russian accounts tells the truth. Or perhaps they are equally true and supplement each other. In any case it is quite understandable that Ignat'ev should have related in Shanghai only the second account, which would reveal nothing of Ignat'ev's negotiations in Peking.

In view of these facts and with our knowledge of the power configuration in Peking, the opposition between the war and peace parties, and the increasing expectation of a renewal of Anglo-French military hostilities, we may perhaps reconstruct the course of events which led to the fifth interview as follows:

There was within the Peking government a conflict of opinion as to how to deal with the Russian demands. Su-shun, a leader of the war party, who conducted the negotiations with both Russian representatives, was a pivotal figure in the group which opposed conciliation. He was categorically against accepting Russian military assistance, at least after he came to suspect that the Russians were using it as a bargaining tool to gain territorial concessions to which he was opposed. The Russians in Peking observed that "he had, as an imperial clansman, almost unlimited influence, and as the head of the war party he was hostile to foreigners in general, but especially inimical to Russia because of her claims on the Manchurian territory." [138]

Su-shun's opponents in Russian affairs were probably not quite the same as the peace party in the Arrow War. Their circle is assumed to have been wider, at least at the decision-making level, because the persistent expectation of the arrival of Russian firearms, which is seen in edicts, must have reflected a relatively moderate attitude toward Russia on the part of the Grand Council, where edicts were drafted. This offers a striking contrast to the situation pertaining to the conflict with Britain and France, where the basic tone of the edicts was warlike and the Grand Council is thus inferred to have been under the control of the war party.[139] As for the boundary problem, it was in all probability unanimously deemed desirable to repudiate the Aigun Treaty, if possible. It is very likely, however, that there was a divergence of opinion as to how far the government should, as a matter of practical politics, admit the established facts that the left bank of the Amur was already actually under the control of Russia and that the Russians were encroaching upon the right bank of the Ussuri.[140]

As for the machinery for negotiations, one reason why the government did not comply with Ignat'ev's demand for Su-shun's dismissal as negotiator was apparently that it did not want to put into full operation the formula stipulated in Article 2 of the Tientsin Treaty. Another and very real factor may have been Su-shun's determination not to let the leadership in Russian affairs go over to the conciliatory group. If we can assume that Hua-sha-na was to have been appointed as a third negotiator and committed suicide because of this entanglement, this may suggest that the conciliatory group was temporarily in the ascendancy, but that Su-shun's position was still so strong and the prospects so gloomy that Hua-sha-na found himself in a hopeless plight. It was possibly because Ignat'ev hoped for the entrance into the negotiations of none other than Grand Secretary Kuei-liang, central figure of the peace party, that from December 1859 he demanded the appointment simply of a grand secretary and no longer used the expression "a grand secretary or a grand councillor." It was perhaps more than a mere coincidence that Kuei-liang vainly asked for permission to retire on January 5, 1860.[141]

The mysterious vacillation which seems to have preceded the January 16 interview may indicate the strength of the impact on the Peking government of Ignat'ev's letter of January 5, which plainly offered mediation with the allies but at the same time included a barely veiled threat that Russia might join Britain and France in their war with China. Under this impact it was probably decided to adopt a conciliatory approach and the reply of January 8 was drafted. That the reply was to be transmitted by the unusual procedure of dispatching "President Su" and "President Jui" as its bearers may have been a tacit admission that Ignat'ev was right in invoking

Article 2. It may also have been an indication of a very delicate balancing of forces between the intransigeants and those who favored conciliation. Then, probably at Su-shun's insistence, an assembly of high officials was called — perhaps a joint session of the Grand Council and the Council of Princes with Su-shun and some other dignitaries also present.[142] As a result of their re-examination of the issue, the reply was redrafted with the addition of an important passage. Because Su-shun was extremely courteous and would not even raise his voice at the interview of January 16, the Russians were convinced that he had been instructed to be cautious and avoid a quarrel.[143] This again may have been an indication that Su-shun's position was at this time relatively precarious and that he did not want to be excluded from the negotiations by provoking another protest from Ignat'ev.

Correspondence between Ignat'ev and the Grand Council continued even after the January 16 interview, but the negotiations had now definitely reached a stalemate.

Now determined to leave Peking as soon as a Russian ship arrived in the Gulf of Peichihli, Ignat'ev wrote to the Grand Council on February 19, 1860, that Russian warships were to arrive off Pehtang in the coming spring and he asked that any letter to him from Russians on board be transmitted to him in Peking. (As we shall see, this request was rejected by the Grand Council.)[144]

The Supplementary Agreement in Operation: Russian Communication Between Peking and Pehtang

As we have seen, the passage of Russian officials to Peking via the seacoast was restricted by the Supplementary Agreement of April 25, 1859, which, among other things, stated that the port of entry would be Pehtang. It also specified that permission to come to Peking by this route would be given only if the seaports were at peace. During Ignat'ev's stay in Peking there were occasional comings and goings of persons and letters between the Russian Hostel and Russian warships appearing off Pehtang. Bound by the Tientsin Treaty and the Supplementary Agreement, the Ch'ing government did not at first oppose Russian contact between Pehtang and Peking. As things developed, however, they became increasingly inclined to prohibit, or at least restrict, contact on the ground that the seaports were not at peace. (The Supplementary Agreement also specified that application for permission to send an official to Peking was to be made through the Chinese authorities at Urga, but the Peking government did not invoke this specification.)

On July 14, 1859, Murav'ev arrived in the Gulf of Peichihli. He landed Lieutenant Colonel Budogovskii and three others and let them proceed to Peking, bearing a map of the right bank of the Ussuri.[145]

The Ch'ing authorities on the coast asked Peking for instructions, stating that they did not know whether there was in the Tientsin Treaty any provision for sending a letter (by an emissary) from the seacoast to Peking (a joint memorial received on July 17 from Heng-fu and the provincial treasurer, Wen-yü). At this time Ward was about to start for Peking via Pehtang. The matter was referred to "the princes and ministers" or "the princes" (probably to the Council of Princes) and an edict of July 17 called attention to the Supplementary Agreement and gave permission for the four Russians to come to Peking. Heng-fu and Wen-yü were ordered to let them start only after Ward had left for Peking. The Russians were to be escorted by two officials, civil and military, who were not "high officials." Furthermore, their travel expenses were not to be defrayed by the Russians (in contradiction to Article 2 of the Tientsin Treaty). Budogovskii and his three companions arrived in Peking on July 24, escorted by Ch'ang-ch'i, a prefect, and Wen-an, an expectant first captain.[146]

In Peking, Ignat'ev sought permission to send Colonel Martynov down to Pehtang to inform Murav'ev of the state of affairs at the capital. But the Peking government refused his request,[147] probably because it wanted to make a distinction between a trip from Pehtang to Peking and return, and a trip from Peking to Pehtang, which it regarded as less relevant to the kind of situation provided for in the Supplementary Agreement.

Prince Dadeshkil'iani, who had accompanied Budogovskii to Peking, returned to Pehtang, leaving the capital on July 29 and meeting interference from Ch'ing local officials on his way. An enormous military man, he frightened local inhabitants by his terrifying appearance and energetic gestures. In early August Colonel Martynov left Peking for Russia by way of Mongolia, carrying with him Ignat'ev's reports. En route he became involved in some friction with local authorities who tried to delay him. (Subsequently, the Court of Dependencies complained to Ignat'ev about the behavior of these two men and asked the Russians in future not to send "such rude people" who disturbed the peace of local inhabitants.)[148]

Budogovskii left Peking in September for Irkutsk by way of Mongolia, accompanied by a Russian official and two soldiers.[149]

On August 5, in expectation of Murav'ev's second arrival off Pehtang, Ignat'ev wrote to Su-shun and Jui-ch'ang asking for compliance with an incidental request of Murav'ev's for permission to send officers to Peking with letters and necessities for Ignat'ev. An edict of August 8 approved the request and instructed Heng-fu and Wen-yü that only "two or three persons" should be sent to Peking. A letter of August 9 from Su-shun and Jui-ch'ang to Ignat'ev also specified that for the sake of convenience in escorting and providing for them, not more than three persons should come to Peking. In reply Ignat'ev asked Su-shun and Jui-ch'ang on August 13 to transmit a letter from him to Murav'ev in which this limitation was mentioned. The letter was sent in care of Heng-fu through the Grand Council. After waiting vainly for over a month for Murav'ev to reappear, Heng-fu, together with Seng-ko-lin-ch'in, asked for further instructions. In accordance with orders received in reply, in an edict of September 27, the letter was returned to the Russian Hostel through the Court of Dependencies. On October 5 Ignat'ev wrote to Su-shun and Jui-ch'ang, taking exception to the return of the letter and requesting transmission to Pehtang of a new letter to be delivered to a Russian ship that would appear off Pehtang. He also insisted that, if the Russians on board wanted to send letters or couriers to him, they should be allowed to do so. His new letter was sent to Pehtang through the Grand Council and as we shall see, was eventually delivered to the Russians on a Russian ship.[150]

While the Peking government, whether reluctantly or not, was not blocking Russian contact either in person or by letter between Pehtang and Peking, Seng-ko-lin-ch'in and Heng-fu both repeatedly suggested to Peking that the contacts should be suspended. In a joint memorial received on August 22, 1859, they advised letting Russian officials and letters come and go by the overland route via Urga for the time being. The reason was that because peace was yet to be made with Britain and France the strengthening of defenses at the various seaports was essential. Peking agreed with their suggestion in principle for the future, but at the same time it reminded them that, with regard to Murav'ev's expected arrival, the promise already given to Ignat'ev should be kept.[151]

A foreign ship appeared on October 6. Seng-ko-lin-ch'in thereupon sent a letter to "Prince Hui and others" in which he stated that if it was a Russian vessel he would send an official to put out a feeler by informing those on board that "if it is necessary to go to the capital on business, the trip should be made via Urga. At this place we are at war with Britain and France, hence we dare not receive here any documents or communications." Seng-ko-lin-ch'in's letter was presented to the throne by the grand councillors ("P'eng Yun-chang and others"). In response, an edict of October 9 stated that if the vessel was Russian, any documents or communications from it might be accepted off Pehtang and any letters to Ignat'ev transmitted. The edict also drew attention to the Supplementary Agreement and stated that a request to send couriers to Peking, if they were only "one or two persons," should be acceded to, after referral to Peking.[152]

The foreign vessel turned out to be a Russian warship. Ignat'ev's letter, which had been kept in Heng-fu's care, was delivered to the Russians on board, who produced a communication addressed to

Heng-fu and four letters to their countrymen in Peking. At one point the Russians insisted upon sending a few persons to Peking for consultation with Ignat'ev, but this plan was dropped. The five letters were all sent to the Grand Council, and the four addressed to the Russians were delivered through the Court of Dependencies on October 13. On October 14 Ignat'ev wrote to Su-shun and Jui-ch'ang enclosing a letter in reply to the Russians on the ship. The Grand Council sent the letter to Pehtang where it was delivered to the Russians. Before sailing off, the crew left two letters, food, and bottles of wine, all to be transmitted to Ignat'ev. By order of an edict of October 22, the letters and the provisions were sent to the Grand Council and then delivered to Ignat'ev through the Court of Dependencies. A joint memorial received on October 22 from Seng-ko-lin-ch'in and Heng-fu had suggested that access to the fortified seaports be temporarily forbidden to Russian vessels until tranquillity had been restored to the seaports, on the ground that since the Russian ships and crews were indistinguishable from those of other countries, an unnecessary conflict could arise where an Anglo-French retaliatory expedition was expected every moment. The edict of the same date dismissed the suggestion for two reasons: first, it would be difficult to reject a Russian demand to send letters to the capital via Pehtang because of the Supplementary Agreement; second, if all the Russian letters were transmitted via Urga, even greater troubles would arise at postal stages.[153]

It was probably because the negotiations with Ignat'ev definitely became deadlocked after the interview of January 16, 1860, and also because of the mounting pressure of an expected Anglo-French military expedition that Peking came to reverse its stand on the subject of communications between Peking and Pehtang. As we have seen, on February 19, 1860, Ignat'ev asked the Grand Council to transmit to him any letter from Russian war vessels which were due to arrive off Pehtang in the coming spring. Citing the very same Supplementary Agreement, the Council rejected his request on February 20, on the following grounds: the seaports were not at peace and it was feared that vessels of other countries might approach, falsely hoisting Russian flags, and spy upon the defenses; secondly, the Tientsin Treaty made no provision for a Russian warship to come to the coast to send letters or to secure provisions.[154]

In the middle of March Ignat'ev wrote to the Grand Council asking that a letter be transmitted to Shanghai. He also asked permission to send some persons to Pehtang after April 10 to meet the expected Russian ships. The Grand Council's reply on March 19 refused these requests, asserting that the Tientsin Treaty made no stipulations for transmitting letters to Shanghai or for Russian warships coming and anchoring off Pehtang. The letter to be transmitted was returned to Ignat'ev,[155] and an edict of March 27 gave detailed orders to Seng-ko-lin-ch'in and others about the measures to be taken should Russian warships appear off Pehtang. The edict also instructed them to arrest and escort back to Peking any Russian who might come to Pehtang from the capital.[156]

The letter that was returned to Ignat'ev was addressed to the captain of the first Russian vessel to put in at Shanghai. It explained the situation in Peking and asked the captain to come to the Gulf of Peichihli as soon as possible. When the Grand Council returned the letter, Ignat'ev got a Catholic missionary to send it through native Christians to Shanghai, where it was put in the care of the Russian consular agent in the city.[157]

When he learned that the letter had reached Shanghai, Ignat'ev wrote the Grand Council (on April 22) and stated that since Russian warships were certainly coming he wanted to send an officer and a student to Pehtang, escorted by a Ch'ing official, in order to prevent a possible misunderstanding between the crews and the local inhabitants. Again invoking the Tientsin Treaty, the Council refused permission, flatly stating that "there should be nothing to be said about it." [158]

Meanwhile Ignat'ev's letter to Shanghai had been delivered to Captain Likhachev, who arrived there on April 2. On the *Iaponets* he arrived off Pehtang on May 11, on the same day that his letter of reply, which had been transmitted from Shanghai through native Christians, happened to reach Ignat'ev.[159]

A memorial from Seng-ko-lin-ch'in and Heng-fu reporting the appearance of Russian vessels was received on May 15. Frankly admitting that the Pehtang area was difficult to defend, the memorialists voiced their suspicion that some British and French barbarians might be mixed with the Russian crews in order to make a reconnaissance. However, they went on to say that if the Russians really had brought letters to be sent to Peking they would be received and forwarded on their behalf "respectfully, in accordance with the previous edict." (It should be noted that Seng-ko-lin-ch'in and Heng-fu were here reversing themselves and invoking the edict which had rejected their suggestion to suspend Russian communication between Pehtang and Peking.) An answering edict of the same date ordered them to receive Russian letters at Pehtang and forwarded them to Peking, and to ask for further instructions if the Russians on board wanted to send "one or two persons" to Peking. The edict also stated that although the government knew that it could reject a request to send persons to Peking, by asserting that the seaports were not at peace, it was rather preoccupied with the possibility of the Russians fishing in troubled waters and was eager to avoid any friction with them and to have them withdraw as soon as possible.[160] The unusual cautiousness displayed by Seng-ko-lin-ch'in and also by Peking becomes understandable against the background of an increasingly tense and ominous situation: foreign warships for some time had often been seen off Taku and along the coast of Shangtung; at the end of April a Chinese officer and two men on reconnaissance off Taku had been kidnapped on a French warship; and the news reached Peking on May 13 that Tinghai had fallen to the Anglo-French forces.[161]

On May 17 two letters addressed to Ignat'ev were handed over at Pehtang. They were sent to the Grand Council and delivered to the Russian Hostel through the Court of Dependencies on May 19. On May 18 a letter (from Ignat'ev?) which had been forwarded by the Grand Council was delivered to the Russians at Pehtang, and on May 24 Ignat'ev's reply to their letters was forwarded to them.[162]

Ignat'ev's Departure from Peking

Ignat'ev received Likhachev's letter from Pehtang on May 19. On May 21 the Grand Council received a communication from him dated May 20, which took the form of an ultimatum. Informing the Council that he had received new instructions from St. Petersburg, Ignat'ev asked them to report to the emperor on the pending issues and to give a definite answer within three days to the Russian demands on the frontier demarcation. If the demands were met, Ignat'ev wanted to hold any necessary negotiations with grand councillors. If they were rejected, he declared, he would leave Peking on May 28, to board a Russian ship at Pehtang.[163]

The Grand Council's reply did not touch upon Ignat'ev's intended departure. It simply argued along previous lines on the border question and added that if everything was not now clear to Ignat'ev, the imperially commissioned high officials might hold another interview with him.[164] Ignat'ev's reply on May 24 to this evasive communication asked for a categorical answer to the point raised in his last letter. When this letter was being sent out, officials came to the Russian Hostel with a message from Su-shun informing him that the Chinese government would not allow him to go to Pehtang.[165]

An edict of May 25 admitted the inevitability of Ignat'ev's departure for Pehtang: "[Ignat'ev] wants to leave the capital on May 28 to board a vessel at Pehtang. There is something unfathomable in the mind of this barbarian chieftain. It cannot be known whether or not his intention is to fish in troubled waters by making disturbances in collusion with Britain and France and then offering to mediate. We cannot know either whether or not he wants to help Britain and France in secret and wage a war against us, thus giving rein to his abnormal insolence. If we hinder him from going, we shall inevitably meet intimidations on his part." The edict then stated that the Office of Gendarmerie and the Metropolitan Prefecture had already been ordered to send officials and petty officers to escort Ignat'ev, that Heng-fu was to see to it that on his arrival in Pehtang Ignat'ev sailed immediately; and that, if Ignat'ev wanted to send Likhachev to Peking in his place, Seng-ko-lin-ch'in was to hinder him from coming and ask Peking for further instructions.[166]

An edict of May 27 stated that Ignat'ev was now scheduled to leave for Pehtang the next day and that the Metropolitan Prefecture had already been ordered that day to send officials to escort him and make necessary arrangements for food and accommodation en route. Seng-ko-lin-ch'in and Heng-fu were to send officers to meet Ignat'ev on the way and take over as escorts, and they were to order the local authorities along the way to make arrangements like those of the Metropolitan Prefecture. Ignat'ev was to be led to Pehtang via the side road from Pei-ts'ang and not be allowed to go through Tientsin and the routes behind the Taku forts. He was also to be required to sail immediately after boarding the ship.[167]

On the evening of May 27, officials came to the Russian Hostel with the information that, since the Russian representative was to leave on May 28, arrangements had been made for providing carriages, horses, and an escort of officials, and that the Grand Council therefore had no further answer to Ignat'ev's letters.[168]

Ignat'ev and his party left Peking on May 28. They were reportedly escorted by officials from the Metropolitan Prefecture as far as Yang-ts'un, and then by officials sent by Heng-fu. Ignat'ev rode in a chair, having managed to hire native bearers in spite of the prohibitory imperial instructions given orally to the grand councillors. (The bearers were subsequently taken to Taku and punished.) On June 1 Ignat'ev reached Pehtang where he was met on behalf of Seng-ko-lin-ch'in and Heng-fu by Te-hsiang, assistant department director of the Court of Dependencies, Ch'ung-hou, salt controller, and Sun Chih, taotai of Tientsin. Three days later Ignat'ev and his party sailed southward.[169]

Before sailing, the Russians handed over to the Chinese authorities three letters: one from Ignat'ev to the Grand Council, one to be forwarded to the next Russian vessel that might come, and one that seems to have been a letter of farewell to the Chinese authorities on the coast (*kuan-mien chin-kao i-chien*). The Chinese authorities accepted the first two, but returned the third.[170]

The edict of May 25 had ordered that if Ignat'ev wanted to send Likhachev to Peking in his place, Seng-ko-lin-ch'in was to hinder him from coming, meanwhile asking for further instructions. In answer, Seng-ko-lin-ch'in and Heng-fu suggested, in a joint memorial received on May 29, that after Ignat'ev's departure the Russians should be strictly prohibited for military reasons from moving to and fro between Peking and Pehtang. Peking's response to this suggestion was rather ambiguous. In the vermilion endorsement on the answering memorial, the government reversed itself and suggested that if adequate precautions were taken, secrets would not be revealed even if the Russians were admitted to the capital; if the Russians were prevented from coming, they might use it as an excuse for making trouble, and the point now was to get Ignat'ev to sail as soon as possible.[171] (Incidentally, the problem of the Supplementary Agreement and communication between Pehtang and Peking again became an issue at a later date, when Ignat'ev sent a courier from Shanghai to Pehtang bearing letters to the Grand Council, and when he himself came north with the Anglo-French expeditionary forces.)[172]

CHAPTER V

Conduct of Peace Negotiations in Peking, Fall 1860

There . . . he saw the Prince and Wan-se-ang, neither of whom seemed much alarmed. Wan-se-ang said to him, "Well, what are we to do with those prisoners, behead them or send them back?" He strongly recommended that the former course should be avoided. The following day he again saw them, and they were then a good deal perturbed, having received notice that in the event of the prisoners not being given up, Peking would be burned.

— *Wen-hsiang and Huang Hui-lien early in October 1860*

When the Anglo-French troops finally approached Peking late in September 1860, the emperor, who had been staying at the Summer Palace in a northwestern suburb of the city, fled to the imperial villa in Jehol, accompanied by Princes Hui, Tun, I, Cheng, and other princes, Su-shun and most of the grand councillors, and the harem.[1] Back in the metropolitan area, in the course of the painful and protracted muddling through of peacemaking, a sizable organization for conducting peace negotiations was formed, with Prince Kung, Grand Secretary Kuei-liang and Wen-hsiang, grand councillor and senior vice-president of the Board of Revenue, as its leaders. The organization also included high-ranking officials (mainly Manchus) such as Heng-ch'i, Ch'ung-hou and Ch'ung-lun, who acted as intermediaries, some Grand Council secretaries, and many subordinates for scouting, liaison, clerical, and other purposes. It had two negotiating branches, one to deal with the British and French diplomats, and the other with the Russian representative, who was then in Peking, ready to take advantage of the confused situation.

ORGANIZATION FOR NEGOTIATIONS
UNDER PRINCE KUNG

Formation of the Controlling Body,
with a Team of Actual Negotiators

On September 21, 1860, the day before he left for Jehol, the emperor announced by edict the appointment of Prince Kung as imperial commissioner in charge of peace negotiations.[2] A vermilion rescript of the same date instructed the prince: "It is generally understood that peace is now difficult to make. It is only to gain time for the present that you are appointed and are to exchange communications in your own name with the barbarian chieftains. As for actual contacts and personal negotiations, there are, as a matter of fact, Heng-ch'i, Lan Wei-wen, etc., to undertake this task. It is not worthwhile for you to meet the barbarian chieftains personally. If peace is yet again not to be made, supervise the military campaign in the rear of the camps. In the event that [the enemy] really cannot be held in check, you should seek personal safety, retreat, and hasten to the imperial traveling lodges." [3]

On the same day, Prince Kung notified the British and the French plenipotentiaries of his appointment as imperial commissioner in place of Prince I and Mu-yin, stating further that "Heng-ch'i, Lan Wei-wen, etc.," were to be sent to discuss the peacemaking.[4]

Prince Kung, a young man of 28 *sui* and a younger brother of the Hsien-feng emperor, thus for the first time came to the fore in foreign affairs, although, as we have seen, he had been an active peace advocate since 1858, participating in policy decisions relating to war and peace.[5]

Heng-ch'i, then about 59 *sui*, was a member of the Manchu Plain White Banner and belonged to the Imperial Household. At the expiration of his term as Hoppo in Canton, he had returned north in the summer of 1860, and was now director of the Imperial Armory with the honorary title of minister of the Household. An edict of August 16, 1860, before the fall of the Taku forts, ordered him to Pehtang to accompany the Anglo-French representatives to Peking. When Taku fell, he was ordered to assist Kuei-liang and Heng-fu in the Tientsin peace negotiations, in the course of which he was given the status of associate commissioner (*pang-pan ta-ch'en*). At Tientsin he dealt especially with Harry Parkes and Thomas Wade. Though he was deprived of his associate commissionership at the breakdown of the Tientsin negotiations, he participated in the subsequent T'ung-chou negotiations under Prince I and Mu-yin, again dealing with Parkes.[6]

Lan Wei-wen had had long experience in Shanghai, where he had served since the opening of the port. From 1855 to 1857 he was acting taotai of Shanghai. In 1859 to 1860, he was active in Shanghai as an expectant prefect and as an important figure close to Ho Kuei-ch'ing, then Shanghai imperial commissioner and governor-general of Kiangnan and Kiangsi. He was sent north in July 1860 by Hsueh Huan, Shanghai imperial commissioner and governor of Kiangsu, and participated in the Tientsin negotiations in August and September. During the T'ung-chou negotiations he was attached to Prince I and Mu-yin as a courier. A letter for Lan to the taotai of T'ung-chou (apparently meant to be shown to Prince I and Mu-yin) was intercepted by the British. In this letter Lan advocated peace.[7]

When the group of negotiators who were to act under Prince Kung is referred to in documents as "Heng-ch'i, Lan Wei-wen, etc." (Heng-ch'i Lan Wei-wen *teng*), or as "either Heng-ch'i, or Lan Wei-wen, etc." (*huo* Heng-ch'i *huo* Lan Wei-wen *teng*) (as in an edict of September 21 giving orders to Seng-ko-lin-ch'in),[8] to whom does "Lan Wei-wen, etc." or, more specifically, "etc." (*teng*), refer?

In a memorial received on July 17, 1860, Hsueh Huan reported that he was sending north Lan Wei-wen, who was bringing with him "Huang Chung-yü, expectant district magistrate, and one or two Chinese merchants."[9] Later only Lan and Huang were mentioned as "the delegates from Kiangsu," or simply as "the delegates," in memorials from the officials in the north and in edicts.[10] But the "one or two Chinese merchants" hardly appeared again in the documents, so it is rather doubtful whether they actually came north. As we have mentioned before, Huang Chung-yü had often worked since 1858 as an unofficial channel of communication between the British and the Ch'ing delegations.[11] When he came north with Lan Wei-wen he served in the Tientsin negotiations as an intermediary between Parkes and the Ch'ing officials. He was then attached to Prince I's headquarters at T'ung-chou.[12]

Now on September 23, 1860, Prince Kung's office asked the Offices of Police Censors to transmit a summons to "the two officials, Lan Wei-wen and Huang Chung-yü, delegates from Kiangsu," to come to the Shan-yuan Temple (that is, Prince Kung's office).[13] Huang Chung-yü presented himself there on September 24, Lan Wei-wen within the next two days.[14] Thus we may safely infer that the same two delegates from Kiangsu — Lan Wei-wen and Huang Chung-yü — had been ordered to serve as negotiators under Prince Kung.

While Heng-ch'i's activities under Prince Kung were extraordinary,[15] Lan Wei-wen's role in the Peking negotiations seems to have been rather inconspicuous.[16] As for Huang Chung-yü, he was sent on at least one or two occasions as an official emissary to the British and the French authorities.[17] It is also certain that late in October 1860 he acted in an unofficial capacity to convey to the British a complaint from the Tientsin people about the occupation of private houses by the British soldiers.[18]

On September 22, prior to his departure, the emperor ordered Kuei-liang and Wen-hsiang to assist Prince Kung in conducting peace negotiations, thus forming a controlling body of three.[19] The earliest memorial in *Ch'ou-pan i-wu shih-mo* from Imperial Commissioner Prince Kung was received by the emperor on September 24.[20] Like most of the memorials from Prince Kung in his new capacity it was also signed by Kuei-liang and Wen-hsiang.

On September 23, an emergency commission was created in the Imperial Palace in Peking to deal with national affairs, with Prince Yü as its senior member or chairman. Prince Yü (I-tao), Kuei-liang, Chou Tsu-p'ei, assistant grand secretary and president of the Board of Revenue, and Ch'üan-ch'ing, president of the Board of Civil Appointments, were named commissioners to conduct national affairs at Peking (*liu-Ching pan-shih wang-ta-ch'en*). Kuei-liang, however, was to remain outside the city, while Chou Tsu-p'ei, who had been charged with civil defense, was to remain in the Chinese City.[21]

On the same day, Wen-hsiang was given a concurrent assignment as acting general commandant of the Gendarmerie, though he was "temporarily to reside outside the city." At the same time Lin K'uei, junior vice-president of the Board of Punishments, and Ch'ing-ying, subchancellor of the Grand Secretariat, were made acting lieutenant-generals, senior and junior, of the Gendarmerie.[22] These high-ranking officials of the Gendarmerie formed the nucleus of the Commission of Defense (Hsun-fang-ch'u), a temporary emergency organ to preserve order in the capital. The office of the commission was in the Fa-hua Temple on Pao-fang Lane, in the middle of the eastern part of the Imperial City.[23] As we shall see, Jui-ch'ang replaced Wen-hsiang in October as acting general commandant of the gendarmerie. Pao-yun, junior vice-president of the Board of Revenue, and Ch'ung-lun were also attached to the Commission of Defense.[24]

The general command of the military forces stationed in Peking was in the hands of Prince K'o-ch'in (Ch'ing-hui), who had been given the title of *ch'in-ming tsung-kuan chiu-ch'eng hsun-shou ta-ch'en* sometime in the seventh Chinese month of the year (August 17 to September 14, 1860).[25] After the emperor's departure Prince K'o-ch'in and his associates, who included Mien-sen, president of the Board of Works, I-shan, and Sai-shang-a, were repeatedly ordered to do their utmost to defend the city.[26] They were often referred to by the generic designation "the prince and high officials for the defense of the city" (*shou-ch'eng wang-ta-ch'en* or *ch'eng-shou wang-ta-ch'en*).[27] In planning the defense, they consulted with Sheng-pao, the Manchu general who had been defeated by the allied troops in the battle of Palikiao on September 21.[28] Though distinct from the Commission of Defense, this group seems to have been functionally connected with that commission.[29]

The administration of civil defense (*t'uan-fang*) had been assigned on August 21 to Chou Tsu-p'ei, Ch'en Fu-en, president of the Board of War, P'an Tseng-ying and Sung Chin, senior and junior vice-presidents of the Board of Works, and the police censors. Ten more censors, who lived in the Chinese City, had been added to the group on August 30. On September 23 Chia Chen, grand secretary, and Chao Kuang, president of the Board of Punishments, were also charged with the management of civil defense. Chou Tsu-p'ei, who on the same day was made an associate of Prince Yü, was instructed to remain in the Chinese City, where the civil defense headquarters were located.[30]

Now we must turn back to the machinery for peace negotiations.

The foreign plenipotentiaries were notified only of the appointment of Prince Kung, with "Heng-ch'i, Lan Wei-wen, etc.," as actual go-betweens. And correspondence with the foreign officials was conducted in the name of the prince. Hence, it appears that the existence of Kuei-liang and Wen-hsiang as associates of Prince Kung in the peace negotiations was not known, or at least was ignored, by the foreign authorities.

Parkes reported that when Heng-ch'i came to see him in the prison of the Board of Punishments on September 22, he informed him that Prince Kung had been appointed to succeed Prince I and Mu-yin and that Kuei-liang might be his colleague.[31] This is probably the only mention of Kuei-liang in the contemporary Western reports on this period. Though no serious attention seems to have been paid him at this stage of affairs, there is hardly any doubt that he played an important part in assisting Prince Kung in the peace negotiations. As we know, Kuei-liang had been the senior member of the Ch'ing delegation at Tientsin and at Shanghai in 1858, had dealt in 1859 in Peking with John Ward, and had again been active as imperial commissioner in the 1860 Tientsin negotiations. Throughout this period he had consistently advocated peace and the foreign officials in China had also considered him the pivotal figure of the peace party. Now he had reached the age of 76 *sui*.[32]

As for Wen-hsiang, his name is referred to in a Russian report as one of the officials attached to the Commission of Defense.[33] This is the only instance in which his name is mentioned in the Western literature I have seen on this particular period. It seems, however, that Wen-hsiang was extraordinarily active behind the scenes during the peace negotiations. While Kuei-liang was probably engaged solely in helping Prince Kung to negotiate peace, Wen-hsiang was extremely busy, concurrently involved in many other duties, as the sole grand councillor remaining in Peking and as the senior member of the Commission of Defense. Though he was expected "temporarily to reside outside the city," in actuality he had to be both inside and outside the city. "In the evening," he recorded, "I entered the city to handle the defense; in the daytime I went out of the city to deal with peace negotiations. Going back and forth through the scene of disturbances, I no longer took concern for my own safety." [34]

The lieutenant-generals of the Gendarmerie asked that Wen-hsiang, as their general commandant, be stationed within the city and that Prince Kung also reside in the city. An edict of September 28 replied that Prince Kung was to remain at his temporary residence in the Summer Palace and was not to be allowed to enter the city. Wen-hsiang might be stationed within the city and go to the Summer Palace whenever Prince Kung and his associate needed to confer with him, but he was expected to return to the city in the evening; should he be unable to go to the Summer Palace, he was to confer with the prince by correspondence.[35] Prince Kung, Kuei-liang, and Wen-hsiang pointed out in a joint memorial received on October 4 that it would be quite inconvenient to comply with these instructions. In view of the urgent nature of the peace negotiations, they asked that Wen-hsiang be stationed outside the city so that he could be available at any time for personal consultation with his two colleagues. They suggested further that the duties of the general commandant of the Gendarmerie be assigned to someone else. They added that Wen-hsiang would be able concurrently to manage the affairs of the Grand Council at the Summer Palace. On October 4 the emperor approved all these suggestions and appointed Jui-ch'ang acting general commandant of the Gendarmerie. Because of the delays and interruptions in traffic between Peking and Jehol these decisions did not become known to Prince Kung's office until October 12.[36] Meanwhile, in Wen-hsiang's words, "there were fewer and fewer people available, with more and more work to do. The situation was really thorny." Wen-hsiang further reminisced about the days of the Peking negotiations: "Affairs as numerous as the spines of a hedgehog accumulated. Furthermore, from the end of the seventh month [lunar calendar] through the ninth month, I could not even ungirdle myself or sleep for over seventy days. Beset with redoubled anxiety and toil, I began to cough and spit blood. Moreover I suffered from asthma."[37]

Expansion of Subordinate Personnel

Prince Kung's office, as a sort of secretariat, had a group of secretaries from the Grand Council. Wen-hsiang, as the only remaining grand councillor, was charged with conducting the affairs of the Grand Council. Thus Prince Kung's office was actually an amalgamation of the remaining part of the Grand Council and the machinery for peace negotiations.

When the emperor left for Jehol there was no Grand Council secretary in his suite. As of September 25 the secretaries were still on duty at the Summer Palace, divided into sections that served in rotation.[38] In due course eight of the secretaries went to Jehol,[39] but Ying-hsiu and five other secretaries remained with Prince Kung throughout the Peking negotiations.[40] With only these six subordinates, there was a shortage of hands in Prince Kung's office, and some other officials were summoned to assist. The office also had a number of clerks and a scouting party to get information on the moves of the foreign troops. The following quotation from a joint memorial from Prince Kung and his associates, received on December 17, 1860, gives a vivid picture of Prince Kung's office in operation, though there is perhaps a degree of exaggeration in this memorial, which requested the grant of honors to the officials and clerks who had served meritoriously under Prince Kung:[41]

We, your officials, received orders on September 22 to manage peace negotiations, and we sought permission at an audience [and received it] to retain Ying-hsiu and some other Grand Council secretaries. Subsequently there was need for additional aides to be sent on errands [or, to attend to official business], because the barbarians were so cunning in all sorts of ways that we became very busy. So we transferred to our office Chou Chia-hsun, secretary of the Grand Secretariat, who had once accompanied your official, Kuei-liang, to Tientsin. We also transferred to our office, to be sent on errands [or, to attend to official business] in his company, Ch'eng-lin, secretary (temporarily appointed by Prince Kung) (*wei-shu chu-shih*)[42] of the Gendarmerie, and others.

After people were dispersed on October 6 [when Anglo-French troops entered the Summer Palace], Ying-hsiu, accompanied by Shih-shun and other clerks, followed us on foot, carrying with them the files of documents. They had no time to sleep or to eat. The situation ever changed kaleidoscopically even within the span of one day. If there was any delay in sending communications, complications were certain to arise on every hand. Peace negotiations were generally deemed anathema. Most people escaped and hid somewhere far away. Scouting was most important, but officers dispatched for this purpose shrank from advancing. As it was feared that the delicate situation might thus be misjudged, we summoned Ch'ang-shan, expectant lieutenant-colonel, and others, and let them scout in various directions.[43] It happened that Te-ch'un, taotai of T'ung-chou, and others arrived in Ch'ang-hsin-tien [i.e., Lu-kou-ch'iao]. As they were well versed in barbarian affairs, we kept them there to transact business. At that time the barbarian miasma (*i-fen*) drew nearer and there were several alarms during one night. People were in fear and perplexity. There were continuous streams of evacuees from the city. Officials of the respective government offices scattered widely. Nine bureaus out of ten became empty. In the midst of the general fear and confusion, the above-mentioned officials had a profound grasp of the great principle of loyalty and would not avoid facing difficulties or dangers. They moved from one place to another enduring privation and other hardships. Their exhaustion was increasingly visible. On October 10 a barbarian chieftain came to the outside of the Hsi pien-men, commanding cavalry men and foot soldiers, and drew right up to the

T'ien-ning Temple. We, your officials, showed that we were keeping quiet and unmoved. The above-mentioned officials transacted business as before, having not the slightest intention of deserting.

According to a joint memorial from Prince Kung and his associates, received on October 19, they had ordered Ch'ung-lun, former superintendent of the government granaries at the capital, who had been on duty with the Commission of Defense, to help Heng-ch'i. This step was taken on the joint recommendation of the commissioners to conduct national affairs at Peking and the Commission of Defense (*liu-Ching hsun-fang wang-ta-ch'en teng*).[44] Ch'ung-lun, then 69 *sui*, was a member of the Chinese Plain White Banner and belonged to the Imperial Household. In the ninth year of Hsien-feng (roughly 1859) he had been deprived of his post because of involvement in a scandal, and his family possessions had been sequestered.[45] Back in 1850 he had been one of the Ch'ing negotiators at Taku when Walter Henry Medhurst was sent there by Bonham, the British minister, bearing a copy of a letter to the Peking government from Lord Palmerston, minister for foreign affairs.[46] In 1854 he had served as a Ch'ing representative in the treaty revision negotiations at Taku with the British, American, and French diplomats.[47] Again in 1858, he had been sent to participate in negotiations at Taku, and then at Tientsin. At that time, however, he was not quite acceptable to the British, because copies of his memorials relating the 1854 negotiations had been among the papers seized at Canton by the British early in 1858 and the inside story of his maneuvers on that occasion had thus been disclosed.[48]

In a supplementary memorial received on October 22, 1860, Prince Kung and his associates reported that there had arrived at their office Ch'ung-hou, Ch'ang-lu salt controller wearing a button of the second rank; Sun Chih, taotai of Tientsin with the honorary title of salt controller; and Te-ch'un, taotai of T'ung-chou with the honorary title of salt controller. All of these they had found sufficiently diligent and competent to be used.[49] Of the three it was Ch'ung-hou who later became an important figure in foreign contact under Prince Kung.

Ch'ung-hou, then 34 *sui*, was a member of the Manchu Bordered Yellow Banner and belonged to the Imperial Household.[50] He had been a minor member of the Ch'ing delegation at the 1858 Taku negotiations.[51] In 1859 he had escorted the Ward party on its trips between Pehtang and Peking, and he had been present at the August 10 meeting at the Chia-hsing Temple between Ward, Kuei-liang, and Hua-sha-na.[52] In the summer of 1860 he had been sent to Pehtang to meet Ignat'ev.[53] Later in 1860 he had served in the Ch'ing delegation at Tientsin.[54] Now under Prince Kung he was first kept in the prince's office and then was sent to join Heng-ch'i in personally contacting foreign officials.[55]

Another supplementary joint memorial, also received on October 22 from Prince Kung and his associates, stated that they had ordered Ch'eng-ch'i, superintendent of the government granaries at the capital, to help Heng-ch'i.[56] Ch'eng-ch'i was a member of the Manchu Plain Yellow Banner,[57] and seems to have had no previous experience of foreign contact. In the fall of 1860 he was put in command of the troops guarding the Kao-miao, a temple in the Imperial City near the Te-sheng Gate, to which Parkes had been moved from the prison of the Board of Punishments. From that time he was active behind the scenes in the peace negotiations. He was more active in later negotiations with Ignat'ev than in contact with the British or the French.[58]

Among the people who served immediately under Prince Kung there was besides Huang Chung-yü another person of a similar type — Huang Hui-lien, who since 1858 had sometimes worked as an unofficial channel of communication between the Chinese and Western officials in China. Huang Hui-lien, who spoke English well, was an interpreter and courier at Taku when the forts fell in August 1860. Subsequently he was summoned to T'ung-chou, arriving there on September 18 just after the breakdown of negotiations. Thereafter he was called to Prince Kung's office, where he seems to have served in an advisory capacity. He seems also to have been sent on occasion to visit the Western officials to pick up information.

When called to Prince Kung's office he was assistant district magistrate of Mi-yun, Chihli.[59]

An edict of December 17, 1860, and another of December 24 announced the grant of honors to all those who had played an active part in the Peking negotiations with the British and the French.[60] Fifty-five names were mentioned in these edicts, among them were Prince Kung, Kuei-liang, Wen-hsiang, and all the others to whom I have referred above, except Ch'eng-ch'i. Judging from the number who received honors on this occasion, the machinery for peace negotiations which had been formed under Prince Kung must have been quite sizable.[61]

Though he was not among those honored on this occasion, the behind-the-scenes activities of Chang Chin-wen, a Tientsin merchant, also merit attention. During the allied occupations of Tientsin in 1858 and 1860, he was an important figure as purveyor for the foreigners; he was also a leading sponsor of the local militia and a mediator in Sino-foreign disputes. In the fall of 1860 he was summoned to Peking by Prince Kung, at whose office he presented himself on October 22. His contribution seems to have been greater after the signing of the Peking Conventions than during the negotiations. Since 1858 he had consistently tried to exert pacifist pressure upon the authorities.[62]

Group for Sino-Russian Negotiations

During the Peking negotiations Ignat'ev, who had followed the allied plenipotentiaries north from Shanghai, entered the city. Established at the Russian Hostel, he kept in touch with the high officials in the city and acted as mediator between the Chinese and the allies in the last stage of the peacemaking.

After the British and the French Peking Conventions had been signed on October 24 and 25, Ignat'ev proposed to Prince Kung that the border negotiations be resumed. The prince's reply stated that Jui-ch'ang, Lin-k'uei, Pao-yun, and Ch'eng-ch'i had been ordered to negotiate with Ignat'ev at the Russian Hostel.[63] Thereafter actual negotiations were carried on between these four officials and the Russians, resulting in the Additional Treaty of Peking, which was signed on November 14 by Prince Kung and Ignat'ev, also at the Russian Hostel.[64] This treaty confirmed the Aigun Treaty and also agreed to the cession to Russia of the land between the Ussuri and the sea.[65] Wen-lien, an official of the Court of Dependencies, who was experienced in Russian affairs, had also been attached to the Ch'ing delegation.[66]

Jui-ch'ang, a member of the Mongol Bordered Red Banner, was then president of the Board of Punishments.[67] Lin-k'uei, a member of the Manchu Bordered White Banner, was junior vice-president of the Board of Punishments.[68] Ch'eng-ch'i, as stated previously, was a member of the Manchu Plain Yellow Banner and was then superintendent of the government granaries at the capital. Pao-yun, a member of the Manchu Bordered White Banner, was junior vice-president of the Board of Revenue.[69] Jui-ch'ang, Lin-k'uei, and Pao-yun were members of the Commission of Defense, Jui-ch'ang having taken over from Wen-hsiang as acting general commandant of the Gendarmerie. The Russians seem also to have counted Ch'eng-ch'i as a member of the Commission.[70]

Ignat'ev entered Peking around October 16 through the An-ting Gate, which had been surrendered to the allied troops a few days before. Thereafter, his mediatory activities were carried on by maintaining contact with Elgin and Gros on the one hand, and with Prince Kung on the other through high officials on the Commission of Defense, who went back and forth between the Russian Hostel within the Imperial City and Prince Kung's office in the suburbs. The ultimatums to Prince Kung from Elgin and Gros were shown to Ignat'ev, who assisted in the drafting of the replies to be sent in the prince's name.[71]

In brief, Jui-ch'ang and the other officials who were appointed to negotiate with Ignat'ev after the signing of the British and the French Conventions had already been acting as channels between Ignat'ev and Prince Kung, in their capacity as members of the Commission of Defense.[72]

Heng-ch'i had also been one of this liaison group before the signing of the Peking Conventions. But the Russians felt that he distrusted them and was manifestly pro-British, and that his dispositions were incompatible with Russia's interests. Furthermore, they feared that the British might keep watch, through Heng-ch'i, on Ignat'ev's maneuvers. Therefore, Ignat'ev dropped a hint to the Chinese authorities and succeeded in excluding Heng-ch'i from the Sino-Russian negotiations.[73]

We thus see that in the course of the Peking negotiations two distinct negotiating bodies came into being under the over-all control of Prince Kung and his two associates, Kuei-liang and Wen-hsiang —one to negotiate with the British and the French (Heng-ch'i, Ch'ung-lun, Ch'ung-hou, and others) and one to negotiate with the Russians (Jui-ch'ang, Lin-k'uei, Pao-yun, and Ch'eng-ch'i).[74] Since the signing of the Tientsin Treaties, negotiations with the British, French, and American diplomats had centered around the peace advocate Kuei-liang; negotiations with Russia, on the other hand, had been in the hands of the uncompromising Su-shun and his associate, Jui-ch'ang, with the persisting implication that Russian affairs continued to be under the jurisdiction of the Court of Dependencies. Now, with the creation of the two negotiating bodies under Prince Kung, Kuei-liang, and Wen-hsiang, the apparatus for Sino-Russian negotiations was absorbed into the machinery dominated by the peace party, though there was a degree of continuity in that Jui-ch'ang was now the senior negotiator with the Russians.[75]

As we know from the preceding chapter, the Peking government had refused to the last to accede to Ignat'ev's repeated demands that it honor Article 2 of the Russian Tientsin Treaty, which provided for interviews between Russia's representative and a grand secretary or a grand councillor. In the negotiations in the fall of 1860, Jui-ch'ang and the other negotiators were neither grand secretaries nor grand councillors, but Ignat'ev did not dispute their qualifications. Perhaps he felt no need to do so because current circumstances had so increased his bargaining power and because so exalted a person

as Prince Kung, a brother of the reigning emperor, was expected to
be the signer of the new treaty.

Shifting Location of Prince Kung's Office

When he was first appointed imperial commissioner Prince Kung
set up his office in the Shan-yuan Temple outside the Jui-i Gate of
the Summer Palace.[76] After the emperor's departure, the location
of Prince Kung's headquarters repeatedly became a three-cornered
issue between the high officials remaining within Peking, the emperor at Jehol, and Prince Kung himself. Prince Kung was driven
to move his office from one place to another according to changing
circumstances.

As we know, the request of the lieutenant-generals of the Gendarmerie that both Wen-hsiang and Prince Kung be stationed
within the city was refused, so far as Prince Kung was concerned,
in an edict of September 28.[77] Prince Yü and other high officials
jointly wrote to Prince Kung around September 25 demanding that
he move into the city. Prince Kung refused.[78] Thereupon Prince Yü
and twenty high officials, in a joint memorial received on October 1,
expressed their fears that Prince Kung, not being firmly determined
to manage peace negotiations, might be "disposed to get away,"
and they asked that he be ordered to remain outside the city (i.e.,
not to run away) and properly manage peace negotiations. (The
memorialists admitted explicitly that making peace was unavoidable under the circumstances.) An answering edict of the same
date assured them that Prince Kung understood the imperial wishes
and would do his utmost to devise stratagems, and that he was not
inclined to hasty flight. The memorialists sent a copy of this edict
and of their memorial to Prince Kung, who referred to the incident
in a joint memorial with his associates, received on October 8:
"Though the inside and the outside of the city are not far apart,
it is undeniable that rumors are liable to get about in this emergency
situation." [79]

Sheng-pao, director of the Banqueting Court, who had been seriously wounded when his forces were defeated at Palikiao, requested

in a warlike memorial received on October 3 that Prince Kung and his associates be ordered to enter the city to raise the morale of the people. The emperor gave no answer to this request.[80]

Prince Kung thus continued to stay in the Shan-yuan Temple. There were in the area a certain number of Gendarmerie soldiers under Wen-hsiang's command, but most of them were sent out on scouting missions or other duties. Thus there was virtually no guard at hand for Prince Kung and his associates. For the protection of the area they depended upon the remnants of defeated troops of Seng-ko-lin-ch'in and Jui-lin, a grand secretary, which now camped on the northern side of the city between Te-sheng Gate and the An-ting Gate. Seng-ko-lin-ch'in's officers served as couriers between Prince Kung and the Anglo-French officials.

On October 6 allied troops routed the forces of Seng-ko-lin-ch'in and Jui-lin and entered the Summer Palace. Prince Kung took refuge in the Wan-shou Temple, south of the Summer Palace and west of Peking. Subsequently he retreated to Lu-kou-ch'iao (Ch'ang-hsin-t'ien), southwest of the city. The original texts of the four Tientsin treaties and some other official papers, which had been brought to the Summer Palace from the Board of Rites, were lost during this confusion. Prince Kung retreated to Lu-kou-ch'iao because Ch'ing forces encamped on the northern side of Peking had been moved to its southwestern suburbs, north of Lu-kou-ch'iao. The emperor feared that correspondence between Lu-kou-ch'iao and Jehol would take too much time, and ordered Prince Kung and his associates to move to the northwestern area of the Summer Palace, making a detour of the occupied area (an edict of October 10). Prince Kung and his associates did not follow these instructions; in a memorial received on October 17 they pointed out the present location of Ch'ing forces and the necessity for keeping in close contact with the authorities inside Peking.[81]

In the meanwhile, Heng-ch'i, who was in Peking, appealed to Prince Kung on October 7 to enter the city.[82] The next day Parkes was released, in the pressing circumstances to be described below. Reporting on Parkes's release, Prince Yü and others requested in a supplementary memorial of October 10 that, in view of the inconvenient distance of forty *li* (about fourteen miles) between Prince Kung's office and the city, the prince should be ordered to enter the city.[83] A similar request was made by Prince K'o-ch'in and others in a memorial received on October 13.[84] Also around October 10, Ch'eng-ch'i, Heng-ch'i, and Lien-ch'eng (a deputy lieutenant-general of a banner) successively went to Prince Kung's office and asked him to move into the city.[85]

On October 13 the An-ting Gate on the northern side of the city was surrendered to the allied armies.[86] That day Prince Yü and others sent a written request to Prince Kung to come to the city. So did the Commission of Defense. Neither request was complied with.[87] However, on the following day Prince Kung moved from Lu-kou-ch'iao to the T'ien-ning Temple, outside the city and quite near the Hsi pien-men, or Western Side Gate, on the northwestern corner of the Chinese City. In the area around the temple, under the command of Sheng-pao, there was a force of 6,000 or 7,000 reinforcements from Chihli and Shensi.[88]

On October 17, having received from Prince Yü and others a report on the surrender of the An-ting Gate and a further request for Prince Kung's entry into the city, the emperor gave orders that Prince Kung and his associates should enter the city immediately to sign the "supplementary conventions" (the British and the French Peking conventions) and exchange the ratifications of the Tientsin treaties.[89]

On October 18 high officials of the Commission of Defense, who had come to the Russian Hostel as bearers of a letter from Prince Kung, orally sounded out Ignat'ev as to whether the prince, who would not enter the city out of fear of the allies, might stay at the Russian Hostel. Ignat'ev dismissed the idea, explaining that such a step would seriously irritate the British and would bring no benefit in any case.[90]

On the same day the British army destroyed the Summer Palace by fire, as a revenge for the atrocities committed on allied prisoners. At the sight of the swirling smoke, which was spreading even over

Peking, Prince Kung, it was reported, wanted to flee from his residence and was barely restrained, almost by force.[91]

On October 22 some reconnoitering cavalry of the British army drew near the T'ien-ning Temple. Their appearance seems to have been quite a shock to the Chinese authorities in the area.[92]

On October 24 Prince Kung entered the city. At the principal hall of the Board of Rites, located near the Cheng-yang Gate in the southern part of the Imperial City, he signed the British Peking Convention and exchanged the ratifications of the Tientsin Treaty with Lord Elgin. This was his first personal contact with a Western representative. The prince had been escorted as far as the Cheng-yang Gate by a force of 400 under Sheng-pao and had continued to the Board of Rites with an escort of twenty guards. On the same day his office was moved to the Fa-yuan Temple in the southwestern part of the Chinese City. On the following day, he exchanged the ratifications of the French Tientsin Treaty with Baron Gros and signed the French Peking Convention, again at the Board of Rites.[93]

On October 31 Prince Kung moved his office to the Jui-ying Temple in the northern part of the Imperial City near the Te-sheng Gate. According to a report from the prince and his associates, he took this step because the foreign authorities seemed to regard his staying in the Chinese City with suspicion.[94] Gros visited Prince Kung on November 1, as did Elgin two days later. On November 8 Elgin again visited Prince Kung, this time bringing Bruce with him. The prince received these visits at the Kuang-hua Temple, not far from the Jui-ying Temple. According to the prince and his associates, the Western diplomats had wanted to visit him at his palace, but he had refused on some pretext. Ignat'ev visited Prince Kung on November 19, also at the Kuang-hua Temple.[95] He had already called on him on November 11, at a place unidentified in the documents — probably the same temple.[96]

Elgin, Gros, and Bruce left Peking on November 9, and Ignat'ev on November 22.[97] On November 26 Prince Kung moved his office to the Chia-hsing Temple,[98] in the northern part of the Imperial City, near the Ti-an Gate on the northern wall of the Imperial

Palace. The temple was located west of the office of Yuan-p'ing district, at a distance of one *li* (about a third of a mile) from Prince Kung's palace." [99] It was the place where Kuei-liang and Hua-sha-na had received John Ward in 1859.[100]

POLITICAL BACKGROUND OF THE NEGOTIATIONS

*Manchu Leadership of the Negotiating Organization:
Political Affiliations of Its Leading Members*

Of the fifty-five persons who received honors for their participation in the Peking negotiations with the British and the French, some thirty-two appear to have been indigenous Chinese; most of the others seem to have been Manchus, with at least one Mongol and one Chinese bannerman.[101] In other words, in the peacemaking machinery as a whole, Chinese constituted a majority. However, the inner core consisted of Prince Kung, Kuei-liang, Wen-hsiang, Heng-ch'i, Ch'ung-hou — all Manchus — and Ch'ung-lun, a Chinese bannerman. Of the Grand Council secretaries who remained to the last with Prince Kung, it is assumed that four were Manchus and the remaining two Chinese.[102] As for the Sino-Russian negotiators, Jui-ch'ang was a Mongol; Lin-k'uei, Ch'eng-ch'i, and Pao-yun were Manchus. In brief, although Chinese constituted a majority, the nucleus was solidly Manchu.

Let us look now at the political backgrounds of the negotiators, beginning with the members of the controlling body. Of Grand Secretary Kuei-liang, it will be sufficient to recall here that he was well known to the allied negotiators as a highly experienced old politician who had persistently advocated peace; that he was the father-in-law of Prince Kung and also of Prince Hui, who was uncle of the emperor and the chairman of the Council of Princes. It must have been under Kuei-liang's influence that Prince Kung, a member of that Council, had maneuvered as a peace advocate from 1858.[103]

Wen-hsiang's position is less clear. Though the Westerners were as yet scarcely aware of his existence, Wen-hsiang gained experience in foreign affairs during the Peking negotiations and later became the pivotal figure in the Tsungli Yamen in its earlier stage. Prince Kung, on October 28, 1860, told the French priest Mouly: "Negotiate in confidence with Wen-hsiang. He is a second self of mine."[104] In his memorial (received on November 14) requesting the recall to Peking of Wen-hsiang, who was then away suppressing local bandits, Prince Kung complained: "There are at present so many barbarian affairs to be dealt with. Kuei-liang, approaching 80 *sui*, is quite enfeebled. Heng-ch'i and Ch'ung-hou should soon proceed to Tientsin. At the office of your official, I-hsin [Prince Kung], there is no one to assist. The situation is really difficult."[105]

Wen-hsiang was a Manchu of the Gualgiya clan and a member of the Plain Red Banner (the same clan, and the same banner, as Kuei-liang, a coincidence that probably meant nothing in those days). He was born in 1818 in Liaoyang, the son of a minor official. After becoming a *chin-shih* in 1845 at the age of 28 *sui* he occupied a series of posts in Peking, without ever being transferred to a provincial or local post, though he was sometimes sent out of the capital on missions. In July 1858, only thirteen years after he had become a *chin-shih*, he was appointed probationary grand councillor. In 1859 he was made a full-fledged grand councillor.[106]

As a grand councillor he naturally dealt with edicts or memorials on foreign affairs and attended important conferences; he thus became versed in foreign affairs at least through official papers, though he had no opportunity for personal contact with foreign officials. It is not known what his position was in the heated conflict between counsels of peace and war up to the time of the Peking negotiations. Wen-hsiang argued strongly against the emperor's planned departure for Jehol in memorials presented jointly with other high officials; he even had a personal audience with the emperor, who was thus moved to change his mind for a time.[107] After the emperor had left and Wen-hsiang had been made acting general commandant of the gendarmerie, it is said that he happened to meet in Tung-ch'eng (the eastern district of Peking) Yin Keng-yun, who had also strenuously opposed the emperor's flight, and they "clung together and wept."[108] Simply from the fact that Wen-hsiang opposed the emperor's flight we cannot of course infer that he was either a war advocate or a peace advocate. But if we take into account the fact that he appears to have been friendly with Yin Keng-yun, we may assume at least that he was rather close to the group of indigenous Chinese officials that formed the nucleus of the war advocates in Peking. It may also be assumed that he had been exposed to the influence of the war advocates by virtue of his position as a grand councillor since the pressure of the war party was acutely felt in the council. Thus, while he may have been rather sympathetic toward the stand of the Chinese war advocates, as a Manchu grand councillor he must have been in a position to facilitate adaptation, to the developing situation, as a matter of practical politics. In brief, though he participated in the peacemaking under Prince Kung in company with the pacifist Kuei-liang, his attitude and approach may have been somewhat different from the latter's.

Heng-ch'i, Ch'ung-lun, and Ch'ung-hou, Prince Kung's actual negotiators, were all bannermen of the Imperial Household. This fact is worth noting, though it may be a mere coincidence. Bannermen of the Imperial Household belonged to the Inner or Household Division of the Three Superior Banners and were, as hereditary bond servants (pao-i), close to the emperor.[109] The most active of the three negotiators was Heng-ch'i, whose work was reported in detail in the joint memorials from Prince Kung and his associates. According to foreign observations in 1861, Heng-ch'i was not a particular favorite with Prince Kung and stood in better with the emperor than with the prince or Wen-hsiang.[110] He was also considered to be a protégé and a spy of Su-shun.[111]

Factors Behind the Tardiness in Concluding Peace

About a month elapsed between Prince Kung's appointment as imperial commissioner and the signing of the Peking Conventions.

After Seng-ko-lin-ch'in's loss of the Taku forts on August 21 the Ch'ing army had lost one battle after another. The allied troops, incomparably superior to the Ch'ing forces in firepower, had already drawn near the walls of Peking when Prince Kung took over the negotiations. The Ch'ing forces were now mere remnants of the defeated troops, without any fighting spirit, [112] and Seng-ko-lin-ch'in was repeatedly advocating peace.[113] From the time of the T'ung-chou negotiations, the conduct of negotiations had been in the hands of princes close to the emperor. Thus Prince I, leader of the war party, had personally gone to T'ung-chou as imperial commissioner and had almost concluded peace. Now Prince Kung was in charge of peacemaking, assisted and presumably influenced by Kuei-liang, the pivotal figure of the peace party. Furthermore, with the flight of the emperor, it is to be assumed that the pressure applied by the emperor and by the war advocates in his entourage must have been reduced to its lowest point. As a matter of fact, the emperor would not give specific directions on the conduct of negotiations. He tended to give instructions that were general in nature, admitting that under the tense and ever-changing circumstances he was not in a position to control from afar. He thus allowed Prince Kung and his associates a good deal of discretion, repeatedly making it clear that the conclusion of peace was urgent.[114] When the emperor fled, half of Peking officialdom disappeared. After the allied troops entered the Summer Palace, "nine offices out of ten became empty." [115] Many of the residents of Peking moved out of the city.[116] The public peace was disrupted and within and outside the city bandits were causing much trouble in the confusion.[117] Straggling soldiers were looting and resorting to violence in the suburbs.[118] The Peking government was short of silver cash and was finding it acutely difficult to pay soldiers' wages.[119] In fear of the possible consequences of an allied attack on the city, the merchants of Peking appealed to Elgin and Gros as well as to Prince Kung to make peace.[120]

Why did the peace negotiations drag on for a month or so, especially with circumstances deteriorating so rapidly?

There were certainly a number of factors that must have hampered progress of the negotiations. For one thing it took four to seven days for a round-trip transmission of correspondence between Prince Kung and the emperor in Jehol.[121] For another, in the initial

stage of the negotiations the allied diplomats insisted on the immediate release of Parkes and other prisoners, while the Manchus were
equally insistent that the prisoners could be returned only after the
suspension of hostilities and the conclusion of peace.[122] Furthermore,
in this initial stage the reserves of ammunition with the allied troops
at the front had been greatly reduced, and the British and the French
were trying to gain time to replenish supplies by exchanging correspondence with Prince Kung. (A memorial from Seng-ko-lin-ch'in
indicates that the Ch'ing authorities were not entirely unaware of
this.)[123] Then came the intrusion of the allied troops into the Summer Palace and the extensive looting of the Palace, which must have
had a staggering impact on Prince Kung and others. As a result
of this notorious event, Prince Kung took refuge as far away as
Lu-kou-ch'iao and communication between him and the officials
remaining inside Peking became all the more difficult. It should also
be taken into account that the fact that twenty of the thirty-nine
allied prisoners were tortured and killed [124] probably delayed completion of the return of all prisoners, alive or dead. (The bodies of
two persons, believed to have been decapitated after the battle of
Palikiao, never were returned.) In reprisal for these atrocities the
allies demanded further indemnities and the British destroyed the
Summer Palace, events that evidently further delayed the conclusion
of peace.

As a final factor, we may assume that in the arena of domestic
politics, extending over Peking and Jehol, Prince Kung and his
associates felt their position to be still precarious so that they had
to proceed slowly and maneuver with the utmost prudence.

Among the memorials in *Ch'ou-pan i-wu shih-mo,* after a memorial received on September 22 from Yin Chao-yung, chief supervisor of instruction,[125] there were no warlike memorials from
metropolitan officials, except for several from Sheng-pao.[126]

Sheng-pao, a member of the Manchu Bordered White Banner,
had been subexpositor of the National Academy, subreader of the
Academy, and libationer of the Imperial Academy of Learning, and
had been famous for his straightforward remonstrances with the

emperor. In the 1850's he had often been in the field fighting the Taipings, sometimes with the status of imperial commissioner. In 1860 he was a field commander near Peking. On September 21 his troops were defeated at Palikiao and he was severely wounded. In 1862 he was sent to Shensi as imperial commissioner to take charge of military affairs there. In the same year he was denounced by various persons for carnal excesses, embezzlement, graft, arrogance, and misrepresentation in memorializing. In 1863 he was put on trial in Peking and was ordered to commit suicide.[127]

After the battle of Palikiao Sheng-pao repeatedly advocated war. He asserted on one occasion that the troops of Seng-ko-lin-ch'in and Jui-lin were all utterly helpless, and indicated the thinly veiled hope that he would be made commander of the reinforcements that were expected to arrive.[128] After he was wounded, his troops were placed under Jui-lin, so that for a time he was without any. On October 10 he was ordered to take command of the reinforcements from several provinces and so he commanded near Peking a force of six or seven thousand.[129] An edict of October 15 conferred on him an imperial commissionership.[130] As we have seen, his troops gave protection to Prince Kung in the later stages of the Peking negotiations. Sheng-pao frequented Prince Kung's office from the outset of the negotiations.[131] He gave advice on the defense of Peking; he also attended meetings of high officials remaining in the city and presented memorials bitterly complaining of their ineffectiveness.[132] Though his troops were competent only to deal with the local bandits and were evidently helpless against the firepower of the Western forces,[133] still it can easily be imagined that his war advocacy and perhaps the very existence of his troops, were enough to restrain Prince Kung.

In reading the joint memorials presented by Prince Kung, Kuei-liang, and Wen-hsiang during the period between the emperor's departure and the signing of the Peking Conventions, one is struck by certain inconsistencies of tone and, in two specific instances, by what seems to be definite misrepresentation of facts (or, at the least, a deliberate misplacement of emphasis). These two instances are their reports on the release of the allied prisoners and on the surrender of the An-ting Gate.

In their memorial received on October 13, which reported the release on October 8 of Parkes and others, they emphasized that the step had been taken as a result of consultation between Heng-ch'i and the princes and high officials remaining in the capital, without the prior knowledge of Prince Kung.[134] According to the memorial, Prince Kung sent a letter to the British on the morning of October 6, in which he announced the Chinese intention to release Parkes. The memorialists feared that this letter had not been delivered to the British, because of the courier's cowardice. Later on the same day the allied troops drew near the Summer Palace. The prince and his associates sought refuge at the Wan-shou Temple, where Heng-ch'i came to see them. Heng-ch'i had seen Parkes, he reported, and had obtained from him a written statement to the effect that if all the prisoners were released the British government would take no retaliatory measures and would demand no additional treaty provisions.[135] Heng-ch'i also stated that he had learned that the barbarians had *not* yet broken into the Summer Palace.

"Thereupon we sent off a second letter to the barbarians," continues the memorial, "accusing them of not suspending hostilities in spite of the already granted permission to release Parkes. We intended to let Heng-ch'i see Parkes again on the following day, in order to give permission for his release and to get another written statement from him. While we were thus consulting, we received intelligence that the barbarians had already invaded and occupied the Summer Palace. The defeated soldiers all streamed in crowds to the Wan-shou Temple. We, your officials, immediately proceeded to Lu-kou-ch'iao for a temporary stay. Heng-ch'i did not come with us."

Between 3:00 and 5:00 p.m. on October 7, Prince Kung received a letter from Heng-ch'i, who was in the city. It asked for instructions, reporting that Heng-ch'i had met Thomas Wade that day outside the city at the latter's invitation and had agreed to release Parkes. The prince replied that Parkes's release had been promised before the occupation of the Summer Palace; the circumstances were now different and so the matter should be reconsidered. The memorialists thus expected that Heng-ch'i would do his best in arguing again with the barbarians. Contrary to expectation, a report came from Heng-ch'i on October 8 that he had returned Parkes on that day. According to Heng-ch'i, the barbarians were going to bombard the city at once if Parkes was not released; so a consultation was held with the princes and high officials remaining in the capital and Parkes was freed.

After giving this account, the memorialists again emphasized that Parkes should not have been hastily released after the Summer Palace had been invaded. They had learnt from Sheng-pao, who had come to Lu-kou-ch'iao, that at the consultation held in the city on October 8 he had strongly opposed Parkes's release, and the memorialists stated that they shared his view. "However, as Parkes has already been released on consultation between Heng-ch'i and the princes and high officials remaining in the capital," they lamented, "it is now too late to resist the force of circumstances!"

This account is probably quite truthful on the whole. If we recall that Heng-ch'i, as actual negotiator, was in constant touch with the princes and high officials in the city as well as with the imprisoned Parkes, it can certainly be considered a natural course of events that he should play a primary role in releasing Parkes.[136] It can also readily be imagined that at the crucial stage close contact could not be maintained between Prince Kung and Heng-ch'i. Reporting on the release of Parkes, Prince K'o-ch'in and others stated in a joint memorial received on October 13 that, since Prince Kung had temporarily moved far away, they had been unable to consult with him by correspondence and consequently had had to make the decision to return Parkes and some other prisoners after consultation with the officials in the city.[137] This explanation was accepted completely in an edict of the same date.[138]

On the other hand, the assertion of Prince Kung and his associates that they were at the last opposed to Parkes's release may not be accepted entirely at face value. There are in their memorial at least some traces of misrepresentation, or of intentionally misplaced emphasis. As early as October 2 an edict had suggested that it would be best to return Parkes and all the other prisoners in order to facilitate peacemaking. This edict reached Prince Kung two days later,[139] and was probably responsible for the drafting of the first letter to the British mentioned in the memorial. The letter, which is in *Pan-li fu-chü an,* stated that Prince Kung would personally meet with Parkes "within two or three days" to decide upon the final peace terms, so that the date for signing the "additional treaty" (the British Peking Convention) could be fixed personally with Parkes and the British prisoners could be returned. It also stated that Prince Kung had already ordered the field commanders to move back their troops and that the falling back of British troops would accordingly be expected.[140] As Prince Kung and his associates feared, this letter did not reach Elgin.[141] The second letter mentioned in the memorial is also in *Pan-li fu-chü an.* This letter expressed the hope, in its latter half, that the British forces would fall back to a distance of several *li* so that a Chinese official might be sent out on October 8 for a conference, when the opportunity would be taken to return the British subjects kept in the city. The letter also enclosed a letter in Chinese (dated "October 6, 1860, 3 P.M.") from Parkes to Thomas Wade in which Parkes wrote that Chinese officials had told him that all the British and French prisoners were to be returned on October 8.[142] It was upon receipt by the British of this letter that the interview between Heng-ch'i and Wade took place on October 7, at which an ultimatum from the allied commanders was placed in Heng-ch'i's hands, and on the following day Parkes and seven other prisoners were returned.[143] Strangely enough, although a copy of the second letter seems to have been enclosed in the memorial from Prince Kung and his associates,[144] the latter half of the letter and the enclosed letter from Parkes were not touched upon in the memorial, which merely stated that after sending the letter Prince Kung and others conferred about the plan to return Parkes. This was indeed a subtle misrepresentation on their part.[145]

Furthermore, although the exact sequence of events on October 6 cannot be reconstructed from the sources consulted, there may also be room for doubt about the truthfulness of the memorialists' assertion that the second letter was sent and the plan for release decided upon because the barbarians were not yet known to have invaded the Summer Palace, and that with the invasion of the Palace the plan should have been dropped. If we recall that Prince Kung himself admitted that he had already taken refuge at the Wan-shou Temple, from which the letter was sent, it may be rather natural to assume that he was at least in a position to foresee the invasion when he was sending the letter.

Prince Kung and his associates stated in the memorial that they shared Sheng-pao's opposition to the release. However, in a memorial received on October 13, Sheng-pao wrote bitterly that Prince Kung and his associates, who had moved to Ch'ang-hsin-tien (Lu-kou-ch'iao) were planning to let Heng-ch'i and others release Parkes in a day or so in order to make peace by any means.[146]

In short, we may at least assert that in reporting on Parkes's release Prince Kung and his associates tried to ascribe responsibility for the decision to Heng-ch'i and other officials in the city. Even if their account was wholly truthful, it still cannot be denied that they tried to emphasize that the development of events had been beyond their control and now the *fait accompli* could not be reversed. It is all the easier to suspect them of misrepresentation or at least of intentionally misplaced emphasis, if we recall that Heng-ch'i was considered a protégé of Su-shun and was not in the favor of Prince Kung.[147]

In reporting the surrender on October 13 of the An-ting Gate, which meant the surrender of Peking, Prince Kung and his associates emphasized that the decision to surrender had been made by the princes and high officials remaining in the capital, independently of Prince Kung. The event was reported by them successively in memorials received on October 17, October 19, and October 22. In these memorials they repeatedly blamed the princes and high officials concerned for having taken this step.[148] Again, Prince Kung and his associates must have intended thus to emphasize that the event had occurred under circumstances beyond their control.[149]

We have said that the memorials from Prince Kung and his associates at this time display a puzzling inconsistency of tone: the memorialists often made very firm (if not warlike) statements, mingled with indignation or lamentation; yet they continuously hinted that the conclusion of a peace was the only feasible course, describing in quite realistic detail the actual state of affairs in and outside the city.[150] In a memorial (received on October 28) that reported on the signing of the Peking Conventions and the exchange of ratifications of the British and the French Tientsin treaties, they went further and begged to be punished for the inadequate measures they had taken.[151]

Why did Prince Kung and his two associates write memorials of this kind? For one thing, they probably thought it necessary to weave belligerent words into their memorials because the emperor and Prince I's clique tended to be warlike and were not on good terms with Prince Kung or with Kuei-liang. For another thing, in addition to the overt war advocacy of such a person as Sheng-pao, there probably still existed around Peking — or at least Prince Kung and his associates felt that there existed — a strong feeling of anti-foreignism, if not downright war advocacy. Ying Chao-yung, a passionate war advocate, was called to Prince Kung's office on September 23 with some other people. He seems to have visited the office regularly until the foreigners invaded the Summer Palace.[152] When the allies broke into the Palace compound, it is reported that Hsü Nai-p'u, Shen Chao-lin, Hsü P'eng-shou, and P'an Tsu-yin had been drinking there together and they ran away helter-skelter. All of them had advocated war in 1858.[153] Whether and to what extent persons like these participated in or influenced decision-making at Prince Kung's office is not known. We may assume, however, that their presence was at least a factor in making Prince Kung more cautious and dilatory.

As for the princes and high officials remaining within Peking, who were responsible for the preservation of the city, it seems undeniable that circumstances compelled them to hasten the conclusion of peace. Their ineffectiveness in defending the city was bitterly scored by Sheng-pao, who specifically named Prince K'o-ch'in and Chou Tsu-p'ei, as well as Heng-ch'i, as the prime movers in surrendering the An-ting Gate.[154] After the surrender of the gate, Ignat'ev entered the city and settled himself at the Russian Hostel. The high officials of the Commission of Defense (except Heng-ch'i) were eager to secure his services as a mediator, and they readily followed his advice.[155] In 1867 Prince Kung and others recalled in retrospect in a memorial refuting the antiforeign views of Wo-jen: "In- and outside the capital criticism was heard against the tardiness of concluding treaties. There was even a succession of joint memorials from officials, Manchu and Chinese, which demanded a prompt conclusion of treaties, missives being transmitted day and night in a continuous flow. We, your officials, perceived the circumstances and were obliged to follow public opinion and prevent further aggravation of the general situation." [156] Also in a memorial of 1873: "The princes and high officials, Seng-ko-lin-ch'in, Chou Tsu-p'ei, Ch'üan-ch'ing, Chia Chen, and others repeatedly presented memorials requesting that we, your officials, be ordered to make peace without delay so that further aggravation of the general situation might be prevented." [157]

While the high officials in the city were compelled to hasten peace, there is some reason to suspect that there still persisted among them the mood of war advocacy or antiforeignism that had prevailed among Peking officialdom since 1858. As we have seen, the war advocate Yin Keng-yun was then in the city and wept with Wen-hsiang. It is stated in an entry for October 9 in the diary of Weng T'ung-ho, a compiler of the first class of the Academy, that Ch'en Fu-en, president of the Board of War, strongly opposed making peace and patrolled various places with several hundred braves, thus evoking the general admiration of the inhabitants.[158] It is also reported that the Grand Secretary Chia Chen "daily sat upright at the T'ien-an Gate [of the Imperial Palace], kept back [sic] the foreign troops, and was uncompromising and sorrowful whenever attending a conference." [159] These fragmentary indications suggest the tenseness of the atmosphere, which was perhaps all the greater because the hopelessness of the situation must have been evident to everyone.

The Kao-miao Temple where Parkes and Loch were confined was guarded by a force of three hundred men under the command of Ch'eng-ch'i.[160] The guard was greatly increased after the invasion of the Summer Palace.[161] When Parkes and Loch were released, their carts were escorted as far as the city gate by a large body of troops, "not under three thousand men." [162] These facts indicate not only the general disorder in the city but also the anticipated resistance to Parkes's release and the degree of the antiforeign feeling.

One more factor behind the uncompromising statements woven into the joint memorials from Prince Kung and his associates was probably Wen-hsiang himself. As we shall see in the Epilogue, Wen-hsiang became in the 1860's the pivotal figure of the Peking government, both in domestic politics and in foreign affairs, and was unanimously praised by foreign observers for his statesmanship, honesty, and perception. This does not necessarily mean, however, that he was from the beginning a flexibly minded peace advocate. Exceptionally for a Manchu official, Wen-hsiang was a regular *chin-shih* with an orthodox education and was apparently on good terms with Yin Keng-yun. This leads us to infer that he was originally rather akin to warlike Chinese scholar-officials by tendency and association, and that he underwent a gradual metamorphosis as a result of his experience as a grand councillor and his participation in the Peking negotiations, which is reflected in these joint memorials. This is of course pure conjecture. But if the inference is reasonable, then the political role he came to play in later years is more easily understood.

In summary, our conclusion is this: the nucleus of the machinery for peace negotiations under Prince Kung consisted of peace advocates of Manchu high officialdom, but they had to maneuver very cautiously, taking into consideration the antiforeign and aggressive mood that prevailed among the emperor and his entourage in Jehol

and also among officials in the metropolitan area. A similar configuration of forces was probably at work even inside Prince Kung's
office.[163] At the same time, in this critical situation, with allied
military pressure at its limit and the pressure of war advocacy at its
lowest point, the peace party was stronger, though temporarily, than
it had ever been before. There was thus in the process of formation
a sizable *de facto* organ for the conduct of foreign affairs, with
Prince Kung as its head and overlapping in part with the Grand
Council.

CHAPTER VI

Developments Following the Peking Conventions

He [Prince Kung] remained about two hours, and a great deal of conversation took place with Lord Elgin, in the course of which he repeatedly admitted the advantages which would accrue from more direct intercourse between foreign ministers and the government in Peking, inaugurated under the new treaties. He is also stated to have remarked in the course of conversation after lunch, that it was not until the expedition of 1860 that the Chinese government was aware that India was a province only of the British empire, their impression formerly having been that Great Britain was a very small island, the population of which was so large that the greater half of the people were compelled to reside afloat.

— *D. F. Rennie*

CHANGE IN ATMOSPHERE AFTER THE SIGNING OF THE CONVENTIONS

After the Peking Conventions were signed on October 24 and 25 there was a marked change in relations between the Anglo-French diplomats and Prince Kung. The atmosphere abruptly changed from one of mutual suspicion and distrust to one of mutual trust and cordiality, or at least of understanding.

A few days before the signing, the British received information that infernal machines had been placed in some of the houses along the street leading to the Board of Rites, where the ceremony was to take place, that the guns on the walls were turned against the building, and that a large force was encamped on the west side of the city. Providing against emergencies, the British field commander posted a field battery at the An-ting Gate. The street from the gate to the Board of Rites was lined with two thousand infantrymen. Elgin rode in a sedan chair with sixteen bearers, accompanied by the field commander and his staff, four hundred infantry, one hundred cavalry, and two bands playing at the head of the procession.[1] Elgin was two and three quarters hours late in arriving at the Board of Rites.[2] Prince Kung, growing impatient, had sent an official to the Russian Hostel for consultation as to whether the appointment should be canceled. A Russian messenger had been sent out to make inquiries at the British camp, and on his way had met the British procession marching through the capital.[3]

At the ceremony hall Elgin was cold and distant. Prince Kung looked sulky and seemed apprehensive. When the photographer in Elgin's suite directed against him the large lens of his camera, which looked rather like a mortar, he was terrified and turned pale as death. When Elgin took leave, the prince gave him a glance full of hatred.[4] The prince had proposed a banquet after the ceremony, but the British had not accepted, fearing that the food might be poisoned.[5]

On October 27 Elgin took up residence in the city in Prince I's palace,[6] escorted by bodyguards.

Baron Gros entered the city on October 24, escorted by two companies of infantry, and took up residence in the Hsien-liang Temple.[7] On October 25 he went out of the city. After forming a procession, he re-entered and proceeded to the Board of Rites, riding in a sedan chair with eight bearers and accompanied by an escort of about two thousand men. Aware that Elgin had acted coldly toward Prince Kung, Gros purposely tried to be seemly and respectful. The prince was gracious and the apprehension that was noticeable at the beginning of the meeting disappeared shortly. After the ceremony, the prince sent a repast to Gros' residence, which Gros shared with the French officers in his escort.[8]

Thus there was a considerable difference in attitude between the British and the French at the moment of signing the conventions.

This is not to say, however, that there was no distrust among the French. General de Montauban records that when Gros moved to the Hsien-liang Temple he offered to share the residence with Montauban, but the latter refused because he distrusted the Chinese government and Prince Kung. On October 25 he at first refused to attend the signing ceremony because he considered it possible that he and Gros might be captured. In the end he changed his mind and accompanied Gros. At the ceremony hall, however, he was still very suspicious. When tea was served, he checked carefully to see that his tea came from the same teapot as Prince Kung's. He dared to sip the tea only after he saw the prince drink. After the ceremony, however, the French general did not fail to enjoy the repast sent by the prince, along with his staff.[9]

Father Mouly called on Montauban on October 28. On that morning the priest had seen Prince Kung at the latter's invitation, extended through the Tientsin merchant, Chang Chin-wen, and he conveyed to Montauban Prince Kung's grave apprehension as to whether the treaty clauses would be faithfully observed by the foreigners, whether, among other things, the allied troops would leave Peking according to their promise. Montauban asked Father Mouly to reassure the prince, affirming that he had every intention of observing all the treaty clauses and that the prince should be equally reassured about the sincerity of the British.[10]

On November 2 Prince Kung visited Elgin. He remained about two hours, and there was a good deal of conversation on various topics. The next day Elgin returned the visit, and they had "a more *coulant* conversation" than Elgin had ever had with any Chinese authority. On November 8 Elgin visited the prince with Bruce, who had just arrived from Shanghai. On the following day the prince returned Bruce's visit. In these interviews, Prince Kung repeatedly admitted the advantages that would result from the direct intercourse between the Peking government and foreign ministers which the new treaties inaugurated. Elgin and Bruce noted that a person as highly placed as Prince Kung was less afraid of being denounced than were provincial functionaries and so could show less reserve in discussing delicate matters.[11]

Robert Swinhoe, who was in Elgin's suite, described the changed atmosphere thus: "Much cordiality now existed between Lord Elgin and Prince Kung, and visits were frequently exchanged. The Prince threw off the nervous restraint and show of bad humour that marked his first interview." [12]

While Elgin waited for Prince Kung to visit him first, Gros took the initiative and called on Prince Kung on November 1. The prince returned his visit on November 2, having called on Elgin earlier in the day.[13] On November 9, immediately prior to Gros' departure from Peking, Prince Kung personally came unannounced to bid him farewell. Gros considered this "extremely obliging" (d'une prévenance extrême). When the prince was leaving, he clasped Gros' hand and thanked him for not having participated in the burning of the Summer Palace.[14]

How did Prince Kung report these exchanges of visits with the British and French diplomats to the emperor?

We know that when the emperor appointed Prince Kung imperial commissioner he anticipated no necessity for the prince to meet the Western representatives personally.[15] His edict of October 5 relating to the release of allied prisoners authorized the prince to receive Parkes before his release in order to break his arrogance by personally showing him the benevolence of the Celestial Empire and letting him understand what his best interests were. This was Prince Kung's first authorization to meet a foreign official.[16] In a joint memorial with his associates received on October 17, the prince stated that since the city had now been surrendered at the discretion of the responsible authorities inside the city, he had no choice but to take the risk of entering the city to argue personally with the barbarians. The emperor's vermilion endorsement on the memorial warned him against the possibility of capture. After receiving further information, however, the emperor issued an edict (also on October 17) explicitly ordering the prince to enter the city at once to sign the Peking Conventions and exchange the treaty ratifications.[17]

"At the beginning of my management," stated Prince Kung in a memorial received on November 14, "I, your official, wondered how, as an imperial prince, I could be willing to associate with persons of a different race." The prince went on to state that after the barbarians entered the city, meeting them became unavoidable and he cited the edict of October 5, which authorized him to interview a foreign official. "Subsequently, when the ratifications were exchanged at the Board of Rites," the prince continued, "it was felt that the barbarians were becoming tame and submissive as a result of the open-heartedness shown by me. Afterward I received them several times. Their demeanor was now quite different from that on previous occasions, when they had behaved like untamed wild horses. The barbarians have already withdrawn [from the capital]. It seems that they will not break their word again . . . I have often measured their real intentions. Since they have already obtained all that they want, if we handle them properly in future there will be nothing to worry about, although for the moment we have no convincing evidence to support this [belief] . . . If in the future we show them our good faith, they will not start new trouble, even if they come to the capital in the spring . . . If the matter is to be discussed on the basis of the present situation, it should be said that now that peace has been made it is indispensable that we act magnanimously toward them. This is the only way to command their confidence so that they will not behave treacherously even in matters not provided for in the treaty clauses." [18] This memorial clearly reflects the change of atmosphere that followed the signing of the Peking Conventions.

While Prince Kung and his associates reported to the emperor his receptions of Elgin, Bruce, and Gros, they did not report his visits to the British and French diplomats.[19] On the other hand, all the visits exchanged between the prince and Ignat'ev were made known to the throne, except the prince's visit of November 10, before the signing of the Additional Treaty of Peking.[20]

SOUNDINGS ON FOREIGN AID
AGAINST THE TAIPINGS

It will be recalled that between May and August of 1860, as the Taipings swept down the Great River to Shanghai, provincial authorities in the Shanghai area had tried, unsuccessfully, to persuade Peking of the necessity for foreign military assistance against the rebels.[21] Now, with the Peking conventions signed and relations with the foreigners greatly improved, Peking's attitude changed.[22]

At the end of October, the French authorities were approached. Though it is difficult, because of the inadequacies and contradictions of the available sources, to establish in detail just what happened, the outline seems to have been as follows. Through the mediation of Chang Chin-wen, Father Mouly and his coadjutor, Father Anouilh, met Sheng-pao. They also met Prince Kung, Kuei-liang, and Wen-hsiang. In compliance with the wish of the Ch'ing authorities, they went to see Montauban and then Gros, sounding them out on the possibility of military assistance against the Taipings. The French were evasive and gave no definite answer. It was apparently the Ch'ing authorities who took the initiative, but Prince Kung and his associates reported to the emperor that the French had made an offer of assistance.[23]

The matter of military assistance was discussed also by Prince Kung and Ignat'ev. The Additional Treaty of Peking was signed on November 14 and Ignat'ev left Peking on November 22 to return overland to Russia. According to Buksgevden, Prince Kung visited the Russian Hostel on November 21 and expressed his deep regret that his government had not accepted Putiatin's offer of military assistance in 1858, and he hinted unmistakably that the Chinese were now willing to receive the weapons they had earlier refused.[24] According to reports to the emperor from Prince Kung and his associates, however, the offer of assistance came again from the Russians. At the signing ceremony on November 14, they asserted, Ignat'ev mentioned that Russia's offer of a gift of firearms was still effective. He added that a number of instructors and engineers would also be sent from Russia to teach the Chinese how to operate and how to cast firearms. When Prince Kung received Ignat'ev at the Kuang-hua Temple on November 19, Ignat'ev suggested among other things that a Russian naval force might be sent out for concerted operation with the Chinese land forces against the Taipings. According to Prince Kung and his associates, they cited to Ignat'ev an earlier communication from the Court of Dependencies to the Russian Senate dealing with where the expected weapons were to be received, and pointed out that the Russian offer of military assistance had never been rejected — perhaps a veiled thrust at Su-shun's opposition to its acceptance. During Prince Kung's visit to the Russian Hostel on November 21, the memorialists stated, Ignat'ev repeated his previous proposals.[25] If we take into account the whole history of the Russian offer we may probably assume that there was more than a grain of truth in this account by Prince Kung and his associates, whereas they may be suspected of misrepresentation in their report on the alleged French offer. In other words, it is most likely that Prince Kung not only expressed willingness to accept military assistance, but that Ignat'ev also entered into active discussion of the matter.

In a memorial reporting on the November 19 interview with Ignat'ev, Prince Kung and his associates recommended acceptance of firearms, instructors, and engineers. As for Ignat'ev's alleged suggestion of concerted Sino-Russian action against the Taipings, they suggested that the governor-general of Kiangnan and Kiangsi, and the governors of Kiangsu and Chekiang should be consulted. An edict of November 23 approved acceptance of firearms, instructors, and engineers. Another edict of the same date mentioned the proposal for concerted action against the rebels, adding that a similar proposal had also been made by the French, and asked advice of Tseng Kuo-fan, governer-general of Kiangnan and Kiangsi, Hsueh Huan, governor of Kiangsu, and Wang Yu-ling, governor of Chekiang.[26] (A copy of an extract from this second edict was obtained by a British merchant in Shanghai, but the British officials in

China doubted its authenticity.)[27] Tseng Kuo-fan approved the idea of concerted action, though with a number of qualifications. Hsueh Huan and Wang Yu-ling (jointly with Jui-ch'ang, Tartar general of Hangchow) expressed unqualified approval. Yuan Chia-san, director-general of grain transport, who had also been consulted, was opposed. Prince Kung and his associates agreed with Yuan, as did the emperor.[28]

There is no tangible evidence that military assistance was discussed in Peking between Prince Kung and the British diplomats late in 1860. When the prince returned Bruce's visit on November 9, Bruce drew attention to the current situation in Kiangsu, asserting that only the presence of allied troops kept Shanghai from the Taipings and that the British occupation could not possibly be prolonged indefinitely. He urged upon the prince the necessity for immediate steps to restore the authority of the imperial government in the province, and also stated that the prince was misled in supposing that British interests would lead the British to hold Shanghai for the Chinese government if the province and its principal centers of commerce remained in Taiping hands.[29] Prince Kung and his associates stated in a memorial received on December 2 that Bruce "bitterly deplored" the fact that the throne had not been informed that Shanghai had been saved through the British assistance extended to the government forces.[30] Thus it seems certain that if the subject of military assistance was not directly raised at least the military situation *vis-à-vis* the Taipings was discussed with the British authorities. (In January 1861 Thomas Wade went to Peking from Tientsin. At interviews with Prince Kung, Wen-hsiang, and others, on January 6 and 19, he was repeatedly sounded out on the possibility of British military assistance against the insurgents. He parried the questions and made no commitment. He even talked about the unfavorable consequences that usually accrued to powers that offered armed intervention in civil wars.)[31]

In short, once peace had been restored in North China and the boundary question with Russia had been settled, the Ch'ing authorities were willing to explore the possibility of foreign aid against the rebels. The misrepresentations of Prince Kung and his associates to the emperor, however, seem to indicate that the matter was still a delicate and touchy one within the Chinese government. On the other hand, we should perhaps consider it a very important development that the emperor explicitly sought the opinions of certain high officials in the provinces.

WESTERN PRESSURE FOR A PERMANENT FOREIGN AFFAIRS ORGAN

At his interview with Prince Kung on November 8, Bruce informed the prince of his resolution not to accept any provincial authority as imperial commissioner for foreign affairs, but to correspond henceforth with Prince Kung or "the Foreign Minister at the capital." He also declared that although he was returning to Tientsin until his residence in Peking was prepared for him, he would be ready to come to the capital at any time if public business required his presence.[32] In a letter to Prince Kung of the same date, Elgin expressed his deep regret that he, who had always wanted peace, had been compelled to resort to hostilities because of the policy recommended by "evil councillors" to the emperor. That hostilities had gone no further he was willing to attribute to the counsels of Prince Kung, and it would be gratifying to him to be able to report that the administration of foreign affairs was to continue in his hands.[33] The British authorities thus pointed to the necessity for creating in Peking a new foreign affairs organ to deal with the foreign legations now to be established there, expressed once more their disapproval of the system of an imperial commissioner on the coast, and finally, made it clear that they wished the new organ to be conducted not by the war party in the emperor's entourage but by Prince Kung and his fellow peace advocates. In other words, they hoped that Prince Kung's peacemaking machinery would become a permanent organ for foreign affairs. A letter of December 2 to Prince Kung from Bourboulon also expressed the wish to see Prince Kung as the head of a forthcoming "Department of Foreign Affairs." [34]

These Western expectations were conveyed to the emperor by Prince Kung and his associates. In a memorial received on November 8, they expressed the wish that the emperor would return to Peking now that the barbarian troops were gradually withdrawing and the weather was becoming cold. They also suggested that Heng-ch'i and Ch'ung-hou be stationed in Tientsin to manage trade affairs. In reply, the emperor ordered Heng-ch'i and Ch'ung-hou to Tientsin, and admonished the memorialists: "Hereafter there will still be many barbarian affairs to be dealt with. How can Prince Kung and others lay down responsibility because of the withdrawal of troops and the return [to the capital] of the imperial chariot?" [35] Prince Kung and his associates explained in a memorial received on November 14 that they had suggested stationing Heng-ch'i in Tientsin with the sole intention that he would manage "trivial matters," negotiate with the foreign ministers there, and thus restrain them from visiting the capital; they had not meant to lay down responsibility themselves. "Furthermore," they took this occasion to state, "the barbarians have often said that if a matter of importance occurs that requires discussion, they want to continue to transact business with the original person in charge (*yuan-pan chih jen*). Therefore we, your officials, can in no way shift responsibility to someone else. We humbly pray that all these complicated circumstances and our predicament may be thoroughly understood by Your Majesty." [36]

The British and French diplomats had left the capital on November 9 because Gros feared that the immediate establishment of legations in Peking might cause Prince Kung's overthrow at the hands of the emperor's entourage and also defer the emperor's return to the capital. He thought it better to establish the legations in Tientsin for the time being announcing that they would pass the winter there. In the meanwhile a convenient place was to be prepared in Peking and the legations would settle there in April, before the withdrawal of the foreign troops from Tientsin. Since Elgin thought it advisable to agree with Gros, the latter's proposal overruled that of Bruce, who was quite ready to remain in Peking.[37]

The British at first requested the use of Prince I's palace, where Elgin had been staying, for their legation, but the Chinese authorities opposed this. After some negotiation, it was finally arranged that the British would rent the palace of I-liang, in the immediate vicinity of the Russian Hostel. So that the Chinese government would have no misapprehension about the British intention to have Bruce settled in Peking in the spring, T. Adkins, a student interpreter, took possession of the building when Elgin and his suite left Peking, ostensibly to oversee house repairs.[38]

The French left no one behind them in Peking. Early in December de Méritens, interpreter of the French legation, came to Peking to arrange the rental of a legation building. He was dissuaded against his initial choice of the palace of Prince Su and finally settled on the former residence of Ching-ch'ung, which was now uninhabited and was also located near the Russian Hostel. After the arrangement was completed, de Méritens returned to Tientsin.[39]

During de Méritens' visit to Peking, Prince Kung gave him clearly to understand that he wanted to see the ministers installed in the capital as soon as possible. Perhaps the prince meant to imply that only a *fait accompli* could put an end to the opposition that was still being offered to the permanent residence of Western envoys in Peking.[40]

APPOINTMENT OF COMMISSIONERS AT TIENTSIN

In proposing that Heng-ch'i and Ch'ung-hou be stationed at Tientsin to "manage trade affairs at the port" (*pan-li hai-k'ou t'ung-shang shih-i*), Prince Kung and his associates had in mind a measure for coping with the new situation that followed on the Peking Conventions: the British and French ministers were to reside in Tientsin for the present, foreign troops were to be stationed there, and the port of Tientsin was to be opened to foreign trade. The memorialists also suggested that Ch'ung-hou be given the honorary title of "expectant metropolitan high official of the third or fourth rank" (*san-ssu-p'in Ching-t'ang hou-pu*), because Ch'ung-hou as a salt controller had not been accepted by the foreign diplomats as a negotiator on a previous occasion since he was not a metropolitan official under an imperial commission.[41] On November 8 the emperor conferred the proposed title on Ch'ung-hou and approved the appointment of Heng-ch'i to "manage trade affairs at the port" with Ch'ung-hou as his associate. An edict of the same date made it clear that in "soothing and bridling barbarians" at Tientsin, Heng-ch'i and Ch'ung-hou were to act as subordinates to Prince Kung. All trivial matters respecting trade were to be disposed of by them, but any matter of importance was to be referred to Prince Kung and his associates, and any reports to the throne were to be made by Prince Kung and his colleagues; Heng-ch'i and Ch'ung-hou were not allowed to memorialize.[42] It is probable that in forbidding Heng-ch'i and Ch'ung-hou to memorialize, the emperor was seeking to forestall the possibility of Prince Kung and his associates shifting responsibility. Under this arrangement the activities of the officials in Tientsin had to be reported in memorials from Prince Kung and his associates.[43]

On November 16 the emperor ordered Wen-ch'ien, provincial treasurer of Chihli, to Tientsin to cooperate with Heng-ch'i and Ch'ung-hou in managing "trade affairs." This step was taken at the suggestion of Heng-fu, who felt that barbarian affairs at Tientsin were now of sufficient importance to require the presence there of a competent high provincial official. He recommended Wen-ch'ien, who had had experience in tax administration at Tientsin as Ch'ang-lu controller-general of the salt gabelle (*Ch'ang-lu yen-cheng*).[44] Wen-ch'ien had had some experience in foreign contact too. During the treaty revision negotiations of 1854, Wen-ch'ien, then in Tientsin as Ch'ang-lu controller-general of the salt gabelle, had been sent to Taku to deal with the Western diplomats.[45] Again when Putiatin came to Taku in 1857, Wen-ch'ien (then in Peking) had been put under the command of T'an T'ing-hsiang, acting governor-general of Chihli, and sent to Taku as a negotiator.[46]

Prince Kung notified Bruce of the appointment of Heng-ch'i and Ch'ung-hou as "commissioners" in Tientsin in a letter on December 15, 1860. Bruce immediately became suspicious. Determined "to show in an unequivocal manner that the principle of direct intercourse with the highest authorities at Peking was irrevocably decided upon, and thus to put an end to any lingering hope that might exist among the Emperor's advisers, that a compromise on this point might be effected," he took no notice of the appointment of commissioners, and sent Thomas Wade to Peking on January 2, 1861, with a formal letter to Prince Kung, empowering Wade to discuss in his name all matters of business. Wade reached Peking on January 4, followed by Heng-ch'i, and remained there maintaining personal contact with Prince Kung, Wen-hsiang, and Heng-ch'i.[47] Early in February, Count Kleczkowski, secretary of the French legation, also moved from Tientsin to Peking, accredited to Prince Kung.[48]

THE EMPEROR'S FAILURE TO RETURN TO PEKING: THE ALLIED OCCUPATION OF TIENTSIN

Even while the Peking negotiations were in progress, voices had been raised requesting the emperor's return to the capital. These requests were in the form of individual memorials of a warlike tone from certain high provincial officials who were not well informed about the current situation in Peking.[49]

Once the Peking Conventions had been signed, Prince Kung and other high officials in Peking repeatedly advised the emperor's return. In a memorial received on November 8, Prince Kung, Kuei-liang, and Wen-hsiang suggested that the emperor come back to the capital at once to allay the people's anxiety. They repeated the proposal in a memorial received on November 11, this time joined by Sheng-pao.[50] On November 10, the day after the withdrawal of the allied forces from Peking had been completed, Prince Kung, other princes, and numerous metropolitan officials gathered at the Grand Secretariat and signed a memorial urging the emperor to return immediately. The memorial was received on November 13.[51]

In reply to this last memorial, an edict of November 13 announced: "This year the cold is becoming severe. We intend to postpone the return of the imperial carriage for the moment. Wait for an edict to be issued next year." Another edict of the same date explained that the emperor would not return so long as the foreigners continued to demand an audience for personal delivery of a "state letter" (*kuo-shu*, that is, credentials) because he would only be compelled to leave the capital again to avoid such an audience. The edict also made it clear that the princes and high officials were not again to dare to request the emperor's return within the current lunar year.[52]

While the requests from high provincial officials assumed a war-like tone, those from Peking were based on an understanding of the actual present situation and were conciliatory. It should be noted in this connection that there was at least one petitioner for the emperor's return who, despite his previous advocacy of war, had squarely faced the realities, clearly perceived the Anglo-French intention to support the dynasty, and thus had become a supporter of a conciliatory foreign policy. Shen Chao-lin, president of the Board of War, had presented in 1858 a firmly warlike memorial especially opposing the resident minister clause and the opening of rivers to foreigners. A memorial from him received on September 22, 1860, however, was rather different in tone. At first sight it may look warlike, but it was actually a counsel of prudence and no longer opposed the terms of the Tientsin treaties.[53] Shen was one of the signers of the joint memorial received on November 13. In response to the answering edict of the same date, Shen presented a memorial refuting its arguments and urging the emperor to return to the capital in the spring. On the basis of his personal observations, he categorically asserted in this memorial that Britain and France had no territorial ambition whatever in China. "Though they entered the city with more than ten thousand soldiers, they withdrew

after the signing ceremonies had taken place. The entire city has
suffered no harm. Thus we can be firmly convinced that their aim
is exclusively to make money and they have no other purpose what-
soever." As for the audience problem, their request could be leni-
ently fulfilled, because "what they beg for is to be honored with a
brief [imperial] address, gracious and soothing." Trade was advantageous to China as well. What the Chinese government should
worry about was its domestic problems. How should the helpless
Banner forces be trained? How could the ever-raging Taipings and
Nien Army be suppressed? How were the financial difficulties to
be overcome? All these problems were "more serious than the
barbarian affairs and more difficult to deal with." Thus Shen Chao-
lin urged in conclusion the necessity of the emperor's return to allay
the people's anxiety, to prevent the deterioration of official discipline,
and to restore peace and order.[54] Shen Chao-lin was probably not
the only official to change his views gradually in response to observation of the actualities.[55]

In a joint memorial received on November 25, Prince Kung,
Kuei-liang, Wen-hsiang, Sheng-pao, and Ying-kuei, governor of
Shensi, presented a detailed project for an imperial tour to Sian.
The project had originally been suggested in secret to the emperor
during the Peking negotiations by Prince Kung and others, and
separately by Ying-kuei, and the emperor had ordered Ying-kuei to
go to Peking to discuss the matter with Prince Kung and others
and report to the throne. Their joint memorial discussed in detail
how the tour should be carried out. (The tour was regarded as
necessary because the severe climate of Jehol and its proximity to
Russian territory made it unsuitable for prolonged residence.) At
the same time, the memorial gave a hint that the plan might now
better be shelved: "The general situation has changed since the
time when we, your officials, previously memorialized. At present
the capital is calm and secure. Danger has been turned into peace.
It is really beyond our initial expectations." The emperor suggested
in reply that in view of the importance of the matter and the careful
planning that would be required, a decision should be made as late

as the second or third month of the next lunar year, after examining the attitudes of the foreigners.[56]

A principal reason for the emperor's unwillingness to return to Peking was the fact that the foreigners were insisting on an imperial audience, and the kowtow problem was still unsolved. In December Prince Kung and his associates succeeded in obtaining written assurance from the British and French ministers in Tientsin that they would not insist upon an audience,[57] thus allaying the emperor's worries, at least for the time being.

An edict of February 11, 1861, announced that the emperor would move homeward on March 23. It was announced on the following day that the emperor would leave the capital on April 11 to pay reverence at the Imperial Tombs to the east of the capital and then return to the Imperial Villa in Jehol. On March 20, however, his scheduled departure was postponed to April 4 because of "a slight indisposition." An edict issued on April 11 — several days after Bourboulon and Bruce had separately entered Peking — announced that because of the emperor's continued ill-health his homeward journey was deferred until the autumn, when another edict would be issued.[58] Whatever may have been the true reason for the postponement, the Hsien-feng emperor did not, after all, return to Peking. He died in Jehol in August 1861.

It is to be assumed that a second major deterrent to the emperor's return to Peking was the fact that Anglo-French troops were stationed in Tientsin. We can imagine also that the presence of these forces in Tientsin probably increased, in the minds of the emperor and his entourage, the menace of the unsolved audience problem.[59]

The occupation of Tientsin was based on Article 9 of the British Convention and Article 8 of the French Convention, according to which Britain and France might keep troops at Tientsin, Taku, the north coast of Shantung, and Canton as a guarantee against full payment of full indemnities. The allied stationary force in Tientsin consisted of some 5,000 or 6,000 men including three batteries of artillery.[60]

The Chinese authorities feared that the allied forces in Tientsin might advance again on the capital. They were all the more sensitive because the foreigners, citing the arrest of Parkes, had suggested that they wanted more than 100 guards for their legations in Peking. The emperor expressed apprehension over the possibility of further diplomatic pressure from the foreigners, backed by force, if he returned to Peking while the allied troops still remained in Tientsin. He was also concerned about the strength of the force there.[61]

In effect, the presence of the allied forces in Tientsin served to support the influence of Prince Kung, because the peace party could be influential only if external pressure continued to be felt. The British and French diplomats had expected that the withdrawal of their troops to Tientsin would encourage the emperor to return to Peking. At the same time, Elgin had thought it probable that there might be some political reaction when the emperor and "the bad advisers whom he had about him" returned, and he expected the presence of the allied forces in Tientsin to strengthen Prince Kung's position sufficiently to prevent his being overwhelmed in this reaction. "Kung will claim credit," wrote Elgin on November 10, 1860, "for having induced us to remove from Pekin to Tientsin, while the fact that we are still as near as Tientsin will be an *in terrorem* argument in support of his policy of conciliation."[62]

If the stationing of allied forces in Tientsin was really instrumental in keeping the emperor away from Peking,[63] then its effect was even greater than Elgin had anticipated. I would venture to suggest that the emperor's flight, which the foreign powers had feared might be fatal to the dynasty, actually served to maintain the new political equilibrium in which the peace party was now able to have a decisive voice. In this delicate power situation, with the return of the emperor and his entourage repeatedly postponed, the *ad hoc* machinery for peace negotiations under Prince Kung was all the more easily institutionalized as a formal standing organ for foreign affairs.

CHAPTER VII

The Tsungli Yamen

Wansiang went on to say that the Decrees had arrived respecting the new Foreign office and the Foreign establishment of the Customs, and that the Prince had prepared Lay's commission and sent it to Hangki. I had heard that the Prince's Memorial about their Foreign office had been objected to in some details. As yet I have not been able to get a copy thereof. The Prince will be the ostensible, Wansiang the working head.

— *Wade to Bruce, Peking, January 23, 1861*

Letters have been received from Tientsin to the 5th February per *Marne*. We have not a line from our correspondent, nor have we any new *Gazettes* . . . The news is favourable, everything is progressing amicably and as a proof of it, an Imperial edict appointed a Foreign Board on the 23rd [sic], under the management, it is reported, of the Prince of Kung and Kwei-liang, and all communications from foreign Ministers are to be seen by the Emperor himself.

— *North China Herald*

ESTABLISHMENT OF THE TSUNGLI YAMEN

In a memorial received on January 13, 1861, Prince Kung, Kuei-liang, and Wen-hsiang proposed the establishment in the capital of an "office for the general administration of the affairs of the different nations" (*tsung-li ko-kuo shih-wu ya-men*), which would be "solely responsible" for the management of "foreign affairs" (*wai-kuo shih-wu*). In view of the imminent residence of Western diplomats in Peking, the memorial strongly urged the necessity for a new approach to the conduct of foreign affairs both in Peking and in the provinces. A detailed plan was presented in an accompanying six-article memorandum (*chang-ch'eng liu-t'iao*) which Bruce later called "a very businesslike document written in a good spirit." Three supplementary memorials were also submitted at the same time.[1]

The principal memorial, written in a dignified conventional style replete with flowery antiforeign rhetoric and citations from history, freely discussed the current political situation.[2] Its major argument was twofold. First, it was the judgment of Prince Kung and his associates that Britain and France had no territorial ambitions in China. "Since the exchange of treaty ratifications [and the signing of the conventions], the barbarians have returned to Tientsin and sailed southward in groups. Moreover, they continue to base their requests on the treaties. This means that they really do not covet our land and people. Hence we can still, through good faith and justice, tame and control their nature, while we ourselves strive for national vigor (*tzu-t'u chen-hsing*)." Second, the memorialists felt that the troubles at home were more serious at the moment than those coming from without, and so it was a matter of practical politics to get along with the foreign powers for the time being. "Among the barbarians, Britain is ferocious and Russia unfathomable, while France and America follow and collude with these countries . . . Against the violent and frenzied behavior of the barbarians this time a voice full of wrath and resentment has been raised in unison by all people who have any spirit at all. We, your officials, roughly know the principles of righteousness. How can we forget the long-term policy of the state?" Having thus displayed moral indignation, the memorialists proceeded to assess the priorities of the problems to be dealt with. "However, the Nien are blazing in the north and the Taipings in the south. Our military funds are drained and our troops are exhausted. The barbarians took advantage of our weakness and we have been drawn under their control. If we cannot restrain our wrath and [re-] open hostilities with them, sudden catastrophe may fall upon us in no time at all. On the other hand, if we forget about the ills they may inflict upon us and take no precautions against them, we shall be leaving a source of misfortune to our posterity. The ancients had a saying, 'A policy of peace and friendship is a temporary measure of expediency; war and defense is the real policy to pursue.' This is indeed a statement of everlasting truth. Let us discuss the situation today. The Taiping and Nien bandits are gaining victories in turns and constitute a disease of our internal organs, so to speak. Russia, with her territory bordering ours, aiming at encroaching upon the Middle Kingdom, may be compared to a threat at our bosom. As for Britain, her aim is trade, but she behaves ferociously and has no conception of human decency. If we do not keep her within limits, we shall not be able to stand on our feet. Hence she may be considered a malady of our limbs. Therefore we should first of all exterminate the Taiping and Nien bandits. And we should get Russia under control next, and the British last." [3] In conclusion Prince Kung and his associates recommended the following short-term foreign policy: "If we act in accordance with the treaties and do not allow [the barbarians] to exceed them by even an inch, if we give an appearance of sincerity and amity while we quietly try to keep them in line, then they will not suddenly cause us great harm for several years to come, even though they may make occasional demands."

This line of argument was quite similar to that in Shen Chao-lin's memorial requesting the emperor's return (see Chap. VI). It was probably persuasive enough to convince the war advocates in Jehol and Peking; indeed, we may say that it was the greatest common measure between the peace party and the war party.

One of the supplementary memorials reported that while the principal memorial was being prepared Thomas Wade came to Peking and asked for an interview with Prince Kung. As we know, Bruce had sent Wade from Tientsin as a countermeasure to the appointment of the commissioners at Tientsin. The memorialists, however, asserted that although Wade pretended to have come to Peking to investigate the legation building, they suspected that his real aim was to find out what the Chinese government would do if the British withdrew their troops from Tientsin. (They believed that the British were inclined to do so because of the heavy expenses involved.) When the memorialists hinted to Wade that an "office for the general administration of the affairs of the different nations" might be established to "take sole charge of foreign affairs," he was delighted and remarked, "[That] is what we have vainly sought for several decades. If the Celestial Empire would thus show that it was not indifferent to the foreign countries, they, on their part, would never try to make further trouble." [4] The memorialists were probably implying that the new formal agency for foreign affairs would be instrumental in ending the occupation of Tientsin, which the emperor so resented. They also implied that since a hint as to the establishment of the new agency had already been given to Wade, rejection of their proposal by the emperor might lead to awkward consequences. This was a skillful presentation of the situation and must have been designed to strengthen the persuasive powers of the principal memorial.

The emperor referred the principal memorial and the six-article memorandum to Prince Hui, the princes and ministers in charge of the temporary imperial residence, the adjutant generals, and the grand councillors, and ordered them to deliberate and report on the matter.[5] A memorial received on January 19 from Prince Hui and others supported the whole plan and submitted it to the emperor's decision.[6] On the following day (January 20, 1861) an edict announced the establishment in the capital of the "Office for the General Administration of the Trade Affairs of the Different Nations" (Tsung-li ko-kuo t'ung-shang shih-wu ya-men — later commonly abbreviated to Tsungli Yamen or Tsung-shu). It also announced the appointment of Prince Kung, Kuei-liang, and Wen-hsiang to "take chief charge of" (*kuan-li*) this office. This edict and another of the same date outlined the new arrangements for the conduct of foreign affairs in Peking and in the provinces.[7]

Whereas Prince Hui and others had endorsed the plan of Prince Kung and his associates *in toto,* these edicts inserted the word "trade" (*t'ung-shang*) into the name of the new office, contrary to the original plan. They also differed from the original plan in several other important respects. This fact suggests that there was a conflict of opinion within the emperor's entourage. The controversy between Peking and Jehol was carried on until a memorial received on February 15 from Prince Kung and his associates and an edict in reply of the same date completed a compromise. The new machinery as formulated through this process of compromise will be described later in this chapter.[8]

One of the supplementary memorials received on January 13 proposed that in order to obtain correct information on foreign activities in the treaty ports and to know the opinions of provincial officials on foreign affairs, copies of the recent edicts on foreign affairs and the recent relevant memorials from Shantung, Kiangnan, and Kwangtung should be sent from the Grand Council (in Jehol) to Prince Kung's office, and also copies of all future memorials concerning foreign affairs. An edict of the same date approved this proposal. It also authorized Wen-hsiang, the sole grand councillor remaining in the capital, whenever necessary, to order a Grand Council secretary on duty in Peking to copy any of the memorials received before September 21, 1860, and kept at the Military Archives Office (these documents had not been carried to Jehol).[9] In short, pending the definitive working out of details relating to the new agency for foreign affairs, arrangements were made to assemble necessary documents in Prince Kung's office, through the Grand Council.

INSTITUTIONAL FEATURES OF THE YAMEN

Relation to Other Government Offices

In the central government of the Ch'ing dynasty, the position of the highest organ for policy integration and decision-making, directly attached to the emperor, was originally shared by the Grand Secretariat, a survival of a Ming institution, and the Council of Princes and High Officials (the so-called I-cheng wang ta-ch'en), a typical Manchu organ based on the banner system, which kept within its jurisdiction military and foreign affairs. The Grand Council, established by the Ch'ing in 1729 as a temporary high military committee, gradually took over the powers of the Grand Secretariat and of the Council of Princes and High Officials, which was discontinued in 1792.

As of 1860 the Grand Secretariat still nominally retained its prestige as the highest statutory government organ under the emperor, but the organ that actually integrated policy and made important decisions was the Grand Council, a sort of privy council whose several members also held other substantive posts. In its daily session in the presence of the emperor, the Grand Council deliberated in an advisory capacity on all political matters of importance, including military and foreign affairs. The council examined the more important memorials and composed all the edicts. The general administration of the government was divided among the traditional Six Boards or Ministries (Civil Appointments, Revenue, Rites, War, Punishments, and Works). There were also such special agencies as the Court of Dependencies and the Court of Judicature and Revision, while the Censorate performed the functions of inspecting the conduct of business by the government agencies and impeaching officials guilty of misconduct. These organs were all under the immediate control of the emperor, and formally they were all equals.

The major provincial offices, such as those of governor-general, governor, and Tartar general, were also directly under the emperor and their position equated with that of the Grand Council or the Six Boards. For example, a Board could not give direct instructions to a governor-general or governor; the standard procedure was to memorialize first and let the emperor issue an edict giving orders to the provincial official concerned. Thus, the Grand Council's formal relation to the Six Boards, to governors-general, or to other high authorities in Peking and in the provinces was that of an equal, but in function it was a superior organ as the emperor's council.

As for foreign affairs, those relating to the Western maritime powers, which were considered tributary states, came under the jurisdiction of the Board of Rites; Russian affairs were under the jurisdiction of the Court of Dependencies, which was responsible for the administration of matters concerning the frontier tribes in

the north and west. However, important matters in foreign relations were all deliberated upon and decided in the Grand Council.[10]

It now became an important issue between the emperor, influenced by his entourage in Jehol, and Prince Kung and his associates
in Peking[11] what the nature of the new office for foreign affairs
should be, and what its position should be in relation to the other
government organs in Peking.

The six-article memorandum received on January 13 proposed
that the controlling board of the new office should be composed of
"prince(s) and high officials" (*wang ta-ch'en*) and should include
all the grand councillors, who would thus serve concurrently in the
Council and in the Tsungli Yamen. For secretaries, eight Manchus
and eight Chinese should be selected from the secretaries of the
Grand Council, the Grand Secretariat, the Six Boards, and the
Court of Dependencies. These sixteen would retain their original
posts and serve in rotation at the Tsungli Yamen. They would transact all the yamen's business according to the practice established in
the Grand Council. All foreign matters were to be communicated
directly to the Tsungli Yamen as well as to the throne by provincial
high officials. The Tsungli Yamen was to be a temporary agency
that would be discontinued as soon as military operations against
the insurgents were concluded and foreign affairs became less complicated. Thereafter foreign affairs were to revert to the Grand
Council. The implication in this memorandum is that the Tsungli
Yamen was expected to be a branch of the Grand Council, or to
put it differently the Grand Council itself was to function in disguise
as a foreign office, with a specially designated prince presiding and a
secretariat which, though differently composed, was definitely connected with that of the Grand Council.[12]

Of the three men appointed in the edict of January 20 to "take
chief charge" of the new office, only Wen-hsiang was a grand councillor. This meant a rejection of the original proposal that all the
grand councillors concurrently serve as Tsungli Yamen ministers.
This edict also ordered that all secretaries selected from the Grand
Council to serve in the new office should immediately cease to serve

at the Council. The relationship between the Tsungli Yamen and the Grand Council, in short, was to be rather remote, in sharp contrast to the original proposal. Furthermore, another edict of the same date prescribed that communications from provincial high officials (including the Shanghai imperial commissioner and the new Superintendent of Trade for the Three Ports to be stationed in Tientsin) were to be sent not directly to the Tsungli Yamen but to the Board of Rites, which in its turn would transmit (*chuan-tzu*) them to the Tsungli Yamen. Though this formula did not necessarily deny formal equality of status between the Tsungli Yamen and the Board of Rites, it certainly implied the functional subordination of the former to the latter, whose jurisdiction included the tributary states. At least Prince Kung and his associates thought it did, as we shall see. The same basic implication appeared in the addition of the term "trade" to the official title of the office; foreign affairs to be handled by the Tsungli Yamen thus fell into the category of "trade," and the principle of interstate equality was thus denied.[13]

In two memorials received on January 26 — one supplementary to the other — Prince Kung and his associates ventured to dispute these imperial modifications to their plan. This time they adapted their line of argument to the conception of the new office suggested by the emperor, ostensibly giving up their initial idea of making it a branch or *alter ego* of the Grand Council.[14]

On the relationship of the Tsungli Yamen to the Board of Rites, the memorialists explained that their initial intention had been to set up an office for foreign affairs at the Board of Rites, because the "overseas tributary states" (*hai-wai fang-feng*) had originally been under the jurisdiction of that board. As a compromise they now proposed that in order to maintain secrecy of vital and confidential matters they should for the moment be reported directly to the Tsungli Yamen as well as to the throne, while ordinary matters should be reported through the Board of Rites. They further suggested that once foreign affairs came to a satisfactory settlement, all matters, vital or not, should be reported through the Board of Rites so that the old system of soothing and pacifying the tributary states (*fan-fu*) might be preserved. This compromise plan the emperor ignored.

The necessity for having a grand councillor serve concurrently as a minister of the Tsungli Yamen they again stressed, though for somewhat different reasons than before. They referred to Article 2 of the Russian Tientsin Treaty and a recent Russian practice of addressing communications solely to the Grand Council, adding that other powers might follow the Russian precedent, which would be quite a nuisance. They also pointed out that the foreigners knew that Wen-hsiang was a grand councillor and respected him highly for that reason; therefore he could meet foreign ministers at the Tsungli Yamen and receive at that office any communications from them addressed to the Grand Council without incurring further complaints from them. Their original request that *all* the grand councillors be in the Tsungli Yamen they no longer insisted upon; they simply added, possibly as a faint protest, that it might bring about no inconvenience for the moment if the emperor did not appoint the grand councillors in Jehol to concurrent duties at the Tsungli Yamen.

On the other hand, they strongly urged that the secretaries to be selected from the Grand Council continue to serve also the Council, because for reasons of secrecy important documents of the Tsungli Yamen should be kept at the Grand Council. In a vermilion endorsement on the memorial the emperor accepted this proposal in principle and asked the memorialists for suggestions as to how to supervise the secretaries who would serve concurrently at both offices.

Their supplementary memorial deprecated the insertion of the term "trade" on the ground that it would arouse profound suspicion among the foreign officials and cause them to refuse to deal with the Tsungli Yamen: "though the real intention of the barbarians is solely to make profit, they pose as officials and will not admit that they are engaged in trade, lest they incur our contempt." Since it would have been very impolite to ask the emperor to alter an edict already issued, the memorialists requested that "trade" be dropped from the official seal of the Tsungli Yamen and from all its communications. The emperor complied in his vermilion endorsement on the memorial. A strange situation was thus created, for domestically both titles remained official while the designation without "trade" was used by the Tsungli Yamen in its correspondence with foreign authorities.[15]

In a memorial received on February 3, which presents a ten-article memorandum (*chang-ch'eng shih-t'iao*) concerning details of organization and procedure for the Tsungli Yamen, Prince Kung and his associates wrote: "We, your officials, planned at first to set up a bureau at the Board of Rites. . . . However, the Board of Rites is the place to discuss the rites and ceremonies and its dignity (*t'i-chih*) is rather exalted; for barbarians to frequent the place, would not be at all compatible with that dignity. Moreover, if we used the principal hall where the high officials of the Board transact business, the reception there of barbarians would cause much inconvenience. But if we used only the secretaries' halls the barbarians would certainly not be satisfied. Therefore, a separate office has been established. The barbarians will think that is the place for 'general administration' with a very dignified designation. We shall consider it like such offices as the Residence for Envoys of the Four Tributary States." Accordingly its personnel and expenditures would be on a very small scale, "with the hidden meaning that it cannot have a standing equal to that of other traditional government offices, thus preserving the distinction between China and foreign countries."[16]

In a separate memorial received on the same day,[17] Prince Kung and his associates discussed the two issues still pending. First, as to the transmission of provincial reports to the Tsungli Yamen, the memorialists retreated a step further. They now rather ambiguously proposed that on vital and confidential matters the established precedent of "only memorializing the throne and not reporting to any other office" (*tsou erh pu-tzu*) be followed;[18] not all matters need be communicated to the Tsungli Yamen. Second, they offered the following compromise on the secretary problem: None of the prescribed sixteen secretaries should be selected from the Grand Council, but eight additional secretaries (four Manchus and four Chinese) would be selected from the Council and treated as supernumeraries (*e-wai hsing-tsou*) of the Tsungli Yamen. These eight secretaries would ordinarily be on duty at the Grand Council and would serve at the Tsungli Yamen only when necessary.

An edict of the same date (February 3)[19] accepted their suggestion on the first point. In vital and confidential matters all provincial reports should be presented to the throne alone; copies of those that concerned foreign affairs would be prepared by the Grand Council and sent to the Tsungli Yamen. (This procedure is roughly the same as the one suggested in the supplementary memorial received on January 13 and approved by the emperor.) In short, the Tsungli Yamen was to receive provincial reports on ordinary matters through the Board of Rites; on vital and confidential matters it would only receive copies of memorials sent to it from the Grand Council.[20]

On the second point, the edict again ordered the memorialists to devise regulations determining the location of responsibility for supervising secretaries who were to serve concurrently the Grand Council and the Tsungli Yamen. In a memorial received on February 15 Prince Kung and his associates submitted in reply a detailed plan which was approved in an edict of the same date. It was thus settled that four Manchu and four Chinese secretaries of the Grand Council would concurrently be supernumerary secretaries of the Tsungli Yamen, to serve ordinarily at the Council and only when necessary at the Yamen. Their exclusive duty at the Grand Council would be to transact business concerning foreign affairs and to take care of the relevant secret documents. One of them was to be stationed in the Military Archives Office of the Grand Council, where the secret documents concerning foreign affairs were to be kept.[21]

The Yamen in Its Initial Stage

The Tsungli Yamen had the hierarchical structure common to government offices in Peking at this time, with the officials (*kuan*) at the top, and ranging down through the yamen clerks (generically called *shu-li, hsü-li,* or simply *li*) to the servants (generically called *i*).

The officials were divided into two groups: the controlling board and the secretaries. The following is a description of the Tsungli Yamen's organization in its initial stage.[22]

The controlling board, the "prince(s) and high officials" (*wang ta-ch'en*) corresponded to the *t'ang-kuan* (the group of presidents and vice-presidents) in other metropolitan offices. It is noteworthy that in the case of the Yamen an imperial prince was appointed senior member of the controlling board. There was a resemblance to the Grand Council in that the controlling board had no fixed number of members. Nor was an equal number of Manchus and Chinese specified, as in the Six Boards. Prince Kung, Kuei-liang, and Wen-hsiang originally constituted the controlling board. At their suggestion Ch'ung-lun and Heng-ch'i were appointed to the board on April 25, 1861, as associate ministers of the Tsungli Yamen (*tsung-li ko-kuo shih-wu ya-men pang-pan ta-ch'en*).[23] The members of the controlling board acted as a group and were all responsible for the conduct of its business. In this the Tsungli Yamen was like the Six Boards and other metropolitan offices.

The originally prescribed fixed number of secretaries (*ssu-yuan* or *chang-ching*)[24] was sixteen, eight Manchus and eight Chinese, selected from those of the Grand Secretariat, the Boards of Revenue, Rites, and War, and the Court of Dependencies. Of these, four (two Manchus and two Chinese) were secretaries-general (*tsung-pan*) and two others were assistant secretaries-general (*pang-pan*). The secretaries served at the Tsungli Yamen on a concurrent basis, retaining their original posts. They were divided into two groups, to be on duty at the Yamen alternately for five-day periods. Except for two of the secretaries-general, all put in night duty at the Yamen in rotation.[25]

In addition to these sixteen, eight of the Grand Councils' secretaries concurrently served as supernumerary secretaries of the Tsungli Yamen.[26]

The selection of the sixteen secretaries was made in April 1861. Among them was Yen-ju, a Manchu assistant director of the Board of Rites, who had been engaged in clerical work in Prince Kung's office during and ever since the Peking negotiations. Eleven others were nominated as reserves against a vacancy. As most of the sixteen secretaries were inexperienced in foreign affairs, Ch'eng-lin, secretary (to be appointed when a vacancy occurred) (*chi-pu chu-shih*) of the Gendarmerie, and Hsiu-wen, official writer (*pi-t'ieh-shih*) of the Gendarmerie, both of whom had also been in Prince Kung's office for half a year, were added as secretaries and treated as being within the fixed number. Since the secretaries recommended from the Court of Dependencies were not competent in both Manchu and literary Chinese and were not conversant with Russian affairs, Hui-lin, superintendent of the Russian Hostel and second-class secretary of the Court of Dependencies, was made an additional secretary and regarded as within the fixed number. Prince Kung and his associates also asked that Ch'ang-shan, expectant lieutenant-colonel, be similarly added, but the emperor replied that Ch'ang-shan was to serve at the Yamen as a supernumerary. Ch'ang-shan, Kuei-liang's son-in-law and so Prince Kung's brother-in-law joined Prince Kung's office during the Peking negotiations, doing clerical work and scouting. He had remained under Prince Kung and at one point had engaged in negotiations with the Archimandrite in the Russian Hostel. Yen-ju, Ch'eng-lin, Hsiu-wen, and Ch'ang-shan were all among the recipients of honors for their participation in the peacemaking.[27] Of these four additional secretaries, Hui-lin was a Mongol; the other three were Manchus.[28]

The sixteen clerks (specifically called *kung-shih* in the Yamen, as in the Grand Secretariat and some other offices) for the Yamen were chosen from the clerks of the State Historiographer's Office and the Military Archives Office, because these two offices were considered to be free of the corrupt practices all too commonly indulged in by the clerks in the Ch'ing government offices. Contrary to general current practice, even documents on ordinary matters were drafted by the Yamen's secretaries; the clerks worked solely as copyists. The sixteen clerks were selected from clerks who had worked under Prince Kung during the Peking negotiations.[29]

As servants (specifically called *su-la* in the Yamen, as in the Imperial Household — the transliteration of a Manchu word), twelve servants from the Imperial Household were selected, and eight banner soldiers were chosen to act as messengers. When the exchange of business between the Yamen and the new foreign legations began, the eight soldiers were found to be insufficient, and eight more were added.[30]

Two offices were attached to the Tsungli Yamen: the Inspectorate General of Customs (Tsung-shui-wu-ssu) and the T'ung-wen kuan (College of Foreign Languages).

The three identical Rules of Trade signed at Shanghai in November 1858 with Britain, France, and the United States stipulated (Rule 10) that a uniform system for the collection of customs should be enforced at all treaty ports. This meant the extension to all treaty ports of the foreign inspectorate system which had been in operation at Shanghai since 1854. H. N. Lay, who had been appointed the first inspector general in 1859 by Ho Kuei-ch'ing, Shanghai imperial commissioner, was now re-appointed as an official directly attached to the new agency for foreign affairs.[31]

Article 50 of the British Tientsin Treaty stipulated that all British official communications to the Chinese authorities were to be written in English; they would be accompanied by a Chinese version for the time being, but the meaning as expressed in the English text would be held as authoritative.[32] Article 3 of the French Tientsin Treaty made a similar provision. Prince Kung and his associates suggested in their six-article memorandum received on January 13 that selected capable boys of the banners be trained in foreign languages.[33] The T'ung-wen kuan was established in Peking in 1862 and was under the direct control of the Tsungli Yamen.[34]

The Chia-hsing Temple, where Prince Kung's office had been finally located, served as the temporary site of the Tsungli Yamen,[35] pending repairs on the deserted office of the Department of Iron Coins (T'ieh-ch'ien-chü), in Tung-t'ang-tzu Lane in the eastern part of the Imperial city, which had been assigned to the Yamen. This was a small and very old building, and repairs were carried out rather sparingly. The front gate, which looked like that of a private

residence, was reconstructed according to the required style for government offices, in order to lend it sufficient dignity for the reception
of foreign diplomats.[36]

Beginning with a memorial received on February 21, Prince Kung
used the title Ch'in-ming tsung-li ko-kuo shih-wu (commissioned by
His Majesty to undertake the general superintendence of foreign
affairs) instead of his previous title of imperial commissioner.[37]
On March 11, a formal ceremony for the reception of the Yamen's
official seal, which had been made ready by the Board of Rites,
marked the official inauguration of the new office.[38] The old T'ieh-
ch'ien-chü building was ceremoniously opened as the new site of the
Tsungli Yamen on November 11, 1861, soon after the *coup d'état*
which got rid of Prince I, Prince Cheng, and Su-shun. The British
estimated that by moving into its new site the Tsungli Yamen became a permanent institution.[39]

Provincial Agencies for Foreign Affairs

When the idea of establishing a new central organ for foreign
affairs was brought up in Peking and Jehol, Hsueh Huan was the
acting imperial commissioner at Shanghai and Heng-ch'i was the
commissioner in charge of trade affairs at Tientsin. In their original
proposal for the establishment of the Tsungli Yamen, Prince Kung
and his associates suggested the creation at Tientsin of a new post
of Superintendent of Trade for the Three Ports (Pan-li san-k'ou
t'ung-shang ta-ch'en), to take charge of the new treaty ports of
Tientsin, Newchwang, and Chefoo. They also suggested that the
jurisdiction of the original "imperial commissioner for the five
ports" (*wu-k'ou ch'in-ch'ai ta-ch'en*) (the Shanghai imperial commissioner) be extended to cover all the new treaty ports along the
Great River and all those along the seacoast south of the mouth of
the Great River, with Hsueh Huan still to be the incumbent. The
Superintendent of Trade for the Three Ports would not be invested
with the title of imperial commissioner. They suggested that either
Ch'ung-hou or Ch'ung-lun be appointed to this new post in Tientsin
and Heng-ch'i come to Peking to serve at the Tsungli Yamen.[40]

The edict of January 20 accepted these proposals and appointed Ch'ung-hou Superintendent of Trade for the Three Ports.[41] As has been stated, the preceding machinery for foreign contact at Tientsin had been subordinate to Prince Kung in the capital and had not been permitted to present memorials. In contrast, the new Superintendent of Trade at Tientsin headed an independent office and had the power to memorialize directly.[42]

There was certainly a geographical justification for creating the new post, in that the treaty ports were dispersed over an area so much extended that it was more expedient to divide their jurisdiction between the Shanghai commissioner and the superintendent of trade in Tientsin. But this was not the sole point taken into account. Prince Kung and his associates stated in their original proposal that their primary intention in requesting the creation of the Tsungli Yamen and the superintendency of trade in Tientsin was "to divide the management of affairs between Shanghai in the south and [Tientsin] in the north and to have the general direction of affairs performed in the capital, so that the effect [of freely operating the whole machinery from Peking] will be achieved in such an untrammeled way as the body uses the arms and the arm uses the fingers. If the management in Tientsin is satisfactory, then the barbarian chieftains will have nothing to do even if they reside in the capital. It is certain that they will thus eventually come to think of returning home in frustration." [43] We may gather from this quotation that while the creation of a metropolitan government office to deal on terms of equality with the foreign ministers in Peking was planned, there still persisted the old hope of preventing the approach of Western diplomats to Peking.[44] Bruce was rather cautious, though a bit optimistic, in appraising the new arrangement. "Two Commissioners of trade are named," he wrote to Lord Russell, ". . . of course I have no ground for objecting to appointments made for the protection of the Revenue, should the Chinese government think them necessary. But it is clearly understood that Foreign Ministers have nothing to do with these trade Commissioners . . ." [45]

The original request by Prince Kung and his associates that the

Shanghai imperial commissioner and the superintendent of trade at Tientsin might send reports directly to the Tsungli Yamen was refused by the emperor. As we know, the final decision was that the Yamen would receive reports on ordinary matters from the Shanghai imperial commissioner, the Tientsin superintendent of trade, and other provincial authorities through the Board of Rites, while on vital and confidential matters it would receive only copies sent from the Grand Council of memorials presented to the throne. Consequently, the institutional relations of the Tsungli Yamen with these two offices were not as close as Prince Kung and his associates had originally intended.[46]

In 1862 the Shanghai imperial commissionership became an independent and full-time post with the designation of Superintendent of Trade Affairs (Pan-li t'ung-shang shih-wu ta-ch'en).[47] The next year it was again made a concurrent post of the governor of Kiangsu.[48] In 1866, for the second time, it became a concurrent post of the governor-general of Kiangnan and Kiangsi.[49] This post was sometimes commonly called Nan-yang t'ung-shang ta-ch'en (Superintendent of trade for the southern ports) or simply Nan-yang ta-ch'en. The latter name at some point became its official designation.

The Superintendent of Trade for the Three Ports came to be called from an unascertainable time Pei-yang t'ung-shang ta-ch'en (Superintendent of trade for the northern ports) or simply Pei-yang ta-ch'en.[50] In 1870 the post was made a concurrent one for the governor-general of Chihli. More precisely, it was abolished as a full-time, independent post and its functions, which were now expanded and were to cover "foreign affairs and maritime defense," were transferred on a concurrent basis to the governor-general of Chihli, on whom the status of imperial commissioner was also conferred.[51]

It should be added here that Prince Kung and his associates, in their original six-article memorandum, had suggested that provincial high officials should circulate among themselves documents (memorials presented and edicts received) concerning foreign affairs and that these documents should be kept on file and transmitted to succeeding incumbents. The emperor promptly approved so far as memorials were concerned. This proposal had been offered as a criticism of current practice, whereby foreign affairs were reported only in secret memorials and were not communicated to provincial high officials. Indeed, in extreme cases matters were kept secret even from colleagues stationed in the same place.[52] It cannot be said without further research whether, or to what extent, the proposal was carried out. But it is noteworthy at least as an indication of a conscious effort to bring about a unified and coordinated national conduct of foreign affairs and to accumulate precedents as a common stock of information.

Epilogue

Having broken into Peking by the most flagitious means, you have now a Minister there who is undertaking to remodel that empire. Read his despatches; what is he doing? Constantly advising the government that they must change their mode of administration. They are to become a centralized government.

— *Richard Cobden, May 31, 1863, House of Commons*

We do not wish to revolutionize the country, for I am convinced that we are more likely to get on with a Manchoo than with a purely Chinese dynasty. We do not wish to turn China into a second India, even if that were possible, and we should not be satisfied were any other foreign Government to make the attempt.

— *Sir Frederick Bruce to Harry Parkes*

In the spring of 1861, Bruce and Bourboulon took up residence in Peking. Bourboulon entered the city on March 25 and Bruce on the following day, each accompanied by a small escort.[1] Thus began the regular official intercourse between the Tsungli Yamen and Western legations.[2] The newly appointed Russian minister, Colonel Balliuzek, arrived in Peking on July 8, 1861.[3] Anson Burlingame, the American minister, arrived on July 20, 1862.[4]

As an epilogue to this study of China's conduct of foreign affairs, culminating in the establishment of the Tsungli Yamen, I should like now to make some observations about the political environment in which the Yamen operated, especially in the earlier stage of its forty-year existence.

CONSOLIDATION OF PRINCE KUNG'S POWER

It will be recalled that the Tsungli Yamen started as a Manchu organ. Originally its controlling board consisted of three Manchus

— Prince Kung, Kuei-liang, and Wen-hsiang — in contrast to the Grand Secretariat and the Six Boards, whose controlling boards were statutorily composed of an equal number of Manchus and Chinese, and also in contrast to the Grand Council, in which there were always Manchu and Chinese councillors, although the ratio between the two fluctuated. In April 1861 Heng-ch'i, a Manchu, and Ch'ung-lun, a Chinese bannerman, joined the controlling board of the Yamen. Prince Kung, Kuei-liang, and Wen-hsiang had formed the nucleus of the peace party at the close of the Arrow War. Their influence rested on a delicate equilibrium of political forces, and there was a possibility that the once-warlike antiforeign party might restore its great influence and overwhelm the peace party, if the emperor and his entourage returned to the capital.

The Hsien-feng emperor died in Jehol in August 1861. When he was dying, a council of regents was formed for the succeeding boy emperor. The council was composed of eight "imperial assistants in national affairs" (*tsan-hsiang cheng-wu ta-ch'en*), among whom were Prince I, Prince Cheng, Su-shun, and the four grand councillors then in Jehol. Any edict issued by this organ, however, was to be approved by the two Dowager Empresses, Hsiao-ch'in (the child emperor's mother) and Hsiao-chen (the senior consort). The co-regents, dominated by Prince I's clique, or rather by Su-shun himself, ignored this restraint and came into conflict with the Dowager Empresses. Finally, the empresses conspired with Prince Kung to overthrow the regency. Early in November 1861, when the court had moved back to Peking, the coregents were arrested and deprived of their offices. After a trial Su-shun was beheaded and Princes I and Cheng were forced to commit suicide.

To replace the regency overthrown in this *coup d'état,* a new arrangement was made whereby the two Dowager Empresses acted as coregents and Prince Kung acted as prince counsellor (*i-cheng-wang*). Prince Kung was also made a grand councillor, together with Kuei-liang, Pao-yun, Shen Chao-lin, and Ts'ao Yü-ying, subdirector of the Court of State Ceremonial.[5] At the end of November Pao-yun and Tung Hsun, junior vice-president of the Board of

Revenue, were ordered to concurrent posts at the Tsungli Yamen.[6]
Thus at the end of 1861 the Grand Council consisted of Prince
Kung, Kuei-liang, Wen-hsiang, Pao-yun, Shen Chao-lin (a Chinese)
and Ts'ao Yü-ying (a Chinese); on the controlling board of the
Yamen were Prince Kung, Kuei-liang, Wen-hsiang, Pao-yun,
Ch'ung-lun, Heng-ch'i, and Tung Hsun. In other words, Prince
Kung headed both the Grand Council and the Tsungli Yamen, and
three others, including his close associates Kuei-liang and Wen-
hsiang, also served in both organs. Tung Hsun's appointment meant
that the Yamen now for the first time had a Chinese minister.

In brief, as a result of the *coup d'état* that destroyed Prince I's
clique, Prince Kung and his close associates achieved dominance
over the Grand Council; and the political equilibrium in Peking
upon which their position depended was now consolidated, at least
temporarily. The Tsungli Yamen, which had heretofore had only
one grand councillor (Wen-hsiang), was now largely interlocked
with the Grand Council and thus in a position to operate as a policy-
making body in foreign affairs.

The *coup d'état* really represented a struggle for power among
the top Manchus. Whichever group held the hegemony, its course
of action in the last analysis had to be determined by consideration
for the survival of the dynasty. Thus Prince Kung and his close
associates took over the policy of adaptation to the emergence of new
regional armies organized against the Taipings by such Chinese
scholar-officials as Tseng Kuo-fan; this was the policy previously
promoted by Prince I's clique. Prince I's clique had advocated war
during the Arrow War, probably because it was in a position to be
influenced by the intense war advocacy that existed especially among
indigenous Chinese scholar-officials. As a background to the ascendancy to power of Prince Kung's clique, which had been put in a
position to advocate peace, we probably should not overlook the
fact that some of the once-warlike Chinese scholar-officials, facing
the stern realities, had come to advocate a conciliatory policy in
foreign affairs.[7]

It was the Manchu élite that saved the situation in the Arrow

War by making peace, and it established the Tsungli Yamen. Certainly they were sensitive to any shift in power relations and ready to adapt. But they do not seem to have been very determined to work out a further positive policy for national reconstruction. More or less systematic discussions of "foreign matters" (*yang-wu*) with a specific policy program, however intertwined they were with strenuous efforts to preserve things traditional, came rather from the Chinese scholar-officials, some of whom had been serious war advocates in the Arrow War. The memorial presented after the signing of the Tientsin Treaties by Wang Mao-yin, a war advocate, to which special attention was given above, may be considered one of the earliest treatises of this kind.[8]

BRITISH ATTITUDES

Perhaps we may assume that a primary factor enabling Prince Kung to effect the *coup d'état* was the friendly relations existing between the Tsungli Yamen and the foreign legations. Had there not been Western support for the conciliatory conduct of foreign affairs by Prince Kung and his associates, they might not have dared to take bold measures. They would also have found it difficult to stabilize the political situation after the *coup d'état*.[9]

The British took a favorable view of the political developments in Peking. Soon after the *coup d'état*, Bruce wrote from Peking to Lord Russell, with visible satisfaction tempered by a tone of caution: "The downfall of the violent party, and the language of the decree of arrest [of Prince I and others], amount to a real ratification of the Treaty of which the formal ratification was executed last year. I have suffered too much from the reaction consequent on the disappointment of Utopian expectation, to be inclined to exaggerate the importance of what has taken place, and to talk as if all our difficulties were at an end. But I shall be certainly mortified, *if* the Prince does not administer foreign affairs in a more reasonable and intelligent spirit than has hitherto characterized the proceedings of the Chinese Government."[10] Several months later he wrote to

Russell: ". . . it is no small achievement within twelve months to have created a party inclined to and believing in the possibility of friendly intercourse, to have effectually aided that party to power. To have established satisfactory relations at Peking and become in some degree the advisers of a government with which 18 months since we were at war."[11]

In a debate on China in the House of Commons on March 18, 1862, A. H. Layard, undersecretary for foreign affairs, delivered a shatteringly critical speech on the Taipings, whom he considered "utterly unable to organize any adequate system of administration." Referring to the current Peking political scene, he stated in the same speech: "Within a very short time a great change had taken place; a *coup d'état* had been effected which led to a change of Ministers, . . . Prince Kung and the two Empresses had called together a new Ministry and had inaugurated a new policy; for the first time a Chinese Government had admitted the rights of foreigners, and consented to treat with them as equals."[12] Apparently based, at least in part, on such an estimate of the political situation in China, the China policy of the Palmerston cabinet moved in the course of 1862 from one of neutrality to one of positive, though decidedly limited, intervention in China's civil war.[13]

At the time of the *coup d'état* Anglo-French troops were still in Tientsin. The presence of these troops was a pillar of support to Prince Kung against his political opponents. It also sustained the weakened authority of the government in North China where disturbances were occurring to a threatening degree.[14] The French troops were evacuated from North China in November 1861, excepting for a small detachment in Taku.[15] The British troops withdrew in May 1862, also leaving behind in Taku a small detachment.[16] Prior to the British withdrawal, British officers had given military instruction in Tientsin to selected Ch'ing troops.[17] It was not until 1865 that the Anglo-French troops finally withdrew from Taku.[18]

We know that it was the British authorities who had been most insistent in demanding permanent diplomatic residence in Peking, hoping among other things that with a minister resident in Peking and with the British thus in a position directly to influence the Peking government, the latter would be persuaded to apply pressure upon the provincial and local authorities so that the observance of treaty obligations might be enforced. The dispatches Frederick Bruce sent home from Peking revealed his persistent expectations, and recurrent disappointments, about the role to be played by Prince Kung and his associates in the Tsungli Yamen.

For instance, in a dispatch of June 23, 1861, he described the atmosphere among the top Peking officials as follows: "The same want of energy and incapacity to carry out comprehensive plans, and the same inability to centralize the resources of the Government and direct them to one end, strike me at Peking [as in the provinces]. Attention here is chiefly directed to the movements of the Shan-tung insurgents, and the spirits of the Imperial authorities are depressed or raised according to the news received of their progress. The course of the far more formidable insurrection in the South is treated with comparative indifference." [19] In a dispatch dated May 13, 1862, he pointed out that the influence of Prince Kung was still rather weak even after the *coup détat*: ". . . the obstacles to a more liberal policy in China have by no means disappeared with the fall of Su-shun and his colleagues. There is still a large party wedded to the ancient traditions of China, and their influence is strong in the Provinces. The action of the imperial Government is but feeble in remote districts, and the position of the Prince of Kung is necessarily the more critical on account of the minority [of the emperor]." [20] The following passage from a dispatch of June 16, 1862, may be considered supplementary to the above statement: "There are parties in China as well as in other countries, and those averse to foreigners' ways hope that the majority of the young Emperor will transfer power to the hands of the Prince's opponents. To defeat these reactionary views, I look rather to connecting visibly the interests of China with the adoption of European improvements than to violent measures against officers of high position who still cling to the traditions of the Empire. Unwearied patience and pertinacity will gradually produce important results." [21]

Regarding the evacuation, already effected, of the British troops from Canton, Tientsin, and the "Miatow" (Miao-tao) Islands, Bruce stated in a dispatch dated July 24, 1862: "Had this Government been strong, I should not have concurred in the policy of abandoning these places, for the Chinese consider that the stipulations of the Treaties were imposed by force, and they would have had no scruple in resisting their exercise at first, had they hoped to do so with success. But the existence of the insurrection and the want of funds prevented any move on the part of the anti-foreign party, and I trust by a friendly and conciliatory attitude so to strengthen the Peace Party, as to render it impossible for China hereafter to revert to the old policy of isolation." [22]

Taking a firm stand against a British consul calling in gunboats to get redress in a case of breach of treaty in a treaty port, Bruce argued in a dispatch of September 8, 1862: "Our true policy is to give weight and authority to the Foreign Board [the Tsungli Yamen], by compelling it to deal with foreign questions and to punish, if necessary, officials who violate Treaties, and thus to teach the latter to tremble when a consul threatens to bring a matter under the notice of the Minister at Peking. In this way, the Foreign Board will come to be looked upon as a powerful Department in the administration of the empire; and the fact that the Prince of Kung is at its head is favourable to giving it the prestige, in the eyes of Local Governors, which is necessary to render it effectual for the purposes designed." [23] (This approach to treaty enforcement, it should be pointed out, indicates a subtle but remarkable change in Bruce's thinking since the Arrow War period. As of April 1860 he had still been convinced of the importance of gunboat diplomacy on the seaboard, and he had looked forward to the use of direct pressure on Peking via a resident diplomat as a supplement to the gunboat approach in cases of breach of treaty in the interior, where foreign warships could not penetrate.) [24]

The British government was not the only one to support the Ch'ing central government under Prince Kung's leadership. In the 1860's the so-called Cooperative Policy was pursued by the major powers in Peking: Britain, the United States, France, and Russia cooperated with one another and with China. The four powers made a joint effort to secure treaty enforcement not by force but through diplomatic pressure exerted upon the Peking government, and they also tried to induce Peking to take steps toward the gradual modernization of China.[25] Furthermore, Robert Hart, inspector general of the Maritime Customs, gave strong support to the Tsungli Yamen and acted as political advisor to Prince Kung. Under its foreign inspectorate, the Maritime Customs was able to secure a generous amount of revenue for the central government, a situation that was instrumental in strengthening the position of Prince Kung and the Peking government and at the same time fitted in beautifully with the interests of Britain.[26]

THE TSUNGLI YAMEN'S LEADERSHIP
AND ITS DECLINE

The Tsungli Yamen did not function as effectively as the British authorities had hoped. Nevertheless, considering the political environment in which it operated, the Yamen did fulfill its function as central organ for the conduct of China's foreign affairs — at least in its earlier phase.[27]

Of the initial trio in command of the Yamen, the astute old Kueiliang passed away in July 1862 at the age of 78 *sui*. Prince Kung, who does not seem to have been a man of great intellect or ability, was yet sufficiently capable to be more than a mere figurehead and to exercise a certain amount of leadership. It was Wen-hsiang who was really the pivotal figure in the 1860's not only in the Tsungli Yamen but also in the Grand Council. "The working man of the F. O. [the Tsungli Yamen] is Wensiang; he is an exceedingly shrewd, intelligent, and, as far as Chinese nature permits it, honest man."[28] Thus wrote Robert Hart in 1861. This is but one of the almost unanimously favorable appraisals by Western observers of Wen-hsiang's ability, intellect, and character.[29]

There seems to be no doubt that Wen-hsiang was a diligent, upright, and incorruptible hard worker. Placed in a position to effectuate a power-balancing integration of conflicting views and influences, he seems to have combined the quality of a skilled politician, sensitive to any change in power relations, with the quality of a solid policy-maker, oriented to positive and reformative programs. The first was a Manchu rather than a Chinese quality (Kuei-liang was a typical example); the second was more evident among the indigenous Chinese scholar-officials.

With the final suppression of the Taiping Rebellion in 1864, the Ch'ing government's position was certainly reconsolidated to some extent. At the same time, however, the political climate underwent a delicate change. "No sooner did the Chinese feel themselves independent of foreigners, after the Taiping Rebellion had been suppressed by their aid," complained foreign merchants in Shanghai, "than the native officials began steadily, though insidiously, to advocate retrogressive views, which . . . there has been a disposition in influential quarters to endorse and to uphold." [30] Since a primary factor sustaining the influence of the Tsungli Yamen had been the expediency of maintaining friendly relations with Western powers as a means of coping with the domestic crisis, it may be said that the achievement of internal peace served to weaken the position of the Tsungli Yamen. Wen-hsiang, whom Thomas Wade referred to in 1867 as "a confirmed coward," [31] must now have been in a more difficult position than ever. For one thing, the antiforeignism of the scholar-officials, which had seemingly dwindled after the *coup d'état* of 1861, had in fact been regaining strength.[32] Anson Burlingame had already observed late in 1862: "There is a strong antiforeign party looking for some large concession to foreigners, as an opportunity of overthrowing the present government, which is friendly to progress, and in need of all our support." [33]

After the fall of the Taipings, the people like Tseng Kuo-fan, Li Hung-chang, and Tso Tsung-t'ang, who had contributed greatly toward the conclusion of the civil war, gained remarkably in political influence, and the tendency toward regionalism gradually gathered momentum. In 1870 Li Hung-chang, who held a large personal army, was appointed governor-general of Chihli with the concurrent post of superintendent of trade for the northern ports. In this position he came into rivalry with the Tsungli Yamen, and eventually he became the real center for China's conduct of foreign affairs.

In 1876, Wen-hsiang died. This meant the loss to the Tsungli Yamen of the mainstay of its influence, but it is probable that by this time the Yamen had already passed the zenith of its effectiveness.[34]

Sources of the Mottoes

The sources of the quotations used at the beginning of each chapter are as follows:

I A. Michie, *The Englishman in China* (Edinburgh and London, 1900), II, 221–222; the source for the motto on p. 42 is given in the end notes.

II Wade to Elgin, Pa-li-chiau. Spetember 23, 1860, *PP: Affairs in China,* p. 169

III IWSM:HF, 38:3; Lay to Bruce, confidential, April 27, 1860, in Bruce to Russell, private, secret and confidential, April 28, 1860, P.R.O. 30/22/49

IV *Russkii Kitai* (Port Arthur, 1902), pp. 38–39

V D. F. Rennie, *Peking and the Pekingese* (London, 1865), II, 77

VI D. F. Rennie, *The British Arms in North China and Japan* (London, 1864), p. 184

VII Bruce to Russell, No. 14, Tientsin, March 12, 1861, FO 17/350; *North China Herald,* March 2, 1861

Epilogue

Hansard's Parliamentary Debates, Third Series, 175:922; Bruce to Parkes, private, Jan. 2, 1864, Elgin Archives, Private Correspondence

CSK   *Ch'ing-shih k̠ao* (Draft history of the Ch'ing dynasty), comps. Chao Erh-hsun *et al.* (photolithographic ed. by Lien-ho shu-tien, 1942).

CSL   *Ta-Ch'ing li-ch'ao shih-lu* (or *Ch'ing shih-lu*) (Veritable records of successive reigns of the Ch'ing dynasty; photo-offset reproduction, Tokyo, 1937–38). Series for the reigns of Hsuan-tsung (Tao-kuang emperor), Wen-tsung (Hsien-feng emperor), Mu-tsung (T'ung-chih emperor).

FO 17   Foreign Office, General Correspondence, China. Filed in the Public Record Office, London.

FO 65   Foreign Office, General Correspondence, Russia. Filed in the Public Record Office, London.

FO *Affairs in China, Confidential (1859)*: *Correspondence Relating to Affairs in China, March to November 1859. Confidential. Printed for the Use of the Foreign Office, Nov. 14, 1859.*

FO *Affairs in China, Confidential (1861)*: *Correspondence Respecting Affairs in China, 1859–61. Confidential. Printed for the Use of the Foreign Office, Jan. 18, 1861.*

IWSM   *Ch'ou-pan i-wu shih-mo* (A complete account of the management of barbarian affairs; photolithographic reproduction, Peking, 1930). Tao-kuang period 1836–50, 80 *chüan*, presented to the emperor 1856; Hsien-feng period 1851–61, 80 *chüan*, presented 1867; T'ung-chih period 1861–74, 100 *chüan*, presented 1880.

PLFC   Pan-li fu-chü tang-an (Documents on the management of peace-making; no date of compilation, no pagination). For subdivisions see Bibliography, Note on Archival Sources.

PP *Affairs in China: Parliamentary Papers*, No. 66 (2754), *Correspondence Respecting Affairs in China, 1859–60.*

PP *Corr. with Bruce: Parliamentary Papers*, No. 69 (2587), *Correspondence with Mr. Bruce, Her Majesty's Envoy Extraordinary and Minister Plenipotentiary in China.*

PP *Elgin's Missions: Parliamentary Papers*, No. 33 (2571), *Correspondence Relative to the Earl of Elgin's Special Missions to China and Japan, 1857 to 1859.*

Reed Corr.: Senate Executive Documents, 36th Congress, 1st Session, No. 30.

SKHT   Ssu-kuo hsin-tang (New files concerning the four powers), deposited at the Institute of Modern History, Academia Sinica, Taipei, Taiwan. For subdivisions see Bibliography, Note on Archival Sources.

Notes

Notes to Introduction: Ch'ing Management of Foreign Relations
Prior to the Arrow War

1. This book has been developed from four articles published previously by me in Japanese: (1) " 'Sōrigamon' setsuritsu no haikei," *Kokusaihō gaikō zasshi*, 51.4:360–402 (Aug. 1952); *ibid.*, 51.5:506–541 (Oct. 1952); *ibid.*, 52.3:89–109 (June 1953). (2) "Tenshin jōyaku (1858-nen) chōin go ni okeru Shinkoku gaisei kikō no dōyō — kinsa daijin no Shanhai ichū kara Beikoku kōshi Wōdo no nyūkyō made," *ibid.*, 55.6:595–616 (Mar. 1957); *ibid.*, 56.1:35–69 (Apr. 1957). (3) "Sōrigamon no setsuritsu katei," in Kindai Chūgoku Kenkyū Iinkai, ed., *Kindai Chūgoku kenkyū*, No. 1:1–105 (Tokyo, 1958). (4) "Pekin ni okeru tai-Ro kōshō kikō no hembō — Tenshin jōyaku (1858-nen) chōin kara 1860-nen 5-gatsu made," *ibid.*, No. 3:1–67 (Tokyo, 1959).

2. For a basic study of the Ch'ing tributary system, see John K. Fairbank and S. Y. Teng, "On the Ch'ing Tributary System," *Harvard Journal of Asiatic Studies*, 6.2:135–246 (June 1941); see also J. K. Fairbank, "Tributary Trade and China's Relations with the West," *Far Eastern Quarterly*, 1.2:129–149 (Feb. 1942).

3. Under "Reception Department of the Board of Rites," in *chüan* 31 of *Chia-ch'ing hui-tien* (1818), there are listed as tributary states Korea, Liu-ch'iu, Annam, Laos, Siam, Sulu, Holland, Burma, and Western Ocean (Hsi-yang). A note inserted under "Western Ocean" enumerates as "the countries of the Western Ocean" Portugal, the Papacy, and England. In short, all the Western powers that had sent delegations to Peking were labeled tributary states, whether or not the kowtow had been performed on these visits. This source also states that "the remaining countries have commercial relations [with China]," and a note lists France, Sweden, and Denmark as "trading countries" (*hu-shih chu-kuo*) along with Japan and various places in Southeast Asia. See also Fairbank and Teng, "Ch'ing Tributary System," pp. 182–190.

4. See *Chia-ch'ing hui-tien, chüan* 52, under "Department of Outer Mongols of the Court of Dependencies." According to the regulations, there were two imperial agents at Urga, but there seems actually to have been one imperial agent and one assistant imperial agent. See *Shinkoku gyōseihō*, Rinji Taiwan Kyūkan Chōsakai (Tokyo and Kobe, 1910–1914), Vol. 1 (revised and reissued in 1914), Part 2, p. 108; H. S. Brunnert and V. V. Hagelstrom, *Present Day Political Organization of China*, trans. from the Russian by A. Beltchenko and E. E. Moran (Shanghai, 1912), p. 453. In translating the names of Chinese offices and titles, I have, so far as possible, used the English

250 Notes to Introduction

equivalents given in Brunnert and Hagelstrom. A primary exception is Li-fan-yuan, for which I have used the term Court of Dependencies. During the Ming the tribes in the north and west were also under the jurisdiction of the Board of Rites. In the Ch'ing a separate government organ was established to deal with them. The technique of control, however, was that of the ancient tributary system. See Fairbank and Teng, "Ch'ing Tributary System," pp. 158–163, 177.

5. On the Russian Hostel, see *Chia-ch'ing hui-tien shih-li, chüan* 751, under "Russian Hostel," in the section for the Court of Dependencies; *Chia-ch'ing hui-tien, chüan* 52, under "Department of Outer Mongols of the Court of Dependencies"; Article 5 of the Kiakhta Treaty of 1727. (Unless otherwise indicated, treaty texts are here cited or quoted throughout from *Treaties, Conventions, etc., between China and Foreign States*, 2nd ed. [Statistical Department of the Inspectorate General of Customs, 1917]). See also Ho Ch'iu-t'ao, "E-lo-ssu-kuan k'ao," in his *Shuo-fang pei-sheng*. For a more detailed discussion of the institutional arrangement for Sino-Russian relations in this period, see S. M. Meng, *The Tsungli Yamen: Its Organization and Functions* (Cambridge, Mass., 1962), pp. 9–11, 110–111; Meng Ssu-ming, "The E-lo-ssu kuan (Russian Hostel) in Peking," *Harvard Journal of Asiatic Studies*, 23:19–46 (1961); Hoo Chi-tsai, *Les bases conventionelles des relations modernes entre la Chine et la Russie* (Paris, 1918), pp. 32ff; Albert Parry, "Russian (Greek Orthodox) Missionaries in China, 1689–1917: Their Cultural, Political, and Economic Role" (Ph.D. thesis, University of Chicago, 1938). See also Yano Jin'ichi, "Pekin no Rokoku kōshikan ni tsuite," *Geimon*, 6.9:884–897 (September, 1915); 6.10:1065–1091 (October, 1915).

6. For regulations governing the treatment of a tribute envoy, see *Chia-ch'ing hui-tien, chüan* 31, "Reception Department of the Board of Rites." A Russian envoy was also supposed to perform the kowtow, according to an "imperial ruling given in the thirty-second year of K'ang-hsi after the question had been referred for deliberation to the proper authorities" (see *Chia-ch'ing hui-tien shih-li, chüan* 746, "Trade with Russia"). On the problem of the kowtow in the Macartney mission, see E. H. Pritchard, "The Kotow in the Macartney Embassy to China 1793," *Far Eastern Quarterly*, 2.2:163–203 (Feb. 1943). Pritchard includes a table of Western missions to China, 1520–1840, in which a documented statement for each mission reaching the capital tells whether or not the kowtow was performed. See also Yano Jin'ichi, *Shina kindai gaikoku kankei kenkyū* (Kyoto, 1928), pp. 151–180; Fairbank and Teng, "Ch'ing Tributary System," pp. 138–139.

7. IWSM:TK, 61:25–26. I have not used the letter *b* when referring to the second side of a Chinese page. Accordingly, "35," for instance, may mean the first or the second side, or both sides, of page 35.

8. *Ibid.*, 66:1–2.

9. *Ibid.*, 70:8–9.

10. CSK, *pen-chi*, under Tao-kuang, 24th year.

11. IWSM:TK, 71:18–19.

12. *Ibid.*, 78:36; CSL:HT, 456:6; CSL:WT, 67:11, 80:18.

13. Thus it is interesting to note that the establishment of this practice was apparently reflected in the appearance in treaty clauses in 1844 of the following titles: the Sino-American Treaty of Wang-hea in 1844 mentioned "the Imperial Commissioner charged with the superintendence of the concerns of Foreign nations with China" (Article 31; the Chinese text reads *Chung-kuo pan-li wai-kuo shih-wu chih ch'in-ch'ai ta-ch'en*); the Sino-French Treaty of Whampoa, signed later in the same year, mentioned "[le] Surintendant des cinq ports" (Article 4; the Chinese text reads *tsung-li wu-k'ou ta-ch'en*), and "[le] Surintendant des cinq ports chargé de la direction des relations extérieures de la Chine" (Article 34; the Chinese text reads *"pan-li wu-k'ou chi wai-kuo shih-wu ta-ch'en"*).

14. For a recent discussion of the imperial commissionership, see J. K. Fairbank, *Trade and Diplomacy on the China Coast: The Opening of the Treaty Ports 1842–1854* (Cambridge, Mass., 1953), I, 96–98. Some aspects of the actual operation of the Canton commissionership are examined in Banno Masataka, "Gaikō kōshō ni okeru Shimmatsu kanjin no kōdō yōshiki: 1854-nen no jōyaku kaisei kōshō o chūshin to suru ichikōsatsu," *Kokusaihō gaikō zasshi*, 48.4:502–540 (Oct. 1949); 48.6:703–737 (Dec. 1949).

15. J. K. Fairbank and S. Y. Teng, "On the Transmission of Ch'ing Documents," *Harvard Journal of Asiatic Studies*, 4.1:43–44 (May 1939).

16. H. B. Morse, *The International Relations of the Chinese Empire* (Shanghai, 1910, 1918), I, 510.

17. A term used by Horatio Nelson Lay in commenting on the general system of stationing an imperial commissioner at a treaty port. Lay to Bruce, confidential, April 27, 1860, in Bruce to Russell, private, secret and confidential, April 28, 1860, P.R.O. 30/22/49. See also H. N. Lay, *Our Interests in China. A Letter to the Right Hon. Earl Russell, K. G., Her Majesty's Principal Secretary of State for Foreign Affairs* (London, 1864), pp. 55, 70.

18. For a full discussion, based on a case study, of the behavior pattern toward Peking of the mandarins on the coast who were charged with foreign contact, see Banno, "Gaikō kōshō . . . kōdō yōshiki," Part 2, pp. 713–737.

19. Banno Masataka, "Ahen sensō go ni okeru saikeikoku taigū no mondai," *Tōyō bunka kenkyū*, 6:32–41 (Oct. 1947).

20. Yano Jin'ichi, *Kindai Shina ron* (Tokyo and Kyoto, 1923), pp. 208–213. CSK, *lieh-chuan* (biographies), No. 150 (Mu-chang-a); No. 157 (Ch'i-ying); No. 172 (Ch'i Chün-tsao). See also Arthur W. Hummel, ed., *Eminent Chinese of the Ch'ing Period* (Washington, D.C., 1943, 1944), I, 125–126, 130–134, 582–583.

21. IWSM:HF, 1:9–26, 28–31, 2:1–3; W. C. Costin, *Great Britain and China 1833–1860* (Oxford, 1937), pp. 142–143; Fairbank, *Trade and Diplomacy*, I, 376–379; II, 33–34. Palmerston's letter was originally to have been addressed to "the Minister for Foreign Affairs at Peking." As there was no such official in Peking, Bonham addressed the letter to Mu-chang-a and Ch'-ying. (See Costin, p. 142; Morse, *International Relations*, I, 398.)

22. IWSM:HF, 1:13 (edict of May 29, 1850); *ibid.*, 1:15–16 (communication in reply to Lu Chien-ying from Mu-chang-a and Ch'i-ying).

23. See Fairbank, *Trade and Diplomacy*, II, 34 (note 32).

24. On the case in 1858, see IWSM:HF, 18:16–35; *PP: Elgin's Missions,* pp. 242 (footnote), 257, 266, 298, 325, 327; *Reed Corr.*, pp. 221–222, 230–231, 233, 236, 245–246, 254–255, 264–265; Henri Cordier, *L'expédition de Chine de 1857–58. Histoire Diplomatique. Notes et Documents* (Paris, 1905), pp. 319, 325, 328–330.

On the case in 1860, see IWSM:HF, 49:12–18, 20, 31–32; *PP: Affairs in China,* pp. 41–43, 52–54; Henri Cordier, *L'expédition de Chine de 1860. Histoire Diplomatique. Notes et Documents* (Paris, 1906), pp. 161–164, 166–167. On this occasion, the governor-general in question also had the status of imperial commissioner for foreign affairs (the so-called imperial commissioner at Shanghai).

25. T. F. Tsiang, "Notes and Suggestions: 1, Origins of the Tsungli Yamen," *Chinese Social and Political Science Review,* 15.1:92 (Apr. 1931).

26. Banno, "Gaikō kōshō . . . kōdō yōshiki," Part 1, pp. 704–711.

Notes to Chapter I. *The Arrow War: Western Demands for Diplomatic Representation in Peking*

1. For a general account of the Arrow War, standard works by Morse, Costin, Cordier, and Tyler Dennett should be consulted. For an excellent recent study, see John F. Cady, *The Roots of French Imperialism in Eastern Asia* (Ithaca, New York, 1954).

2. Theodore Walrond, ed., *Letters and Journals of James, Eighth Earl of Elgin* (London, 1872), pp. 209, 213. On his way to China in the 1860 expedition, Elgin said to Gros, "If all the business should drag on, it would be rather better to let the people of Nanking triumph and thus make an end. This war is unpopular in our country, it must be ceased within this year." (Gros to Thouvenel, May 25, 1860, P. S., May 26, 1860, in Cordier, *L'expedition, 1860,* p. 197; cf. *ibid.*, p. 200.) This remark piqued Gros. In October of the same year, when Elgin advocated strong measures of revenge for the atrocious murder of English and French prisoners, Gros worried about the possible collapse of the Ch'ing dynasty. And remembering Elgin's earlier remark, he suspected that Elgin might have received secret instructions ordering, or at least permitting, the overthrow of the dynasty. (Gros to Thouvenel, private letter, Oct. 19, 1860, in *ibid.*, pp. 397–398. Cf. Gros to Thouvenel, Oct. 19, 1860, *ibid.*, p. 402; Gros to Thouvenel, Oct. 26, 1860, *ibid.*, pp. 443–444; Costin, p. 339.)

3. Nathan A. Pelcovits, *Old China Hands and the Foreign Office* (New York, 1948), pp. 1–31. For a recent discussion of the Mitchell Report, see Etō Shinkichi, "Mitcheru hōkoku ni tsuite," *Tōyō bunka,* 20:25–40 (Jan. 1956).

4. See Cady, pp. 294–296.

5. Clarendon to Elgin, Apr. 20, 1857, *PP: Elgin's Missions,* pp. 1–4.

Western Demands for Representation   253

There are also two supplementary letters of instruction with the same date in *ibid.*, pp. 4–7; one discusses in detail the trade facilities to be demanded, the other covers negotiations with Japan. Diplomatic representation in Peking was a perennial British official demand dating back to the abortive mission in 1787–1788 of Lieutenant-Colonel Cathcart, who died en route to China. The expedition to Tientsin in 1759 of James Flint, an agent of the British East India Company, to deliver a memorial for the emperor, may be considered the earliest British effort at direct contact with Peking. See Cathcart's instructions, dated Nov. 30, 1787, in H. B. Morse, *The Chronicles of the East India Company Trading to China 1633–1834* (Oxford, 1926–1929), II, 160–167. On Flint's expedition, see *ibid.*, I, 298–299, 301–305; V, 68, 75, 80–84.

6. Cordier, *L'expédition, 1857–58*, pp. 145–151.

7. Tyler Dennett, *Americans in Eastern Asia* (New York, 1922), pp. 298–307.

8. Cass to Reed, May 30, 1857, *Reed Corr.*, pp. 6–11.

9. Cordier, *L'expédition, 1857–58*, pp. 168–170. The Russian foreign minister told the British ambassador that "he was not prepared to determine at present whether it would be better to establish resident ministers or send Envoys from time to time, but he thought that the Russian Government would probably not think it necessary to appoint a Resident Minister" (Wodehouse to Clarendon, No. 263, June 5, 1857, FO 65/495.)

10. On the background of Putiatin's mission, see A. Popov, "Tsarskaia diplomatiia v epokhu Taipinskogo vosstaniia," *Krasnyi Arkhiv*, 21:182–199 (1927).

11. Cady, p. 196. In the fall of 1860, Ignat'ev, Russian minister to China, felt that the permanent residence of other Western ministers in Peking would be incompatible with Russian interests. A British representative, for instance, would have overwhelming influence there because of British wealth, connections, and military power. Ignat'ev thus maneuvered strenuously, but vainly to prevent the materialization of permanent residence. (Baron A. Buksgevden, *Russkii Kitai: Ocherki diplomaticheskikh snoshenii Rossii s Kitaem, I, Pekinskii dogovor, 1860 g.* [Port Arthur, 1902], pp. 172–175, 214–215, 222, 225–228.)

12. Elgin to Malmesbury, July 12, 1858, *PP: Elgin's Missions*, p. 346.

13. Reed to Cass, June 30, 1858, *Reed Corr.*, p. 352.

14. Reed to Cass, Official, No. 23, June 30, 1858, Diplomatic Dispatches, China (U.S. Department of State), Vol. 17. This is the dispatch cited in note 13 but in its original, unexpurgated version. S. Wells Williams, secretary and interpreter to the American legation to China, wrote on July 22, 1858: "By and by, when foreign Ministers live at Peking, how easy it will be for them to mix themselves up in all these intrigues, take parties [sic] in Court and Cabinet cabals, and thus intermeddle to the disorder of China!" (F. W. Williams, ed., "The Journal of S. Wells Williams, L.L.D. . . . ," *Journal of the North-China Branch of the Royal Asiatic Society*, 42:89 [1911]).

15. Reed to Cass, Oct. 21, 1858, *Reed Corr.*, pp. 438–441. Reed also says, "They [these documents] are certainly the most painful revelation of the

mendacity and treacherous habits of the high officials of this empire yet given to the world; they cannot be read without contemptuous resentment, and I have no such confidence in my own equanimity and self-control as to determine what might have been my inclination before and after the fall of the Taku forts had the contents of these papers been known to me."

16. R. Alcock, "Memorandum on suggested Heads of a new Treaty," *PP: Elgin's Missions*, pp. 54–61.

17. Cf. Reed to Cass, July 29, 1858, *Reed Corr.*, p. 383.

18. Bruce to Russell, Apr. 7, 1860, *PP: Affair in China*, pp. 37–39. H. N. Lay's comment in 1864: "The trade of the ports was beyond the reach of interference; they were accessible to our ships of war, and therefore secure. Not so the trade in the interior; that would need to be protected by other means, and mainly through the moral influence attained by our Minister at Pekin" (*Our Interests in China*, p. 49).

19. Laurence Oliphant, *Narrative of the Earl of Elgin's Mission to China and Japan in the Years 1857, '58, '59*, 2nd ed. (Edinburgh and London, 1860), I, 413–414.

"The real nature of the Chinese government is a mixture of despotism and democracy, *which is difficult to explain to those who have not seen its actual workings*" (italics mine). Reed to Cass, Sept. 4, 1858, *Reed Corr.*, pp. 429ff. In this report, Reed laid stress on the decentralized character of China's polity.

20. Bruce to Russell, Apr. 7, 1860, *PP: Affairs in China*, pp. 37–39.

21. *Hansard's Parliamentary Debates*, Third Series, Vol. 161, Cols. 577–578. Lay in 1864: "In a country despotically ruled as China is, there is but one source of authority, the throne, where sits the 'Father of the people,' the 'Son of Heaven,' who is worshiped with Divine honours. The Emperor alone permits, or interdicts. Officials and people await his mandate in obedient attitudes: no spontaneity of thought or action on their part is possible. Hence we often see what we have been accustomed to look upon as deep-seated hostility, transmuted as by magic upon a nod from Pekin, into hearty goodwill" (*Our Interests in China*, pp. 57–58).

22. Oliphant, I, 413. D. B. Robertson, British consul at Shanghai, in a memorandum submitted to Elgin on Jan. 19, 1858: ". . . an arbitrary Government, the chief support of which is prestige . . ." (*PP: Elgin's Missions*, p. 168).

Reed, in a report to Cass dated Feb. 13, 1858: "the pleasure of the Emperor . . . , which will be obeyed as heretofore by all, officials and others, with the strange sort of superstitious loyalty which characterizes this nation" (*Reed Corr.*, p. 125).

To Charles Elliot, in May 1840, the Chinese government was "dependent upon feeling, and the whole fabric would probably fall to pieces under the effect of a blow, notorious to the people" (to Palmerston, May 20, 1840, quoted in Costin, p. 78).

23. I originally owed this point to the insight of the late Professor Harley F. MacNair: "Rarely had China had anything approaching truly centralized

government. The people and the local officials have always opposed such. This was a fact that westerners and their governments were especially slow to appreciate in the nineteenth century. In general, the West pictured old China as an absolute monarchy; it held that all that was necessary was to bring pressure to bear on the imperial government in order to get what it wanted. This accounts largely for the determination of the British government in 1858 and 1860 to obtain the right of residence at Peking for its envoy — a right which the other powers insisted upon as soon as England had won it" (*China in Revolution: An Analysis of Politics and Militarism under the Republic* [Chicago, 1931], pp. 20–21). See also Costin, pp. 12ff.

In contrast we may notice, as a more realistic but exceptional observation, a report by S. W. Williams supplementing Reed's report cited above in note 19, in which he stresses the importance of "a middle class of *literati* and gentry" in China's politics (Williams to Cass, Jan. 28, 1859, *Reed Corr.*, pp. 545–547). He emphasizes the resistance of this group to the officials, and their influence on local politics. But he does not say much about how the literati and gentry controlled the common people.

Sir John Bowring, governor of Hong Kong, also pointed out that the power of the emperor was far from unlimited, and he called attention to instances in which pressure was exerted upon the authorities by the local elders and literati (Bowring to Clarendon, May 5, 1852, quoted in Costin, p. 18; Bowring to Clarendon, Nov. 5, 1855, quoted in Costin, pp. 19–20).

24. Elgin to Clarendon, July 9, 1857, *PP: Elgin's Mission,* pp. 19–22.

25. Bruce to Alston, private, Dec. 31, 1860, FO 17/339. See also Costin, pp. 341–342.

26. Costin, pp. 246–247, 345. The view, rejected by Bruce, that China should be "treated as a congeries of separate States" was originally expressed in an article on China in the *Abeille du Nord* of St. Petersburg. This view, Bruce felt, could lead to "a result no doubt very favorable to nations, who seek to aggrandize themselves territorially at her expense." This criticism by Bruce was omitted when his report was published in *PP: Affairs in China,* pp. 37–39 (Bruce to Russell, Apr. 7, 1860). Cf. Bruce to Russell, No. 89, Apr. 7, 1860, FO 17/337.

27. Cf. Reed to Cass, June 30, 1858, *Reed Corr.,* p. 351.

28. *PP: Elgin's Missions,* pp. 324–331, 336–339.

29. Extracts from a journal kept in Peking during the year 1858, trans. from the *Morskoi Sbornik* (Naval magazine) for Sept. 1860, in Erskine to Russell, No. 100, Oct. 7, 1860, FO 65/554. On the authorship of the journal, see below, Chap. IV, note 78.

30. Lay's note of the conversation between him and Kuei-liang, in *PP: Elgin's Missions,* p. 327. Lay, in a pamphlet written in 1893, also recalls an instance of a personal appeal made to him in a private interview at Tientsin by one of the Ch'ing commissioners; the context of the narrative seems to indicate that this instance occurred on a different occasion, later than June 7 (*Note on the Opium Question, and Brief Survey of Our Relations with China* [London, 1893], p .12).

31. Elgin to Malmesbury, No. 142, July 5, 1858, FO 17/289; Cordier, *L'expédition, 1857–58,* pp. 436–438; Reed to Cass, Official No. 23, June 30, 1858, Diplomatic Dispatches, China, Vol. 17. Cf. Williams, "Journal," pp. 76–79; Walrond, p. 253; W. A. P. Martin, *A Cycle of Cathay,* 3rd ed. (New York, 1900), pp. 186–188.

32. Lay, *Note on the Opium Question,* p. 11.

33. Walrond, pp. 252–253. According to Mr. Jack Gerson of the University of Toronto, who has checked the original letter in the archives of Elgin's family estate in Scotland, the "fellow-countrymen" reads "fellow creatures" in the original.

34. *Ibid.,* pp. 253–254.

35. Hansard, 156:1463. Cf. Clarendon to Elgin, Apr. 20, 1857, *PP: Elgin's Missions,* pp. 1–4.

36. Cady, pp. 194–195, 200–201, 204–205. See also Cordier, *L'expédition, 1857–58,* p. 322; Malmesbury to Elgin, Mar. 25, 1858, *PP: Elgin's Missions,* p. 166; Malmesbury to Elgin, Sept. 25, 1858, *ibid.,* p. 361.

37. Malmesbury to Elgin, No. 51, Sept. 25, 1858, FO 17/284. This passage was omitted when the document was published in *PP: Elgin's Missions,* p. 361. For a further discussion of the British attitudes on the resident minister issue on three different levels — Foreign Office, Elgin, and Lay — see Immanuel C. Y. Hsü, *China's Entrance into the Family of Nations: The Diplomatic Phase, 1858–1880* (Cambridge, Mass., 1960), pp. 24–26, 46–49, 77, 83–88, 95–98, 105.

38. Reed to Tan, May 11, 1858, *Reed Corr.,* pp. 315–316; Tan and others to Reed, May 13, 1858, *ibid.,* pp. 316–317.

39. Cordier, *L'expédition, 1857–58,* pp. 364–365; *Reed Corr.,* pp. 318–321; Williams, "Journal," pp. 30–31, 33.

40. IWSM:HF, 21:3, 10–11, 17–18, 34–35.

41. *Ibid.,* 22:8–9. See also another memorial from the same officials, received on the same day (*ibid.,* 22:11). All translations of Chinese documents herein are my own, but I should like to register my gratitude especially to Professor Earl Swisher for his *China's Management of the American Barbarians: A Study of Sino-American Relations, 1841–1861, with Documents* (New Haven, 1953), which contains translations of 544 documents from IWSM. I have always benefited by consulting his translations.

42. *Ibid.,* 22:9–10.

43. *Ibid.,* 22:12–13.

44. *Ibid.,* 24:27–28, 35, 37–38; 25:3–4, 16–17, 27–28, 36–38; 26:6–7, 24–25, 28–29; 26:1–6.

45. *Ibid.,* 27:1–6.

46. *Ibid.,* 28:8. The concessions made on June 11 had marked an important turning point in the Sino-British Tientsin negotiations. Kuei-liang and Hua-sha-na first reported this event briefly in a memorial received on June 14 (*ibid.,* 25:16–17), and gave a detailed account of it later in a memorial received on June 20 (*ibid.,* 25:36–38). Thereupon, detailed instructions were issued from Peking (*ibid.,* 25:39–41), in response to which Kuei-liang and

Hua-sha-na withdrew their statements to the British and tried to recover the ground lost.

47. *Ibid.*, 21:22, 40; 22:3, 10, 13, 20–21. See also a discussion of the concept of *t'i-chih* in Hsü, *China's Entrance*, pp. 109–118. In nineteenth-century Ch'ing administrative practice two types of imperial edict were used: the *ming-fa shang-yü* and the *chi-hsin shang-yü*. Both were drafted at the Grand Council. The *ming-fa shang-yü,* as reproduced in CSL or IWSM, began with the opening phrase *"Yü Nei-ko"* (Edict to the Grand Secretariat, or lit., "We order the Grand Secretariat"). This kind of edict was promulgated through the Grand Secretariat, and was used for the public announcement of various matters — for example, personnel changes, rewards or punishments, or scheduled imperial tours. The opening phrase of the *chi-hsin shang-yü,* as compiled in CSL or IWSM, was *"Yü chün-chi ta-ch'en teng"* (Edict to the Grand Council, or lit., "We order the grand councillors"). This kind of edict was used for instructions on confidential matters and was communicated to the specific offices concerned. It was transmitted to the provinces through the Couriers Office of the Board of War in the form of a "court letter" (*t'ing-chi*).

Most of the edicts cited or quoted herein come within the category of *chi-hsin shang-yü,* and these I have referred to simply as edicts. By way of distinction, when referring to the *ming-fa shang-yü* I have, so far as possible, used some such formula as "an edict of Jan. 13, 1861, announced," or "it was announced in an edict of Jan. 13, 1861 that."

48. IWSM:HF, 22:31.

49. The memorandum was attached to a memorial from "Tsai-yuan (Prince I) and others" received on May 28, 1858 (IWSM:HF, 23:10–13). The same memorial is in SKHT:YCLT, 10:10, without the names of the memorialists; according to the system used in this compilation, this presumably shows that it was presented from the Grand Council. I therefore infer that the memorial was presented jointly by Prince I and the grand councillors, with or without some others. The version in SKHT, which is longer than the one in IWSM, also states that the memorandum had been prepared by secretaries of the Grand Council and it was to be presented to the emperor on the following day, after the memorialists had given it a thorough re-examination. The memorandum also appears in SKHT:YCLT, 10:11–14; this version indicates that a slight addition was made to a passage in the document by order of the emperor.

50. IWSM:HF, 25:39–41.

51. *Ibid.*, 26:25–26.

52. *Ibid.*, 27:6.

53. Memorial by Ch'ien Pao-ch'ing, vice-director of the Imperial Clan Court, received on June 23, *ibid.*, 26:15–17.

54. *Ibid.*, 25:9.

55. *Ibid.*, 26:13–15. This memorial is also printed, under the title "Ch'ou-i-su erh," in Yin Keng-yun, *Hsin-pai-jih-chai chi* (1884). The co-signers of the memorial are listed in Yin Keng-yun, "Hsien-feng wu-wu

wu-yueh shih-san-jih t'ing-ch'en hui-i lueh," *ibid., chüan* 3. The drafters were Yin himself and Lu Ping-shu, junior censor (*Ch'ing-shih lieh-chuan*, 76:47).

56. See, for example, a memorial entitled "Tsai-lun i-wu su" by Shen Chao-lin, in his *Shen Wen-chung kung chi* (1869), 1:15–16. This memorial is undated, but its content indicates that it must have been presented during the 1858 Tientsin negotiations. See also a memorial received on November 7, 1860, from Ch'ing-lien, governor of Honan, IWSM:HF, 68:7.

57. *Ibid.*, 50:16.

58. *Ibid.*, 29:8; 30:28, 31, 38–40, 42–46; 31:18–19, 21–22, 29–31, 33–36, 41–42, 44–46, 48–51; 32:1–11, 15–19, 23–24; 33:44–45. See also T. F. Tsiang, "Notes and Suggestions: The Secret Plan of 1858," *Chinese Social and Political Science Review*, 15.2:291–299 (July 1931); Hsü, *China's Entrance*, pp. 71–75.

59. Kweiliang, etc., to Elgin, Oct. 22, 1858, *PP: Elgin's Missions*, pp. 408–410.

60. Elgin to Kweiliang, etc., Oct. 25, 1858, *ibid.*, p. 410.

61. Kweiliang, etc., to Elgin, Oct. 28, *ibid.*, p. 411.

62. Elgin to Kweiliang, etc. (undated), *ibid.*, pp. 411–412.

63. Elgin to Kweiliang, etc. (undated), *ibid.*, pp. 484–485. According to Morse, *International Relations*, I, 573, footnote, the dispatch was dated March 2, 1859. On the negotiations leading to the British agreement not to exercise the right of permanent residence, see also IWSM:HF, 31:49–51; 32:1–4, 15–16; 36:12–14, 16.

64. *Ibid.*, 33:10–11.

65. *Ibid.*, 33:32.

66. *Ibid.*, 35:40–41. In the spring of 1859 Kuei-liang tried to ascertain, through an unofficial channel, whether the British would consent to proceed *overland* to Peking. This the British interpreted as a design to follow "the time-honoured form of introducing the periodical missions from Annam, Lewchew, and other dependent States, into Pekin." Bruce to Malmesbury, July 13, 1859, *PP: Corr. with Bruce*, p. 23; Memorandum by T. Wade, *ibid.*, p. 35. According to Kuei-liang's report, the British, when sounded out by the Chinese officials, made it clear that their envoy would "get down only on one knee" in the presence of the Chinese emperor. IWSM:HF, 38:13.

67. *Ibid.*, 36:17–19.

68. Kweiliang, etc., to Bruce, June 12, 1859, *PP: Corr. with Bruce*, p. 16.

69. IWSM:HF, 38:21. Ignatieff to Ward, Pekin, July 7 (19), 1859, *Reed Corr.*, pp. 610–612. Crampton to Russell, Sept. 12, 1859, *FO: Affairs in China, Confidential* (1859).

70. IWSM:HF, 38:17–18.

71. Malmesbury to Bruce, Mar. 1, 1859, *PP: Corr. with Bruce*, pp. 1–3. See also Cady, pp. 226, 228–229.

72. IWSM:HF, 38:31.

73. Costin, p. 292; see also IWSM:HF, 38:52.

74. Costin, pp. 292–293.

75. *Reed Corr.*, pp. 570, 588–589, 592. Bruce to Malmesbury, July 13, 1859,

PP: Corr. with Bruce, p. 24; *ibid.*, pp. 37–38. Secretary of State Cass stated, apparently through a misunderstanding, that "The Treaty provides for the exchange of its ratifications at Peking." Cass to Ward, No. 1, Jan. 18, 1859, Diplomatic Instructions, China, (U.S. Department of State), Vol. 1.

76. On Ward's visit to Peking see below, Chap. III.

77. See below, Chap. IV.

78. IWSM:HF, 39:1–2, 39, 42–43; 40:13–15, 20–23; 41:5–7, 16–18, 20–23, 48–50. Cordier, *L'expédition, 1860*, pp. 95–97. *PP: Corr. with Bruce*, pp. 40–43, 45–47. La Servière, R.P.J. de, S. J., *Histoire de la mission du Kiangnan* (Shanghai, 1914), I, 12–13.

Soon after the Taku incident, the Chinese government sounded out John Ward in Pehtang as to whether he could mediate to this end, but to no purpose, since Bruce and Bourboulon had already sailed away. (IWSM:HF, 39:23–24, 26, 36–38; 40:4–6; *Reed Corr.*, pp. 601–602.) Though there seems to have been no specific order from Peking, in August and September 1859 such people in Canton as Heng-ch'i, superintendent of Customs for Kwangtung (the so-called "Hoppo"), also took soundings for peace. (Winchester to Hammond, Aug. 22, 1859, FO: *Affair in China, Confidential* (1859); Winchester to Hammond, Sept. 9, 1859, *ibid.*; Cordier, *L'expédition, 1860*, pp. 97–98; IWSM:HF, 39:5–6, 43–44; 41:23–24.) The conciliatory orientation of Peking was reported also by Ignat'ev, who was in Peking at that time. (Montebello to Thouvenel, Feb. 15, 1860, Cordier, *L'expédition, 1860*, pp. 122–123.)

79. IWSM:HF, 41:9–10, 18–20.

80. *Ibid.*, 48:14–15. See also *ibid.*, 48:31.

81. *Ibid.*, 49:20–21.

82. *Ibid.*, 50:16. See also *ibid.*, 50:22.

83. *Ibid.*, 53:44–45 (edict of July 17); 54:25–26 (edict of July 27); 54:34–35 (edict of July 31); 55:3–4 (edict of Aug. 1).

84. *Ibid.*, 55:5–6, 13, 16, 22, 30–31, 34.

85. *Ibid.*, 55:40–41.

86. *Ibid.*, 58:8–9.

87. *Ibid.*, 59:12.

88. See below, Chap. II.

89. Cf. notes by T. Wade, appended to the translation of the letter from Tsai and Muh to Elgin, Sept. 10, 1860, *PP: Affairs in China*, p. 163.

90. *Ibid.*, pp. 168–171.

91. Cordier, *L'expédition, 1860*, pp. 313, 316–317, 323.

92. Weng T'ung-ho, *Weng Wen-kung kung jih-chi* (Shanghai, 1925), *chüan* 1, *keng-shen*, p. 35.

93. IWSM:HF, 62:5.

94. *Ibid.*, 62:13–14, 18, 21; *PP: Affairs in China*, pp. 172–174, 178–180, 227–230; Cordier, *L'expédition, 1860*, pp. 317–321. On the capture of Parkes and the thirty-eight others, see Morse, *International Relations*, I, 600–602; Costin, pp. 327–329; Cordier, *L'expédition, 1860*, pp. 319–321. The number of captured persons is given in Cordier, *L'expédition, 1860*, p. 384. For an

analysis of Parkes's arrest, based on Chinese sources, see Hsü, *China's Entrance*, pp. 100–102.

95. IWSM:HF, 62:14–15.

96. *Ibid.*, 69:4–5. This problem is discussed in some detail in Chap. VI, below.

97. *Ibid.*, 70:23–27, 30–33. Bruce to Russell, No. 199, Dec. 13, 1860, FO 17/339. Bourboulon to Thouvenel, No. 90, Dec. 13, 1860, Correspondance Politique, Chine (Ministère des Affaires Etrangères), Vol. 32.

98. "The restriction as to the number of the Legation, and the obligation not to enter this River, protected as it is by a bar which our ships cannot approach nearer than six or eight miles, with men of war, I had no difficulty in agreeing to." (Reed to Cass, Official No. 23, June 30, 1858, Diplomatic Dispatches, China, Vol. 17.) This passage was omitted from the published version, possibly because it would have sounded naïve to some critics.

99. Reed to Cass, Nov. 9, 1858, *Reed Corr.*, p. 498.

100. Memorandum by Wade, etc., *PP: Corr. with Bruce*, pp. 36–37. See also Bruce to Malmesbury, July 15, 1859, *ibid.*, p. 38.

101. IWSM:HF, 27:6.

102. Reed to Cass, June 30, 1858, *Reed Corr.*, pp. 354, 362.

103. J. W. Foster, *American Diplomacy in the Orient* (Boston and New York, 1903), p. 241; Cordier, *L'expédition, 1857–58*, p. 433.

104. Memorandum of a Conference between Commissioners Kweiliang and Hwashana, and Mr. Bruce, in the suburb of Tien-tsin, on June 24, 1858, *PP: Elgin's Missions*, p. 338.

105. *Shinkoku gyōseihō*, Vol. 1, Part 1, p. 193 and Vol. 1, Part 2, p. 187. See also *Chia-ch'ing hui-tien*, 6:1, 3.

106. Tsiang, "Origins of the Tsungli Yamen," p. 93.

107. Russell to Bruce, Oct. 29, 1859, *PP: Affairs in China*, pp. 1–2; Bruce to Pang Wan-chang, Mar. 8, 1860, *ibid.*, pp. 34–36.

108. This treaty was drafted in Russian, Manchu, and Chinese, the Manchu text being considered authentic (Article 12). For a discussion of the various texts of the treaty and of discrepancies between them, which became an issue before the exchange of ratifications in 1859, see Chap. IV, especially note 15.

109. Of the four Tientsin treaties only the Russian treaty provided for correspondence not only with a grand secretary but also with a grand councillor. This may indicate that the Russians knew better than others where the real seat of power was in China's central government at this time. Reed, for instance, referred to the Grand Secretariat — "the privy council, (Nui Koh)" — as "the most powerful of the official boards . . . the fit organ of correspondence with the highest diplomatic representative of the United States" (*Reed Corr.*, p. 353).

In a memorandum of April 10, 1858, Thomas Wade gave a rather pedestrian description of the operation of the Grand Council ("the Great Council, literally the Council of War"), but he seems to have been somewhat aware of the relative positions of the Grand Council and the Grand Secretariat (*PP: Elgin's Missions*, pp. 271–272).

110. Putiatin in April 1857 had arrived in Kiakhta as a Russian representative, and had sought permission to proceed to Peking. After he had waited for six weeks in Kiakhta, his request was refused. He then sailed down the Amur River and to the mouth of the Peiho, where he renewed his demand for admission to Peking. Peking again refused, saying that only a tribute bearer could come to the capital and that in no circumstances could the kowtow be dispensed with. See Buksgevden, pp. 1–3; Petr Shumakher, "K istorii priobreteniia Amura, snosheniia s Kitaem s 1848 po 1860 god," *Russkii Arkhiv* (1878), III, 286–288, 290–293, 294; Ivan Barsukov, *Graf Nikolai Nikolaevich Muraviev-Amurskii po ego pis'mam, offitsial'nym dokumentam, razskazam sovremennikov i pechatnym istochnikam (materialy dlia biografii)* (Moscow, 1891), I, 494–496, 498, 503. See also IWSM:HF, 15:7–9, 11–18, 20–30, 37; 16:1–14, 23–29, 34–35; 17:1–3, 14–16.

111. The expenses had previously been shared by the Chinese and the Russian governments. See E. F. Timkovskii, *Puteshestvie v Kitai chrez Mongoliiu v 1820 i 1821 godakh* (St. Petersburg, 1824), I, 7–9. See also Hoo Chi-tsai, pp. 51–52, 228–229.

112. The customary length of residence had previously been roughly ten years (*ibid.,* pp. 52–53, 227).

113. Elgin to Russell, private, Talienwan, July 12, 1860, P.R.O. 30/22/49.

114. The Russian attitude was somewhat different. In an 1860 letter of instruction sent to Ignat'ev in Peking, the Russian government expressed fear that the overthrow of the dynasty would result in the transfer of the center of gravity of Chinese politics from Peking to the south; China would thus move away from Russian influence toward that of the maritime powers, primarily of Great Britain (Buksgevden, p. 51).

For a survey of the tsarist government's policy *vis-à-vis* the Chinese domestic strife, see Popov.

For a survey of the relations between the Taipings and the Western powers, see Ueda Toshio, "Taiheiran to gaikoku," published in three parts in *Kokka gakkai zasshi,* 62.9:464–494 (Sept. 1948); 62.12:669–687 (Dec. 1948); 63.1–3:31–78 (Mar. 1949). For a condensed English translation of this article, see Ueda Toshio, "The International Relations of the T'ai P'ing Rebellion," *Japan Annual of Law and Politics,* No. 2:119–148 (1953). A recent critical study, based on British primary sources, is John S. Gregory, "British Intervention against the Taiping Rebellion," *Journal of Asian Studies,* 19.1:11–24 (Nov. 1959).

115. Ueda, "Taiheiran," Part 1, pp. 479–494; Costin, pp. 158–161, 181–184; Dennett, pp. 210–216, 232–234; Morse, *International Relations,* I, 453–454.

116. On the French military action, see Ch. B. Maybon and Jean Fredet, *Histoire de la concession française de Changhai* (Paris, 1929), pp. 112–136; see also Cady, pp. 130–134.

117. Malmesbury to Bruce, No. 5, Mar. 1, 1859, FO 17/311; see also Cordier, *L'expédition, 1860,* pp. 47–49.

118. *Reed Corr.,* p. 10.

119. IWSM:HF, 32:5–8.

120. *Ibid.*, 32:18; 34:24–25, 36:20–23.

121. *Ibid.*, 32:22–23; 35:39–40. Thomas Wade gave the following explanation for the acquiescence "with a great grace" of Kuei-liang and others to Elgin's intention to proceed up the Great River: "This was . . . partly, I feel sure, from words that fell from the Judge [Hsueh Huan], in the hope that we should have a profitable collision with the insurgents at Nankin" (memorandum by Mr. Wade, etc., *PP: Corr. with Bruce*, p. 32). This may be another indication that the Chinese authorities on the spot were aware of the British intention not to support the Taipings.

122. IWSM:HF, 39:43 (edict of July 14, 1859); see also *ibid.*, 40:20, 22.

123. *Ibid.*, 40:21–22.

124. *Ibid.*, 40:22–23.

125. *Ibid.*, 40:36–37.

126. On the events reviewed in this paragraph, see Kuo T'ing-i, *T'ai-p'ing T'ien-kuo shih-shih jih-chih*, 1st ed. (Shanghai, 1946). On the Anglo-French moves relating to the defense of Shanghai and the Chinese requests for military assistance, see also *PP: Affairs in China*, pp. 60, 65–74, 129–133, 149, 199, 250–251; Cordier, *L'expédition, 1860*, pp. 174ff., 216, 218–219, 224, 280, 298.

127. On the pattern of distortion in these reports, see Banno, "Gaikō kōshō . . . kōdō yōshiki," Part 2, pp. 728–730, 735–736.

128. IWSM:HF, 51:40–41. The memorial is printed also in Ch'iao Sung-nien, *Ch'iao Ch'in-k'o kung ch'üan-chi* (1877), *tsou-i, chüan* 1. The latter version is dated June 12, 1860, which indicates the date the memorial was dispatched. Ch'iao Sung-nien, like Ho Kuei-ch'ing, was a *chin-shih* of 1835. See Fang Chao-ying and Tu Lien-che, comps., *Tseng-chiao Ch'ing-ch'ao chin-shih t'i-ming pei-lu* (Peking, 1941). (Hereafter in this book, the year given for any official's becoming a *chin-shih* will be derived from this source.)

Ch'iao Sung-nien, as acting toatai of Shanghai, worked under Chi-erh-hang-a, governor of Kiangsu, when the latter besieged and recaptured the native city of Shanghai (*Hsü pei-chuan-chi*, 27:5). In 1859 Ch'iao was in Shanghai as a deputy (*wei-yuan*) under Ho Kuei-ch'ing, dealing with a street fight in Shanghai between foreigners and Chinese, which had been caused by coolie-trade kidnapings (IWSM:HF, 42:22, 25–26).

129. *Ibid.*, 52:14–17. According to Bruce, there was a long discussion between Ho Kuei-ch'ing, Provincial Judge Hsueh Huan, and Wu Hsü, taotai of Shanghai. In this discussion, Ho (who was prepared even for his own possible execution because of the reverses suffered by the imperial troops within his jurisdiction as governor-general) urged that a memorial be presented to the emperor pointing out the necessity for compliance with the allies' demands and that this memorial first be communicated to Bruce for his approval. Hsueh objected to sending such a memorial. Unlike Ho, he was not in a position to be blamed for the recent military misfortunes in the province, and so he was probably not ready to be involved in this risky project of telling the truth to Peking. Ho's proposal thus resulted in a joint memorial with Wang Yu-ling (Bruce to Russell, No. 124, June 12, 1860,

FO 17/338; Bruce to Russell, No. 127, June 26, 1860, FO 17/338; Bruce to Russell, June 29, 1860, *PP: Affairs in China,* p. 71; see also Cordier, *L'expédition, 1860,* pp. 185–186). The British obtained a copy of this memorial — a copy that had been altered from the original so as to be more satisfactory to the foreigners and had apparently been thrown in the way of the British. Compare the English translation of this version (*PP: Affairs in China,* pp. 71–75) with the original memorial in IWSM:HF.

Wang Yu-ling became an official through the purchase of a title. He was trusted and patronized by Ho Kuei-ch'ing because of his ability to raise military funds. See CSK, *lieh-chuan,* No. 182 (under Wang Yu-ling), and No. 184 (under Ho Kuei-ch'ing); *Hsü pei-chuan-chi,* 57:12–14.

130. IWSM:HF, 51:41.

131. *Ibid.,* 52:17–18; see also *ibid.,* 52:1 (edict of June 19).

132. *Ibid.,* 52:45, 53:20, 54:7. On F. T. Ward, see Robert S. Rantoul, *Frederick Townsend Ward (Historical Collection of the Essex Institute,* Vol. 44, Salem, Mass., 1908).

133. Wade to Elgin, Pa-li-chiao, Sept. 23, 1860, *PP: Affairs in China,* p. 169.

134. Elgin to Clarendon, Apr. 15, 1858, *PP: Elgin's Missions,* p. 265.

135. Poutiatine to Elgin, June 15, 1858, *ibid.,* pp. 332–333. Poutiatine to Gros, June 15, 1858, in Cordier, *L'expédition, 1857–58,* p. 412.

136. Elgin to Poutiatine, June 17, 1858, *PP: Elgin's Missions,* p. 333; Gros to Poutiatine, June 16, 1858, in Cordier, *L'expédition, 1857–58,* pp. 413–415.

137. Elgin to Malmesbury, July 13, 1858, *PP: Elgin's Missions,* p. 356.

138. Persigny to Walewski, London, Oct. 15, 1859, in Cordier, *L'expédition, 1860,* p. 103.

139. *PP: Affairs in China,* pp. 209, 216, 218, 247.

140. Elgin to Russell, Oct. 25, 1860, *PP: Affairs in China,* p. 214. As a matter of fact it was with great difficulty that the Peking government contrived to find the funds for the indemnities, which totaled a million and a half taels, one million to be paid soon at Tientsin and half a million to be paid instantly as indemnities for the atrocities. See IWSM:HF, 67:4, 7, 11–12, 36–38.

141. Russell to Elgin, Apr. 17, 1860, *PP: Affairs in China,* pp. 29–30. Discussion had been under way inside the British government as to the march on Peking. The Prime Minister, Palmerston, was rather in favor of taking the risk of capturing Peking, whereas Sidney Herbert, secretary of state for war, was strongly against it. In the end the advance on Peking was left to the discretion of the commanders of the allied forces, subject to consultation with the diplomats as to the political expediency of such a move. See Arthur H. G. Stanmore, *Sidney Herbert, Lord Herbert of Lea* (New York, 1906), II, 295–296, 301–308, 313–315, 320–321, 350.

142. Instructions to Baron Gros, Apr. 21, 1860, in Cordier, *L'expédition, 1860,* pp. 136–137.

143. Russian note, Feb. 15, 1860, in *ibid.,* p. 121; Montebello to Thouvenel, St. Petersburg, Feb. 15, 1860, in *ibid.,* pp. 122–123.

144. Gros to Elgin, July 17, 1860, *ibid.*, p. 242.

145. Gros to Montauban and Charner, Aug. 30, 1860, *ibid.*, p. 289; cf. Gros to Montauban and Charner, Sept. 7, 1860, *ibid.*, pp. 302–303.

146. G. J. Wolseley, *Narrative of the War with China in 1860* (London, 1862), pp. 74–76.

147. Elgin to Russell, Oct. 25, 1860, *PP: Affairs in China*, pp. 213–215; Montauban to Grant, Oct. 17, 1860, in Elgin to Russell, No. 67, Oct. 23, 1860, FO 17/331; Grant to Montauban, Oct. 18, 1860, *ibid.;* Montauban to Grant, Oct. 18, 1860, *ibid.;* Elgin to Gros, Oct. 19, 1860, in Elgin to Russell, No. 79, Oct. 26, 1860, FO 17/332; Gros to Elgin, Nov. 4, 1860, in Elgin to Russell, No. 91, Nov. 4, 1860, FO 17/332; Foley to Russell, Oct. 26, 1860, *FO: Affairs in China, Confidential* (1861), p. 316; Gros to Elgin, Oct. 16, 1860, in Cordier, *L'expédition, 1860,* pp. 371–373; Elgin to Gros, Oct. 16, 1860, *ibid.,* pp. 373–374; Gros to Elgin, Oct. 17, 1860, *ibid.,* pp. 374–375; Gros to Thouvenel, private, Oct. 19, 1860, *ibid.,* pp. 397–398; Gros to Thouvenel, the same date, *ibid.,* pp. 400–404. See also César Lecat, Baron de Bazancourt, *Les expéditions de Chine et de Cochinchine d'après les documents officiels* (Paris, 1861–1862), II, 295–304; Montauban, *L'expédition de Chine de 1860: souvenirs du Général Cousin de Montauban, Comte de Palikao,* published by his grandson le Comte de Palikao (Paris, 1932), pp. 348–355; Comte Maurice Hérisson, *L'expédition de Chine, d'après la correspondance confidentielle du Général Cousin de Montauban, Comte de Palikao* (1883), pp. 215–217, 221; Baron J. B. L. Gros, *Négociations entre la France et la Chine en 1860: livre jaune du Baron Gros* (Paris, 1864), pp. 147–150.

148. Buksgevden, pp. 195–196.

149. Cordier, *L'expédition, 1860,* pp. 368, 372, 374, 398; Montauban, pp. 358–359.

150. Elgin to Russell, Oct. 25, 1860, *PP: Affairs in China*, pp. 213–215. At the sight of the smoke swirling over the Summer Palace, which was spreading even as far as Peking, Prince Kung, it was reported, wanted to flee from his residence and was barely, and almost forcibly restrained. Gros to Elgin, Nov. 4, 1860, *FO: Affairs in China, Confidential* (1861), pp. 332. See also Gros, pp. 150, 191–193, 199.

151. Buksgevden, pp. 192–218; Ignatieff to Elgin, Peking, Oct. 6/18, 1860, in Elgin to Russell, No. 69, Oct. 23, 1860, FO 17/331; Ignatieff to Gros, Oct. 16 [sic]/18, 1860, in Cordier, *Histoire des relations de la Chine avec les puissances occidentales 1860–1900* (Paris, 1901–1902), I, 94–95. On Ignat'ev's activities at this stage Prince Kung and his colleagues reported to the emperor only briefly, citing the reports of such officials as Ch'ung-hou and Heng-ch'i (IWSM:HF, 66:11).

The mediatory maneuvers of Ignat'ev, who went even so far as to help, or meddle, in the drafting of communications from the Chinese authorities to the British and the French, were calculated to pave the way for a favorable solution of the Sino-Russian boundary dispute with which he had been grappling for more than a year (Buksgevden, pp. 192–218). On Ignat'ev's earlier activities in Peking and their background, see below Chap. IV.

152. Gros to Thouvenel, Oct. 19, 1860, P.S., in Cordier, *L'expédition, 1860,* p. 403. See also Montauban, pp. 362–363.

153. Reed to Cass, July 29, 1858, *Reed Corr.,* pp. 382–383.

154. Kweiliang, etc., to Elgin, Oct. 28, 1858, *PP: Elgin's Missions,* p. 411; Elgin to Malmesbury, Nov. 5, 1858, *ibid.,* pp. 406–408.

155. Bruce to Russell, June 10, 1860, *PP: Affairs in China,* pp. 65–67.

156. Elgin to Bruce, Oct. 12, 1860, in Elgin to Russell, No. 59, Oct. 12, 1860, FO 17/331.

Notes to Chapter II. The Arrow War: The Domestic Political Scene

1. Prince I, Tsai-yuan (1816–1861), was a great-great-grandson of Prince I, Yun-hsiang, who was the thirteenth son of the K'ang-hsi emperor. For his biography, see *Ai-hsin chueh-lo tsung-p'u* (Mukden, 1938), *chia-ts'e,* pp. 879–882. (This compilation is the most authentic source for the biographies of the Ch'ing princes and imperial clansmen, though I have not cited it below in each case.) See also CSK, *lieh-chuan,* No. 7; Arthur W. Hummel, ed., *Eminent Chinese of the Ch'ing Period* (Washington, D.C., 1943–1944), II, 924.

2. Prince Cheng ("the Prince of Ching" according to the romanization used in reports in the Blue Books), Tuan-hua (1807–1861), was a descendant, after seven generations, of Prince Cheng, Chi-erh-ha-lang (Jirgalang), who was a nephew of Nurhaci. See CSK, *lieh-chuan,* No. 2.

3. For biographies of Su-shun (1816–1861), see CSK, *lieh-chuan,* No. 174; *Ch'ing-shih lieh-chuan,* 47:27ff.; Hummel, II, 666–669.

4. On the decisive role of the personally led regional armies in suppressing the Taipings and its impact on the Ch'ing power structure, see Lo Erh-kang, "Ch'ing-chi ping wei chiang-yu ti ch'i-yuan," *Chung-kuo she-hui ching-chi shih chi-k'an* 5.2:235–250 (June 1937); Lo Erh-kang, *Hsiang-chün hsin-chih* (Changsha, 1939), pp. 21–30, 118–137, 216–232, 243–245; Franz Michael, "Military Organization and Power Structure in China during the Taiping Rebellion," *Pacific Historical Review,* 18.4:469–483 (Nov. 1949). For a recent critical discussion of this subject, see Ralph L. Powell, *The Rise of Chinese Military Power 1895–1912* (Princeton, 1955), pp. 32–36. See also Mary C. Wright, *The Last Stand of Chinese Conservatism: The T'ung-chih Restoration, 1862–1874* (Stanford, 1957), pp. 57–59, 206, 221.

5. Lo Erh-kang stresses the suspicion that the Ch'ing court and the emperor entertained toward Tseng Kuo-fan and their persistent reluctance to give him the status of governor or governor-general (*Hsiang-chün hsin-chih,* pp. 49, 194–197, 202, 204).

6. Hsueh Fu-ch'eng, "Shu Ch'ang-pai Wen Wen-tuan kung hsiang-yeh" in *Yung-an-wen hsü-pien (Yung-an ch'üan-chi).* See also Hsueh Fu-ch'eng, "Shu tsai-hsiang yu-hsueh wu-shih," *ibid.* As Hsueh Fu-ch'eng was a follower of Tseng Kuo-fan and later of Li Hung-chang, we may have to discount to some extent his report of Wen-ch'ing's role. For Wen-ch'ing's biography, see CSK, *lieh-chuan,* No. 173.

7. In a sense, there was in operation at this time a sort of division of

labor between the authority of the Manchus and the military power of the Chinese. As an example, we may cite the case mentioned by Hsueh Fu-ch'eng of friction and reconciliation between Kuan-wen (a Manchu), governor-general of Hunan and Hupei, and Hu Lin-i (a Chinese), governor of Hupei ("Shu I-yang Hu Wen-chung kung yü Liao-yang Kuan Wen-kung kung chiao-huan shih," in *Yung-an wen-pien, chüan* 4). Yen Ching-ming, who persuaded Hu Lin-i to become reconciled with Kuan-wen by stressing the necessity of this division of labor, had served on the Board of Revenue under Wen-ch'ing as president. In those days Wen-ch'ing used to seek his counsel (Hsueh Fu-ch'eng, "Shu Ch'ang-pai Wen Wen-tuan kung hsiang-yeh.")

8. See references cited in notes 1 and 2 above. See also Meng Sen, "Pa-ch'i chih-tu k'ao-shih," *Li-shih yü-yen yen-chiu-so chi-k'an* 6.3:343–412 (July 1936).

9. CSL:HT, 476:15, 17–18. The eight others who received the testamentary decree were Tsai-ch'üan (Prince Ting), presiding controller of the Imperial Clan Court; Seng-ko-lin-ch'in, adjutant-general; Mu-chang-a, grand councillor; Sai-shang-a, grand councillor; Ho Ju-lin, grand councillor; Ch'en Fu-en, grand councillor; Chi Chih-ch'ang, grand councillor; and Wen-ch'ing, minister of the Imperial Household.

10. Hsueh Fu-ch'eng thus describes the process by which these three ingratiated themselves with the emperor and assumed power: "Tsai-yuan and Tuan-hua gradually clouded the emperor's intellect by means of music and sensual pleasure. They recommended Su-shun to the emperor, and he got him to attend in the inner court. They used to cater to the imperial wishes better than anyone else. The emperor began to discuss public affairs with them. The three villains inquisitively asked questions and thus they all meddled in state affairs. The power of the Grand Council gradually declined. All the grand councillors looked on with folded arms, just following orders and doing nothing." ("Hsien-feng chi-nien san-chien fu-chu," in *Yung-an pi-chi, chüan* 1).

11. Hsueh Fu-ch'eng, "Su-shun t'ui-fu Ch'u-hsien," in *Yung-an pi-chi, chüan* 1. For a recent appraisal of Su-shun's activities, see Wu Hsiang-hsiang, *Wan-Ch'ing kung-t'ing shih-chi*, 2nd ed. (Taipei, 1953), pp. 6–13.

12. CSK, *lieh-chuan*, No. 174 (Su-shun). On the rather close relationship between Yin Keng-yun and Tseng Kuo-fan, see "Kuo-shih hsun-li chuan" reprinted in the later edition of Yin, *Hsin-pai-jih-chai chi* (preface by Wang K'ai-yun dated Kuang-hsü 21st year). A certain Cheng Tun-chin, sometime president of the Board of Punishments, who, according to a biographer, was "famous for his integrity," never accepted the eager invitations of Su-shun, although "many notables or high officials readily hastened to be Su-shun's guests" (*Hsü pei-chuan-chi*, 12:22).

13. CSK, *lieh-chuan*, No. 172.

14. For a critical comment on this inference as originally propounded in my article " 'Sōrigamon' setsuritsu no haikei," see Hsü, *China's Entrance*, pp. 65–66.

15. For biographies of Mien-yü, see CSK, *lieh-chuan*, No. 8; Hummel, II, 968.

16. Charles Gützlaff, *The Life of Taou-Kwang* (London, 1852), pp. 42, 64–65, 102, 212–215, 270–271. Ignat'ev, who had then been in Peking for almost a year, told Frederick Bruce at Shanghai in June 1860 that Prince Hui was "a man of eighty [sic] years of age notorious for his rapacity and corruption and who owes much of his influence to the facilities he enjoys from his position for pandering to the taste of the Emperor" (Bruce to Russell, No. 127, June 26, 1860, FO 17/338). In Nov. 1861 Heng-ch'i, then a member of the Tsungli Yamen, told Thomas Wade at Peking that Prince Hui was "a fat, proud, stupid man" (Memorandum . . . by Thomas Wade, Nov. 8, 1861, in Bruce to Russell, No. 161, Nov. 12, 1861, FO 17/356).

I am not equal to the task of a really thorough critique of the various sources cited in this book concerning court politics, many of which may be based on little more than hearsay. It should be understood that I have used these sources merely as suggestive material.

17. According to an edict of June 1, 1858, Princes Hui, I, and Cheng had already been charged with the defense of the capital (IWSM:HF, 23:36). An edict of June 3 formally announced the appointment to this task of the three princes and two of the grand councilors (*ibid.*, 24:9). The appointment of yet another high official to the commission was announced by edict on June 17 (*ibid.*, 25:27). Although in these edicts the designations "Hsun-fang-ch'u" or "Hsun-fang Wang-ta-ch'en" were not used, they were used in some edicts or memorials in reference to this commission.

"Hsun-fang Wang-ta-ch'en" (princes and high officials in charge of the Commission of Defense) probably referred to this group of three princes and two or three high officials. But it could certainly mean the three princes only. See for instance IWSM:HF, 25:22–23.

The Hsun-fang-ch'u was discontinued on July 23, 1858 (CSL:WT, 256:26). Prince Cheng was appointed general commandant of the Gendarmerie on June 2, 1858, thus coming to control the police force of the metropolis (*ibid.*, 252:3). He and his policemen were not popular in the city (Buksgevden, p. 82).

18. Yin Keng-yun, "Hsien-feng wu-wu wu-yueh shih-san-jih t'ing-ch'en hui-i lueh," *Hsin-pai-jih-chai chi, chüan* 3.

19. IWSM:HF, 25:22–23; see also *ibid.*, 25:24.

20. *Ibid.*, 29:17, 30; 30:12–16.

21. Chi-p'u, *Ssu-pu-kuo-chai chu-jen tzu-hsü nien-p'u* (undated), pp. 43–44.

22. SKHT:MLCT, 4:52. While the addressors' names are given, that of the addressee is not indicated.

23. Chu Shih-chia, comp., *Shih-chiu shih-chi Mei-kuo ch'in-Hua tang-an shih-liao hsuan-chi* (Peking, 1959), I, 88.

24. SKHT:MLCT, 4:57. The memorial as reproduced in SKHT is undated, being a memorial from the grand councilors. The vermilion endorsement is stated to have been put on it on August 15. However, the edict thus drafted was issued on August 9 (*ibid.*, 4:58; IWSM:HF, 41:29–30). Therefore, the late date here of "August 15" must have been a mistranscription. It is thus tentatively aissumed that the vermilion endorsement was made on

August 9 and the memorial had probably been presented earlier on the same day.

25. CSL:WT, 305:18. This attendance is worth noticing as representing the probable inner core of the Peking government: the nucleus of the Council of Princes, the grand councillors, and the most important military figure.

26. IWSM:HF, 58:4–5; 59:1. Weng T'ung-ho, *chüan* 1, *keng-shen,* p. 30.

27. Wade to Elgin, Pa-li-chiau, Sept, 23, 1860, *PP: Affairs in China,* p. 169. Apparently on the basis of this same report, H. B. Morse described these three princes as "the camerilla [*sic*] of three Imperial princes in whose hands lay the actual government of the empire." (*International Relations,* I, 599).

28. PLFC: Pan-li fu-chü an, *chüan* 1, under Sept. 25, 1860.

29. Prince Kung (1833–1898) was the sixth of the nine sons of the Tao-kuang emperor, of whom the Hsien-feng emperor was the fourth. See Hummel, I, 380–384; CSK, *lieh-chuan,* No. 8.

30. IWSM:HF, 24:1–2. I-tsung (Prince Tun) (1831–1889) was the fifth son of the Tao-kuang emperor. As of 1858 he was a prince of the second degree (*chün-wang*), and was promoted to prince of the first degree (*ch'in-wang*) in 1860. See Hummel, I, 393; CSK, *lieh-chuan,* No. 8.

31. Weng T'ung-ho, *chüan* 1, *keng-shen,* pp. 33, 35, 37.

32. *Ibid.,* p. 32.

33. IWSM:HF, 25:24, 25; 26:1. Princes Hui, I, and Cheng acted here in their capacity as Hsun-fang Wang-ta-ch'en.

34. Weng T'ung-ho, *chüan* 1, keng-shen, p. 32.

35. *Ibid.,* p. 37. Prince Ch'un (I-huan, 1840–1891) was the seventh son of the Tao-kuang emperor. See Hummel, I, 384–385; CSK, *lieh-chuan,* No. 8. It is recorded in Weng T'ung-ho, *chüan* 1, *keng-shen,* p. 35, that on Sept. 13 Prince Ch'un had an audience together with Prince Cheng, in which he "strongly opposed in tears" the plan for the imperial flight. But his name never appears in the IWSM volumes for the Arrow War period. Hence we may safely neglect him when we talk about the Council of Princes.

Among the audiences of princes during the days just preceding the emperor's departure, which are listed in Weng T'ung-ho, *chüan* 1, keng-shen, p. 36, there are three in addition to those which have already been mentioned either in the text or in the notes: on September 18 Prince I had audience twice and Prince Cheng once.

36. Yin Chao-yung, *Yin P'u-ching shih-lang tzu-ting nien-p'u* (undated), p. 37.

37. Translation of a paper forwarded to the Earl of Elgin in Parkes's dispatch of Jan. 15, 1859, *PP: Corr. with Bruce,* pp. 25–28. Cf. *PP: Elgin's Missions,* pp. 475–477. On the seizure of this letter and other papers on the same occasion, see also IWSM:HF, 34:1–2.

38. In short, we are assuming that the expression "Prince Hui and others" referred to one of the three groupings mentioned in the text. There were also some instances in which "Tsai-yuan (Prince I) and others" or simply "Tsai-yuan and others" were mentioned without the name of Prince Hui. For ex-

ample, a joint memorial by "Tsai-yuan (Prince I) and others" was received on May 28, 1858, to which there was attached a memorandum on the foreign demands, apparently prepared for the guidance of Kuei-liang and Hua-sha-na when they went to Tientsin (IWSM:HF, 23:10–12; SKHT:YCLT, 10:10–14 — see above, Chap. I, note 49). This was before Princes Hui, I, and Cheng were made Hsun-fang Wang-ta-ch'en, and Prince Hui probably did not yet have a voice in foreign affairs (see above, note 17). There were several other instances of "Tsai-yuan and others" between mid-August and the beginning of September 1860. See IWSM:HF, 55:36; 56:7; 57:21; 59:11, 13.

39. SKHT:ELST, 16:47.

40. *Ibid.*, 18:68; see also an edict of the same date in IWSM:HF, 43:8–10.

41. *Ibid.*, 32:5–8.

42. SKHT:YCLT, 11:102.

43. IWSM:HF, 34:17.

44. *Ibid.*, 37:13; 38:51; 41:52.

45. *Ibid.*, 42:31.

46. *Ibid.*, 46:32.

47. *Ibid.*, 33:5.

48. SKHT:ELST, 14:20. This passage is not reproduced in IWSM.

49. IWSM:HF, 60:6–7; CSL:WT, 326:9–11. See also IWSM:HF, 60:21, 36. This vermilion rescript was seized by the British at the Summer Palace. Thomas Wade, in his notes to its English translation, pointed out that Prince I, Prince Cheng, and Su-shun were, "according to common report, the real Government of the country for some time past" (*PP: Affairs in China,* pp. 272–273). Incidentally, Su-shun was an adjutant-general as of 1860.

50. IWSM:HF, 62:12.

51. *Ibid.*, 25:22.

52. *Ibid.*, 36:1, 17.

53. In addition to the cases already cited, see *ibid.*, 24:2, 25–27; 28:50; 29:1–8; 60:1.

The *North China Herald* (Aug. 13, 1859) reported, on a basis of the *Peking Gazette,* that at the july 20 audience given to Kuei-liang and Hua-sha-na, both of whom had come back from Shanghai, there were also present "the Emperor's uncle, prince Hwui, and two others of the chief princes." This can be considered another example of "Prince Hui and others."

We have one indication that the Council of Princes functioned also in purely domestic politics: the *North China Herald* (Sept. 17, 1859) quotes the *Peking Gazette* to the effect that on Aug. 17, 1859, the emperor summoned Prince Hui, Prince I, Prince Cheng, Ch'en Fu-en (president of the Board of War), and the grand councillors, in order to discuss the scandal relating to the Peking provincial examination of 1858, in which the Mongol Grand Councillor Po-chün was involved. Cf. CSL:WT, 288:15–18.

54. IWSM:HF, 31:22.

55. *Ibid.*, 60:21–22.

56. *Ibid.*, 43:26; 50:3, 4; 54:27, 35. On the occasion of Ch'i-ying's impeachment in 1858, Ch'i-ying first wrote to Seng-ko-lin ch'in, explaining why

he had had to leave Tientsin. Seng-ko-lin-ch'in sent this letter to Prince Hui. Prince Hui consulted with Prince I and Prince Cheng, and the three princes then presented a joint memorial impeaching Ch'i-ying. This may also be considered an instance of Seng-ko-lin-ch'in's contact with the Council of Princes. See IWSM:HF, 25:22–23.

57. *Ibid.,* 59:15.

58. There are also some instances of the use of the expression "princes" (*wang teng*) or "princes and ministers" (*wang-ta-ch'en* or *wang-ta-ch'en teng*), by which perhaps "Prince Hui and others" was meant; e.g., see *ibid.,* 40:1–12; 56:2, 13; 58:15; see also CSL:WT, 286:5.

Archimandrite Palladii of the Russian Ecclesiastical Mission in Peking recorded, as of January 1858, that all affairs were "in the hands of the Supreme Council [the Grand Council] and of the Council of princes and ministers, composed of narrow-minded men with very little depth of intellect" (Extracts from a Journal kept at Peking during the years 1858, trans. from the *Morskoi Sbornik* (Naval Magazine) for August 1860, in Erskine to Russell, No. 81, Sept. 17, 1860, FO 65/554. On the authorship of the journal, see below, Chap. IV, note 78).

59. In writing this section I owe much to the ideas developed by Professor Miyazaki Ichisada in his article "Shinagawa shiryō yori mitaru Ei-Futsu rengōgun no Pekin shinnyū jiken, tokuni shusenron to waheiron," *Tōa kenkyū shohō,* No. 24:852–884 (Oct. 1943). Professor Miyazaki, however, does not mention Prince Hui.

60. A memorial received on May 27 from Hsü Nai-p'u, president of the Board of Works, began by stating that appeasement was the best policy. After a brief discussion of the gloomy military prospects the memorialist skillfully shifted his position and advocated war, expounding upon how to use the militia forces. This would seem to suggest that there was at this time a good deal of pacifism (IWSM:HF, 23:4–5). A warlike memorial on the following day from P'an Tsu-yin, expositor of the National Academy, referred to the current reasoning of the pacifists (*ibid.,* 23:8–10). A short memorial on May 30 from Tu Ch'iao, junior vice-president of the Board of Revenue, advanced a counsel of prudence and enclosed a memorandum by an expectant salt controller named Chin An-ch'ing who was familiar with the earlier Sino-foreign negotiations at Shanghai. Tu Ch'iao recommended that this man be sent to Tientsin as an advisor to the Chinese delegation (*ibid.,* 23:19–21).

For the period between May 20, when Taku fell, and June 26, when the British treaty was finally signed, there are some eleven memorials on the problem of war or peace in SKHT which are not included in IWSM. Among these, eight are warlike, including one on May 26 from Fan Ch'eng-tien, drawing attention to the prevalence of a short-sighted advocacy of peace (SKHT: YCLT, 9:73–74). Of the remaining three, a memorial on May 27 from Ts'ai Hsieh presents a well-considered counsel of prudence (*ibid.,* 10:20–21). One on June 7 from Chu Wen-chiang is seemingly bellicose but suddenly changes in tone, concluding with a somber counsel of peace (*ibid.,*

10:137), perhaps an indication that war advocacy had by that time gained much strength. On the other hand, Tu Ch'iao, now departing somewhat from his previous position, took a firmer stand in a memorial of June 7, in which he ventured to suggest that the militia in Kwangtung be ordered to attack and exterminate the foreigners in Canton so that those in Tientsin would hasten to withdraw (*ibid.,* 10:134).

Fan Ch'eng-tien was a censor as of 1859 (*Ta-Ch'ing chin-shen ch'üan-shu,* winter of Hsien-feng 9 [1859], 1:58). Ts'ai Hsieh certainly served as a censor for some years (*Te-hua hsien-chin* [1872], 29:8), though I have not been able to ascertain his position in 1858 or 1859. The position of Chu Wen-chiang, a *chin-shih* of 1850, remains to be identified.

61. For warlike memorials by Yin Chao-yung, see IWSM:HF, 63:4; "Yin Chao-yung ch'ing pa T'ien-chin fu-i yuan-tsou" in Chiang-shang-chien-sou, *Chung-hsi chi-shih* (postscript to the table of contents dated 1865), *chüan* 22. Copies of this memorial were widely circulated among the literati, and an English translation of it appeared in the *North China Herald* (July 23 and Aug. 13, 1859). Guillaume Pauthier's French translation, published with an introductory note, is far from impeccable (*Mémoire secret adressé à l'empereur Hsien-Feng actuellement régnant par un lettré Chinois sur la conduite à suivre avec les puissances européennes* [extract from the *Reveue de l'Orient;* Paris, 1860]). Yin Chao-yung in his autobiography, p. 32, admits that this memorial was widely circulated, he did not know how, after the Taku incident of 1859.

62. For warlike memorials by Hsü P'eng-shou, see IWSM:HF, 24:11, 26:19–22.

63. Yin Keng-yun, *chüan* 1, includes nine warlike "memorials on how to deal with the barbarian problems" ("Ch'ou-i su" in the original ed., or "Ch'ou-yang su" in Kuang-hsü 21 ed.). The third memorial in the series is also printed in IWSM:HF, 25:8–9. The second in the series is a joint memorial drafted by him and Lu Ping-shu (see above, Chap. I, note 55). In Sept. 1860 Yin also drafted a joint memorial against the emperor's anticipated flight. See *PP: Affairs in China,* p. 263; "Tsai-chien hsun-hsing Mu-lan su," in Yin Keng-yun, *chüan* 2.

64. On the antiforeign hostility in Kwangtung which had been raging intermittently from the time of the Opium War, see Morse, *International Relations,* I, 367ff., 397ff., 435ff., 530ff.; see also Costin, pp. 280ff. There is much material also in IWSM.

65. One embarrassing problem here is that we probably must discount to some extent the fierceness of the war advocacy. It is possible that the aggressive memorials, especially those by censors or officials at the National Academy, were drafted for effect, at least in part, according to certain accepted rules of the contemporary political game.

66. The discussions on strategy and tactics by war advocates are entertainingly summarized in Miyazaki Ichisada, "Pekin shinnyū jiken," pp. 877–878.

67. See, for instance, IWSM:HF, 26:21 (Hsü P'eng-shou's memorial);

63:4 (Yin Chao-yung's memorial). An edict of Aug. 21, 1860 (*ibid.*, 56:28) discriminatingly summarizes the various ideas suggested by many memorialists as to how to cope with Western firearms.

In this period, there were fantastic stories about foreigners circulating among the Chinese in North China. For instance, even educated persons reportedly believed that the English were webfooted and their limbs had no joints. See D. F. Rennie, *Peking and the Pekingese* (London, 1865), I, 99, 174–175.

68. See, for example, a memorial by Wang Chin-jung, reader of the Grand Secretariat, in IWSM:HF, 27:25–26. This is just one of many memorials suggesting the same idea.

69. Feb. 21, 1860, House of Lords, Hansard, 156:1467. See also Oliphant, I, 434–435.

70. For the numerous memorials by these officials, see IWSM:HF, *passim* in the vols. for 1858–1860.

71. Miyazaki Ichisada, "Pekin shinnyū jiken," attaches much importance to the role played by Kuei-liang and analyzes in detail his maneuvers *vis-à-vis* Peking. On Kuei-liang, see Hummel, I, 428–430. In 1858, or more correctly in Hsien-feng 8, his age was 74 *sui*.

72. IWSM:HF, 9:12–20, 23–25.

73. *Ibid.*, 71:7–8.

74. *Ibid.*, 23:27, 36–37; 24:23–24.

75. *Ibid.*, 57:21–22; 58:9–11, 60:22–26.

76. Ting Yun-shu, Ch'en Shih-hsun and Ko Yü-ch'i, comps., *Chang-kung hsiang-li chün-wu chi-lueh* (preface dated 1862; postscript dated 1910), 5:17, 21, 22, 23, 26. The greater part of this six-*chüan* work records the activities in 1858 and 1860 of Chang Chin-wen in Tientsin, who played an important role as a purveyor for the foreigners, a leading sponsor of the local militia in Tientsin, a mediator in Sino-foreign disputes, and as a peace advocate behind the scenes.

77. *PP: Elgin's Missions*, pp. 328, 338; Cordier, *L'expédition, 1857–58*, pp. 396, 422–434; *Reed Corr.*, pp. 339, 347; Williams, "Journal," pp. 52, 61, 62, 66, 76, 78, 81; Martin, p. 169. Chang Chin-wen reportedly thought much of Pien Pao-shu, in spite of his impudent behavior, because he "really surpasses others in courage and ideas" (Ting Yun-shu *et al.*, 3:31).

On the other hand, Pien was denounced in June and July 1858 by some officials in Peking for his allegedly ingratiatory associations with the foreigners (SKHT:YCLT, 10:137; 12:104–105).

78. In April 1860 Prince I orally reported to the emperor some information he had received from Pien (IWSM:HF, 50:5). This may be an indication that Pien was a follower of Prince I's clique which, as we shall see, represented the war party in the Council of Princes.

79. A memorial by Ho Kuei-ch'ing (*ibid.*, 32:5). See also CSK, *lieh-chuan*, No. 181 (Huang Tsung-han). Ho and Huang were both *chin-shih* of 1835.

80. Joint memorial with Chao Te-ch'e (IWSM:HF, 19:21–22; 20:3–8).

The Domestic Political Scene

273

81. *Ibid.*, 25:4–6. A copy of the letter was enclosed in a memorial by Kuei-liang and his colleagues.

82. *Ibid.*, 9:12–13; 15:28; 19:22–23.

83. See *Ta-Ch'ing chin-shen ch'üan-shu* (winter, Hsien-feng 6), under "provincial treasurer of Chihli." CSK, *lieh-chuan*, No. 184 (Ho Kuei-ch'ing).

84. See the Chinese letter on the Shanghai scene cited above in note 37.

85. IWSM:HF, 32:5–8. According to the letter mentioned in note 84, Ho Kuei-ch'ing reportedly suggested in one of his memorials that if the emperor did not agree with his view, Princes Hui, Kung, and Cheng should be sent to Shanghai to manage things themselves; and he was scolded by the emperor in the vermilion endorsement.

86. On Wang Yu-ling see above, Chap. I, note 129. According to Thomas Wade, Wang and Hsueh Huan were "intimately liés" and Ho Kuei-ch'ing drew his inspiration from them (Memo. by Mr. Wade, etc., *PP: Corr. with Bruce*, p. 31). The vermilion endorsement on a joint memorial by Kuei-liang and his colleagues, received on Nov. 9, 1858, expresses suspicion that Wang Yu-ling tends to monopolize the handling of affairs on every occasion. It complains also that this time Ho and Wang have fixed ideas of their own on the management of barbarian affairs and will not permit others to interfere — "What audacity!" "Kuei-liang and others are tamely obeying their suggestions. It is still more incomprehensible" (IWSM:HF, 32:5).

87. Hsueh Huan was a native of Hsing-wen-hsien in Szechwan. After becoming a *chü-jen*, he entered officialdom through purchase of an office. He climbed the bureaucratic ladder through the purchase of offices. Since 1849 he had been serving in Kiangsu. He was appointed taotai of Shanghai in 1857, provincial judge in 1858, provincial treasurer in 1859, and governor of Kiangsu in 1860. Earlier in 1860 he had been given the status of acting Shanghai imperial commissioner (*Ch'ing-shih lieh-chuan*, 53:22).

Thomas Wade's comment on him (July 1859): He is "one of the few Chinese I have met who, notwithstanding much ignorance and prejudice still remaining, really appreciate the power and probity of the foreigners, or who appear soberly to contemplate, without abatement of pride in their own country, the possibility of utilizing barbarian ability to her advantage." (Memo. by Mr. Wade, etc., *PP: Corr. with Bruce*, p. 30.) The originally favorable appraisal of Hsueh Huan's role by the British eventually began to change. The following comment by Bruce in June 1860, concerning the report of Hsueh Huan's refusal to be a cosigner with the Ho Kuei-ch'ing of a memorial advocating compliance with the foreign demands (see above, Chap. I, note 129), is probably the earliest indication of this change: "I am inclined to think that . . . he [Hsueh Huan] has only preserved his influence by echoing the sentiments of the War-party and pledging himself to induce us to abate our demands. There is no doubt that he and Ho are not on good terms, I have reason to believe that the latter has been urgent in favor of peace" (Bruce to Russell, No. 127, June 26, 1860, FO 17/338).

88. Wu Hsü was a native of Jen-ho-hsien in Chekiang. His *chien-sheng*

274 Notes to Chapter II

degree was probably purchased. He served at Shanghai as assistant prefect
for coastal defense in 1854–1855, and then as taotai in 1859–1862. (*T'ung-chih
Shang-hai hsien-chih, chüan 12, chih-kuan-piao, shang.*)

Rennie reports that Wu was "a Tartar by birth" and was reputed to be
one of the richest mandarins in China, allegedly worth about a million
pounds sterling (*The British Arms in North China and Japan* [London,
1864], p. 144).

According to Hsueh Fu-ch'eng, Wu Hsü was the real power-holder under
Hsueh Huan ("Shu Ho-fei po-hsiang Li-kung yung Hu p'ing Wu"). The
North China Herald (July 21, 1860) refers to Wu as "that extraordinary man
the Taotai, who had the purse of Fortunatus," but states that he is "merely
the mouthpiece and money-bag" of Hsueh Huan.

89. Wu Chien-chang was originally a Canton merchant in foreign trade.
He could speak English. He became an official through purchase of an office.
See Hummel, II, 865–866 (an article by J. K. Fairbank); Fairbank, *Trade
and Diplomacy*, Chap. 21. In 1858–1859 Wu was still actively a part of the
Shanghai diplomatic machinery in his capacity as expectant taotai. See
IWSM:HF, 18:17, 19:10, 20, 20:2–3, 45:37; Williams, "Journal," p. 226; *PP:
Elgin's Missions*, p. 271. See also the *North China Herald* (Oct. 16 and Oct.
23, 1858).

90. Lan Wei-wen was a native of Ting-hai subprefecture in Chekiang. He
served as magistrate in Shanghai in 1843–1846, as assistant prefect for coastal
defense in 1849–1854, as acting official in the same post in 1855, and as acting
taotai in the capacity of expectant prefect in 1855–1857. (*T'ung-chih Shang-hai
hsien-chih, chüan 12, chih-kuan-piao, shang.*) In 1859–1860 he was active in
Shanghai as expectant prefect (IWSM:HF, *passim* in *chüan* 40ff.). As of 1859
he was participating in diplomatic negotiations as an important figure close
to Ho Kuei-ch'ing (Bourboulon to the Ministry of Foreign Affairs, July 30,
1859, in Cordier, *L'expédition 1860*, p. 93). Thomas Wade states that Lan
was "as determined an anti-barbarian, but a polished, and, *à la Chinoise,* a
well-educated Chinese: sagacious and capable" (Memo. by T. Wade, Apr. 10,
1858, *PP: Elgin's Missions*, p. 271).

See also a biography in *Ting-hai-t'ing chih* (1855), *chüan* 10; Fairbank,
Trade and Diplomacy, I, 194–195, 457; II, 32.

91. On Yang Fang, see Toyama Gunji, "Shanhai no shinshō Yō Bō,"
Tōyōshi kenkyū (new series), 1.4:17–34 (Nov. 1945). Yang Fang was an
influential figure in the Ningpo Guild in Shanghai. See Negishi Tadashi,
Shanhai no girudo (Tokyo, 1951), pp. 55, 65. On the influence of Wu Hsü
and Yang Fang as the central figures of the Chekiang clique in Shanghai,
see Ono Shinji, "Ri Kō-shō no tōjō — Waigun no seiritsu o megutte," *Tōyōshi
kenkyū,* 16.2:107–134 (Sept. 1957).

92. Morse, *International Relations*, I, 356–358.

93. When Elgin gave a speech to the British merchants in Shanghai, he
anticipated that the Chinese were sure to receive a translation (Walrond, p.
239).

94. In a memorial received on May 19, 1858 (IWSM:HF, 22:16–17; a longer version in SKHT:YCLT, 9:23–24), Huang Tsung-han, a firm anti-foreignist, counseled prudence, stating that pacifist leanings among the Shanghai merchants, who were under pressure from foreign plenipotentiaries, had been reported from Shanghai by Chang T'ing-hsueh, compiler of the second class of the National Academy. According to the memorial, Chang had been stationed in Shanghai as an informant for the memorialist until he sailed for Kwangtung, and he was close to such wealthy Shanghai merchants as Yang Fang. This indicates that the pacifist views of the Shanghai merchants, who had been exposed to pressure by the foreign officials, indirectly influenced a firmly antiforeignist high official and reached the ears of the emperor.

Chang T'ing-hsueh was favored by Wu Hsü and was a good friend of Yang Fang (*Yin-hsien chih* [1877], 44:36; IWSM:HF, 10:3).

In February 1860 Yang Fang stated to the Shanghai manager of Jardine, Matheson and Co. that, at the suggestion of the peace party, "the industrious [*sic*] and commercial classes" had sent a petition for peace to the emperor (Bruce to Russell, No. 44, Feb. 19, 1860, FO 17/336).

95. IWSM:HF, 36:14, 18; 38:14–15; 39:1–2, 39; 40:13, 14, 20–22; 41:5, 16–20, 46; 42:23; 45:27–30; 47:10–11; 48:11–16, 27–31; 49:11–14, 20, 22, 31–33; 50:1, 13–17, 19, 31; 51:11, 14, 15, 39; 52:14, 15, 43, 44; 53:18–20, 41–45; 54:7, 25. Bruce to Russell, No. 44, Feb. 19, 1860, FO 17/336; Cordier, *L'expédition, 1860*, pp. 149–151.

96. See Chap. I, p. 46. See also Toyama Gunji, *Taihei Tengoku to Shanhai* (Kyoto, 1947), pp. 69ff.

In April 1860 the Chinese authorities and merchants in Shanghai asked the French field commander General de Montauban, through a French Jesuit, what his intentions would be should the government of the Middle Kingdom fall (Hérisson, pp. 317–318).

97. Bruce to Russell, Apr. 17, 1860, *PP: Affairs in China*, pp. 44–46; Memo. by Bruce, Apr. 14, 1860, *ibid.*, pp. 47–49. The chairman of the Shanghai Chamber of Commerce to Bruce, Apr. 13, 1860, *ibid.*, pp. 49–50.

98. Bruce to Russell, Apr. 7, 1860, *PP: Affairs in China*, p. 40; Bruce to Russell, Mar. 6, 1860, *FO: Affairs in China, Confidential* (1861), p. 45.

T'an T'ing-hsiang and his colleagues in a memorial: "As for the junk crews, many of them are vagrants from such places as Shanghai. They dwell on boats. Usually they have occasional intercourse with various barbarians. They never dare to give up their jobs and to work for the government. They fear resentment and reprisal on the part of the barbarians" (IWSM:HF, 23:19).

99. See references cited above in note 97. See also IWSM:HF, 50:13–14 (a memorial from Ho Kuei-ch'ing). Bruce had been instructed to institute a blockade of this kind (Russell to Bruce, Oct. 29, 1859 *PP: Affairs in China*, pp. 1–2). According to Ho Kuei-ch'ing's memorial, when Bruce was holding a conference with the British merchants the Chinese merchants staged a demonstration involving more than 1,000 junk men. Pressure was also applied to

General de Montauban by Chinese merchants in Shanghai, Christian and pagan, through a French priest. See La Servière, II, 16–17.

For a recent study, based on Chinese sources, of the maritime transport of tribute grain and the shipping merchants involved in the 1850's and after, see Yamaguchi Michiko, "Shindai no sōun to senshō," *Tōyōshi kenkyū*, 17.2:180–196 (Sept. 1958). This article mentions the events described here.

100. IWSM:HF, 22:29; *PP: Elgin's Missions,* p. 311; Cordier, *L'expédition, 1857–58,* pp. 379–380.

101. IWSM:HF, 14:17; 17:39–40; 18:1; 19:13, 17, 20; 22:39–40; 28:36; 31:14, 15; 41:32; 42:9–10; 49:28; 62:30, 32–33. Liang Chia-pin, "Ying-Fa lien-chün chih i Kuang-tung chiu shih-san-hang hang-shang t'iao-t'ing chan-shih shih-liao," *Kuo-li Chung-shan ta-hsueh wen-shih-hsueh yen-chiu-so yueh-k'an,* 1.1:77–82 (Jan. 1933); reprinted in Liang Chia-pin, *Kuang-tung shih-san-hang k'ao* (1937). On Wu Ch'ung-yueh, see Hummel, II, 867–868; Liang Chia-pin, *Kuang-tung shih-san-han k'ao,* pp. 294–296.

102. S. W. Williams reports that Lo (Tun-yen), Lung (Yuan-hsi) and Su ("So") (T'ing-k'uei), the three gentry leaders of the antiforeign movement, were unpopular among "the trading people, who suffer their exactions" (Williams to Cass, Feb. 12, 1859, Diplomatic Dispatches, China, Vol. 18).

103. IWSM:HF, 29:9.

104. *Ibid.,* 33:31, 44–45; 45:29; 49:32; 50:31. See also *PP: Elgin's Missions,* p. 477; *PP: Corr. with Bruce,* pp. 21–28.

P'an Shih-ch'eng was a wealthy man descended from a hong merchant family. He was given a *chü-jen* degree in recognition of a contribution of money to the government. Through purchase of offices, he eventually became salt controller of Kwangtung. During the first half of the 1840's he helped Ch'i-ying in diplomatic affairs (Hummel, II, 605–606).

105. J. Jardine to Elgin, Oct. 1, 1857, *PP: Elgin's Missions,* pp. 83–84; Elgin to Clarendon, Nov. 27, 1857, *ibid.,* p. 82.

106. Hummel, I, 380. Wang K'ai-yun, "Wang Hsiang-ch'i hsien-sheng lu Ch'i-hsiang ku-shih," *Tung-fang tsa-chih,* 14.12:93 (Dec. 1917). Lo Tun-jung, "Hsiao-ch'üan Huang-hou tz'u-ssu," K'ang-tz'u'u T'ai-hou tsun-hao," in his "Pin-t'ui sui-pi," *Yung-yen,* 2.5:15–16 (May 1914).

107. J. O. P. Bland and E. Backhouse, *China under the Empress Dowager* (new rev., ed., Peking, 1939), p. 30.

We may infer from the very fact that antagonism developed between the two princes during the period from the emperor's flight to the *coup d'état* in November 1861 (in which Prince I, Prince Cheng, and Su-shun were put to death), that their enmity derived from something more than a difference in policy.

108. IWSM:HF, 23:10–13; SKHT:YCLT, 10:10–14. I infer that the memorialists ("Tsai-yuan [Prince I] and others"), who also oversaw the preparation of the memorandum, were Prince I and the grand councillors, with or without some others; see Chap. I, note 49.

109. *Ibid.,* 25:22–23; 26:31–32. Miyazaki Ichisada, "Pekin shinnyū jiken," pp. 860–861, 864–865.

110. CSK, *lieh-chuan*, No. 174 (Su-shun); No. 210 (Yin Keng-yun).

111. *Ibid.*, No. 181 (Huang Tsung-han).

112. As a nearly first-hand observation, we may cite a report by Ignat'ev in June 1860 to the allied authorities then in Shanghai. According to him, a warlike party of civilian officials, led by Su-shun and Princes Cheng, I, and Hui, was controlling the Peking government, and Kuei-liang had no real influence at all. (Bruce to Russell, No. 127, June 26, 1860, FO 17/338; Bourboulon to Thouvenel, June 16, 1860, in Cordier, *L'expédition, 1860*, pp. 186–187; H. Knollys, ed., *Life of General Sir Hope Grant, with Selections from his Correspondence* [Edinburgh, 1894], II, 70–71.) According to what Harry Parkes heard from Heng-ch'i in September 1860 while he was held prisoner in Peking, the majority of the princes and ministers, including Prince Cheng, Prince I, and Seng-ko-lin-ch'in, favored the continuation of war (Parkes to Elgin, Oct. 20, 1860, *PP: Affairs in China*, p. 236.) According to the Chinese letter on the Shanghai scene cited in note 37, Princes Hui, Kung, and Cheng, in whose hands rested the administration of barbarian affairs, were warlike. This information can be interpreted as indicating that the predominant mood was warlike in the Council of Princes, which was definitely affecting the drafting of edicts.

113. On the Hsien-feng emperor, see Hummel, I, 378–380. In 1858 his age was 28 *sui*. Wang K'ai-yun states in his preface to Yin Keng-yun, *Hsin-pai-jih-chai chi* (Kuang-hsü 21 ed.) that the Hsien-feng emperor "really did not want peace." An intelligence report which the British received from a Chinese informant who had just returned from Peking tells of the emperor's aversion to such foreign demands as the residence in the capital of a Western diplomat; see Memorandum by R. Hart, Canton, May 22, 1859, *PP: Corr. with Bruce*, pp. 7–8.

114. CSL:WT, 269:31–32; 278:16–17; CSK, *lieh-chuan*, No. 209 (Sung Chin). Williams, "Journal," p. 35; R. Swinhoe, *Narrative of the North China Campaign of 1860* (London, 1861), p. 290; Montauban, p. 148; Memo. by Hart, Canton, May 22, 1859, *FO: Affairs in China, Confidential* (1859), p. 9. In 1858 Archimandrite Palladii recorded that, not withstanding his poor health, the emperor daily attended to state affairs. (Extracts from a journal kept at Peking during the year 1858, trans. from the *Morskoi Sbornik* [Naval Magazine] for Aug. 1860, in Erskine to Russell, No. 81, Sept. 17, 1860, FO 65/554. On the authorship of the journal, see below, Chap. IV, note 78.)

115. IWSM:HF, 24:1–2, 16–19; 26:10–15.

116. T. F. Tsiang, "Notes and Suggestions: I, Origins of the Tsungli Yamen," pp. 93–94; Ch'en Kung-lu, "Ssu-kuo T'ien-chin t'iao-yueh ch'eng-li chih ching-kuo," *Chin-ling hsueh-pao*, 1.2:411, 419 (Nov. 1931); Hummel, I, 380; Hsü, *China's Entrance*, pp. 38–39, 58, 60, 64–65, 89, 233, note 31.

117. For the most part, I am here following the analysis in Miyazaki Ichisada, "Pekin shinnyū jiken."

118. Hummel, I, 428.

119. Miyazaki Ichisada, "Pekin shinnyū jiken," p. 860. When Ch'i-ying, on the recommendation of the war party, was appointed a third representative,

Prince Kung stated in one of his warlike memorials that Ch'i-ying, who was to blame for the previous week-kneed diplomacy, should assume sole responsibility for the negotiations (IWSM:HF, 24:17). When Ch'i-ying was impeached, Prince Kung opposed the very severe penalty suggested by the war party (ibid., 26:31–32). These two moves can be interpreted as efforts to defend indirectly the viewpoint of Kuei-liang (Miyazaki Ichisada, "Pekin shinnyū jiken," pp. 860, 864–865).

120. Ignat'ev represents Prince Hui as a leading war advocate. See above, note 112. The following passage from the autobiography of Yin Chao-yung, a passionate war advocate, may be taken as an indication of Prince Hui's role: " . . . the barbarian bandits occupied the Tientsin forts [Taku forts], and were insatiable in making demands. The men in power (chih-cheng) strongly advocated peace. Prince Hui came to the Palace School for Princes ([Shang-] shu-fang) [where select scholar-officials of orthodox learning like Yin Chao-yung were serving as tutors to young princes] to inquire about public opinion" (Yin Chao-yung, p. 32, under the fourth Chinese month [May 13–June 10] of 1858).

121. Ai-hsin chueh-lo tsung-p'u, chia-ts'e, pp. 87, 91.

122. On Seng-ko-lin-ch'in, see Ch'ing-shih lieh-chuan, 45:1–10; CSK, lieh-chuan, No. 191; Hummel, II, 632–634, 968.

On the institutions and historical background of the Korchin tribe, see Yano Jin'ichi, Kindai Mōkoshi kenkyū (Kyoto, 1925); Kamenofuchi Ryūchō, comp., Mō-chi, (1914; a new printing, Sinkyō [Hsinking], 1935); in Minami Manshū Tetsudō Kabushiki Kaisha, Manshū kyūkan chōsa hōkoku, 9 vols., 1913–1915.

123. See above, note 9.

124. Bruce's comment on Seng-ko-lin-ch'in's army: "According to the observations of competent persons, during the Peking campaign [of 1860], the army under Sung-ko-lin-tsin was organized in the same manner [as Tseng Kuo-fan's]; the men were paid and no pillage was permitted. The villages, where they had been quartered, were untouched, and his troops, even in their retreat, neither injured the houses, nor the standing crops" (Bruce to Russell, No. 9, Feb. 23, 1862, FO 17/370). See also Rennie, Peking and the Pekingese, II, 32; Rennie, British Arms, p. 260.

125. See Case 9, in the early part of Chap. II.

126. Extracts from a journal kept in Peking during the year 1858, trans. from the Morskoi Sbornik (Naval Magazine) for Sept. 1860, in Erskine to Russell, No. 100, Oct. 7, 1860, FO 65/554. (On the authorship of this source, see below. Chap. IV, note 78.) Bruce to Malmesbury, July 5, 1859, PP: Corr. with Bruce, p. 17. Memo. by Mr. Wade, etc., ibid., p. 37; Bruce to Russell, No. 35, Feb. 6, 1860, FO 17/336; Bruce to Russell, No. 44, Feb. 19, 1860, FO 17/336; Bruce to Russell, No. 93, Apr. 17, 1860, FO 17/337; Parkes to Elgin, Oct. 20, 1860, PP: Affairs in China, p. 236; Wolseley, p. 56; Dispatch from Bourboulon, June 30, 1859, Cordier, L'expédition, 1860, p. 82; Hérisson, p. 30; Martin, p. 193; Montauban, pp. 277, 296. Mgr. Mouly to Montauban, between Peking and Tientsin, Apr. 29, 1860, ibid., pp. 119–123.

127. Most of the sources cited in note 126 are based on reports by Chinese informants. For a report affirming that he was *not* warlike, see Bruce to Russell, secret and confidential (unnumbered), Jan. 21, 1860, FO 17/335. Incidentally, Thomas Wade reported as follows in January 1861: "Was Ho [Kuei-ch'ing], I asked, the *bona fide* advocate of peace with us? Yes, said Wan [i.e., Wen-hsiang], and another whom you would not suspect, and he wrote the name of Sang [Seng-ko-lin-ch'in] on the inkstone. He said Sang urged (not from fear of us) that the empire had war enough without embroiling itself with foreign powers" (Wade to Bruce, Peking, Jan. 23, 1861, in Bruce to Russell, No. 14, Tientsin, Mar. 12, 1861, FO 17/350).

128. Elgin to Russell, Aug. 25, 1860, *PP: Affairs in China,* p. 115. English translations of the two memorials are in *ibid.,* pp. 120–124.

129. IWSM:HF, 49:22–25. The other of these two memorials, the one presented by Seng-ko-lin-ch'in alone, is not included in IWSM:HF.

130. For an English translation of this memorial, see *PP: Affairs in China,* p. 260. The original Chinese text is not in IWSM: HF.

131. The Chinese text in IWSM:HF, 38:40–41, 43–45. English translations are in Cordier, *L'expédition, 1860,* pp. 74–76; enclosures no. 2 and no. 3 in Winchester to Hammond, Canton, Aug. 8, 1859, *FO: Affairs in China, Confidential* (1859); *North China Herald* (July 30, 1859), p. 207.

The *North China Herald* (July 23, 1859), p. 202, comments on these two memorials as follows: "We are assured by a gentleman to whom we have submitted them that they have been most probably made up from the accounts published by ourselves, they are so remarkably free from the exaggerated compliments to native skill and valour which usually characterise compositions of the sort." This comment is noteworthy as paradoxically revealing the realistic characteristics of Seng-ko-lin-ch'in's ideas presented in his memorials. The *North China Herald* thus temporarily entertained an impression that these documents "were manufactured down here [in Shanghai] for the foreign market." See *North China Herald* (Aug. 6, 1859), p. 3; cf. *ibid.* (Aug. 27, 1859), p. 14.

The Peking government became quite nervous when it heard that the barbarians had obtained copies of Seng-ko-lin-ch'in's memorials on the Taku victory. See IWSM:HF, 41:7; 42:22, 30–31; 50:30.

132. Cordier, *L'expédition, 1860,* pp. 152–155.

133. IWSM:HF, 39:11–14 (a principal memorial and an additional memorial received on July 3, 1859). The Chinese text of the principal memorial is considerably shorter than the French version. There are also some differences in phraseology. Furthermore, the French version seems to contain some errors of translation. However, it appears to be indisputable that, in substance, these two versions are of the same document.

134. Williams, "Journal," pp. 212–217. Williams himself may have been the translator.

135. *North China Herald* (Sept. 10, 1859), p. 22. On this memorial by Yin Chao-yung see above, note 61.

136. Seng-ko-lin-ch'in's memorials of the kind examined here had been kept

confidential by the Chinese authorities and reached the foreigners by seizure or purchase. There were, of course, other memorials by him, which had been published in the *Peking Gazette* and so could easily come to the notice of foreign observers. See Enclosure in Bruce to Russell, Sept. 20, 1859, *PP: Corr. with Bruce*, p. 54.

137. Cf. Miyazaki Ichisada, "Pekin shinnyū jiken," pp. 862–863, 873. Seng-ko-lin-ch'in seems to have been unable to use literary Chinese, or at least he was "not very good" at it according to a memorial by Yuan Chia-san in 1861 (*Yuan Tuan-min kung chi, tsou-i,* 15:12 [in Ting Chen-to, comp., *Hsiang-ch'eng Yuan-shih chia-chi* (1911)]. I owe this reference to Chiang Siang-tse, *The Nien Rebellion* [Seattle, 1954], p. 84).

On the other hand, Harry Parkes reported that just after his capture on Sept. 18, 1860, he was taken to Seng-ko-lin-ch'in and there was an exchange of harsh words between them. Parkes gives a somewhat *verbatim* transcript of the dialogue, from the context of which it appears that Seng-ko-lin-ch'in spoke in Chinese and probably talked directly to Parkes: "The Prince then continued in a very forbidding tone, 'Listen! . . . ' "; " . . . when the Prince interrupted me by saying . . . "; "I then heard him give directions to take Mr. Loch, the Sowar, and myself to the Prince of I . . . " (Parkes to Elgin, Oct. 20, 1860, *PP: Affairs in China,* pp. 229–230).

Perhaps we should assume that he could speak Mandarin fairly well, but had difficulty in handling literary Chinese. This language handicap of his raises the embarrassing question of how far the ideas presented in his memorials were his own. As we shall see, however, his memorials were on the whole rather pessimistic and restrained, except for some memorials after the Taku victory which were quite understandably exalted and rather aggressive. This consistency in tone, whether or not he was assisted by the peace advocate Kuo Sung-tao (see below, note 139), may safely lead to the assumption that the memorials presented under his name substantially represented his own ideas on war and diplomacy.

138. IWSM:HF, 25:29–31; 26:38–40.

139. *Ibid.,* 40:18–19. Kuo Sung-tao, then a compiler of the second class of the Academy, who had been working for some time under Seng-ko-lin-ch'in, brought this memorial to Peking. He explained the memorial in the presence of the emperor (*ibid.,* 40:19–20).

In his autobiographical recollections, Kuo Sung-tao recalls that early in Hsien-feng 9 (roughly 1859) he advised peace in answer to Seng-ko-lin-ch'in's personal inquiry and he opposed the latter's building up defenses. When he was working for him later, all his advice was rejected. He also angered the Mongol prince by repeatedly presenting to him memoranda in which he seemed to oppose a plan for "sniping at the enemy" (*Yü-chih lao-jen tzu-hsü* [1893], pp. 8–9).

140. IWSM:HF, 49:22–25 (with Heng-fu).

141. *Ibid.,* 55:26–30 (with Heng-fu). See also a memorial (with Heng-fu) of Aug. 6, 1860, printed in Chu Shih-chia, I, 160–161.

142. IWSM:HF, 55:32–33, 35, 38–39; 56:33; 57:1; 62:34–35.

143. *Ibid.*, 57:17.

144. *Ibid.*, 60:8.

145. *Ibid.*, 63:31; 65:27; 66:27.

146. *Ibid.*, 63:12–14.

147. *Ibid.*, 64:8 (memorial from Prince Kung and others). Two communications from Seng-ko-lin-ch'in to Prince Kung's office in PLFC: Pan-li fu-chü an, *chüan* 2, under Oct. 1, 1860, and *chüan* 3, under Oct. 12, 1860.

148. See Cases 10, 36 and 37 in the early part of Chap. II.

149. Ignat'ev's remark to General Grant, field commander of the British forces, quoted in H. Knollys, *Life of Grant,* II, 70–71. The French version of Ignat'ev's observation is somewhat different in nuance. It describes Seng-ko-lin-ch'in as "desiring the war, solely because he is a military chief, and as a means of augmenting his influence," but at the same time it sharply distinguishes him from "the party of the war to the knife" led by people like Su-shun and Prince Cheng (Bourboulon to Thouvenel, June 16, 1860, in Cordier, *L'expédition, 1860,* pp. 186–187).

150. See Chap. I, p. 48. On similar soundings undertaken by Prince Kung and his associates in Peking after the signing of the Peking Conventions see Chap. VI, pp. 207–210.

151. See for instance, Reed to Cass, June 2, 1858, *Reed Corr.,* p. 330; Williams, "Journal," pp. 46, 48, 50; Walrond, p. 251; Marquis de Moges, *Souvenirs d'une Ambassade en Chine et au Japon en 1857 et 1858* (Paris, 1860), pp. 214, 216. Similar observations may easily be found in many other Western sources cited in this book.

During the occupation by the allied troops in 1858, the people in Tientsin were at first quiet, but they grew restive as time passed. On June 10 there occurred two antiforeign incidents. (Williams, "Journal," pp. 63–64, 164; IWSM:HF, 25:21, 33–34; Ting Yun-shu *et al.,* 4:1–2; Lay, *Note on the Opium Question,* pp. 11–12; G. M. Wrong, *The Earl of Elgin* [London, 1905], p. 103.) Lay, rightly or not, ascribes one of these disturbances to instigation on the part of the Ch'ing negotiators. However, a more substantial cause of this kind of tension seems to have been that the port of Tientsin had been in a state of virtual blockade since foreign warships had arrived in the river; business was at a standstill; the price of rice had meanwhile risen three and a half times, and the populace had thus become desperate. This tense situation frightened Kuei-liang and Hua-sha-na, and was a factor in driving them to submission. See Martin, p. 180, Moges, p. 221; IWSM:HF, 26:25, 27:27.

152. For instance, see Williams, "Journal," pp. 40–41; Elgin to Russell, Aug. 26, 1860, *PP: Affairs in China,* pp. 125–126. However, they would hesitate to accept money when they feared reprisals by the mandarins (Moges, p. 205; Swinhoe, p. 22).

153. Elgin to Russell, Oct. 9, 1860, *PP: Affairs in China,* p. 189.

154. Williams, "Journal," p. 39.

155. Bruce to Russell, No. 93, Apr. 17, 1860, FO 17/337.

156. Wolseley, pp. 92–93; *North China Herald* (Aug. 18, 1860), p. 131.

157. Swinehoe, pp. 159–160.

158. IWSM:HF, 59:15.

159. Shen Chao-lin, 1:16–19; see also *Ch'ing-shih lieh-chuan*, 47:5–6.

160. IWSM:HF, 22:23; 57:29–34; 58:24–25. These are memorials by vehement war advocates like Wang Mao-yin, Pi Shu-t'ang, and Lu Ping-shu. See also Williams, "Journal," p. 29.

At T'ung-chou Prince I asked Harry Parkes to supply the capital with grain at a reasonable price (Wade to Elgin, Sept. 23, 1860, *PP: Affairs in China*, p. 169).

161. Ward to Cass, Shanghai, June 29, 1860, Diplomatic Dispatches, China, Vol. 19. See also Bruce to Russell, No. 127, June 26, 1860, FO 17/338.

162. Walrond, p. 350; Wolseley, p. 16; Williams, "Journal," pp. 48, 50; Hérisson, "Introduction," p. iv.

163. IWSM:HF, 26:42 (memorial from T'an T'ing-hsiang); 46:2 (joint memorial from Seng-ko-lin-ch'in and Heng-fu); 60:22–25 (joint memorial from Chiao Yu-ying and Chang Chih-wan).

164. *Ibid.*, 24:30 (memorial from T'an T'ing-hsiang); 56:26 (edict).

165. *Ibid.*, 25:8–9; also printed in Yin Keng-yun, *chüan* 1, as "Ch'ou-i su san." In a memorial presented in 1859 he stated: "Your Majesty lives within the palace remote from the outside. How can your Majesty know [the anxieties of the men in the street]? Your Majesty relies upon either the reports in the memorials by Kuei-liang and his colleague or the whitewashing mutual praises of the princes. They say either that the barbarians are very submissive, or that there is no other way than this [to meet the situation]" ("Ch'ou-i su ch'i," *ibid., chüan* 1).

166. Unless otherwise indicated, the following narrative concerning the assembly of courtiers and the events preceding it on the same day is based on Yin Keng-yun, "Hsien-feng wu-wu wu-yueh shih-san-jih t'ing-ch'en hui-i lueh," *Hsin-pai-jih-chai chi, chüan* 3. See also Miyazaki Ichisada, "Pekin shinnyū jiken," pp. 861–862.

167. SKHT:YCLT, 11:102. See also Case 26 in the early part of Chap. II and its context.

168. On this memorial, see Chap. I, pp. 26–27 and note 55. The Commission of Civil Defense was established on June 2 and discontinued on July 23, 1858. It was composed of Ch'ou Tsu-p'ei, Chao Kuang, Hsü Nai-p'u, Wang Mao-yin, Sung Chin, and the police censors. See IWSM:HF, 24:1, 10; CSL:WT, 256:26.

169. This description of the attendance is vague. Yin Ken-yun's biography in *Ch'ing-shih lieh-chuan*, 76:47, says more specifically: "the grand councillors, princes and high officials (*wang-ta-ch'en*), Nine Chief Ministries of State (*Chiu-ch'ing*) and the censors (*k'o-tao*)."

According to Archimandrite Palladii's diary for 1858, the "Supreme Council" (the Grand Council) was joined in any emergency by the princes, ministers, and other high officers of state. He records that on June 2, 1858 (assuming that the date "21 May" given in the English translation quoted here is in the Julian calendar), there was held "an extraordinary meeting of the Supreme Council, at which the princes, ministers, and superior functionaries of the capital were present." As a result of this meeting the emperor gave orders to place the capital in a state of defense, a militia was to be raised, Seng-ko-lin-ch'in was appointed commander-in-chief of the troops defending the capital, and Ch'i-ying was ordered to take part in the Tientsin negotiations. (Extracts from a journal kept at Peking during the year 1858, trans. fr. the *Morskoi Sbornik* [Naval Magazine], for Aug. and Sept. 1860, in Erskine to Russell, No. 81, Sept. 17, 1860, and No. 100, Oct. 7, 1860, FO 65/554. — On the authorship of the diary, see below, Chap. IV, note 78.) — (In fact, on June 2 the grand councillors presented a memorial on the defense of the city, and three edicts were issued, which respectively announced the establishment of the Commission of Civil Defense, the appointment of Seng-ko-lin-ch'in, and that of Ch'i-ying [IWSM:HF, 24:1, 2–5]). The assembly of courtiers on June 23, 1858, and that of September 9, 1860 (mentioned later in this chapter), were apparently the same kind of extraordinary meeting of the Supreme or Grand Council as that referred to by Palladii.

170. See above, note 17.

171. Sung Chin was subchancellor of the Grand Secretariat and acting junior vice-president of the Board of Revenue. He was one of the cosigners of the joint memorial from the Commission of Civil Defense. In a memorial received on June 17, 1858, he suggested bribing Lay (IWSM:HF, 25:32–33). In IWSM and SKHT there is no memorial indicating his opposition to the demand for free navigation of rivers.

172. The memorial by Wan Ch'ing-li referred to here is not in IWSM or SKHT. According to Yin's "T'ing-ch'en hui-i lueh," Wan was then vice-president of the Board of Punishments. According to CSK, *pu-yuan ta-ch'en nien-piao*, however, he was not in that post, but was appointed senior vice-president of the Board of War in the seventh month of Hsien-feng and was transferred in the tenth month to the junior vice-presidency of the Board of Civil Appointments.

173. This vermilion rescript is also in IWSM:HF, 26:24; this version is slightly different from Yin Keng-yun's.

174. IWSM:HF, 58:24.

175. Postscript by his son Yin Yen-ho to Yin Keng-yun, "Yü ta-ch'en Su-shun shu", *Hsin-pai-jih-chai chi* (Kuang-hsü 21 ed.), *chüan* 3.

176. *Ibid.; Hsü pei-chuan-chi,* 37:10, 14; CSK, *lieh-chuan*, No. 210 (Yin Keng-yun). On his demotion, see CSL:WT, 292:24–25.

177. Later in the same year he was promoted to chief supervisor of instruction. See CSK, *lieh-chuan,* No. 209.

178. See also the quotation from Yin Chao-yung's autobiography in note 120 above. The memorial quoted in the text is in Chiang-shang-ch'ien-sou (Hsia Hsieh), 22:11–17, as "Yin Chao-yung ch'ing pa T'ien-chin fu-i yuan-tsou." The date of the memorial is based on Yin Chao-yung, p. 32.

As stated in note 61 above, copies of this memorial circulated among the literati after the 1859 Taku victory, the *North China Herald* printed an English translation, and G. Pauthier published a French translation. The *North China Herald* (July 23, 1859, p. 202; Aug. 13, 1859, p. 7) referred to this memorial as "the tremendous war-memorial" and commented that the policy it recommended was that of "the old school of China statesmen."

179. Yin Chao-yung, p. 32. See also his biography in Min Erh-ch'ang, comp., *Pei-chuan-chi pu*, 4:3-4.

180. IWSM:HF, 28:45-49. Also included in the collection of his memorials, *Wang Shih-lang tsou-i*, ed. I P'ei-shen (editor's preface dated eleventh month of Kuang-hsü 13), 9:20-23. Wang Mao-yin was a typical scholar-official with a reputation for integrity and straightforwardness. See CSK, *lieh-chuan*, No. 209; *Hsü pei-chuan-chi*, 11:2-3. For a modern analysis of his career and thinking, with special attention to his expert knowledge of currency problems, see Wu Han, "Wang Mao-yin yü Hsien-feng shih-tai ti hsin pi-chih," *Chung-kuo she-hui ching-chi-shih chi-k'an*, 6.1:113-146 (June 1939). (Reprinted with slightly changed title in Wu Han, *Tu-shih cha-chi* [Peking, 1957]). Professor Miyazaki Ichisada asserts, without giving documentation, that Wang Mao-yin was a follower of Su-shun ("Pekin shinnyū jiken," p. 861).

For warlike memorials by him, see IWSM:HF, 23:22-25 (received on May 30, 1858) (cf. a longer version in Wang Mao-yin, 9:11-14); *ibid.*, 9:18-19 (a memorial dated June 6, 1858, which is not in IWSM:HF or SKHT). As stated above, he served on the Commission of Civil Defense and was a co-signer of the joint memorial from the Commission presented on June 23. He also supported Yin Keng-yun at the assembly of courtiers held on the same day. In August 1858 he was relieved of his post for reasons of health, on his own request (Wang Mao-yin, 9:23-24; CSL:WT, 258:11). It is possible that he made this request in order to evade the displeasure of the emperor or of the princes, which was possibly brought on by this memorial quoted in the text.

181. On Ch'i Kung's memorial, see *Hsü pei-chuan-chi*, 24:2; Li Yuan, comp., *Kuo-ch'ao ch'i-hsien lei-cheng ch'u-pien*, 197:33.

182. This translation of the quotation from the Book of History (*Shu-ching*) is taken from James Legge, *The Chinese Classics* (London and Hong Kong, 1861-74), Vol. 3, Part 2, p. 490.

183. Bourboulon to Thouvenel, June 16, 1860, in Cordier, *L'expédition, 1860*, pp. 186-187. Frederick Bruce in Feb. 1860: "I am now more convinced than ever that from the period of our departure from Tien-tsin in 1858, the war party assumed the ascendant, and deliberately determined to set aside the engagements entered into by the Emperor. . . . I feel bound to record my conviction that nothing short of the complete defeat of this hostile party . . . will enable us to place our relations for the future on a secure basis" (Bruce to Russell, Feb. 6, 1860, PP: *Affairs in China*, p. 28.) See also Gros, p. 9.

184. IWSM:HF, 55:35. One of the edicts issued in response to this report remarked that the grand councillors had presented to the emperor a letter to "Tsai-yuan [Prince I] and others" from Seng-ko-lin-ch'in (*ibid.*, 55:36). In all probability Seng-ko-lin-ch'in had sought to apply pressure to the Council of Princes by telling them about the disastrous situation.

185. *Ibid.*, 55:35-38. The vermilion rescript was to be shown to Prince I,

Prince Cheng, and the grand councilors and then sent posthaste to Seng-ko-lin-ch'in.

186. See the English translation of the memorial in *PP: Affairs in China,* p. 260. The Chinese text is not in IWSM:HF, probably because the original copy was seized by the British at the Summer Palace.

187. Wade to Elgin, Sept. 23, 1860, *PP: Affairs in China,* p. 169.

188. IWSM:HF, 62:5–6 (with Mu-yin).

189. *Ibid.,* 60:30–31; 61:18; Weng T'ung-ho, *chüan* 1, *keng-shen,* p. 32; *PP: Affairs in China,* pp. 260–261.

190. On September 12: a joint memorial from Ch'üan-ch'ing, president of the Board of Civil Appointments, and forty other officials (*ibid.,* pp. 261–262); and a joint memorial from Ai-jen, senior president of the Censorate, and seventy-four other officials of the same organ (*ibid.,* pp. 264–265). On September 13: a joint memorial from Ch'üan-ch'ing and twenty-three other officials (*ibid.,* p. 263); a joint memorial from Ai-jen and seventy-six other officials of the Censorate (*ibid.,* p. 265); and a joint memorial from the Grand Councillors K'uang Yuan, Wen-hsiang, and Tu Han (IWSM:HF, 61:18–19). There was also a joint memorial, of which the date cannot be ascertained, from the Nine Chief Ministries of State and the censors ("Chiu-ch'ing k'o-tao chien hsing Mu-lan su," in Chiang-shang-chien-sou [Hsia Hsieh], *chüan* 15). In addition there were many memorials presented individually by various officials.

On the course of events in the court preceding the emperor's departure, see Weng T'ung-ho, *chüan* 1, *keng-shen,* pp. 32–38; Wen-hsiang, *Wen Wen-chung kung tzu-ting nien-p'u* (printed in his collectanea, *Wen Wen-chung kung shih-lueh* [1882]), p. 32.

191. Elgin to Russell, Nov. 15, 1860, *PP: Affairs in China,* p. 259; R. J. L. M'Ghee, *How We Got to Pekin: A Narrative of the Campaign in China of 1860* (London, 1862), p. 283.

192. Montauban, p. 431.

193. Weng T'ung-ho, *chüan* 1, *keng-shen,* p. 33; CSK, *lieh-chuan,* No. 174 (Su-shun); Hsueh Fu-ch'eng, "Hsien-feng chi-nien san-chien fu-chu"; Bland and Backhouse, p. 283. See also Chao Kuang, *Chao Wen-k'o kung tzu-ting nien-p'u* (postscript dated Kuang-hsü 16), pp. 114–115.

194. *PP: Affairs in China,* p. 263 (English translation). Yin Keng-yun, "Tsai chien hsun-hsing Mu-lan su," *Hsin-pai-jih-chai chi, chüan* 2. The two quotations are from the English translation. "Some about your Majesty's person" reads in the corresponding passage of the Chinese text: "princes of the first degree in your Majesty's entourage like Tuan-hua" (*tso-yu ch'in-wang ju Tuan-hua teng*). Perhaps this daring expression in Yin Keng-yun's original draft was toned down in the final version presented to the throne.

195. "Chien hsun-hsing Mu-lan su," *ibid., chüan* 2.

196. "Yü ta-ch'en Su-shun shu," *ibid.,* (Kuang-hsü 21 ed.), *chüan* 3.

197. Oliphant, I, 351–376; Martin, pp. 171, 174–176, 186.

198. Cordier, *L'expédition, 1857–58,* p. 387.

199. The earliest use of the expression "the war party" in Elgin's dispatches

is probably in Elgin to Malmesbury, No. 193, Oct. 22, 1858, FO 17/291 (also in *PP: Elgin's Missions*, pp. 403–404).

200. Elgin to Malmesbury, Nov. 5, 1858, *PP: Elgin's Missions*, p. 407.

201. *Ibid.*, pp. 460–466, 478–479, 482–483; IWSM:HF, 33:30–34, 42–44. In May 1859 Huang Tsung-han was transferred from the governor-generalship of Kwangtung and Kwangsi to become governor-general of Szechwan (CSL:WT, 280:7). On Kuei-liang's maneuver in exploiting the secret edict in order to persuade the emperor, see Miyazaki Ichisada, "Pekin shinnyū jiken," pp. 848–849.

202. Bruce to Russell, No. 44, Feb. 19, 1860, FO 17/336.

203. IWSM:HF, 48:14–15, 31. See Chap. I, p. 32.

204. See the sources cited in note 97. See also Bruce to Russell, Feb. 6, 1860, *PP: Affairs in China*, pp. 27–28; Montauban, pp. 83–84.

205. Cordier, *Histoire des relations*, I, 43–45, 48; Gros, pp. 199, 201–203; Gros to Elgin, Nov. 7, 1860 (enclosed in the following dispatch of Elgin); Elgin to Russell, No. 89, confidential, Nov. 13, 1860, FO 17/332.

206. Walrond, pp. 371–372.

Notes to Chapter III. The Conduct of Foreign Affairs Following the Tientsin Treaties

1. Kweiliang, Hwashana, etc. to Elgin, Oct. 22, 1858, *PP: Elgin's Missions*, pp. 408–410.

2. IWSM:HF, 31:48–51. A British request "to have an imperial commissioner dispatched for a tour of the various ports" is not mentioned in the Blue Books. Something akin to this idea appears in Article ("rule") 10 of the agreement containing rules of trade, signed at Shanghai by Elgin and Kuei-liang and his colleagues, on Nov. 8, 1858: "The High Officer appointed by the Chinese Government to superintend Foreign trade [*tsung-li wai-kuo t'ung-shang shih-i ta-ch'en* in the Chinese text] will accordingly, from time to time, either himself visit, or will send a deputy to visit, the different ports." In his report on this agreement Elgin offered no explanation of this "High Officer." As we shall see, the British were never willing to accept an imperial commissioner in the provinces or at the ports as a substitute for the arrangement stipulated in Article 5 of the British Tientsin Treaty. Hence, Elgin's "High Officer" must have meant the officer supervising foreign *trade*, as distinguished from official diplomatic business, which should be the responsibility of a different body. If the British really made the request quoted here by Kuei-liang, they must have had in mind the appointment of a roving superintendent of trade. We may thus infer that Kuei-liang and his colleagues here subtly distorted the facts by giving the impression that the British had first demanded a roving imperial commissioner for foreign affairs and that the Ch'ing delegation, in reply, had suggested stationing an imperial commissioner at Shanghai. It is thus quite understandable that the Peking government treated this as a request from the British.

Incidentally, there had earlier appeared, during the Tientsin negotiations, in "A memorandum on the management of barbarian affairs" by Chin An-ch'ing, expectant salt controller, the germ of the idea of stationing a high official for foreign affairs in Shanghai. The memorandum was enclosed in a memorial received on May 30, 1858, from Tu Ch'iao, junior vice-president of the Board of Revenue. A copy of the memorandum was then sent to Kuei-liang and Hua-sha-na at Tientsin. See IWSM:HF, 23:21–22. On Chin An-ch'ing, see, for example, *Ch'ung-hsiu Chia-shan hsien-chih* (preface dated 1894), 19:74.

3. IWSM:HF, 32:1–4.

4. *Ibid.*, 32:5–8. See above Chap. II, note 85.

5. Vermilion endorsement on this memorial (*ibid.*, 32:8). See Case 25 in the early part of Chap. II.

6. IWSM:HF, 32:9; italics mine.

7. *Ibid.*, 32:15–18.

8. *Ibid.*, 32:18–19.

9. *Ibid.*, 32:8–10.

10. *Ibid.*, 33:10–11; italics mine.

11. *Ibid.*, 32:14–16.

12. *Ibid.*, 32:16–17.

13. When Ho stated in his memorial urging appointment of a full-time imperial commissioner, "therefore I have previously suggested the idea of dispatching a full-time official (*chuan-yuan*)" (*ibid.*, 35:15), he was probably referring to the repeated joint requests from Kuei-liang and his colleagues (including Ho) for an imperial commissionership at Shanghai.

14. PP: *Elgin's Missions*, pp. 460–466, 478–479, 482–483; IWSM:HF, 33:30–34, 42–44.

15. Elgin to Malmesbury, April 19, 1859, PP: *Elgin's Missions*, p. 488. As "a spontaneous act on the part of the Imperial Government," Elgin attached considerable importance to the publication.

16. IWSM:HF, 35:18–19.

17. *Ibid.*, 35:14–17.

18. *Ibid.*, 35:17–18.

19. In this sense, this memorial constitutes an important treatise on the machinery for foreign affairs in the period of transition from the Canton commissioner system to the Tsungli Yamen. Besides the points already noted, the memorial made the following recommendations: (1) The imperial commissioner's term of office should not be too long, lest the official come to be made light of by Western officials through familiarity. (2) Correspondence on foreign affairs between the imperial commissioner and the Peking government, and between the provincial authorities in charge of respective treaty ports and the Peking government, should be circulated among the authorities concerned. (3) Copies of the Sino-foreign treaties should be distributed to the authorities concerned.

20. Malmesbury to Bruce, March 1, 1859, PP: *Corr. with Bruce*, p. 1.

21. Cordier, *L'expédition, 1860*, pp. 40–43, 47. It was not until the beginning of June 1859 that Bruce and Bourboulon actually arrived in Shanghai.

22. Ward to Cass, Paris, March 17, 1859, Diplomatic Dispatches, China, Vol. 18.

23. *North China Herald* (Jan. 22, 1859).

24. Elgin to Malmesbury, Feb. 26, 1859, *PP: Elgin's Missions,* p. 482. See below, however, note 26.

25. *North China Herald* (Feb. 26, 1859).

26. Elgin to Kweiliang, Hwashana, etc., *PP: Elgin's Missions,* pp. 484–485; IWSM:HF, 36:15–16. In this communication Elgin took exception to the use, in the edict which announced the transfer, of the expression "management" (lit., "soothing and bridling" [*ju-yü*]), as denying equality.

27. IWSM:HF, 36:17. Kuei-liang and his colleagues described this French protest as "an arrogation of greatness" (*yeh-lang tzu-ta*) (*ibid.,* 36:13).

28. Bruce to Kweiliang, May 16, 1859, *PP: Corr. with Bruce,* pp. 5–6; Bruce to Kweiliang, June 8, 1859, *ibid.,* pp. 13–14; Bruce to Kweiliang, June 11, 1859, *ibid.,* p. 14; a note by T. Wade to a communication of Aug. 13, 1859, from Ho Kuei-ch'ing to Bruce, *ibid.,* p. 46.

29. *Ibid.,* p. 12.

30. *Ibid.,* p. 12.

31. Memorandum by Mr. Wade, etc., Enclosure 2 in Bruce to Malmesbury, July 13, 1859, *ibid.,* p. 37.

32. Ho to Bruce, Aug. 1, 1859, *ibid.,* pp. 42–43.

33. Bruce to Ho, Aug. 9, 1859, *ibid.,* p. 43; IWSM:HF, 41:48–49. The exact Chinese official title used here by Ho Kuei-ch'ing cannot be ascertained because the original document is not available. The Chinese title that I have given in the text is the title he used in 1859 in his communications to Ward, of which the originals are filed at the National Archives. See Ho to Ward, Aug. 31, 1859 (original in Chinese), Enclosure in Ward to Cass, Sept. 1, 1859, Diplomatic Dispatches, China, Vol. 18; Ho to Ward, Nov. 5, 1859 (original in Chinese), Enclosure in Ward to Cass, Nov. 18, 1859, *ibid.*

34. Ho to Bruce, Aug. 13, 1859, *PP: Corr. with Bruce,* p. 46; IWSM:HF, 41:49.

35. *PP: Corr. with Bruce,* p. 46. This exchange of communications bothered the British because the Chinese authorities seemed to be treating diplomatic intercourse entirely as an affair of trade. The sensitive Westerners regarded this as a sinocentric denial of equality. Ho Kuei-ch'ing himself may not have had this intention, but certainly this idea persisted tenaciously. For instance, later when the Tsungli Yamen was established, there arose a controversy over whether the word "trade" (*t'ung-shang*) should or should not be inserted in the official designation of the new organ (see IWSM:HF, 72:22). Also, in the early debate between Peking and Shanghai on whether, when, and how an imperial commissioner was to be appointed at Shanghai, Shanghai talked about "the affairs concerning various countries" (*ko-kuo shih-wu*) or "the affairs concerning foreign countries" (*wai-kuo shih-wu* — see IWSM:HF, 33:15) to be handled by the Shanghai commissioner, while Peking referred to the same topic as "trade affairs" (*t'ung-shang shih-wu*). Yet

Peking chose to use the expression "the affairs concerning various countries" when it drafted the edict announcing the transfer of the commissionership, of which the foreign authorities were to be notified.

In brief, when Ho Kuei-ch'ing used the word "trade" in his official title as imperial commissioner, the British interpreted trade in a narrow sense, sharply distinguishing it from diplomatic intercourse. They thus sought to block the Ch'ing authorities by recognizing the authority of the Shanghai commissioner only over trade in its narrower meaning.

36. Bruce to Pan Wan-chang (i.e., P'eng Yun-chang), Mar. 8, 1860, *PP: Affairs in China*, pp. 34–36; Bourboulon to P'eng Yun-chang, Mar. 8, 1860, in Cordier, *L'expédition, 1860*, pp. 158–160.

37. Ho to Bruce, Apr. 5, 1860, *PP: Affairs in China*, p. 41; Great Council of State to Ho, *ibid.*, pp. 42–43, 52–53; Ho to Bourboulon, Apr. 5, 1860, Cordier, *L'expédition, 1860*, p. 162; Grand Council to Ho, end of March 1860, *ibid.*, pp. 162–163; IWSM:HF, 49:15–18.

38. See an edict of May 8, 1860, *ibid.*, 50:17.

39. An edict of May 13, 1860, *ibid.*, 50:22. This edict was issued in reply to a memorial in which Ho Kuei-ch'ing had stated that, in Bruce's opinion, Ho was qualified to deal only with trade; Bruce could deal only with a grand secretary or a president of a Board on more important matters (see *ibid.*, 50:19). A memorial from Hsueh Huan received on July 17 reported that the British and the French still persisted in their assertion that the Shanghai commissioner could claim authority only in "trade affairs" and not in "the important matters of the state" (*kuo-chia ta-shih*) (*ibid.*, 53:41–42).

40. Bruce to Russell, Apr. 7, 1860, *PP: Affairs in China*, pp. 37–39. This dispatch constitutes an important analysis of the Ch'ing political structure; see passages quoted in Chap. I, pp. 15, 16: see also Chap. I, note 26.

41. Bruce refers here to the interview which took place at "the Municipal Temple" (*ch'eng-huang-miao kung-so*) in Kunshan on the Great River. Apart from the point raised by Bruce, the etiquette connected with the interview was based on equality and the reception was cordial. Ho had chosen Kunshan as the meeting place in accordance with the precedent in 1854 of the interview between I-liang, governor-general of Kiangnan and Kiangsi, and R. M. McLane, American envoy, and also with a view to preventing the foreigners from coming to Ch'ang-chou. See Williams, "Journal," pp. 217–222; IWSM:HF, 43:6–7; 44:33–36.

42. See Chap. I, p. 29; IWSM:HF, 35:40–41.

43. *Ibid.*, 38:1–2, 3–4; Bruce to Kweiliang, Hong Kong, May 16, 1859, *PP: Corr. with Bruce*, pp. 5–6.

44. IWSM:HF, 38:4.

45. *Ibid.*

46. *Ibid.*, 38:2–3. The same vermilion endorsement restated the conditions under which the envoys might come to Peking: (1) they should anchor their vessels outside the bar; (2) they could bring with them only a small number of attendants; (3) they should come in person to Peking (military com-

manders were not allowed to come in their place); and (4) since they would be coming to the capital primarily for the exchange of ratifications, they should not stay long.

47. According to two communications from the Grand Council to the Metropolitan Prefecture (ibid., 38:21) (under June 18, 1859), the government was looking for spacious vacant buildings, at first among schools (*shu-yuan*), guild halls (*hui-ḳuan*), and the like in the Chinese City, and then among such buildings as temples in the eastern suburbs of the city. However, Ward was accommodated in the Tartar City in the former residence of a high official.

According to a report received in London of information supplied to St. Petersburg by Ignat'ev, "there appeared to be every disposition to extend the same friendly treatment to the English, French, and American Representatives." "A handsome residence was prepared for the English Minister, and commodious lodging for the French and American Legations" (Crampton to Russell, St. Petersburg, Sept. 12, 1859, *FO: Affairs in China, Confidential* [1859]).

Also, according to a letter from Ignat'ev to Ward, when the latter was en route to Peking, "Lodgings had been arranged, by order of the Emperor, for the three embassies," and an eyewitness account indicated that the house set aside for Ward was "though spacious . . . not very comfortable, and badly kept" (Ignatieff to Ward, July 7 (19), 1859, *Reed Corr.*, p. 611). (Hereafter dates will be indicated, whenever possible, according to the Gregorian calendar only; dates given in the Julian calendar in the sources will be converted to the Gregorian calendar.)

48. IWSM:HF, 38:32. Of the members of the Ch'ing delegation at Shanghai, Ho Kuei-ch'ing remained in the Shanghai area as Shanghai imperial commissioner and governor-general of Kiangnan and Kiangsi, with Ch'angchou as his official seat. Ming-shen, director of the Imperial Armory, had already been called back to the capital by an edict of January 29, 1859 (*ibid.*, 33:34). It was the remaining three members — Kuei-liang, Hua-sha-na, and Tuan Ch'eng-shih — who left for Peking this time.

49. In the latter stage of the journey Hsueh Huan and Huang Chung-yü were ordered by Peking to proceed to Seng-ko-lin-ch'in's camp. But this change in destination being no longer necessary, they were again ordered to come to Peking directly (*ibid.*, 39:21, 22–23, 38; 40:3).

Huang Chung-yü was a native of Kwangtung (*ibid.*, 30:28). At the time of the Tientsin negotiations he had been working for Elgin's mission as a clerk handling Chinese documents when he was bought over by the Chinese side. Thus he maintained contact with the Ch'ing delegation too (*ibid.*, 26:29; 27:5–6; 32:3; Ting Yun-shu *et al.*, 3:36–37; 4:5, 9–10). At that time he had the status of prefectural commissary of record, which he had secured by purchase. Thanks to his services during the Tientsin negotiations, he had been made, at the request of Kuei-liang and Hua-sha-na, expectant district magistrate with an honorary title of assistant prefect (IWSM:HF, 29:14). Later he was in Hong Kong. Early in 1859 he had been invited to come to

Shanghai. Since then he had been serving there under Kuei-liang and his colleagues as an informal channel of communications between the Chinese and Western officials (*ibid.*, 33:29–31, 34, 44–45; 34:1–2, 8–9, 28, 30–31; 35:37; 36:13, 39; 38:2, 4, 37). He was active in Shanghai in the same way in 1860 (*ibid.*, 51:12; 53:19, 42). In 1860 he was sent to North China by Hsueh Huan, along with Lan Wei-wen (*ibid.*, 53:44, 45; 54:22–25, 33; 56:15; 57:35; 58:16–17; 60:38; 61:14; Ting Yun-shu *et al.*, 5:15; 6:6, 8). When rewards were granted after the conclusion of the Peking negotiations, he was promoted to the status of expectant department magistrate (IWSM:HF, 70:23). In the contemporary Western reports he was referred to as a certain "old Chang," who had formerly taught Chinese to Thomas Wade. While working among the foreigners he called himself Chang T'ung-yun. He could not speak English. ("Memorandum of some papers seized in the I-li shop, the residence of 'Ng' Ts'ün, a Canton linguist, about the 25th November, 1857," by Thomas Wade, Dec. 2, 1857, in Elgin to Clarendon, No. 75, Dec. 9, 1857, FO 17/277; Oliphant, I, 441–443; Bruce to Russell, Jan. 6, 1860, FO 17/335; Bruce to Russell, secret and confidential, unnumbered, Jan. 21, 1860, *ibid.*; Memorandum by Mr. Wade, etc., *PP: Corr. with Bruce*, p. 35; Ting Yun-shu *et al.*, 3:36; Hsueh Fu-ch'eng, "Shu Han-yang Yeh-hsiang Kuang-chou chih pien," *Yung-an wen hsü-pien.* According to this last account, he once worked as a spy for Yeh Ming-ch'en.) For further biographical detail on Huang Chung-yü, see Banno Masataka, "Kō Chūyo (Chō Tōun) to Arō sensō — Shin-Ei kōshō kikō no ichi sokumen," in Hanabusa Nagamichi Hakushi Kanreki Kinen Ronbunshū Henshū Iinkai, ed., *Hanabusa Nagamichi hakushi kanreki kinen ronbunshū, gaikōshi oyobi kokusai seiji no shomondai*, pp. 75–103 (Tokyo, 1962).

50. In Shanghai in the spring of 1860, when H. N. Lay urged upon Hsueh Huan the necessity of instituting at Peking a foreign office composed of men of experience in foreign affairs, the latter observed, "with you as go-between on your side, and me on ours, what great things we would accomplish!" Lay to Bruce, confidential, Apr. 27, 1860, in Bruce to Russell, private, secret and confidential, Apr. 28, 1860, PRO 30/22/49.

51. CSL:WT, 299:8.

52. IWSM:HF, 45:14.

53. Bruce to Hope, Jan. 6, 1860, *PP: Affairs in China*, p. 13; *North China Herald* (Dec. 31, 1859; Jan. 14, 1860).

54. IWSM:HF, 48:26.

55. CSL:WT, 312:29–30. The first such memorial presented by Hsueh Huan after the receipt of this order was received on May 19, 1860 (see IWSM:HF, 50:30–33)

56. CSL:WT, 314:24.

57. IWSM:HF, 48:14–15.

58. *Ibid.*, 49:21.

59. *Ibid.*, 51:26; CSL:WT, 316:22.

60. CSL:WT, 317:33, 35.

61. *Ibid.*, 318:5.

62. *Ibid.,* 323:13.

63. The following American sources provide a detailed record of Ward's visit to Peking: *Reed Corr.,* pp. 585–617; Williams, "Journal," pp. 130–210; S. W. Williams, "Narrative of the American Embassy to Peking," *Journal of the North-China Branch of the Royal Asiatic Society* (Old series, Vol. 1), No. 3:315–349 (Dec. 1859); Martin, pp. 194–203. Relevant materials are also in IWSM:HF, *chüan* 39–41, *passim.,* though they are scanty on Ward's stay in Peking and contain nothing on the audience problem. CSL:WT also has nothing on the problem of Ward's audience. The *North China Herald* (Aug. 27, Sept. 5, 10, 17, Oct. 8, and Nov. 19, 1859) also has some materials concerning Ward's mission.

64. IWSM:HF, 39:18, 24–26, 35–38; 40:4; *Reed Corr.,* pp. 592, 594–595, 599–600; Williams, "Journal," pp. 142, 143, 146, 147–148, 150–151; Williams, "Narrative," p. 323. Actually Kuei-liang and his party arrived in Peking on July 17 (IWSM:HF, 40:4). Williams, apparently on the basis of what he had heard in Peking from the Ch'ing officials, wrote that it was July 20 ("Journal," p. 168).

65. *Reed Corr.,* p. 600; Williams, "Journal," pp. 150, 154, 172, 175; IWSM:HF, 39:25, 35, 38: 40:3.

66. *Reed Corr.,* pp. 599–600; Williams, "Journal," pp. 150–151; IWSM:HF, 40:3, 4, 15–16. On Ch'ung-hou, see Hummel, I, 209–211. Ch'ung-hou later became famous as an expert on foreign affairs under Prince Kung. He was appointed to head the escort because, having been under Heng-fu at the time of the Taku repulse and of the later negotiations at Pehtang, he was familiar with the situation (IWSM:HF, 40:15). He had been a minor member of the Ch'ing delegation at the Taku negotiations in 1858 (Martin, p. 153; Williams, "Journal," p. 151).

67. IWSM:HF, 39:37, 38, 40; 40:2–3; Williams, "Journal," p. 159.

68. IWSM:HF, 39:34–35, 40–41, 42; 40:6; Williams, "Journal," pp. 140, 148–149, 155; Williams, "Narrative," pp. 324–325; Martin, pp. 198, 203 (which contains a picture of the carts used by Ward's party). Both Williams and Martin were inclined to insist on the use of sedan chairs, but dropped the idea because Ward himself was not so insistent (Williams, "Journal," p. 148). Actually in this period sedan chairs were rarely used in Peking. Even the high officials were going around in carts (Swinhoe, pp. 163–165, 367–368).

Incidentally, when Ward went to see Ho Kuei-ch'ing at Kunshan in Kiangsu in November 1959, he rode in a sedan chair, preceded by three marines holding an American flag. (Williams, "Journal," p. 220).

For regulations on the use of sedan chairs — by whom and on what occasions they might be used, and the permitted number of bearers, which varied according to the situation (for example, thirty-two bearers for a certain type of sedan chair for the emperor) — see *Chia-ch'ing hui-tien shih-li, chüan* 326, 327, 835.

69. Williams, "Journal," pp. 165, 166–167.

70. *Ibid.,* pp. 158–159; Martin, p. 197 and the facing illustration.

71. Williams, "Journal," pp. 159, 170, 179, 180, 185, 190, 196, 206, 207, 208–209; IWSM:HF, 39:26–27, 35.

72. *Reed Corr.*, pp. 594–599; Williams, "Journal," pp. 170–172, 174ff., 209.

73. Tung Hsun, *Huan-tu-wo-shu-shih lao-jen shou-ting nien-p'u* (1892), 1:27; *Reed Corr.*, pp. 595, 598, 602, 606; Williams, "Journal," pp. 174, 194.

74. Williams, "Narrative," p. 326; Williams, "Journal," pp. 168, 169. In Chinese sources this place is referred to as Lao-chün-t'ang Ti-fang Kuan-fang (Tung Hsun, 1:27), or Lao-chün-t'ang Kuan (IWSM:HF, 41:12), or Lao-chün-t'ang Mi-li-chien Shih-kuan (*ibid.*, 41:13).

For communications from the Grand Council to the Metropolitan Prefecture or the Board of Revenue, transmitting the emperor's oral instructions relating to the preparations for lodging the American delegation in this house, see SKHT:MLCT, 4:31–32, 40. The house is referred to here as Lao-chün-t'ang Ti-fang Fang-wu or simply Lao-chün-tang Fang-wu.

75. Martin, p. 199.

76. Williams, "Journal," pp. 169–170, 181–182. Whether or not Ignat'ev hoisted a flag on the compound of the Russian Hostel at this time cannot be ascertained. It seems, however, that Perovskii, his predecessor, put up a Russian ensign while he was staying in Peking (Cordier, *L'expédition, 1860*, p. 45).

77. Williams, "Journal," p. 170. A Russian account stated that the street on which the American residence was located was barricaded, that the inhabitants of the neighboring houses had all been evacuated, and that the residence was surrounded by guards (Buksgevden, p. 29).

78. Williams, "Journal," p. 170. Williams here questions the wisdom of this decision and writes that, if the Americans went abroad as a matter of course, the responsibility of stopping them would fall on the Chinese and the Americans could demand to know their reasons.

79. *Ibid.*, p. 179.

80. Ward to Cass, Aug. 20, 1859, *Reed Corr.*, p. 596. According to a letter from Ignat'ev to Ward, written before Ward's arrival in Peking, the Chinese government had notified Ignat'ev that the American legation would not be authorized to circulate in the town, or to receive any Europeans, until the ratifications had been exchanged; to prevent their doing so, soldiers would be stationed at the entrance of the American residence (Ignatieff to Ward, Pekin, July 26, 1859, *ibid.*, pp. 612–613).

81. Williams, "Journal," p. 185.

82. *North China Herald* (Sept. 10, 1859), p. 23 (a letter to the editors from "The Other Side"). "The Other Side" was a pen name of Lieutenant Habersham, who had been in Peking as a member of Ward's suite. See Williams, "Journal," p. 211; see also below, note 141.

83. Williams, "Journal," pp. 172, 180, 181, 185, 188.

84. The Americans themselves understood that this was the case. (*ibid.*, p. 179; Williams, "Narrative," p. 334). At the request of Hsueh Huan, who came to the lodgings on July 29, the Americans promised to defer visits to

the Russians until after their interview with Kuei-liang and Hua-sha-na on the next day (Williams, "Journal," p. 171). But, as we know, at that interview Kuei-liang forbade the American to go out before the exchange of ratifications.

85. Ignat'ev understood that the Chinese had purposely assigned the Americans a house far from the Russian residence in order to prevent contact between them (Ignatieff to Ward, Aug. 7, 1859, *Reed Corr.*, pp. 614–615). Having heard from Ward about his experience in Peking, Bourboulon came to the same conclusion (Cordier, *L'expédition, 1860*, p. 89).

86. Ward to Perowsky, July 6, 1859, *Reed Corr.*, p. 610; Williams, "Journal," p. 143; IWSM:HF, 39:36.

87. IWSM:HF, 39:37–38. To judge from the context of this report, Heng-fu may have been influenced by Seng-ko-lin-ch'in and changed his mind.

88. *Ibid.*, 39:38.

89. *Ibid.*, 39:41.

90. *Ibid.*, 39:42.

91. Ignatieff to Ward, Pekin, July 19, 1859, *Reed Corr.*, pp. 610–612.

92. Ward to Ignatieff, Pekin, July 28, 1859, *ibid.*, p. 612.

93. Williams, "Journal," p. 170.

94. A letter from Ignat'ev to the Grand Council, IWSM:HF, 41:11–13. According to the English translation printed in *Reed Corr.*, pp. 615–616, this letter was dated July 30.

95. Ward to Ignatieff, Pekin, Aug. 3, 1859, *Reed Corr.*, pp. 613–614.

96. Ignatieff to Ward, Pekin, Aug. 7, 1859, *ibid.*, pp. 614–615.

97. Ward to Ignatieff, Aug. 10, 1858 [*sic*], *ibid.*, pp. 616–617.

98. This is the letter cited above in note 94; see also the letter from Ignat'ev to Ward, cited above in note 96.

99. Buksgevden, pp. 29–30; Bruce to Russell, No. 19, Sept. 20, 1859, FO 17/314; *Reed Corr.*, pp. 612–613, 615–616; Williams, "Journal," pp. 187–188; Martin, p. 199; Cordier, *L'expédition, 1860*, p. 87; IWSM:HF, 41:11–12. The accounts given in these sources differ and it is difficult to establish the facts. It seems undeniable, however, that Ignat'ev sent men to the American lodgings once or twice (the first occasion seems to have been before the arrival of Ward) and that they were repelled by the guards.

100. *Reed Corr.*, p. 595; Williams, "Journal," p. 171.

101. Williams, "Journal," p. 194; *Reed Corr.*, p. 598.

102. Williams, "Journal," p. 173.

103. Ibid., pp. 194, 196. When Kuei-liang and Hua-sha-na came to see Ward, they rode in similar carriages. There was no music and no military escort, and the entire suite did not exceed thirty men (*ibid.*, p. 181).

104. *Reed Corr.*, pp. 595, 596, 597; Williams, "Journal," pp. 170ff., 174ff., 181ff., 186–189, 191–192.

105. The letters exchanged between them in Peking are in *Reed Corr.*, pp. 602–609.

106. *Ibid.*, pp. 595–596; Williams, "Journal," pp. 171, 175–178, 181–184,

186–187, 188–189; Williams, "Narrative," pp. 329–335; Martin, pp. 199–200.

107. Williams, "Journal," pp. 183–184.

108. *Ibid.,* pp. 177–178; Williams, "Narrative," p. 329.

109. Williams, "Journal," pp. 186–187. See also Williams, "Narrative," pp. 334–335; Martin, p. 200.

110. Williams, "Journal," pp. 188–189; Williams, "Narrative," p. 335. According to Martin, p. 200, when Ward was about to leave for the court on the day scheduled for the audience, Hsueh Huan came to say that the emperor insisted on the kowtow. This is probably a slip of memory on Martin's part. The records kept by Williams in the form of a diary must be more accurate.

111. Kweiliang and Hwashana to Ward, Aug. 6, 1859, *Reed Corr.,* p. 604–605; Williams, "Journal," p. 190; Williams, "Narrative," p. 337.

112. Ward to Kweiliang and Hwashana, Aug. 8, 1859, *Reed Corr.,* p. 605; Williams, "Journal," pp. 191–192; Williams, "Narrative," p. 337. See also *Reed Corr.,* p. 597.

113. IWSM:HF, 41:28–29; Kweiliang and Hwashana to Ward, Aug. 9, 1859, enclosing "One inclosure of the Imperial Rescript," *Reed Corr.,* pp. 606–607; Williams, "Journal," p. 193; Williams, "Narrative," pp. 337–338. The edict was published in the *Peking Gazette,* and the *North China Herald* (Aug. 27 and Sept. 3, 1859) carried a full English translation of it.

114. Ward to Cass, Aug. 20, 1859, *Reed Corr.,* p. 598; Williams, "Journal," p. 194; Williams, "Narrative p. 338. The president's letter is in IWSM:HF, 41:36–37; the emperor's reply is in *ibid.,* 41:36. The emperor's reply was transmitted to W. L. G. Smith (Shih-mi Wei-liang), United States consul at Shanghai, through Wu Hsü, taotai of Shanghai (*ibid.,* 41:42; 43:6, 18–19).

115. Williams, "Journal," p. 195; Williams, "Narrative," p. 338. There is no record in IWSM or CSL of the conclusion of the imperial commissionership of Kuei-liang and Hua-sha-na.

116. Kweiliang and Hwashana, Aug. 9, 1859, *Reed Corr.,* p. 608; Williams, "Journal," p. 193.

117. Williams, "Journal," pp. 196–206. Heng-fu reported on the exchange: "We, your slaves, immediately prepared a banquet at a post hotel (*i-kuan*) and received the said envoy (*kung-shih*). His words were extremely respectful and submissive. And then we exchanged the ratifications." (IWSM:HF, 41:39).

118. Williams, "Journal," pp. 210–211.

119. *Ibid.,* p. 199.

120. IWSM:HF, 40:18–19.

121. *Ibid.,* 40:19–20.

122. Williams, "Journal," p. 189; Williams, "Narrative," pp. 335–336.

123. Wiliams, "Journal," pp. 174–175, 178; Williams, "Narrative," pp. 327–328. Martin, p. 201, interprets the event differently.

124. Williams, "Journal," pp. 171, 192; see also Martin, pp. 199, 200.

125. Williams, "Journal," p. 179.

126. *North China Herald* (Sept. 10, 1859), p. 23 (letter to the editors from

"The Other Side"). Bruce to Russell, No. 19, Sept. 30, 1859, FO 17/314. On this letter see also notes 82 and 141.

127. Williams, "Journal," pp. 179–180.

128. *Ibid.*, p. 192.

129. Lay to Bruce, confidential, Apr. 27, 1860, in Bruce to Russell, private, Apr. 28, 1860, P.R.O. 30/22/49.

130. Williams, "Journal," pp. 144, 154–155, 156, 157, 158, 164, 196, 203; Williams, "Narrative," p. 321.

An edict of February 25, 1859, discussing the selection of the officials to be dispatched to meet the Western diplomats off Taku and persuade them to return to Shanghai for the exchange of ratifications, reads in part: "The officials, such as Pien Pao-shu, who were dispatched last year, were all awed by the craft and fierceness of the barbarian chiefs, with whom they have become familiar. We are afraid that they would be trifled with by the barbarians" (IWSM:HF, 35:36). Possibly because of this edict, the memorials from Taku and Pehtang during the period leading to the exchange of ratifications at Pehtang never mentioned the name of Pien Pao-shu.

131. Williams, "Journal," p. 209. Williams refers to this man simply as "Li." On July 23 "Li" told Williams about his experience of June 25 when he and "Jin," his aide, went on a vessel to deliver to Bruce a communication from Heng-fu (*ibid.*, p. 162). This account coincides with Heng-fu's report to the effect that he had dispatched Li T'ung-wen, department magistrate of I-chou, and Jen Lien-sheng, lieutenant of the military post at Pehtang, to convey to the barbarian ship a communication from him to Bruce (IWSM: HF, 38:52). Hence we may safely identify Williams' "Li" as Li T'ung-wen.

Some officials, who served as guardians of Ward's lodgings, are reported to have said that the emperor rather desired the audience and was not particularly concerned about the etiquette while Hsueh Huan stuck to the necessity of the kowtow (Williams, "Journal," pp. 180, 189).

The *North China Herald* (July 16, 30 and Sept. 10, 1859) carried reports or rumors to the effect that about the time of the Taku repulse the emperor was rather anxious for peace and did not agree with the aggressive opinions of Seng-ko-lin-ch'in.

132. Bruce to Russell, secret and confidential, unnumbered, Jan. 21, 1860, FO 17/335. Huang Hui-lien was a native of Kwangtung, who had been educated at an American mission school in Shanghai and spoke English well. He worked under Thomas Wade for some time as "linguist," and accompanied Elgin to Tientsin in 1858. He then went over to the Chinese side and served under Seng-ko-lin-ch'in. In 1859 he was an interpreter at Taku and Pehtang. At that time he was an expectant assistant district magistrate. Seng-ko-lin-ch'in sent him to Shanghai early in 1860, and when the allied troops later attacked the Taku forts he was in Taku. He was called to Peking for the subsequent Peking negotiations. Then he was assistant district magistrate of Mi-yun, Chihli. When rewards were granted after the signing of the Peking Conventions, he was promoted to expectant district magistrate. In 1861 he was serving at the Tientsin Customs. In 1862 he was

an interpreter in connection with the British artillery drill of Ch'ing forces. He is another example of informal channel of communications. The range of his activities seems to have been wider than that of Huang Chun-yü, who did not speak English. On Huang Hui-lien, see further: IWSM:HF, 38:26; 39:6, 41; 40:15, 19, 37–38; 44:5–6, 8; 50:8, 22–23, 28; 64:9–15; 70:23; Kuo Sung-tao, pp. 8–9; Bruce to Russell, No. 35, Feb. 6, 1860, FO 17/336; "Memorandum Major Brabazon," by Thomas Wade, Oct. 19, 1861, in Bruce to Russell, No. 149, Oct. 26, 1861, FO 17/355; Williams, "Journal," pp. 151, 153, 172, 205, 206; Reed Corr., p. 598. Martin, p. 202; Henry B. Loch, Personal Narrative of Occurrences during Lord Elgin's Second Embassy to China in 1860, 2nd ed. (London, 1870), pp. 86–87, 94, 100–101, 204, 283; Swinhoe, p. 134; Rennie, British Arms, pp. 117–119; Rennie, Peking and the Pekingese, II, 31–33, 76–78, 279–280. As a detailed account of Huang Hui-lien's activities, based on the above-cited sources and some others, see Banno Masataka, "Kō Keiren to Arō sensō — eigo no hanaseru ichi seinen no yakuwari," Tokyo Toritsu Daigaku Hōgakukai zasshi, 3.1–2:343–385 (March 1963).

133. As to the origin of the compromise plan, Williams wrote in his journal (p. 186), "we could not decide who was at the bottom of it." However, in his "Narrative" (read before the Royal Asiatic Society, Shanghai, on October 25, 1859), he stated: "This unexpected concession of the whole point was supposed to be chiefly due to the personal wish of the emperor to see the foreigners himself, cooperating with the well-known desire of Kweiliang and Hwashana for the audience on political grounds" (p. 335). Furthermore, in his biography by his son, it is positively stated: "Either from motives of curiosity or from a real desire to retain by gracious condescension the friendship of the Americans, Hienfung had evidently a strong desire to see the strangers now at his capital, and in order to do so had consented to waive all but the mere semblance of a prostration" (F. W. Williams, The Life and Letters of S. Wells Williams [New York and London, 1889], p. 318).

134. Williams, "Journal," pp. 186–187; Williams, "Narrative," pp. 334–335.

135. PP: Affairs in China, pp. 205–206. Nothing similar to this document is found in IWSM, CSL, or SKHT.

136. Chu Shih-chia, I, 88. Also on August 5, 1859, the emperor gave orders to affix the imperial seal to the originals of the American treaty, in preparation for the exchange of ratifications. See SKHT:MLCT, 4:56; Hsien-feng t'iao-yueh (published by Wai-chiao-pu T'u-shu-ch'u, no date), 4:17.

137. IWSM:HF, 27:6. See Chap. I, p. 37.

138. Williams, "Narrative," pp. 341–342.

139. Cass to Ward, Dec. 30, 1859, Diplomatic Instructions, China, Vol. 1.

140. Bruce to Russell, No. 13, Sept. 3, 1859, FO 17/314. This dispatch encloses English translations of the Sino-American communications obtained by the British. The Americans knew of this British acquisition (Williams, "Journal," p. 212).

On October 6, 1860, Parkes discovered in the temple in Peking named Kao-miao, where he was being detained with Loch, a small piece of paper pasted on the leg of a chair. The Chinese writing on it declared that this chair had been supplied for the use of "the American Tribute-bearer, Ward." Loch, pp. 221–222, comments on this discovery: "This was a curious confirmation of the wisdom of Sir F. Bruce's policy in declining to go to Peking, in 1859, on the conditions accepted by the United States Minister."

During the debates on China policy in the House of Commons in February and March, 1860, as well as in February 1861, the treatment accorded Ward was also discussed. Those who attacked the administration tended to assert that the treatment of Ward (for example, the use of carts) had not been degrading (Hansard, 156:926–927, 943ff; 157:806, 925; 161:412).

In the debates of March 1860, Lord Palmerston stated that Ward's having to travel in a cart was a degradation. Rear Admiral Sir Michael Seymour, who had been the British naval commander in the China expedition of 1858 and had not then been on good terms with Lord Elgin, disputed this assertion and defended Ward. This discussion prompted Ward, who had been piqued by Palmerston's remark, to send a letter of thanks to Seymour, with whom he was not personally acquainted. (Ward to Cass, Hongkong, May 15, 1860, enclosing a letter from Ward to Seymour of the same date, Diplomatic Dispatches, China, Vol. 19; Ward to Cass, Shanghai, Oct. 4, 1860, enclosing a letter in reply from Seymour to Ward of Aug. 7, 1860, ibid.).

141. Bourboulon to the Minister of Foreign Affairs, Sept. 1, 1859, in Cordier, L'expédition, 1860, pp. 87–92.

S. W. Williams, vexed by the unfavorable way in which the Hong Kong newspapers generally had reported Ward's mission, was impelled to contribute to the North China Herald an unsigned account of the Peking visit. Lieutenant Habersham, who had accompanied Ward, wrote a letter to the North China Herald under the pen name "The Other Side." In this letter Habersham claimed that the account (by Williams), written by a person who was "known to be a great admirer of the Chinese," while it was not untruthful, was calculated to impart a one-sided view or a wrong impression. Habersham's letter went on to disclose some nuances of details of the visit that had not been mentioned in Williams' account. In his journal William complained about Habersham's letter, but did not question the validity of his points. (North China Herald [Aug. 27 and Sept. 10, 1859]; Williams, "Journal," p. 211; F. W. Williams, Life and Letters, p. 323.)

The North China Herald (Nov. 19, 1859) carried a letter of appreciation to Ward from the American residents in Shanghai, and a reply from Ward. The same issue, however, sympathetically reported a general dissatisfaction among the Americans in Shanghai with the American Tientsin Treaty. See also the editorial comment in the issue of Aug. 27, 1859.

In a confidential dispatch bitterly critical of the amateurism of American diplomacy and of the Americans in China, Bruce stated that he used his influence with the editor of the North China Herald to prevent Ward's visit to Peking becoming a topic of discussion. The letter from Habersham cited above, according to Bruce, was the only controversial item to be published on the visit (Bruce to Russell, No. 49, confidential, Nov. 22, 1859, FO 17/315).

Notes to Chapter IV. Sino-Russian Contact in Peking
(1859–1860)

1. The account of Sino-Russian negotiations in this chapter is based mainly on IWSM, SKHT, Buksgevden, and Shumakher. According to his preface, Buksgevden was a naval lieutenant and wrote his book while on service with the Russian Pacific Fleet. He asserts that he used numerous materials "which existed also in the Foreign Office" and which he procured in 1900, but he gives no specific documentation in his book. Shumakher gives no indication of his sources. Though both Shumakher and Buksgevden are evidently based on primary Russian sources and their accounts are in many cases corroborated by IWSM and by Barsukov's documented study, they sometimes differ from one another in their accounts of specific events.

All dates originally given in the Julian calendar will here be rendered in the Gregorian calendar.

2. For a solid general account of Russia's advance toward the Amur, see Miyazaki Masayoshi, Kindai Ro-Shi kankei no kenkyū, en Kokuryū chihō no bu (Dairen, 1922).

3. Buksgevden, pp. 5–7; Shumakher, pp 300–302; Barsukov, I, 510–512, 537–538; II, 166, 170–172, 175–176, 204; SKHT: ELST, 13:53–58, 68–70; 14:1–8, 12, 14. For an informative study of Murav'ev's activities in Siberia, based principally on Barsukov, see Joseph Lewis Sullivan, "Count N. N. Muraviev-Amursky" (Ph.D. thesis, Harvard University, 1955), which I cite with the permission of the author.

Perovskii probably left Irkutsk on August 5, 1858 (Barsukov, II, 183). He arrived in Urga on August 20 and left five days later (SKHT: ELST, 13:37). He reached Peking on October 10 (ibid., 15:1; 16:50).

4. Buksgevden, pp. 14–15.

5. SKHT:ELST, 14:17–19. Perovskii enclosed a communication to the Grand Council from the Russian foreign minister. According to the editorial notes in SKHT, the originals of the two communications were in Manchu.

6. IWSM:HF, 33:5; see also Buksgevden, pp. 14–15. Until October 16, 1858, Su-shun had been president of the Court of Dependencies; Jui-ch'ang was his successor. On February 1, 1859, Jui-ch'ang was transferred to the post of president of the Board of Punishments, and on the same day Su-shun became president of the Board of Revenue (see CSK, pu-yuan ta-ch'en nien-piao).

7. IWSM:HF, 33:5.

8. SKHT:ELST, 14:20. See also Case 33 in the early part of Chap. II.

9. Murav'ev to Kovalevskii, Mar. 3, 1859, in Barsukov, II, 247. Murav'ev commented: "This is also progress!"

10. Cordier, L'expédition, 1860, p. 45. The same information was reported by Bruce more briefly (Bruce to Malmesbury, May 4, 1859, PP: Corr. with Bruce, p. 3).

It is possible that the Chinese deceived the Russians on the matter of the emperor's equipage: according to *Chia-ch'ing hui-tien* (*chüan* 66, "Imperial Equipage Department") an emperor's chair was to be borne by sixteen bearers. Riding in a chair with four bearers in the city of Peking was appropriate to the status of an indigenous Chinese civilian official of the third rank and up (*ibid.*, chüan 22, item on the Board of Rites, subitem concerning the equipage of princes and officials).

11. Memorandum by Hart, May 22, 1859, *PP: Corr. with Bruce*, p. 8. Bruce also reported an account by a certain French traveler named Russell who, after having stayed at the Russian Hostel, came to Shanghai by way of Kiakhta, the Amur River, and the sea route. According to this account, the situation was very different: the Russians were cut off from the respectable classes; they were depressed and demoralized by their isolated and monastic life; they wore Chinese dress when they went out on foot lest they be stoned by boys and surrounded by curious crowds; they were treated with arrogance by the Manchus and were not allowed to enter their houses (Bruce to Malmesbury, No. 38, July 31, 1859, FO 17/313). The accuracy of this account is open to question: it asserts, for instance, that the French traveler found Ignat'ev at Kiakhta, where the latter had been detained for a month awaiting Peking's permission to continue his journey, and that he parted from him "about the middle of April"; the actual date of Ignat'ev's arrival in Kiakhta was April 29.

12. Yin Keng-yun, "Ch'ou-i su wu," in *Hsin-pai-jih-chai chi, chüan* 1. The memorial is undated, but its content would indicate that it was written during Hsien-feng 8th year (ending on February 2, 1859) and after Perovskii's arrival in Peking.

13. IWSM:HF, 34:18–23. As of May 1859 a rumor was current in Hong Kong that the Russians established at the capital had been massacred (Bruce to Malmesbury, Hong Kong, May 30, 1859, *PP: Corr. with Bruce*, p. 7). This may have been indicative of the intense resentment felt by the antiforeign scholar-officials and evidenced in the memorials just cited.

14. SKHT: ELST, 16:50–51; 17:4.

15. IWSM:HF, 33:17–18, 46–49; 35:2, 11–12; 36:26–27; SKHT:YCLT, 15:76; SKHT:ELST, 14:47–52, 58–61; 15:1, 8–9; Shumakher, pp. 303–305; Buksgevden, pp. 8–9. The definitive Chinese version is in IWSM:HF, 36:27–31, and SKHT:ELST, 15:62–67 (the editorial comment states that this is a translation from Manchu). The original Chinese version is in IWSM:HF, 27:8–12, and SKHT:ELST, 12:75–80. The Russian text is in *Sbornik dogovorov Rossii s Kitaem, 1689–1881 gg.* (St. Petersburg: Ministerstvo Inostrannykh Del, 1889), and in *Treaties, Conventions, etc., between China and the Foreign States*, I, 92–100. The Chinese text printed in these two collections of treaties and in *Hsien-feng t'iao-yueh*, 3:15–19, is roughly the same as the original Chinese version in IWSM:HF and SKHT, with some minor variations.

There are two Manchu versions printed in *Sbornik dogovorov*. Mr. Jun Matsumura of Nihon University, Tokyo, has kindly taken the trouble of romanizing these two versions for me and translating them into Japanese. Footnotes in the collection state that one of the Manchu versions was "given from the Russian side" and the other one from the Chinese side. Curiously enough, the two texts agree almost verbatim, with the following exceptions: The rules of *alternat* are followed for the names of the two countries, sovereigns, plenipotentiaries, and government offices. In some places the text given from the Chinese side is closer to the Russian text. The Russian version of the text ends with the signatures, the seals, the date of June 13, 1858 (given in the Julian and lunar calendars), and the name of the Russian translator, whereas the Chinese version ends with the expression, "The Great Emperor of the Great Ch'ing Empire has put on the treaty of peace the vermilion endorsement 'Let it be as recommended!' and has affixed the imperial seal," the date (given in the lunar calendar) of April 24, 1859 (the date of the exchange of ratifications), and the emperor's seal.

The definitive version of the Chinese text in IWSM:HF, 36:27–31, and SKHT:ELST, 15:62–67, is evidently a faithful translation from this Manchu version given from the Chinese side (see also a memorial from the Grand Councillors on April 22, 1859, in IWSM:HF, 36:26). This version of the Manchu text must be a newly drafted document different from the Manchu text which was presented by the Chinese in 1858 for the signatures of the plenipotentiaries. (So far as can be ascertained from the consulted documents, there remains some mystery with regard to how the four texts were drafted in Tientsin in 1858 and how the problem of discrepancies were solved in 1859—partly because there was apparently a certain amount of whitewashing on the part of the Ch'ing officials involved.)

In January 1859 the possibility of exchanging the ratifications elsewhere than in Peking was considered by Kuei-liang and his colleagues in Shanghai and the Peking government (IWSM:HF, 33:29, 34). It is not known whether Peking broached the subject to Perovskii.

16. IWSM:HF, 36:26, 41:53; Shumakher, p. 305; *North China Herald* (Oct. 1, 1859), p. 35.

17. Bruce to Malmesbury, Aug. 10, 1859, *PP: Corr. with Bruce,* p. 42. See also *North China Herald* (Aug. 6, 1859). On the efforts of the Ch'ing government to keep the matter secret, see IWSM:HF, 33:18, 47.

18. IWSM, 33:48.

19. *Ibid.,* 36:17–19.

20. Full text is in *ibid.,* 36:32 (under Apr. 25, 1859, the text itself being undated); SKHT:ELST, 15:68 (with the date of Apr. 25, 1859). See also Shumakher, p. 305.

21. IWSM:HF, 36:33 (under Apr. 25, 1859); SKHT:ELST, 15:82 (undated; the original was in Manchu).

22. SKHT:ELST, 15:69 (undated and placed immediately after the agreement of April 25; the original was in Manchu).

23. *Ibid.,* 15:51–53. The draft, which is undated, appears between an edict of April 6, 1859, and a memorial received on April 9. There is in SKHT, 16:3–4, another draft with substantially the same content, which is also undated and placed right after a communication of May 4, 1859, from Perovskii to Su-shun and Jui-ch'ang (the original was in Manchu).

24. IWSM:HF, 36:37; 37:15–17, 22–23; 38:9–10; SKHT:ELST, 16:16–17, 44–46; 17:21–23, 50; Buksgevden, pp. 8–9, 14–15; Shumakher, p. 308.

25. SKHT:ELST, 16:47. See also Case 23 in the early part of Chap. II.

26. Perovskii to the Grand Council, Jan. 28, 1859, SKHT:ELST, 14:47–51.

27. An appointment for that date is mentioned in Grand Council to Perovskii (draft), May 16, 1859, *ibid.*, 16:22. See also Perovskii to the Grand Council, May 21, 1859, *ibid.*, 16:28–29.

28. See the Grand Council's communication to Perovskii, IWSM:HF, 35:11–12 (under Mar. 10, 1859).

29. SKHT:ELST, 14:48, 49, 59, 60; 15:8; 16:17.

30. *Ibid.*, 16:17, 21–22.

31. The Russian Hostel (E-lo-ssu-kuan) in Peking had two compounds, far apart but both within the Imperial City. One was near Cheng-Yang Gate, the southern front entrance to the Imperial City. The other was in the northeastern corner of the Imperial City near T'ung-chih Gate. As of 1859–1860, the first, where the residence of the Ecclesiastical Mission and the Convent of Candlemass were located, was called the Southern Hostel, or Yuzhnoe podvor'e (Buksgevden, pp. 13 and *passim*) or Nan-kuan (IWSM:HF, 44:12; 69:21, 23–24). The second, where the Church of the Assumption and the living quarters of the mixed-blooded descendents of the Russian war prisoners (the so-called Albazinians) were situated, was called the Northern Hostel, or Severnoe podvor'e (Buksgevden, p. 200), or Pei-kuan (IWSM:HF, 44:12; 66:11; 70:1–2). When later the Russian legation was permanently installed in the Southern Hostel, the principal station of the Ecclesiastical Mission was transferred to the Northern Hostel. (For this and other information about the Russian Hostel, see Introduction, note 5.)

Hereafter, "Russian Hostel," unless otherwise specified, will refer to the Southern Hostel. The contemporary Chinese term E-lo-ssu-kuan also seems to have referred to Nan-kuan. E.g., IWSM:HF, 43:17.

32. SKHT:ELST, 14:48; Shumakher, p. 303.

33. IWSM:HF, 35:2, 11–12; 37:15–17, 22–23; 38:9–10.

34. SKHT:ELST, 14:17–18, 47–52, 58–61; 15:1–2, 8–9, 11; 16:1–2, 16–18, 20, 22, 28–29, 44–46, 50–51; 17:4, 8–9, 21–23, 50.

35. *Ibid.*, 14:17–18.

36. Referred to in Perovskii to the Grand Council, Jan. 28, 1859, *ibid.*, 14:47–51.

37. *Ibid.*, 14:47–51; Shumakher, p. 303.

38. SKHT:ELST, 14:52 (dated Jan. 30, 1859).

39. Perovskii to the Grand Council, May 15, 1859, *ibid.*, 16:16–17.

40. *Ibid.*, 15:11 (dated Mar. 14, 1859); 16:1–2 (dated May 4, 1859), 18 (dated May 16, 1859).

41. *Ibid.*, 14:52, 61; IWSM:HF, 35:2, 11–12.

42. IWSM:HF, 36:33; SKHT:ELST, 15:82. The original was in Manchu.

43. SKHT:ELST, 16:1–2.

44. IWSM:HF, 37:3 (under May 8, 1859); SKHT:ELST, 16:7. The original was in Manchu.

45. Grand Council to the Board of Rites, undated, SKHT:ELST, 16:6 (placed immediately before the communication to the Russian foreign minister). Later communications from the Grand Council to Perovskii mentioned that communications from him were transmitted through the Board of Rites.

46. *Ibid.*, 16:22. See also Perovskii to the Grand Council, May 15, 1859, *ibid.*, 16:20. Perovskii stated that he returned the silver because Article 12 of the Tientsin Treaty required all the expenses for the Russians in Peking to be defrayed by his government.

47. The Grand Council's memorial, undated, whose vermilion endorsement is dated May 16, 1859, in *ibid.*, 16:21.

48. IWSM:HF, 37:15-17. Referred to in Perovskii's letter of May 28 as having been received on May 24 (SKHT:ELST, 16:44).

49. IWSM:HF, 37:22-23 (under May 28); 38:9-10 (under June 11).

50. SKHT:ELST, 16:50-51; 17:4.

51. *Ibid.*, 17:9.

52. Shumakher, p. 305. The letter of protest from the Court of Dependencies is in IWSM:HF, 36:9-10.

53. SKHT:ELST, 16:28-29. In this communication Perovskii also protested against the use in the Court of Dependencies' letter of the designation "king" instead of "emperor" for the tsar.

54. IWSM:HF, 37:15-17.

55. While Murav'ev had intercepted the Court of Dependencies' letter about the Russian penetrations, he had transmitted to St. Petersburg an earlier letter from the same organ relating to the anticipated delivery to China of Russian firearms, which also had not passed through the hands of Perovskii or the Ecclesiastical Mission. See Shumakher, pp. 303, 305; see also Murav'ev's letter of May 1, 1859, to the Court of Dependencies, in Barsukov, II, 260-261, and SKHT, 16:27 (the original was in Manchu).

56. IWSM:HF, 37:23.

57. *Ibid.*, 41:15, 50-52; 43:19-20; 44:15-17. See also Cases 28, 29, and 30 in the early part of Chap. II. The final outcome in this case is not known, though it seems certain that the Russian governor at Kiakhta refused at least once to send to St. Petersburg a communication from the imperial agent at Urga to the Russian Foreign Office.

58. The Court of Dependencies' reply is in IWSM:HF, 37:21 (under May 27, 1859), and SKHT:ELST, 16:43 (which states that the original was in Manchu). The addressee is not clearly indicated, though from the context it is assumed to have been Perovskii rather than the Senate. See also the Grand Council's memorial on the matter, in SKHT, 16:42 (undated; the original was in Manchu), from which I have quoted in the text.

59. For example, see IWSM:HF, 38:33-34, 48-49; 40:26; 70:1, 13-15. Article 9 of the Sino-Russian Additional Treaty of Peking of 1860 stipulated that, in particularly important matters, the governor-general of Eastern Siberia might correspond either with the Grand Council, or with the Court of Dependencies as the principal office in charge of frontier relations and administration—another example of the limited survival of the old practice.

See also the account on p. 146 of Ignat'ev's protest against the Court of Dependencies sending him a communication.

60. Buksgevden, p. 7; Shumakher, p. 304; Vladimir (Zenone Volpicelli), *Russia on the Pacific and the Siberian Railway* (London, 1899), p. 262.

61. Buksgevden, pp. 7–8.

62. Shumakher, p. 304.

63. Buksgevden, pp. 4–6; IWSM:HF, 21:6, 27–28, 30, 49; 22:11; 23:10; 25:39, 40–41; 27:5, 7, 23–25, 30, 33–34; 28:1–2.

64. Buksgevden, p. 7; Barsukov, II, 261. The date of arrival at Kiakhta is given in Barsukov, I, 552; according to *ibid.*, II, 253, Ignat'ev arrived in Irkutsk on April 17.

65. Shumakher, p. 304. The same account as Shumakher's, almost verbatim, appears in Barsukov, I, 552, but see also *ibid.*, II, 259, 265.

66. Buksgevden, pp. 8–10. Barsukov, II, 262, gives the date of Khitrovo's return to Kiakhta as May 11. On the refusal of Russian arms, see also *ibid.*, I, 555–556; II, 263.

67. Shumakher, p. 304; Barsukov, I, 554.

68. Buksgevden, pp. 10, 50; on p. 90, Buksgevden gives Ignat'ev's new title as minister resident.

69. IWSM:HF, 37:3–4; SKHT:ELST, 16:8. This is the earliest mention of Ignat'ev's coming in IWSM and SKHT. The Russian major mentioned in this memorial is probably the frontier commissar, Karpov. See also IWSM:HF, 38:1.

70. IWSM:HF, 37:4–5.

71. *Ibid.*, 37:5.

72. A Chinese informant, who had left Peking on March 22, 1859, and had returned to Canton, informed Robert Hart that the emperor had declined a Russian present of 10,000 muskets, fearing that muskets might be brought by an equal number of Russians (Memorandum by R. Hart, Canton, May 22, 1859, *PP: Corr. with Bruce*, pp. 7–8). On the other hand, the *North China Herald* (May 21, 1859) reported that Russia had given 800 pieces of cannon to the Chinese government in consideration of the land cession at the Amur. In memorials presented presumably a few days before the Taku incident of June 25, 1859, Yin Keng-yun expressed concern over the expected arrival of Russian firearms ("Ch'ou-i su ch'i" and "Ch'ou-i su pa," in Yin Keng-yun, *chüan* 1.).

73. Buksgevden, pp. 10–13. According to Shumakher, p. 304, permission to come to the capital reached Kiakhta on May 25. On the escort and other travel arrangements by the Chinese authorities, see also IWSM:HF, 38:33, 48–49; 40:26. IWSM gives the date of Ignat'ev's departure from Kiakhta as June 4.

74. Buksgevden, p. 14; Shumakher, p. 308; IWSM:HF, 40:26.

75. Buksgevden, p. 29.

76. *Ibid.*, pp. 43, 123–124, 161–162; Sir Henry Knollys, *Incidents in the China War of 1860, compiled from the Private Journals of General Sir Hope Grant, G.C.B., Commander of the English Expedition* (Edinburgh, 1875),

pp. 120–121, 135–136. See also G. Allgood, *China War 1860: Letters and Journal* (London, New York, and Bombay, 1901), p. 54.

77. Buksgevden, p. 16. E. P. Kovalevskii (1811–68) was a Russian traveler, writer, and diplomat. He came to Peking twice, in 1849–1850 and again in 1851, and published in 1853 a book about travel in China (*Bol'shaia Sovetskaia Entsiklopediia* [2nd ed., Moscow, 1949–1957], XXI, 503). During the Arrow War period he was head of the Asiatic Department of the Russian Foreign Office. See, for example, Barsukov, II, 148, and *passim*.

78. In 1858 Archimandrite Palladii recorded many inside accounts that he had heard from Ch'ing officials who were in contact with him (Extracts from a journal kept at Peking during the year 1858, trans. fr. the *Morskoi Sbornik* [Naval Magazine] for Aug. and Sept. 1860, in Erskine to Russell, No. 81, Sept. 17, 1860, and No. 100, Oct. 7, 1860, FO 65/554). For the author's name this translation gives only "A.P.," which can be identified as Archimandrite Palladii because the journal's accounts of the author's trips in 1858 from Peking to Taku and Tientsin fit in with the references to Palladii in IWSM:HF, 21:3–4, 5, 19, 27, 34–35, 44–45, 49, 50; 25:7–8, 38–39; 27:23; 28:1–2, 45. There are also many statements in a letter of June 11, 1858, from Palladii to Murav'ev, that are consistent with what is recorded in the journal. See V. Kryzhanovskii, comp., "Perepiska Nachal'nika Pekinskoi Dukhovnoi Missii Arkhimandrita Palladiia s General-Gubernatorom Vostochnoi Sibiri Gr. N. N. Muravievym-Amurskim," *Russkii Arkhiv* (1914), III:201–206. Shumakher, p. 325, records an instance where Ignat'ev received information from Mongolian lamas.

79. IWSM:HF, 44:12. On the Northern Hostel, see above, note 31. In response to Fu-chia's suggestion, an edict of the same day directed the general commandant of the Gendarmerie and its senior and junior lieutenant-generals to confer and memorialize for further instructions (IWSM:HF, 44:12). The sequel to the occurrence is not known.

80. Buksgevden, p. 14; Shumakher, p. 308.

81. Buksgevden, p. 14; Shumakher, p. 308; IWSM:HF, 39:27; 42:17; 46:14. Ignat'ev's letter to the Grand Council is in SKHT:ELST, 17:51. The communication from the Grand Council is in *ibid.*, 17:52. For the status of Su-shun and Jui-ch'ang, see note 6 above.

82. Buksgevden, p. 16; see also *ibid.*, pp. 173–174.

83. *Ibid.*, p. 20.

84. This date for the second interview is given in IWSM:HF, 40:28 (a letter from Su-shun and Jui-ch'ang to Ignat'ev), and *ibid.*, 41:12 (a letter from Ignat'ev to Su-shun and Jui-ch'ang). According to Shumakher, p. 309, the date is July 21. Buksgevden's account (p. 26) suggests still a third date. In any case, the difference in date does not matter here.

The date of the third interview is not given specifically in any source consulted. According to Buksgevden, p. 39, Ignat'ev demanded the replacement of Su-shun and Jui-ch'ang in a letter to the Grand Council the "next day" after the third interview, and received a reply from the Council "four days later" ("five days later" according to Shumakher, p. 311). What seems to be

Ignat'ev's letter is in IWSM:HF, 42:14–19, under Sept. 1. The Council's reply, which also states that Ignat'ev's letter was received on Sept. 1, is in IWSM:HF, 42:26–27, under Sept. 5. Furthermore, another letter from Ignat'ev (in *ibid.*, 42:31) states that he received the Grand Council's reply on Sept. 5. Hence, we assume that the third interview took place on August 31.

85. That the three documents were presented at the first interview is mentioned in Ignat'ev to Su-shun and Jui-ch'ang, July 19, 1859, SKHT:ELST, 17:67. According to Buksgevden, p. 23, however, they were sent to the Chinese plenipotentiaries the day after the first interview. These three documents are in IWSM:HF, 39:27–33, anachronously placed under July 9, immediately after the edict announcing that Su-shun and Jui-ch'ang were to see the Russian representative.

86. Shumakher, p. 308. The four-point memorandum, without date, appears in IWSM:HF, 39:33–34, and SKHT:ELST, 17:66, as a "communication in reply from the Grand Council." However, in a letter to Su-shun and Jui-ch'ang of July 19 and a lengthy memorandum enclosed therein, Ignat'ev repeatedly referred to the four-point memorandum as a reply from Su-shun and Jui-ch'ang (SKHT:ELST, 17:67–71). It was probably prepared at the Grand Council and sent to Ignat'ev as a reply from the two high officials.

87. For this period there are thirteen communications between Ignat'ev and Su-shun and Jui-ch'ang in IWSM:HF, 40:28–32; 41:1–3, 11, 25–26, 30–32, 34–35, 37–38, 41–42, 52–53. There is in SKHT one more communication from Ignat'ev to Su-shun and Jui-ch'ang, dated July 19 (see note 86).

88. A letter from Su-shun and Jui-ch'ang three days after the second interview definitely came through the Court of Dependencies (Buksgevden, p. 27). Probably the same may be said of other correspondence between Ignat'ev and Su-shun and Jui-ch'ang.

89. This exchange of correspondence between Ignat'ev and the Grand Council is in IWSM:HF, 41:11–13, under Aug. 2, 1859; see also above, Chap. III, note 94. The full text of the Court of Dependencies' letter is not available; it is quoted in summary in Ignat'ev's communication to the Council.

On the Russian attempts to effect personal contact with the Americans, see Chap. III, note 99.

90. Buksgevden, p. 17. We cannot enter here into a detailed discussion of Ignat'ev's protracted and complicated negotiations in Peking, which constitute an independent topic for research. For such a study, see Mark Mancall, "Major-General Ignatiev's Mission to Peking, 1859–1860," *Papers on China* (Harvard University, East Asian Research Center), 10:55–96 (1956).

91. Compare Ignat'ev treaty draft (IWSM:HF, 39:28–29) with Perovskii's drafts (SKHT:ELST, 15:51–53; 16:3–4) and the Grand Council's reply to Perovskii's demands (IWSM:HF, 37:16–17).

92. Buksgevden, pp. 24–25; Shumakher, pp. 305–307, Barsukov, II, 267–276; Hanawa Sakura, "Roshia teikoku no Kyokutō shinshutsu," Part 2, *Rekishigaku kenkyū*, 10. 10:61 (Oct. 1940).

93. IWSM:HF, 25:15, 18, 28; 40:28–30; 41:3, 30; 42:15, 18, 33; 43:1;

46:14–15, 41, 44; 51:1; Chiang T'ing-fu, "Tsui-chin san-pai-nien lai Tung-pei wai-huan shih (shang), ts'ung Shun-chih tao Hsien-feng." *Ch'ing-hua hsueh-pao*, 8. 1:46–48 (Dec. 1932); Buksgevden, pp. 19, 35, 38. See also Cordier, *L'expédition, 1857–58*, pp. 420–421. Perovskii also referred to the fact that Putiatin had been informed of this edict (see SKHT:ELST, 16:17–18).

94. Chiang T'ing-fu, pp. 49–51; Hanawa, Part 2, p. 58.

95. IWSM:HF, 37:15–17 (under May 25, 1859).

96. *Ibid.*, 38:11; Buksgevden, p. 15. See also IWSM:HF, 35:28, 36:6, 9.

97. Buksgevden, p. 22.

98. *Ibid.*, pp. 18–20.

99. IWSM:HF, 39:33–34.

100. Buksgevden, pp. 26–27; Shumakher, p. 309.

101. Of the thirteen communications in IWSM between Ignat'ev and his Chinese counterparts between the second and third interviews (see above, note 87), five concern the Manchurian border problem. See IWSM:HF, 40:28–32; 41:1–3, 30–31, 37–38.

102. *Ibid.*, 41:1–3 (under July 31, 1859).

103. Buksgevden, pp. 38–39.

104. IWSM:HF, 42:14–19; see also Buksgevden, p. 39.

105. IWSM:HF, 42:26–27.

106. For the period between this exchange and Ignat'ev's departure from Peking, IWSM reproduces eighteen communications between him and the Grand Council (IWSM:HF, 42:31–33, 37–38; 43:1–4, 11–12; 45:37–38; 46:7, 13–17, 23, 27–28, 40–45; 47:1–2, 34–36; 48:20, 26, 31–32; 50:5; 51:1–3). There are three more communications in SKHT:ELST, 20:22–24, 32. There are some five or six further communications which are not reproduced in IWSM or SKHT but are mentioned in those that do appear. There are also several more communications which are referred to in Buksgevden, pp. 42, 55, 57–58, 65. That letters were transmitted through the Board of Rites is mentioned here and there in the communications reproduced in IWSM; see also Shumakher, pp. 311, 327.

107. Two letters addressed to Su-shun and Jui-ch'ang in IWSM:HF, 43:20; 44:6–7.

108. *Ibid.*, 42:31–33 (under Sept. 10, 1859).

109. *Ibid.*, 42:37–38 (under Sept. 13).

110. *Ibid.*, 43:1–4 (under Sept. 17).

111. Buksgevden, p. 41. According to Buksgevden, the officials came on October 6 (Julian calendar), which does not make sense in the context of the narrative. It is therefore assumed here that this is an erratum for "September 6" in the Julian calendar, which is September 18 in the Gregorian calendar.

112. Buksgevden, pp. 41–42. The date of the interview is given in Shumakher, p. 312, and in IWSM:HF, 43:11–12 (a communication from the Grand Council, under Sept. 24). Incidentally this communication from the Council alludes to the needlessness of an interview with a grand councillor or a grand secretary.

113. Shumakher, p. 312.

114. SKHT:ELST, 18:68; IWSM:HF, 43:8–10 (an edict of Sept. 21, 1859). See also Case 24 in the early part of Chap. II.

115. Buksgevden, p. 42; Shumakher, p. 314. The Russians also suspected that the return to the capital of Kuei-liang and Hua-sha-na had had unpleasant consequences, since the British in Shanghai had instilled in them a deep distrust of Russia and had disseminated utterly false information about Russia (Shumakher, p. 312).

116. IWSM:HF, 45:37–38 (under Dec. 23, 1859); SKHT:ELST, 20:20 (dated Dec. 23, 1859); Buksgevden, pp. 43–44. Buksgevden's version of the communication is longer than IWSM's version and touches upon another topic besides the request for an interview with a grand secretary.

117. IWSM:HF, 46:7 (under Dec. 27, 1859); Buksgevden, p. 44.

118. SKHT:ELST, 20:22–23. A later communication from Ignat'ev to the Grand Council mentioned that he had sent a letter (its content is not cited) on December 31 to which the Council's latest communication did not reply (IWSM:HF, 46:40, under Jan. 20, 1860).

119. SKHT:ELST, 20:24 (undated). That the Council's reply was delivered on January 1, 1860, is mentioned in Ignat'ev's letter of January 5 (see note 120).

120. IWSM:HF, 46:13–17 (under Jan. 5, 1860); SKHT:ELST, 20:26–29 (dated Jan. 5, 1860); see also Shumakher, p. 316.

121. SKHT:ELST, 20:32 (undated). The brief note is also cited in a communication from Ignat'ev to the Grand Council in IWSM:HF, 46:27–28, according to which Ignat'ev received the brief note "on the 26th day of this month [the 12th month in the lunar calendar]," that is to say, on January 18, 1860, in the Gregorian calendar, and had vainly awaited Su-shun and Jui-ch'ang for five days. This communication of Ignat'ev's is reproduced in IWSM under the 21st day of the 12th month in the lunar calendar (January 13 in the Gregorian calendar). Hence it is assumed here that "on the 26th day of this month" is an erratum for "on the 16th day of this month" (January 8 in the Gregorian calendar). (The same presumed error also appears in the version in SKHT:ELST, 20:39–40.) Shumakher, pp. 316–317, also refers to the brief note from the Grand Council and discusses it somewhat at large.

122. See also Shumakher, p. 317.

123. Shumakher, p. 317; IWSM:HF, 46:27–28 (Ignat'ev's letter, under Jan. 13, 1860). Though Shumakher gives the date of this letter as January 15, we follow IWSM here.

Incidentally, another communication from Ignat'ev, whose content is unknown, was sent to the Grand Council on January 9 (see IWSM:HF, 46:40, under Jan. 20).

124. Shumakher, p. 317.

125. Buksgevden, p. 45; Shumakher, pp. 317–321; IWSM:HF, 46:40–45 (Ignat'ev's communication to the Grand Council, under Jan. 20).

126. IWSM:HF, 46:23; SKHT:ELST, 20:31 (undated). The two versions

here are identical, save for two added characters in SKHT which make no substantial difference.

127. Buksgevden, p. 45. Probably taking exception to this particular passage, Ignat'ev stated in his reply: "It is almost two years since the treaty was signed. Now after so long a time your Council has for the first time repudiated it *(Chin kuei-ch'u shih yen pu-chun)*. In managing important state affairs, can it be reasonable to change [previous agreements] arbitrarily?" (IWSM:HF, 46:41).

The version of the Council's communication cited in Shumakher, pp. 317–318, is roughly the same as IWSM's.

128. IWSM:HF, 33:28; Shumakher, pp. 303, 305. In this document Peking had proposed receiving the arms not at Taku but at Urga. An edict issued a few days later instructed the imperial agents at Urga to this effect (SKHT: ELST, 14:46; this edict is not in IWSM or CSL).

129. *Ch'ing-shih lieh-chuan*, 47:28; CSK, *pu-yuan ta-ch'en nien-piao*.

130. IWSM:HF, 38:9; 49:15.

131. Buksgevden, p. 45. According to Shumakher, pp. 322–323, two meetings were held at the Grand Council, with Su-shun and Seng-ko-lin-ch'in present (Shumakher gives what purports to be the content of the debates at these meetings), and on February 5 the Grand Council reported to the emperor that it was deemed unnecessary to accede to Russia's demands. Although the context would indicate that both meetings took place after the fifth interview (January 16), the earlier one might have been the one to which Buksgevden refers. (Incidentally, we know that Seng-ko-lin-ch'in was back in Peking during this period; see IWSM:HF, 44:28–30; 45:6; 46:6, 22–24; 55:35).

132. CSL:WT, 303:25–26; also in Hua-sha-na's official biography in *Ch'ing-shih lieh-chuan*, 41:30–34.

133. An extra grant for the funeral expenses of a high official, in addition to the customary grant (whose amount varies according to the official's status) was not unusual. A perusal of *Ch'ing-shih lieh-chuan, chüan,* pp. 40–48 (which I selected arbitrarily) indicates that this kind of extra grant was bestowed on such persons as an emperor's tutor (for example, 5,000 taels on Tu Shou-t'ien), a grand secretary or a grand councillor of outstanding achievement (for example, 1,000 taels on Wen-ch'ing), a person who had done great service in suppressing the Taipings (for example, 3,000 taels on Tseng Kuo-fan), or a person who had died while fighting the Taipings or the Nien rebels (for example, 500 taels on Li Hsing-yuan, who died at the front [of an illness], and 5,000 taels on Seng-ko-lin-ch'in, who fell in action).

In comparison, the 300 taels to Hua-sha-na was a small grant. Why it was made is not known. Was it because of his achievements as an administrator? Or perhaps as a token of compassion for his supposedly tragic end? See Buksgevden, p. 45.

134. An edict of May 13, 1860, ordered Ho Kuei-ch'ing to inform the British and the French that there would be no one to negotiate with in North China, since Kuei-liang was no longer an imperial commissioner and Hua-sha-na "died of illness" (IWSM:HF, 50:22).

135. Buksgevden, pp. 44–45.

136. Shumakher, p. 322.

137. Ward to Cass, June 29, 1860, Diplomatic Dispatches, China, Vol. 19. See also Bruce to Russell, private and confidential, June 27, 1860, P.R.O. 30/22/49; Bourboulon to Thouvenel, June 16, 1860, Cordier, *L'expédition, 1860*, pp. 184–188.

In discussing the fate of Ch'i-ying, Martin, p. 186, says: "A year later Hwashana met the same fate, swallowing gold to escape a judicial process."

138. Buksgevden, pp. 16–17.

139. According to Shumakher, p. 326, Su-shun urged that a force of 20,000 be moved to the Russian frontier as a precaution against a possible break with Russia, but this proposal was blocked by the Grand Secretary P'eng Yun-chang (who was also the senior grand councillor).

140. An edict of Sept. 24, 1859, which issued orders to the provincial authorities of Kirin and Heilungkiang, had tacitly admitted the inevitability of ceding the left (north) bank of the Amur (IWSM:HF, 43:10–11); see also Hanawa, Part 2, p. 68.

141. *North China Herald* (Feb. 11, 1860), quoting from the *Peking Gazette* of Jan. 5, 1860. According to Shumakher, p. 317, Kuei-liang was the only grand secretary who had no special commission to execute in these days; but when he heard at the Grand Council that he would inevitably have to comply with Ignat'ev's insistent demands, he became ill and applied for retirement. Thus Su-shun and Jui-ch'ang were the only high officials available to negotiate with Ignat'ev, and he had therefore to receive them, if only as bearers of the Council's communication.

142. Cf. Shumakher's account cited in note 131.

143. Shumakher, p. 319.

144. Buksgevden, pp. 46–47; IWSM:HF, 47:34–36.

145. Buksgevden, p. 25, mentions only Budogovskii and two others; according to IWSM:HF, 40:2, 17, four Russians proceeded to Peking. Shumakher, pp. 306–307, mentions only Budogovskii. See also Barsukov, II, 272–274, 276.

146. IWSM:HF, 40:1–2, 16–17, 30; CSL:WT, 286:5; Shumakher, p. 307.

147. Buksgevden, pp. 25–26. Murav'ev had sent Martynov to Peking from Irkutsk, as a courier in advance of Ignat'ev (Barsukov, II, 259, 265).

148. Buksgevden, pp. 25, 27–28; IWSM:HF, 41:25. Buksgevden says that Prince Dadeshkil'iani left Peking on June 17 (Julian calendar). This must be an erratum for July 17 (Julian calendar).

149. Buksgevden, p. 34; IWSM:HF, 43:4.

150. IWSM:HF, 41:25–26, 28, 30, 31–32, 40, 43; 43:16–17, 20; 44:4–5.

151. *Ibid.*, 41:43–44.

152. *Ibid.*, 43:26.

153. *Ibid.*, 44:4–7, 8–9; Grand Council to Seng-ko-lin-ch'in and Heng-fu, Oct. 28, 1859, SKHT:ELST, 19:10.

154. IWSM:HF, 47:34–36 (under Feb. 20, 1860); Buksgevden, pp. 46–47.

155. IWSM:HF, 48:31–32 (Grand Council to Ignat'ev, under Mar. 19, 1860). Since Ignat'ev's original letter is only quoted in this reply, its date is unknown.

According to Buksgevden, p. 48, it was sent "at the end of March" (Julian calendar), which is perhaps an erratum for "at the end of February" (Julian calendar). After citing from Ignat'ev's reply (not in IWSM) to the Grand Council's letter, Shumakher, p. 324, states that correspondence between Ignat'ev and the Chinese government was again discontinued after March 20.

156. IWSM:HF, 49:14–15.

157. Buksgevden, pp. 48–49; Shumakher, pp. 324, 325. Shumakher states in one place that the letter was addressed to "our consular agent" (at Shanghai) to be forwarded to Captain Likhachev, and elsewhere that it reached Captain Likhachev through Russell and Co. According to Buksgevden, it was delivered to "the American Consul Gard" [sic]. The apparent confusion here may be explained as follows. We know that the United States consul at Shanghai at that time was W. L. G. Smith (see Eldon Griffin, *Clippers and Consuls, American Consular and Commercial Relations with Eastern Asia 1845–1860* [Ann Arbor, 1938], p. 364). We also know that it was reported in June 1860 that "an American gentleman, Mr. Albert Heard, head of the Firm of Heard and Co.," had been appointed Russian consular agent at Shanghai (Bruce to Russell, No. 125, June 15, 1860, FO 17/338). (On Heard's appointment as Russian consular agent, see also W. L. G. Smith to A. F. Heard, Shanghai, June 9, 1860, Records of Foreign Service Posts of the State Department, Consulate, Shanghai, Miscellaneous; Ward to Cass, Shanghai, June 29, 1860, Diplomatic Dispatches, China, Vol. 19; Ho Kuei-ch'ing to Ward, June 14, 1860, in Chu Shih-chia, I, 92; Griffin, p. 368.) The Heard family had interlocking personal, social, and commercial relations with the Russells and the Forbes (Griffin, p. 244). Since the initial H becomes a G when transliterated into Russian, we may assume that "Gard" is a transliteration for Heard. The "American Consul" could be an ambiguous expression for "the Russian consul, or consular agent, who is an American citizen." We may thus infer that the letter was sent in care of Albert Heard, who was, or was going to be, Russian consular agent at Shanghai, and who was also closely connected with Russell and Co.

158. Buksgevden, pp. 49–50; IWSM:HF, 50:5 (under Apr. 23, 1860).

159. Buksgevden, pp. 51–53; Shumakher, pp. 325–326.

160. IWSM:HF, 50:22–25.

161. *Ibid.*, 50:3–9, 18–22.

162. *Ibid.*, 50:28–30; 51:8–9; Shumakher, p. 326. Cf. Buksgevden, p. 53.

163. IWSM:HF, 51:1–2; Buksgevden, pp. 54–55; Shumakher, p. 326. The Chinese text of the letter in IWSM:HF is somewhat longer than the Russian version quoted in Buksgevden, which gives the date of the letter.

164. IWSM:HF, 51:2–3 (under May 22, 1860).

165. Shumakher, pp. 326–327.

166. IWSM:HF, 51:4.

167. *Ibid.*, 51:5.

168. Shumakher, p. 327.

169. Shumakher, p. 327; IWSM:HF, 51:22–24. According to the account he gave Bruce in Shanghai, Ignat'ev hired carriages and horses to convey him-

self and his suite, refused a Chinese escort or conveyances from the government, and traveled sometimes in a chair and sometimes on horseback, escorted by a few Cossacks. (Bruce to Russell, No. 127, June 26, 1860, FO 17/338; see also Cordier, *L'expédition, 1860,* p. 187).

On the events between the sending of the ultimatum and Ignat'ev's sailing, Buksgevden's account (pp. 55–65) is much more detailed than the one that can be reconstructed from the data in IWSM and in Shumakher, and it sometimes differs in nuance. It also seems to embody certain inconsistencies. For instance, Buksgevden states that the Grand Council's reply to the ultimatum categorically forbade Ignat'ev to proceed to the coast; this is not mentioned in the version reproduced apparently in full in IWSM or that cited by Shumakher. Furthermore, according to Buksgevden, the reply was made one week after the ultimatum was sent, that is, on May 27 or 28. He also states that Ignat'ev sent two further communications to the Grand Council *before* his departure, which took place, as Buksgevden himself admits, on May 28. It is rather difficult to imagine that such a chain of events could occur in the span of one or two days.

Among other things, Buksgevden relates in detail Ignat'ev's last-minute efforts to persuade the Council to accede to his border demands in a somewhat moderated form, and the various attempts of the Peking government to prevent Ignat'ev from going by way of Pehtang. For example, Buksgevden says that in Ignat'ev's last days in Peking a disquieting rumor spread that orders had been issued to detain him at the city wall by shutting his chair in between the outer and inner doors of the gate. The Russians promptly took precautions. They sawed in two the rear axles of two carriages that were to be loaded with baggage and joined the pieces of each axle with a pin in such a way that by pulling out the pins they could cause the carriages to break down immediately. By this device they intended to prevent the shutting of the outer and inner doors, thus enabling Ignat'ev and his suite to slip out of the city gate. At 8 a.m. on May 28 the party left the Russian Hostel. At the city gate the two carriages played their assigned role, causing great confusion among the gate guards. Ignat'ev's chair proceeded through the gate, surrounded by the suite and escort on horseback. As a matter of fact, the chair was empty; Ignat'ev was also on horseback. Buksgevden's account thus gives the impression that the Russians themselves thought that they had forced their way out of the city. Buksgevden then tells of the Ch'ing officials' efforts to persuade the Russians to return to Peking.

170. IWSM:HF, 51:23. On the letter to the Grand Council, see Buksgevden, p. 65.

171. IWSM:HF, 51:10–11.

172. *Ibid.,* 53:27, 28–32; 54:1; 59:14; 61:1; Buksgevden, pp. 77–78, 80–83, 105, 137.

Notes to Chapter V. Conduct of Peace Negotiations in Peking, Fall 1860

1. CSL:WT, 327:35; Weng T'ung-ho, *chüan* 1, *keng-shen*, pp. 37–38; Meng Sen, "Ch'ing Hsien-feng shih-nien yang-ping ju-Ching chih jih-chi i-pien," *Shih-hsueh chi-k'an*, No. 2:179–180 (Oct. 1936).

2. IWSM:HF, 62:34.

3. *Ibid.*, 62:34.

4. *Ibid.*, 62:37; Prince Kung to Elgin, Sept. 21, 1860, *PP: Affairs in China,* p. 175; Prince Kung to Gros, Sept. 21, 1860, in Cordier, *L'expédition, 1860,* p. 327.

5. See Chap. II. On Prince Kung, see Hummel, I, 380–384.

6. *Ch'ing-shih lieh-chuan,* 47:35–36; IWSM:HF, 55:40; 56:17–18, 21–22, 35; 57:5–7, 10–14, 20–21, 29, 34–36; 58:2, 9, 15–16; 59:7–11, 16–21; 60:1–4, 12–21, 31–33, 36–39; Parkes to Elgin, Oct. 20, 1860, *PP: Affairs in China,* pp. 227–228; Hummel, I, 381.

7. See Chap. II, note 90. See also IWSM:HF, 53:44, 45; 54:22–25, 33; 56:15; 57:19; 60:21, 36–39; 61:7, 14, 20; Elgin to Russell, No. 53, Sept. 18, 1860, FO 17/331; Parkes to Elgin, Oct. 20, 1860, *PP: Affairs in China,* p. 240; Swinhoe, pp. 222–223; Gros, pp. 80, 83–85.

8. IWSM:HF, 62:37.

9. *Ibid.*, 53:44. See also *ibid.*, 54:45 (an edict in reply).

10. *Ibid.*, 54:25, 33; 56:15; 57:19, 60:21, 36–37, 38; 61:7, 20.

11. See Chap. III, p. 108 and note 49.

12. IWSM:HF, 57:35; 58:16–17; 60:38. Ting Yun-shu *et al.,* 5:15.

13. To the Offices of Police Censors, Sept. 23, 1860, PLFC: Pan-li fu-chu an, *chüan* 1. In a supplementary memorial of the same day, Prince Kung and his associates stated: "The delegates from Kiangsu, Lan Wei-wen Huang Chung-yü *teng*, have received imperial orders to attend upon us in managing peace negotiations. We have repeatedly sent officials to inquire about them, but they have not yet arrived in the Summer Palace. Nor do we know where they are staying" (PLFC: Pan-li fu-chü an. *chüan* 1, under Sept. 23, 1860; the same document is in *Shih-liao hsun-k'an* [Peking: Palace Museum, 1930–31], 17:596, with no date, but it is placed immediately after a memorial from the same people dated Oct. 19, 1860, as if it were supplementary to the latter). In this quotation the character *teng* must have been used not to mean "etc." or "and others" but simply to indicate the end of an enumeration of persons.

14. Prince Kung to Seng-ko-lin-ch'in, Sept. 24, 1860, PLFC: Pan-li fu-chü an. *Chüan* 1; the Offices of Police Censors to Prince Kung's office, Sept. 26, 1860, *ibid.;* a supplementary memorial from Prince Kung and his colleagues, Sept. 28, 1860, *ibid.* The memorial shows also that the memorialists were rather doubtful of Lan's and Huang's usefulness as emissaries and wanted to let the two serve for the moment at Prince Kung's office.

15. IWSM:HF, 63:7, 13, 25–26, 33; 64:16; 33–36; 65:3–4, 18, 21, 26–27, 28, 30, 31; 66:10–11, 12, 13; 67:4, 9, 28, 44. Among many contemporary Western

references to Heng-ch'i, see, for example, Parkes to Elgin, Oct. 20, 1860, *PP: Affairs in China*, pp. 226–244.

16. Lan Wei-wen came to see Parkes and Loch while they were detained at the Kao-miao Temple, in company with Heng-ch'i on October 1, 3, and 5, and alone on October 4 (*PP: Affairs in China*, pp. 240–241; see also IWSM:HF, 64:16). A communication of October 2, 1860, from Prince Kung's office to the Board of Punishments stated that Lan Wei-wen was to be sent with another official to escort French prisoners from the Board of Punishments to the Kao-miao Temple (PLFC: Pan-li fu-chü an, *chüan* 2). On October 22 Chang Chin-wen, a noted Tientsin merchant, stayed in the same inn as Lan Wei-wen in Peking and discussed the situation with him (Ting Yün-shu *et al.*, 6:6). There is no other positive mention of Lan's activities in the sources consulted. When requesting a grant of honors to Lan Wei-wen, Huang Chung-yü, and Huang Hui-lien, in a supplementary memorial of December 15, 1860, Prince Kung and his colleagues extended to Lan only the general praise accorded to the other two: they were all equally versed in barbarian conditions, had participated in the peacemaking under Prince Kung for the last several months, and had endured all sorts of hardships with assiduity and perseverance. The memorialists were more specific in describing the merits of Huang Chung-yü and Huang Hui-lien (PLFC: Huang-yüeh chiang-li, under Dec. 15, 1860).

17. Huang was instructed on October 12 to meet British and French officials at the Hua-yen Temple outside the Te-sheng Gate; he was to be escorted by several of Jui-lin's soldiers (PFLC: Pan-li fu-chü an, *chüan* 3, under Oct. 12, 1860).

The British Museum has a name card (7.8 cm x 16.6 cm) of Huang Chung-yü with woodcut black characters on a vermilion ground. The card is kept in the same album as the original letter (with the envelope) from Prince Kung to General Hope Grant, dated Oct. 19, 1860 (call number: Oriental 6597). Perhaps Huang accompanied the courier or was himself the bearer of the letter.

The supplementary memorial of December 15, 1860, cited in note 16 asserts that Huang was ordered several times to visit the barbarian lodgings to pick up information, that he was fearless and had managed to get the foreign demands softened (lit., "canceled").

18. Ting Yun-shu *et al.*, 6:6, 8.

19. In a joint memorial received on December 12, 1860, Prince Kung, Kuei-liang, and Wen-hsiang stated that they had received orders to conduct peace negotiations from the emperor on September 22 (IWSM:HF, 70:20). See also Wen-hsiang, p. 33; Weng T'ung-ho, *chüan* 1, *keng-shen*, p. 38. *Ch'ing shih-lu*, IWSM, and PLFC contain no edict ordering Kuei-liang and Wen-hsiang to undertake this duty.

20. IWSM:HF, 63:5–7.

21. *Ibid.*, 63:5. The office of the commissioners seems to have been set up in the Grand Secretariat in the Imperial Palace. See Meng Sen, "Ch'ing Hsien-feng shih-nien," p. 180.

22. CSL:WT, 327:37.

23. A supplementary memorial of Sept. 28, 1860, from Wen-hsiang, PLFC: Pan-li fu-chü an, *chüan* 1; Chen-chün, *T'ien-chih ou-wen* (1907), 3:19–20.

24. IWSM:HF, 64:11, 65:30; CSL:WT, 330:15–16; 336:9–10. The Commission of Defense was eventually discontinued by an edict of January 2, 1861 (CSL:WT, 336:9–10).

According to a Russian observation (perhaps not quite accurate) "the temporary military commission (Hsun-fang-ch'u)" (Commission of Defense) ruled Peking after the emperor's departure. "This commission had been entrusted with military, diplomatic, and administrative affairs." It consisted of eight senior and several junior high officials, among whom were Jui-ch'ang, Wen-hsiang, Pao(-yun), Lin-k'uei, Ch'eng(-ch'i?), Heng-ch'i, Ch'ung-lun, and Chu (Tsun? Buksgevden gives Chu as "Cha" in the genitive), "president of the Board of Rites" (Buksgevden, p. 202).

The 1860 Commission of Defense seems to have been rather different in scope and function from the 1858 organ of the same name. The latter, headed by Princes Hui, I, and Cheng, took general command of the government forces in Peking (for example, see IWSM:HF, 24:25–27); in the fall of 1860 corresponding functions were performed by Prince K'o-ch'in and others.

25. *Ai-hsin chueh-lo tsung-p'u, i-tse,* p. 3167. For Prince K'o-ch'in in this capacity, such titles as *tsung-t'ung hsun-shou chiu-men, tsung-t'ung hsun-shou ta-ch'en,* or simply *hsun-shou ta-ch'en* and *chiu-men tsung-t'ung* were also used (PLFC: Pan-li fu-chü an, *chüan* 1, under Sept. 24, 1860; *chüan* 3, under Oct. 6 and 12, 1860). There are several instances in documents before the emperor's departure, in which the generic designations *ch'in-p'ai wang-ta-ch'en* or *pan-fang wang-ta-ch'en* seem to indicate Prince K'o-ch'in and his associates. See IWSM:HF, 56:32, 58:2–3, 59:3, 61:20.

26. IWSM:HF, 63:15; 64:11, 37–38; 65:9. Under Oct. 2, 1860, in his diary, Liu Yü-nan, director of the Banqueting Department of the Board of Rites, recorded that he had learned that there were twenty-four high officials, including Prince K'o-ch'in, Sai-shang-a, and I-shan, in charge of defense of the Imperial City and four others responsible for the defense of the Chinese City (Meng Sen, "Ch'ing Hsien-feng shih-nien," p. 181).

27. IWSM:HF, 63:12, 23; 64:8, 9, 11, 15, 17, 22, 38; 66:2, 16.

28. *Ibid.,* 64:1, 38–39; see also *ibid.,* 64:11.

29. An edict of September 28 ordered Wen-hsiang, Lin-k'uei, Ch'ing-ying, and "the prince and high officials responsible for the defense of the city" (*shou-ch'eng wang-ta-ch'en teng*) to work together in making all the necessary arrangements (*ibid.,* 63:23). In planning the defense, Sheng-pao worked on one occasion with Lin-k'uei, Pao-yun, Prince K'o-ch'in, I-shan, and Mien-sen, and on another with Prince K'o-ch'in and Lin-k'uei (*ibid.,* 64:1, 39).

30. IWSM:HF, 56:23, 58:5–7; CSL:WT, 327:37; Meng Sen, "Ch'ing Hsien-feng shih-nien," p. 181. See also Chao Kuang, pp. 116–118.

31. Parkes to Elgin, Oct. 20, 1860, *PP: Affairs in China,* p. 235.

32. On Kuei-liang's activities from 1858 on, see above, Chaps. I, II, and III, *passim.* For his biography, see Hummel, I, 428–430.

33. Buksgevden, p. 202; see also note 24 above.
34. Wen-hsiang, p. 33. Weng T'ung-ho stated in his diary entry for
September 25 (*chüan* 1, *keng-shen*, p. 38): "The acting general commandant
of the Gendarmerie, Wen-hsiang, a man of loyalty and assiduity, goes around
inspecting the nine gates. The city guards number less than ten thousand.
Many of the officials in charge of the gates are Manchu dignitaries of the
first or second rank. They do not take orders [from Wen-hsiang]."
35. IWSM:HF, 63:23.
36. *Ibid.*, 64:9–11; Wen-hsiang, p. 34; Prince Kung's office to the acting
junior lieutenant-general of the Gendarmerie, Oct. 12, 1860, PLFC: Pan-li
fu-chü an, *chüan* 3.
On October 1 and again on October 2, Prince Kung wrote to Wen-hsiang
(in the city) asking him to come to his office for consultation on an urgent
matter (PLFC: Pan-li fu-chü an, *chüan* 2). On October 9 Prince Kung asked
Lin-k'uei, acting senior lieutenant-general of the Gendarmerie, to perform
the duties of the general commandant in Wen-hsiang's place until a new
appointment was made by the emperor (*ibid., chüan* 3).
37. Wen-hsiang, pp. 34–35.
38. Weng T'ung-ho, *chüan* 1, *keng-shen*, p. 38. The emperor, en route
to Jehol, pointed out in an edict of September 25 that no Grand Council
secretary had yet joined him and he ordered the secretaries to come on a
forced march (IWSM:HF, 63:12).
In a letter of September 25 to the grand councillors in the emperor's suite,
Wen-hsiang explained that two secretaries had presented reasons for not
being able to go to Jehol, and it was not yet known whether the other
secretaries could proceed (PLFC: Pan-li fu-chü an, *chüan* 1).
39. Li Tz'u-ming, *Yueh-man-t'ang jih-chi pu* (1936), *hsin-chi shang*, p. 1
(under Feb. 10, 1861).
40. An edict of December 17, 1860, which announced the granting of
honors to the officials who had been active in the peace negotiations
(IWSM:HF, 70:21–23), mentioned six persons who are assumed to have been
secretaries of the Grand Council: Ying hsiu (Manchu), Ying-hsiang (Manchu), Jui-lien (Manchu), K'un-yü (Manchu), Chu Hsueh-ch'in (Chinese),
and Tu Lai-hsi (Chinese) (Compare with lists of Grand Council secretaries
in Chu Chih *et al.*, comps., *Shu-yuan chi-lueh*, rev. ed. [preface dated 1875],
chüan 17, 19). "The six secretaries of the Grand Council, Ying-hsiu and
others, who had remained and taken care of the business of the peace negotiations" are referred to in a joint memorial from Prince Kung and his associates, received on January 26, 1861 (IWSM:HF, 72:21).
According to Liu Yü-nan's diary, when the allied troops approached the
Summer Palace, "the Grand Council secretaries, Ts'ao Yü-ying, Tseng Hsieh-
chün, Fang Ting-jui, T'ieh Ying-p'u [sic], Wang Cheng, and Tu Lai-hsi also
ran away on the alarm (Meng Sen, "Ch'ing Hsien-feng shih-nien," p. 182).
(T'ieh Ying-p'u must be an error for Ch'ien Ying-p'u. These six secretaries
were all Chinese, not Manchus. See Chu Chih *et al., chüan* 19.) Tu Lai-hsi,

whose name is mentioned in the above edict, must have rejoined Prince Kung's office after having run away. Ts'ao Yü-ying and the other four had possibly also been on duty under the prince.

In these days the Grand Council had a fixed number of thirty-two secretaries, with several additional supernumeraries (Chu Chih *et al., chüan* 13).

41. IWSM:HF, 70:20–21.

42. Mr. Chao-ying Fang suggests that after the emperor's departure Prince Kung must have held the power to make temporary appointments to lower offices, which were to become permanent by imperial approval, and that the term *wei-shu chu-shih* probably indicates here that Ch'eng-lin temporarily held the status of secretary under such an appointment. As of the spring of 1860, Ch'eng-lin held the substantive post of official writer (*pi-t'ieh-shih*) of the Gendarmerie. See *Ta-Ch'ing chin-shen ch'üan-shu,* spring of Hsien-feng 10, 1:82.

A communication of October 9, 1860, from Prince Kung's office to the lieutenant-generals of the Gendarmerie states that two officials of the Gendarmerie, Ch'eng-lin and Hsiu-wen, official writer, were on duty at the office on October 6, that after the barbarian invasion of the Summer Palace Prince Kung brought them to Lu-kou-ch'iao to handle correspondence; and that he also brought with him six scouts of the Gendarmerie (PLFC: Pan-li fu-chü an, *chüan* 3).

43. On scouting, see also IWSM:HF, 64:10, and note 42 above.

44. IWSM:HF, 65:30. Instructions from Prince Kung to Ch'ung-lun to assist Heng-ch'i are in PLFC: Pan-li fu-chü an, *chüan* 4, under Oct. 15, 1860. Ch'ung-lun had already gone with Heng-ch'i to see Parkes on the morning of October 13 to arrange for the surrender of the An-ting Gate (the Commission of Defense to Prince Kung, Oct. 13, 1860, PLFC: Pan-li fu-chü an, *chüan* 3). On further activities of Ch'ung-lun in the Peking negotiations, see IWSM:HF, 67:28; 70:33, 36. See also a letter of October 20 from Ch'ung-lun and Heng-ch'i (to Wen-hsiang?), PLFC: Pan-li fu-chü an, *Chüan* 5.

45. *Ch'ing-shih lieh-chuan,* 52:33–35.

46. IWSM:HF, 9:6, 7, 11, 12–13.

47. Banno, "Gaikō kōshō . . . kōdō yōshiki."

48. IWSM:HF, 19:22–23; 20:14, 23:18, 24:21; Oliphant, I, 282–287. Cordier, *L'expédition, 1857–58,* p. 337. During the Taku negotiations, he signed the memorials jointly with T'an T'ing-hsiang, Wu-erh-kun-t'ai, and Ch'ien Hsin-ho (IWSM:HF, *chüan* 20–22, *passim*).

49. IWSM:HF, 66:12. Ch'ung-hou seems already to have been participating in the handling of correspondence at Prince Kung's office prior to October 12, while holding a commission under the governor-general of Chihli. On October 12, princes and high officials in Peking suggested that the governor-general be asked to send Ch'ung-hou to assist Heng-ch'i. Prince Kung, however, wanted to keep Ch'ung-hou at his office for the time being (Prince Kung to commissioners to conduct national affairs at Peking, Prince K'o-ch'in,

and the Commission of Defense, Oct. 12, 1860, PLFC: Pan-li fu-chü an, *chüan* 3). Prince Kung's intention of keeping Ch'ung-hou under him was formally communicated to the governor-general and to Ch'ung-hou a few days later (a communication of Oct. 15, 1860, to the governor-general of Chihli and instructions of the same date to Ch'ung-hou, *ibid., chüan* 4).

Sung Chih had been acting as paymaster in military camps and was summoned to Prince Kung's office on October 9 (*ibid., chüan* 3). Te-ch'un had apparently been ordered by Prince I to go to Peking to handle correspondence but had probably not obeyed. A summons was thus issued by Prince Kung on September 26 (Prince Kung to Seng-ko-lin-ch'in, Jui-lin, Heng-fu, Tung Hsun, and Te-ch'un, Sept. 26, 1860, *ibid., chüan* 1). It seems, however, that he did not join Prince Kung's office (then in Lu-kou-ch'iao) until after October 6.

50. CSK, *lieh-chuan,* No. 233.

51. Williams, "Journal," p. 151; Martin, p. 153.

52. Williams, "Journal," pp. 150, 151, 163, 164, 168, 195, 196, 209; *Reed Corr.,* pp. 599–600; IWSM:HF, 40:3, 4, 15–16; 41:39.

53. *Ibid.,* 51:22.

54. *Ibid.,* 57:9–11.

55. See note 49; see also IWSM:HF, 66:11; 67:4, 8, 9, 44, 53; 68:11; 70:36.

56. *Ibid.,* 66:13.

57. *Ta-Ch'ing chin-shen ch'üan-shu,* winter of Hsien-feng 9, 1:27.

58. Ch'eng-ch'i was summoned to Prince Kung's office by instructions of September 28 and was ordered next day to take command of the troops guarding the Kao-miao (PLFC: Pan-li fu-chü an, *chüan* 1; see also IWSM:HF, 63:33). It was on October 19 that Prince Kung gave orders to Ch'eng-ch'i to assist Heng-ch'i in peace negotiations (PLFC: Pan-li fu-chü an, *chüan* 5). But Ch'eng-ch'i had already been involved in the peace maneuver of the high officials remaining in the city: around October 10 he went to Lu-kou-ch'iao to see Prince Kung and conveyed the request of the princes and high officials in the city that Prince Kung should enter the city to make peace (Prince Kung to Prince K'o-ch'in and his associates, Oct. 11, 1860, PLFC: Pan-li fu-chü an, *chüan* 3; IWSM:HF, 65:21); in the morning of October 13 Ch'eng-ch'i was among the high officials who went in Heng-ch'i's company to see Parkes to arrange for the surrender of the An-ting Gate (the Commission of Defense to Prince Kung, Oct. 13, 1860, PLFC: Pan-li fu-chü an, *chüan* 3); in the morning on October 19 Ch'eng-ch'i went with Ch'ing-ying and Ch'ung-hou to see Prince Kung and told him about what they had personally heard from General de Montauban (IWSM:HF, 66:11; *Shih-liao hsun-k'an* No. 17, pp. 595–596).

59. Rennie, *British Arms,* pp. 118–120; Rennie, *Peking and the Pekingese,* II, 76–77; Loch, pp. 86–87, 94, 100–101, 203–204, 283; Swinhoe, pp. 61, 134; IWSM:HF, 50:22–23, 28–29; 64:9, 15. On Huang Hui-lien, see p. 122 and note 132 of Chap. III in this volume.

From September 25 Prince Kung's office repeatedly sent out orders to let Huang Hui-lien hasten there (to the governor-general of Chihli, Sept. 25, 1860, PLFC: Pan-li fu-chü an, *chüan* 1; to the department magistrate of T'ung-chou, Sept. 30 and Oct. 2, *ibid., chüan* 2). On September 29 Parkes, imprisoned in the Kao-miao Temple, wrote a letter in Chinese to Elgin, at Heng-ch'i's dictation. Across the letter Loch, his coprisoner, wrote in romanized Hindustani: "This letter is written by order of the Chinese Government. — H. B. Loch." He wrote in Hindustani because he was aware that the letter might be seen by Huang Hui-lien. As a matter of fact, Huang Hui-lien was shown the letter. Upon perusal, he stated that the barbarian words represented a name and date; there was nothing important in them (Loch, pp. 203–204; IWSM:HF, 64:9, 14, 15). In the supplementary memorial of December 15, 1860, in which Prince Kung and his associates requested the grant of honors to Lan Wei-wen, Huang Chung-yü and Huang Hui-lien it is stated that Huang Hui-lien was ordered several times to visit the barbarian lodgings to pick up information and was fearless (PLFC: Huang-yueh chiang-li; see also above, notes 16 and 17).

60. IWSM:HF, 70:21–23, 36; see also note 74 of this chapter.

61. As a matter of fact, fifty-two names are mentioned in these edicts, with two instances of "So-and-so and others" in the first edict. However, the "others" referred to can be identified from the list of recommended persons that was attached to the memorials, principal and supplementary, of December 15 (received on December 17) from Prince Kung and his associates, requesting the grant of honors (PLFC: Huang-yueh chiang-li, under Dec. 15, 1860; only the principal memorial is reproduced in IWSM:HF, 70:20–21).

As for people who were meritorious to a lesser degree, Prince Kung's office recommended, with imperial sanction, some twenty-one persons — mainly soldiers or braves — to their respective superior authorities as worthy of awards (PLFC: Huang-yueh chiang-li, under Dec. 27, 1860).

62. On Chang Chin-wen, see Chap. II, p. 69 and note 76. On his career and activities, see also *Hsü T'ien-chin hsien-chih* (preface dated 1870), *chüan* 20, *tsa-chi,* pp. 5–9; *T'ien-chin-hsien hsin-chih* (1931), *chüan* 21, Part 3, pp. 42–44. His name is occasionally mentioned in IWSM documents for the Arrow War period, and in contemporary Western sources. On his activities in Peking in 1860, see Ting Yün-shu *et al.,* 6:2–13.

63. Buksgevden, p. 223; IWSM:HF, 67:7–9, 10–11, 12, 21–23.

64. Buksgevden, pp. 224–234; IWSM:HF, 67:55–56; 68:12–15, 17–26; 69:21–25.

65. Ignat'ev's activities in Peking in the fall of 1860 are described in detail in Buksgevden; see also IWSM:HF, *chüan* 66–70, *passim.*

66. IWSM:HF, 67:10–11. Prince Kung to the Court of Dependencies, Oct. 26, 1860, PLFC: Pan-li fu-chü an, *chüan* 6.

67. *Ch'ing-shih lieh-chuan,* 46:24–28.

68. *Ibid.,* 46:39–42.

69. *Ibid.*, 46:39–42.

70. Buksgevden, p. 202; see also note 24 of this chapter.

71. Buksgevden, pp. 201-218; cf. IWSM:HF, 66:11, 14; 67:7–9.

72. As to which members of the Commission of Defense actually acted as contacts with Ignat'ev at this stage: on October 20 Jui-ch'ang and Ch'ing-ying visited Ignat'ev at the Russian Hostel (Jui-ch'ang and Ch'ing-ying to Prince Kung's office, Oct. 20, 1860, PLFC: Pan-li fu-chü an, *chüan* 5); on October 22 Pao-yun, Ch'eng-ch'i, Lin-k'uei, and Ch'ung-lun were ordered to visit Ignat'ev as bearers of a letter from Prince Kung (Prince Kung's office to Pao-yun, Ch'eng-ch'i, Lin-k'uei, and Ch'ung-lun, Oct. 22, 1860, *ibid.*, *chüan* 5).

73. Buksgevden, pp. 210–211; cf. IWSM:HF, 66:11. Ch'ung-hou had also been a contact man between Ignat'ev and Prince Kung before the signing of the British and the French Peking Conventions (*ibid.*, 66:11, 67:8).

74. Incidentally, Jui-ch'ang, Lin-k'uei, Pao-yun, and Ch'eng-ch'i were not among the recipients of honors granted by the edicts of December 17 and 24, 1860, though the first three were awarded honors in their capacity as members of the Commission of Defense (CSL:WT, 336:9–10).

As for Wen-lien, the grant of honors to him was announced in an edict of December 30, 1860, on the recommendation of Prince Kung and his associates in a supplementary memorial of December 28 (PLFC: Huang-yueh chiang-li).

75. In December 1860 Prince Kung and his associates requested the inclusion of either Pao-yun or Ch'eng-ch'i in the Ch'ing delegation to the coming Sino-Russian negotiations in the Eastern frontier zone for the actual fixing of the boundary in accordance with Article 3 of the Additional Treaty of Peking. In response the emperor appointed Ch'eng-ch'i (IWSM:HF, 71:4–6).

In April 1861, a few months after the establishment of the Tsungli Yamen, Jui-ch'ang, Lin-k'uei, Pao-yun, and Ch'ung-lun (who was soon thereafter appointed minister of the Tsungli Yamen — see *ibid.*, 76:12–13), were engaged, under commission from Prince Kung and his associates, in negotiations with the Archimandrite Gurii, on a problem relating to overland trade (*ibid.*, 76:6–8).

When the new Russian minister, Balliuzek, arrived in Peking in July 1861, Prince Kung and his associates reported to the emperor their intention to send "Jui-ch'ang and others" to meet with him if anything occurred that required discussion (*ibid.*, 80:6–7).

As a consequence of the *coup d'état* early in November 1861 which got rid of Prince I, Prince Cheng, and Su-shun, Ch'eng-ch'i was dismissed from government service on November 9, accused of having been a follower of Prince I's clique (CSL:MT, 6:24–26). Pao-yun, on the other hand, became a grand councillor on November 3, 1861 (CSK, *chün-chi ta-ch'en nien-piao*), and was concurrently appointed minister of the Tsungli Yamen on November 30 (IWSM:TC, 2:43–44).

76. IWSM:HF, 64:23. On the Shan-yuan Temple and other temples that successively housed Prince Kung's office, see references in Hsü Tao-ling, *Peip'ing miao-yü t'ung-chien* (Peking, 1936).

77. IWSM:HF, 63:23.

78. *Ibid.*, 64:23. "Metropolitan officials jointly sent a letter to Prince Kung, requesting that he enter the city. [The prince] did not accede to the request" (Weng T'ung-ho, *chüan* 1, *keng-shen*, p. 38, under Sept. 25, 1860).

79. IWSM:HF, 63:29; 64:23–24. The memorial from Prince Yü and others is not in IWSM; it is in PLFC: Pan-li fu-chü an, *chüan* 1, under Sept. 29, 1860. The cosigners included Prince Yü's colleagues as commissioners to conduct national affairs at Peking, members of the Commission of Defense, and members of the Commission of Civil Defense.

It will be recalled that the vermilion rescript of September 21 to Prince Kung had stated: "If peace is yet again not to be made, supervise the military campaign in the rear of the camps. In the event that [the enemy] really cannot be held in check, you should seek personal safety, retreat, and hasten to the imperial traveling lodges" (IWSM:HF, 62:34). Perhaps Prince Yü and the others wanted to warn the emperor and Prince Kung, having either got an incorrect report of this rescript or having read into this passage the possibility of Prince Kung's desertion. Weng T'ung-ho recorded in his diary, under September 29, 1860: "It is said that Prince Kung has been ordered to hasten to the traveling lodges and that princes and high officials have presented a joint memorial requesting that he should stay in his present location" (Weng T'ung-ho, *chüan* 1, *keng-shen*, pp. 40–41).

80. IWSM:HF, 64:3–4.

81. *Ibid.*, 62:37; 64:9, 15, 26–28, 33–36, 39–41; 65:20; 66:13. On the loss and partial recovery of the treaty originals and other official papers see *ibid.*, 69:17–18, 23, 33, 43; 70:6–8, 72:37; IWSM:TC, 7:7–10; Cordier, *L'expédition, 1860*, pp. 447–448; Wolseley, p. 242.

82. Heng-ch'i to Prince Kung, Oct. 7, 1860, PLFC: Pan-li fu-chü an, *chüan* 3.

83. *Ibid., chüan* 6, under Oct. 26, 1860.

84. *Ibid., chüan* 4, under Oct. 17, 1860.

85. IWSM:HF, 65:21; Prince Kung to Prince K'o-ch'in and his associates, Oct. 11, 1860, PLFC: *Pan-li fu-chü an, chüan* 3. It seems that as of October 7 Lien-ch'eng had been stationed at the Kao-miao Temple where Parkes had been confined (see Heng-ch'i to Prince Kung, Oct. 7, 1860, *ibid., chüan* 3).

86. The French military authorities in China had once wished to take "the West gate" of the city, which was the only open one. The British had opposed this on the ground that Prince Kung would not then be able to enter the city should he be induced to return from the country, to which he had fled ("Allied Army before Peking, etc.," dated Oct. 9, 1860, *North China Herald*, Oct. 20, 1860).

87. Weng T'ung-ho, *chüan* 1, *keng-shen*, p. 45; The Commission of Defense to Prince Kung, Oct. 13, 1860, PLFC: Pan-li fu-chü an, *chüan* 3; Prince

Kung to the Commission of Defense, Oct. 14, 1860, *ibid., chüan* 4; see also IWSM:HF, 65:29.

88. IWSM:HF, 65:27, 30; Tung Hsun, 1:31.

89. IWSM:HF, 65:23.

90. Buksgevden, p. 209.

91. Gros to Elgin, Nov. 4, 1860, *FO: Affairs in China, Confidential* (1861), p. 332; see also Gros, pp. 150, 191–193, 199. Contemporary foreign reports assert that in these days Prince Kung was changing his residence from day to day (Buksgevden, pp. 189–190; Cordier, *L'expédition, 1860*, pp. 364, 401).

92. IWSM:HF, 67:23–25; 70:21; Wolseley, pp. 290–291; Swinhoe, p. 343. According to Wolseley and Swinhoe, Prince Kung then happened to be on his way into the city. Frightened by the appearance of the cavalry, he turned about and fled in the direction from which he had started.

93. IWSM:HF, 67:5–6, 25; Meng Sen, "Ch'ing Hsien-feng shih-nien," p. 186. As a matter of fact, the signing of the British Convention had first been scheduled for October 23. Though Prince Kung had been informed that the British wanted a postponement, he went to the Board of Rites on the twenty-third and waited in vain for the British plenipotentiary. In the evening a letter from Elgin was delivered, proposing that the ceremonies be held on the following day. Prince Kung to the Office of Gendarmerie, Oct. 22, 1860, PLFC: Pan-li fu-chü an, *chüan* 5; Prince Kung to the Board of Rites, Oct. 23, 1860, *ibid., chüan* 5; (Wen-hsiang) to Pao-yun and others, Oct. 23, 1860, *ibid., chüan* 6; (Wen-hsiang) to Mu-yin, K'uang Yuan, and Tu Han, Oct. 25, 1860, *ibid., chüan* 5. Meng Sen, "Ch'ing Hsien-feng shih-nien," p. 186; Grant to Herbert, Oct. 25, 1860, quoted in Stanmore, II, 348; *PP: Affairs in China,* pp. 209–210; IWSM:HF, 66:9, 14; 67:4–5; Fu Yü-pu, *Tu-ch'eng chieh-yen shih-chi,* (handwritten copy at the Oriental Library, Tokyo), p. 13.

94. IWSM:HF, 67:54; Tung Hsun, 1:31.

95. IWSM:HF, 67:55, 57; 68:1; 69:29; Meng Sen, "Ch'ing Hsien-feng shih-nien," p. 187; Prince Kung to Elgin, Nov. 8, 1860, *PP: Affairs in China,* p. 258.

96. Buksgevden, p. 232.

97. Cordier, *L'expédition, 1860,* p. 450; IWSM:HF, 68:36; 69:42. According to Buksgevden, p. 237, Ignat'ev left Peking on January 10 (1861) (Julian calendar). From the context I assume that this is an error for November 10 (1860) (Julian calendar) or November 22 in the Gregorian calendar.

98. Tung Hsun, 1:31; Prince Kung had already ordered the Metropolitan Prefecture on October 6 or 7 to prepare the temple for use as his office (*ibid.,* 1:31; Prince Kung to the Metropolitan Prefecture, Oct. 7, 1860, PLFC: Pan-li fu-chü an, *chüan* 3).

The chapter on the Tsungli Yamen in *Kuang-hsü hui-tien shih-li, chüan* 1220, begins: "In Hsien-feng tenth year there was established the Fu-chü [lit., 'soothing office'] at the Chia-hsing Temple outside the Ti-an Gate." According to this statement, Prince Kung's office appears to have been called the "Fu-chü." However, the use of the term current in 1860 seems to suggest that *fu-chü* was not a name for an office. As is seen in such expressions as *pan-li fu-chü, ch'ou-pan fu-chü, fu-chü nan-ch'eng,* or *fu-chü yu lieh,* the term apparently meant diplomatic or peace negotiations. Examples are abundant in IWSM. See also S. M. Meng, *The Tsungli Yamen: Its Organization and Functions* (Cambridge, Mass., 1962), pp. 113–114, note 27.

Citing what is called "Tsung-li ya-men hui-tien ti-kao" (Draft statutes of the Tsungli Yamen), Professor Teng Tzu-ch'eng states that the Fu-i-chü was established at the Chia-hsing Temple in Hsien-feng tenth year. From his citations I infer that what he is referring to here is the Tsungli Yamen itself in its initial stage. Again it is rather doubtful that the term Fu-i-chü was in current use in 1860 or 1861 as a name for a government office (Teng Tzu-ch'eng, *Ku-tung so-chi ch'üan-pien* [Peking, 1957], p. 507; cf. IWSM:HF, 71:19; 72:28, 29).

99. *Kuang-hsü Shun-t'ien fu-chih* (rev. ed., 1889), 16:20.

100. Tung Hsun, 1:27.

101. IWSM:HF, 70:21–23, 36. List of recommended persons attached to the memorial of Dec. 15, 1860, from Prince Kung and his associates (PLFC: Huan-yueh chiang-li, under Dec. 15, 1860). See also above, note 61. By consulting biographies, Red Books, and other sources, I have been able to establish in the case of twenty-six of the fifty-five persons whether they were Chinese, Manchus, Mongols, or Chinese bannermen. The rest I have classified on the basis of a rough inference from the appearance of their names. But I believe the margin of error is small enough not to affect my conclusion that, although Chinese constituted a majority of the group, the inner core was predominantly Manchu.

102. See above, note 40.

103. See Chap. II.

104. A. Thomas, *Histoire de la mission de Pékin* (Paris, 1923–1925), II, 395–396.

105. IWSM:HF, 69:7–8. The emperor granted the request (*ibid.,* 69:8).

106. On Wen-hsiang, see his *Wen Wen-chung kung tzu-ting nien-p'u; Ch'ing-shih lieh-chuan, chüan* 51; CSK, *lieh-chuan,* No. 173; Hummel, II, 853–855.

107. Wen-hsiang, pp. 32–33; IWSM:HF, 61:18–19; Wen T'ung-ho, *chüan* 1, *keng-shen,* p. 35.

108. *Ch'ing-shih lieh-chuan,* 76:47; CSK, *lieh-chuan.* No. 210.

109. On the *pao-i,* see Meng Sen, "Pa-ch'i chih-tu k'ao-shih," pp. 375–377, 389–390; Cheng T'ien-t'ing, "Ch'ing-tai pao-i chih-tu yü huan-kuan," in his *Ch'ing-shih t'an-wei* (1946). See also Brunnert and Hagelstrom, pp. 24–25; W. F. Mayers, *The Chinese Government,* 3rd ed., rev. by G. M. H. Playfair (Shanghai, 1897), pp. 5, 8, 55–56; *Shinkoku gyōseihō,* Vol. 1, Part 1, pp. 130–131; Part 2, pp. 200–201.

110. Wade to Bruce, private, Peking, Jan. 20, 1861, in Bruce to Russell, No. 14, Tientsin, Mar. 12, 1861, FO 17/350; Rennie, *Peking and the Pekingese,* I, 260.

111. "Memorandum of conversations with Chinese officials on the subject of

the late *coup d'état* and other matters, secret and confidential," by T. Wade, Peking, Nov. 8, 1861, in Bruce to Russell, No. 161, Nov. 12, 1861, FO 17/356; Rennie, *Peking and the Pekingese,* II, 159–160. See also Bruce to Russell, No. 174, Nov. 25, 1861, FO 17/357. The same sources also assert that Heng-ch'i's attitude changed markedly after the *coup d'état* of November 1861, and that he now ostentatiously pretended to be liberal and conciliatory on foreign affairs.

112. IWSM:HF, 63:25, 31, 33; 64:27, 38–40; 65:21, 27; 67:23–24.

113. *Ibid.,* 63:12–14; 64:8. Prince Kung to Seng-ko-lin-ch'in and Jui-lin, Sept. 24, 1860, PLFC: Pan-li fu-chü an, *chüan* 1; Seng-ko-lin-ch'in to Prince Kung, Oct. 1, 1860, *ibid., chüan* 2; Seng-ko-lin-ch'in to Prince Kung, Oct. 12, 1860, *ibid., chüan* 4.

114. For example, see IWSM:HF, 63:12–14; 64:8.

115. *Ibid.,* 63:34; 70:21.

116. Wu K'o-tu, "Wang-chi p'ien," in his *Hsi-hsueh t'ang ch'üan-chi;* Meng Sen, "Ch'ing Hsien-feng shih-nien," p. 180.

117. IWSM:HF, 63:6, 14, 25; 64:36–37, 40; 66:13–14.

118. *Ibid.,* 63:34; Weng T'ung-ho, *chüan* 1, *keng-shen,* pp. 39, 40.

119. IWSM:HF, 67:6.

120. On their representations to Elgin and Gros, see Weng T'ung-ho, *chüan* 1, *keng-shen,* p. 42; Meng Sen, "Ch'ing Hsien-feng shih-nien," p. 181; Chiang-shang-ch'ien-sou (Hsia Hsieh), 15:9; Gros, pp. 123–124; Cordier, *L'expédition, 1860,* pp. 345–346; Knollys, *Incidents in the China War,* pp. 123–124; Wolseley, p. 211; Allgood, p. 57. Seng-ko-lin-ch'in supported them and even suggested that they make personal representations at Prince Kung's office (Seng-ko-lin-ch'in to Prince Kung, Oct. 1, 1860, PLFC: Pan-li fu-chü an, *chüan* 2).

On their pressures on Prince Kung, see *North China Herald* (Oct. 20, 1860); Knollys, *Incidents in the China War,* pp. 196–197; Stanmore, II, 346; Cordier, *L'expédition, 1860,* p. 366; Gros, p. 142.

121. For instance, a joint memorial from Prince Kung and others acknowledging receipt of an edict of September 30 reached Jehol on October 5, five days after the edict was issued (IWSM:HF, 64:14). An edict of October 2 was reported to have been received by Prince Kung on October 4 *(ibid., 64:22).* (Note that both of these memorials were written before the invasion of the Summer Palace.) The vermilion endorsement on a memorial received on October 8 reached Prince Kung on October 11, while an edict of October 10 was received on October 12 *(ibid.,* 65:19; see also *ibid.,* 64:24). A memorial acknowledging receipt of an edict of October 22 was received on October 28 *(ibid.,* 67:8). A memorial acknowledging receipt of an edict of October 15 was received on October 22 *(ibid.,* 66:13; see also *ibid.,* 65:3).

Within a week or so after the invasion of the Summer Palace there seem to have been several instances of the loss of edicts or memorials while in transit. See IWSM:HF, 64:38; a supplementary memorial of Oct. 8 from

Prince Kung and his associates, PLFC: Pan-li fu-chü an, *chüan* 3; Prince Kung and his associates to the Grand Council in Jehol, Oct. 16, 1860, *ibid.*, *chüan* 4.

122. Morse, *International Relations*, I, 604–606; Costin, pp. 330–332; Cordier, *L'expédition, 1860*, pp. 333–348.

123. Morse, *International Relations*, I, 603, 606; Cordier, *L'expédition, 1860*, pp. 331, 334; IWSM:HF, 63:30.

124. Cordier, *L'expédition, 1860*, p. 384.

125. IWSM:HF, 63:4.

126. However, a number of warlike memorials were still presented by provincial officials: for example, a memorial received on October 15 from Ch'ing-lien, governor of Honan (*ibid.*, 65:10–13); also a memorial received on October 24 from Yuan Chia-san, imperial commissioner and director-general of grain transport (*ibid.*, 65:22–25).

127. *Ch'ing-shih lieh-chuan*, 47:39–47; CSK, *lieh-chuan*, No. 190. It was reported that Sheng-pao had all along been a consistent enemy of Prince I's clique (Rennie, *Peking and the Pekingese*, II, 139).

128. IWSM:HF, 63:8–11; 64:2–4, 38–40; 65:5–8; Ting Yun-shu *et al.*, 6:6. Early in 1859 Sheng-pao presented a very belligerent memorial jointly with Weng T'ung-shu, governor of Anhwei (IWSM:HF, 34:18–25).

129. IWSM:HF, 63:26, 30; 64:1, 5, 15–17, 28, 37, 38–39; 65:5–6, 8, 21; 66:15–16, 18.

130. *Ibid.*, 65:8. The edict cautiously stressed that Sheng-pao might open hostilities only at the request of Prince Kung, and only if sufficient forces were at hand.

Later on Sheng-pao boasted, in a memorial received on October 28, that in his opinion the barbarians had suddenly become inclined to make peace in fear of his new troops. The emperor retorted in the vermilion endorsement on the memorial that the barbarians had consented to the conclusion of peace because their demands had been fully satisfied: "How should they fear your force of several thousands!" (*ibid.*, 67:25, 27).

131. *Ibid.*, 64:1, 2–3, 24, 35; 65:21; Weng T'ung-ho, *chüan* 1, *keng-shen*, p. 40.

132. IWSM:HF, 64:35; 65:6–7; 66:18.

133. Cf. *ibid.*, 65:21; 72:12–13.

134. *Ibid.*, 64:33–37.

135. This coincides with what is stated in Parkes's report to Elgin. See *PP: Affairs in China*, p. 242.

136. On the consultations between Heng-ch'i and princes or high officials in the city which preceded Parkes's release, see two reports from Heng-ch'i to Prince Kung, PLFC; Pan-li fu-chü an, *chüan* 3, under Sept. 7 and 8, 1860; a memorial received on October 13 from Prince K'o-ch'in and others, *ibid.*, *chüan* 4, under Oct. 17, 1860. On Heng-ch'i's contacts with Parkes in the same period, see *PP: Affairs in China*, pp. 242–243. For contemporary ac-

counts of Heng-ch'i's positive role in freeing Parkes, see Weng T'ung-ho, *chüan* 1, Keng-shen, p. 44; Chiang-shang-chien-sou (Hsia Hsieh), 15:7, 9; Meng Sen, "Ch'ing Hsien-feng shih-nien," p. 182.

137. PLFC: Pan-li fu-chü an, *chüan* 4, under Oct. 17, 1860. According to Loch, imprisoned with Parkes, about noon on October 8 when Heng-ch'i was with them an official appeared and held a long whispered conversation with Heng-ch'i. The latter then explained to Parkes that Prince Kung had decided to release them at once (Loch, pp. 228–229). Th veracity of Heng-ch'i's statement is open to question. Parkes does not mention this incident in his report.

138. IWSM:HF, 64:37–38.

139. *Ibid.*, 63:34–35; 64:22.

140. PLFC: Pan-li fu-chü an, *chüan* 3, under Oct. 5, 1860.

141. *PP: Affairs in China*, p. 179.

142. PLFC: Pan-li fu-chü an, *chüan* 3, under Oct. 6, 1860. An English translation of both documents is in *PP: Affairs in China*, pp. 187–188. Parkes's letter was written at the Kao-miao Temple at the alleged request of Prince Kung and was given to Heng-ch'i (*ibid.*, p. 242).

143. *PP: Affairs in China*, pp. 178–179, 187–189, 242–243; Heng-ch'i to Prince Kung, Oct. 8, 1860, PLFC: Pan-li fu-chü an. *chüan* 3; a memorial from Prince K'o-ch'in and others, received on Oct. 13, 1860, *ibid., chüan* 4, under Oct. 17, 1860. The last two documents emphatically refer to Prince Kung's written promise to return prisoners, given to the foreign authorities in the first and second letter of October 6, as an irreversible step taken. Prince Yü and others also stated in a supplementary memorial of October 10 that they had heard that Heng-ch'i and others had released Parkes "in accordance with the communication [the second letter of October 6] from Prince Kung to the barbarian camps" (*ibid., chüan* 6, under Oct. 26, 1960).

144. Mentioned in a supplementary memorial presented together with the memorial in question from Prince Kung and others. See IWSM:HF, 64:37.

145. Misrepresentation is also detected in the way Prince Kung and his associates quoted in the same memorial from Heng-ch'i's two reports to Prince Kung (Oct. 7 and 8), which are reproduced in PLFC: Pan-li fu-chü an, *chüan* 3. For instance, the interview of October 7 between Heng-ch'i and Wade was covered in Heng-ch'i's report of October 8; the memorial quoted some of the relevant passages in it as coming from the report of October 7. What is again very strange is that copies of Heng-ch'i's reports seem to have been enclosed in the memorial (see a longer version of the memorial in PLFC: Pan-li fu-chü an, *chüan* 3, under Oct. 10, 1860).

146. IWSM:HF, 64:40. In Chiang-shang-chien-sou (Hsia Hsieh), 15:9, while it is stated that Heng-ch'i repeatedly tried to persuade Prince Kung to release Parkes, it is also recorded that after he moved to Lu-kou-ch'iao the prince ordered Heng-ch'i to escort Parkes back to the barbarian camps.

147. According to Parkes, Heng-ch'i came to see him and Loch several times during the morning of October 8; he showed considerable uneasiness; at one time he whispered to Parkes, "I am particularly anxious to get you

away for reasons that I will tell you of at a future time, and I will not wait for the hour named to send you off" (*PP: Affairs in China*, p. 243). According to Loch, pp. 237–238, Heng-ch'i told Parkes several months later, that he had learned in the morning of October 8 through his spy at Jehol, that, at the insistence of the war party there, the emperor had finally signed an order for the immediate execution of the prisoners and the order was being sent to Peking; consequently Heng-ch'i persuaded Prince Kung to order the release. The emperor's order from Jehol arrived within fifteen minutes after Parkes and Loch had safely passed through the gates. No such edict, however, is found in IWSM, CSK, or PLFC.

As early as September 24 the emperor had certainly suggested that it would be best to execute Parkes immediately (IWSM:HF, 63:7, vermilion endorsement). An edict of September 26 retreated somewhat, stating that Parkes should be executed in the event that Peking fell (*ibid.*, 63:15). This edict was a response to the suggestion of Seng-ko-lin-ch'in and Jui-lin that Parkes should be neither killed nor released, but retained and generously treated (*ibid.*, 63:13). In further retreat, an edict of October 2 suggested, that it would be best to return all the prisoners, which opinion was reaffirmed in an edict of October 5 (*ibid.*, 63:34–35; 64:16–17). An edict of October 13 issued upon receipt of the news of Parkes's release, treated the event simply as the execution of a prearranged plan (*ibid.*, 64:37–38).

Thus the account that Loch attributes to Heng-ch'i is rather unbelievable. On the other hand, if it is truthful, then Prince Kung and his associates must have felt it all the more necessary to try to evade responsibility.

148. IWSM:HF, 65:18–22, 28–30; 66:9–12.

149. From communications exchanged on October 11, 12, 13, and 14 between Prince Kung's office and Prince K'o-ch'in and his colleagues, Prince Yü and his colleagues, and the Commission of Defense, it is quite clear that, while the various officials in the city tried to involve Prince Kung with them in their decision to surrender the gate, Prince Kung evaded any definite commitment, pretending that the defense of the city was not his affair (PLFC: Pan-li fu-chü an, *chüan* 3, under Oct. 11–13, 1860; *chüan* 4, under Oct. 14, 1860).

Many other Chinese sources also assert that the An-ting Gate was surrendered on the decision of the officials remaining in the city. For instance, Sheng-pao complained in a memorial received on October 15 that Prince K'o-ch'in and Chou Tsu-p'ei were very definitely willing to surrender the city (IWSM:HF, 65:7); he also stated in a memorial received on October 22 that the high officials for the defense of the city had been misled by Heng-ch'i into surrendering the gate (*ibid.*, 66:18). Chiang-shang-chien-sou (Hsia Hsieh), 15:9, records that Chou Tsu-p'ei advocated surrender. Weng T'ung-ho wrote in his diary entries for October 11 and 12 that the princes and high officials remaining in the city held a meeting with the Six Boards and Nine Ministries on each of these days; he also stated in his entry for October 16 that the surrender of the city derived solely from Heng-ch'i's ideas (Weng

T'ung-ho, *chüan* 1, *keng-shen,* pp. 44–45, 46). On October 12, the day before the surrender, proclamations that the foreigners were to enter the city the next day appeared in the streets (*ibid.,* p. 45; Meng Sen, "Ch'ing Hsien-feng shih-nien," p. 183). A British report states that the merchants of Peking went in a body to Prince Kung and urged him to give up the gate (Knollys, *Incidents in the China War,* pp. 196–197).

150. For example, see IWSM:HF, 64:8, 35–36; 65:29–30.

151. *Ibid.,* 67:7–8. The emperor dismissed this suggestion, stating that he fully understood the predicament Prince Kung was in (*ibid.,* 67:12).

152. Yin Chao-yung, p. 37. In the entries for September 23 to October 5, Yin Chao-yung briefly narrates the day-to-day progress of the peace negotiations; in those for October 6 and after he records the hardships he and his family experienced in the area haunted by foreign soldiers or local bandits. His account indicates that he attended Prince Kung's office daily until the Summer Palace was invaded.

153. Meng Sen, "Ch'ing Hsien-feng shih-nien," p. 182. On Hsü Nai-p'u see CSK, *lieh-chuan,* No. 208; *Ch'ing-shih lieh-chuan,* 47:12–17; he was then president of the Board of Civil Appointments. See his independently presented warlike memorial, received on May 27, 1858 (IWSM:HF, 23:4–5).

On Shen Chao-lin, see *Shen Wen-chung kung tzu-ting nien-p'u,* in *Shen Wen-chung kung chi;* CSK, *lieh-chuan,* No. 208; *Ch'ing-shih lieh-chuan,* 47:1ff. In 1858 Shen presented a warlike memorial opposing in particular the resident minister clause and the opening of rivers to foreigners (Shen Chao-lin, 1:15–16). The memorial is undated but judging from the content, it was evidently written during the 1858 Tientsin negotiations, though *Ch'ing-shih lieh-chuan,* 47:4–5, quotes it as having been presented in the fall of 1860. See also another warlike memorial presented jointly with two other officials in 1858 (IWSM:HF, 27:31–32).

A memorial from him received on September 22, 1860, is rather different in tone. At first sight it may look warlike, but it is in fact a counsel of caution and does not oppose the Tientsin treaty terms (IWSM:HF, 63:24; also in Shen Chao-lin, 1:13–15, and *Ch'ing-shih lieh-chuan,* 47:3–4). According to IWSM, Shen presented this memorial as president of the Board of War. Actually he was then senior president of the Censorate and became president of the Board of War on October 16, 1860 (see CSK, *pu-yuan ta-ch'en nien-piao*). After the invasion of the Summer Palace he sent his family to the suburbs, while he remained in his residence in the city (*Shen Wen-chung kung tzu-ting nien-p'u,* p. 14).

On Hsü P'eng-shou, see CSK, *lieh-chuan,* No. 208, under Hsü Nai-p'u, who was his father. IWSM contains two warlike memorials from him in June 1858, when he was subexpositor of the National Academy (IWSM:HF, 24:11; 26:19–22).

P'an Tsu-yin, subdirector of the Court of Judicature and Revision, presented a warlike memorial in May 1858 and in the fall of 1860 presented one opposing the emperor's departure (IWSM:HF, 23:8–10; *Ch'ing-shih lieh-chuan,* 58:1ff).

154. IWSM:HF, 65:7; 66:18; see also above, note 149.

155. Buksgevden, p. 210.

156. IWSM:TC, 48:1; see also *ibid.,* 50:30.

157. Chou Chia-mei, *Ch'i-pu-fu-chai ch'üan-chi* (1895), *cheng-shu,* Part 1, pp. 6–7. The memorial, drafted by Chou Chia-mei, is undated, but its content indicates that it was presented in 1873.

Ch'üan-ch'ing, president of the Board of Civil Appointments, was an associate of Prince Yü as commissioner to conduct national affairs at Peking. In July 1859, as president of the Board of War, he presented a warlike memorial jointly with Lien Chao-lun, superintendent of the government granaries in the capital (39:11–13).

158. Weng T'ung-ho, *chüan* 1, *keng-shen,* p. 44.

159. CSK, *lieh-chuan,* No. 177. Both Ch'en Fu-en and Chia Chen were among the high civil defense officials. Jointly with twenty-five other officials Chia Chen presented a warlike memorial opposing the emperor's flight (received on Sept. 9, 1860) (IWSM:HF, 60:30–31; *PP: Affairs in China, pp.* 260–261).

160. Yin Chao-yung, p. 38.

161. Loch, p. 228. Loch says the prisoners heard that their guard had been increased to between four and five thousand (which was probably an exaggeration).

162. *Ibid.,* p. 231.

163. According to Loch, Heng-ch'i "appeared distressed and anxious" when he came to see him and Parkes on the afternoon of October 5. Heng-ch'i stated that there had been a long and heated debate at "the council intrusted under Prince Kung with the government of the Empire," and that despite Heng-ch'i's strenuous efforts the council had decided to reject the allied demands, to declare war to the knife, and to execute Parkes and Loch that evening. Heng-ch'i then let them write farewell notes. Later they were told that their execution had ben postponed to the morning. Heng-ch'i's "look was so bright" when he called the next morning, Loch reports. He said that he had been up all night with Prince Kung and had persuaded him to reverse the decisions cited above (*ibid.,* pp. 216–221; see also *ibid.,* p. 227). The fact that their execution had been decided upon and that they wrote farewell notes is not mentioned in either Parkes's official report to Lord Elgin or in the one written by Loch (see *PP: Affairs in China,* pp. 190–195, 226–244). If we recall that the edict of October 2 which suggested the release of the prisoners reached Prince Kung's office on October 4 (IWSM:HF, 63:34–35; 64:22), we are forced to suspect that there was some amount of exaggeration and untruthfulness in Heng-chi's story. From it, however, perhaps we may at least assume that there was a conflict of opinion within Prince Kung's office as well.

Notes to Chapter VI.
Developments Following the Peking Conventions

1. Knollys, *Incidents in the China War*, pp. 207–208; *North China Herald* (Nov. 10, 1860), report dated Oct. 24, 1860.

2. Gros, p. 165. Prince Kung and his associates reported that the British came to the Board of Rites in the "eighth double-hour" (1 to 3 p. m.) (a memorial of Oct. 28, 1860, PLFC: Pan-li fu-chü an, *chüan* 6), while Jui-ch'ang and others reported their arrival in the "ninth double-hour" (3 to 5 p. m.) (IWSM:HF, 67:28). The appointment was for 2 p. m. (*PP: Affairs in China*, p. 210).

3. Buksgevden, pp. 220–221. Buksgevden also indicates that Elgin was about five hours late for the appointment.

4. Wolseley, p. 296; Loch, pp. 287–288; Knollys, *Incidents in the China War*, pp. 209–210; Montauban, p. 372; *North China Herald* (Nov. 10, 1860), report dated Oct. 24, 1860.

5. Swinhoe, pp. 348–349. According to Prince Kung and his associates, the prince sent a repast to "the British chieftain," who accepted only the cakes and the fruits, and sent in return on November 1 bottles of liquor and Western dishes (IWSM:HF, 67:56–57).

The British Museum has the "Menu of a repast sent by Prince Kung to Sir Hope Grant, Oct. 28, 1860" (call number: Oriental 6598). (The date is written on the back of Prince Kung's name card in a different hand.) The repast was a dinner for several people, one jar of Shaohsing wine, two kinds of fruit, and two kinds of cake. Liu Yü-nan records in his diary under Oct. 27 that Prince Kung sent to Prince I's palace (Elgin's temporary residence) exactly the same kinds of food, in double the quantities given above (Meng Sen, "Ch'ing Hsien-feng shih-nien," p. 187). Perhaps the same kind of repast was sent simultaneously to Elgin and Grant, and the date is wrong either in the diary or on the menu.

6. Walrond, p. 367; Loch, pp. 277–280; Meng Sen, "Ch'ing Hsien-feng shih-nien," pp. 186–188; Swinhoe, p. 349; *North China Herald* (Dec. 1, 1860) article dated Nov. 7, 1860. According to the last two sources, Elgin moved to Prince I's palace on October 25. But here we follow Elgin's own statement in Walrond.

7. Gros, pp. 152, 154–155, 160–161, 163; Meng Sen, "Ch'ing Hsien-feng shih-nien," pp. 185–188. The French had at first wanted to use Prince Su's palace but had been dissuaded. The British had not considered satisfactory any of the various places offered and eventually had chosen Prince I's palace despite strong objections by the Chinese authorities (a supplementary memorial of Oct. 28, 1860, from Prince Kung and his associates, PLFC: Pan-li fu-chü an, *chüan* 6).

It seems that a battalion of 500 men with two "guns," which apparently means cannons, remained in Peking as an escort for Gros when most of the

French army departed from the city (Colonel Foley to Russell, Nov. 17, 1860, *PP: Affairs in China*, p. 274). According to Prince Kung and his associates, three or four hundred men formed Gros's escort as of the beginning of November (IWSM:HF, 67:55).

8. Gros, pp. 165–169; Montauban, pp. 373–374; IWSM:HF, 67:56.

9. Montauban, pp. 370–371, 375.

10. *Ibid.*, pp. 383–384; Thomas, II, 395–396; Ting Yun-shu *et al.*, 6:8–9. According to Thomas, Father Mouly met Prince Kung for the first time on October 28, when he found the prince very apprehensive. The priest took the prince's hands in his, leaned on the table, and talked with him thus for a good half hour, successfully allaying his fears. Prince Kung and his associates reported in a memorial of October 28 that the French and the British were apparently of one mind but divided in heart, and a French priest wanted to discuss the situation confidentially with the prince (PLFC: Pan-li fu-chü an, *chüan* 6).

Montauban, p. 368, states that Father Mouly came to see him on October 21, at Prince Kung's wish, to report a conversation he had had with the prince. This contradicts Thomas's account (p. 395), according to which the priest left Tientsin on October 21 and stayed on that evening in T'ung-chou.

11. *PP: Affairs in China*, pp. 253–255, 273; Walrond, p. 370; Rennie, *British Arms*, p. 184.

12. Swinhoe, p. 378.

13. Walrond, p. 369; Elgin to Russell, No. 87, confidential, Pekin, Nov. 4, 1860, FO 17/332; Gros to Thouvenel, No. 26, Nov. 17, 1860, Correspondance Politique, Chine, Vol. 34.

The account in Liu Yü-nan's diary, which must be based on hearsay, says that on November 4 Prince Kung called on Elgin and returned a visit to Gros (Meng Sen, "Ch'ing Hsien-feng shih-nien," p. 188). But we follow here the accounts of Elgin and Gros.

14. Gros, p. 206.

15. IWSM:HF, 62:34.

16. *Ibid.*, 64:16–17.

17. *Ibid.*, 65:22, 23.

18. *Ibid.*, 69:8–9.

19. *Ibid.*, 67:55, 57; 68:1, 35. Cf. *ibid.*, 68:4.

20. *Ibid.*, 69:9, 29, 41; Buksgevden, pp. 231, 232, 237.

21. See Chap. I, pp. 46–47.

22. As a matter of fact, it will be recalled that already on September 14, 1860, Prince I had tried in T'ung-chou to sound out Parkes on the possibility of British aid against the Taipings. But Parkes had avoided an answer. See *PP: Affairs in China*, p. 169.

23. Gros to Thouvenel, Oct. 26, 1860; Cordier, *L'expédition, 1860*, p. 444; Gros to Thouvenel, No. 25, Nov. 1, 1860, and No. 26, Nov. 17, 1860, Correspondance Politique, Chine, Vol. 34; Hérisson, pp. 232–233, 295; Montauban, pp. 393–394, 398; Ting Yun-shu *et al.*, 6:7–9, 11–12; IWSM:HF, 66:1, 3–4;

67:55. Elgin seems to have got wind of the French priests' maneuver. See Elgin to Russell, private, Oct. 31, 1860, P.R.O. 30/22/49.

When de Méritens was in Peking in early December 1860, to arrange for the rental of a legation building for the French, Prince Kung interviewed him at length and questioned him about the possibility of effective assistance either to crush the insurrection or to reorganize the Chinese armies. Méritens avoided a definite answer by stating that good offices would be offered by his government when the French minister had been granted an audience by the Chinese emperor and China had also sent a mission to Paris. See de Méritens to Bourboulon, Dec. 20, 1860, in Bourboulon to Thouvenel, No. 92, Dec. 28, 1860, Correspondance Politique, Chine, Vol. 32.

24. Buksgevden, p. 237. On the date of Ignat'ev's departure, see above, Chap. V, note 97.

25. IWSM:HF, 69:22–23, 29–31, 41–42. The communication from the Court of Dependencies is in *ibid.*, 33:28.

26. *Ibid.*, 69:30–32. Early in 1862 the Russian gift of 10,000 rifles and 8 cannons was delivered overland to China through Kiakhta, where selected Chinese soldiers were given some instruction in operating and repairing the arms (Bruce to Russell, No. 87, July 2, 1862, FO 17/372). But the instruction given was quite unsatisfactory to the Chinese, so the Peking government saw to it that the Russian firearms were used in the military training given to Ch'ing troops in Tientsin by British officers in 1862 (IWSM:TC, 3:6–8, 24–26, 45; 5:17). Thus, equipped with these Russian presents the Peking Field Force (Shen-chi-ying) was organized in the same year (Hummel, I, 382).

27. Elgin to Russell, No. 107, Shanghai, Dec. 21, 1860, FO 17/332; Wade to Bruce, private, Peking, Jan. 20, 1861, in Bruce to Russell, No. 14, Tientsin, Mar. 12, 1861, FO 17/350.

28. IWSM:HF, 70:18–20; 71:1–4, 9–12, 15–17, 34–36; 72:3–8, 9–10. The idea of Russian and French assistance was favorably viewed also by Feng Kuei-fen in "Chieh-ping E-Fa i," *Chiao-fen-lu k'ang-i* (1885 and 1897).

29. Bruce to Russell, Nov. 16, 1860, *PP: Affairs in China,* p. 273.

30. IWSM:HF, 70:5.

31. Wade to Bruce, private, Jan. 11, 1861, in Bruce to Russell, No. 14, Tientsin, Mar. 12, 1861, FO 17/350; Wade to Bruce, private, Jan. 20, 1861, in the same.

32. Elgin to Russell, Nov. 13, 1860, *PP: Affairs in China,* p. 255; Bruce to Russell, Nov. 16, 1860, *ibid.,* p. 273.

33. Elgin to Prince Kung, Nov. 8, 1860, *ibid.,* p. 257.

34. Bourboulon to Prince Kung, Dec. 2, 1860, in Bourboulon to Thouvenel, No. 90, Dec. 13, 1860, Correspondance Politique, Chine, Vol. 32.

35. IWSM:HF, 68:10–12, 17.

36. *Ibid.*, 69:7. This explanation skillfully quoted key words from the edict to which it replied, which stated that, while "trivial matters" relating

to trade were to be disposed of by Heng-ch'i and Ch'ung-lun, any "matter of importance" should be referred to Prince Kung and his associates.

37. Cordier, *Histoire des relations,* I, 43–45, 48; Gros, pp. 199–200, 201–203; Gros to Elgin, Nov. 7, 1860, enclosed in the following dispatch of Elgin; Elgin to Russell, No. 89, confidential, Nov. 13, 1860, FO 17/332; Elgin to Russell, Nov. 13, 1860, *PP: Affairs in China,* p. 254; Elgin to Russell, private, Nov. 17, 1860, P.R.O. 30/22/49; Bruce to Alston, private, Dec. 31, FO 17/339.

Ignat'ev had maneuvered in the background to bring Elgin and Gros to their decision. Their original intent had been to establish the legations in Peking immediately, a prospect displeasing to Ignat'ev, who felt that the presence in Peking of the British, French, and American ministers would be disadvantageous to Russia. During the Peking negotiations he emphasized to the British and French diplomats the uselessness of permanent residence and finally prevailed upon them to station their ministers in Tientsin for the moment. Moreover, for fear that the secrets of the forthcoming Sino-Russian negotiations would be revealed if the British and French protracted their stay in Peking, he tried to advance the withdrawal of the allied forces by pointing out to General Hope Grant that the severe Peking winter with the north-west seasonal wind was rapidly approaching. His maneuvers were threatened by the arrival of Bruce, who urged the immediate establishment of the legation. When Bruce visited him in company with Elgin, Ignat'ev tried to persuade him to pass the winter in Tientsin, asserting that friendly relations with China could be maintained only if the Western diplomats left the capital for the moment and returned at the invitation of the Chinese government. To assure success, Ignatiev called on Gros and applied pressure on him (Buksgevden, pp. 172–175, 214–215, 222, 225–228).

Bourboulon, who had been summoned from Shanghai by Gros and had arrived in Tientsin on November 11, at first regretted the decision to postpone establishment of the legation (Bourboulon to Thouvenel, No. 85, Tientsin, Nov. 15, 1860, Correspondance Politique, Chine, Vol. 32).

38. IWSM:HF, 68:2–3, 36–37; *PP: Affairs in China,* pp. 254, 257, 259, 273. Ignat'ev suspected that Adkins remained in Peking to keep an eye on his activities. So he daily invited Adkins to dinner in order to lull his suspicions. On November 14, the day the Sino-Russian treaty was signed, Adkins was taken by the Russians to visit the Yung-ho-kung, a famous Lamaist temple. Then he was invited to dinner at the Northern Hostel, where he was made quite drunk (Buksgevden, pp. 233–234).

39. IWSM:HF, 68:3; 70:33–34; 71:6; Bourboulon to Thouvenel, No. 86, Dec. 1, 1860, Correspondance Politique, Chine, Vol. 32; Bourboulon to Thouvenel, No. 92, Dec. 28, 1860, *ibid.,* Vol. 32; de Méritens to Bourboulon, Dec. 20, 1860, in Bourboulon to Thouvenel, No. 92.

40. Méritens to Bourboulon, Dec. 20, 1860, in Bourboulon to Thouvenel, No. 92.

41. IWSM:HF, 68:10–12, 15.

42. *Ibid.,* 68:16–17.

43. *Ibid.,* 69:43; 70:2, 6–7, 10–11, 33, 35.

44. *Ibid.,* 69:15–16.

45. Banno, "Gaikō kōshō . . . kōdō yōshiki."

46. CSL:WT, 227:8; IWSM:HF, 15:28–30, 37; 16:1–14, 23–24, 26–29, 34–35; 17:1–3. Wen-ch'ien was a member of the Bordered Yellow Banner and belonged to the Imperial Household. See *Ta-Ch'ing chin-shen ch'üan-shu* (winter of Hsien-feng 9), 2:7.

47. Bruce to Russell, No. 201, Dec. 27, 1860, FO 17/339; Bruce to Russell, No. 7, Feb. 20, 1861, FO 17/350; Bruce to Russell, No. 14, Mar. 12, 1861, FO 17/350; Bruce to Russell, No. 25, Apr. 8, 1861, FO 17/351 (on Wade's activities in Peking, see the letters from him to Bruce, enclosed in the last two dispatches). See also IWSM:HF, 71:28–29.

Bourboulon appears to have been less suspicious, though he, like Bruce, avoided direct contact with Heng-ch'i and Ch'ung-hou. See Bourboulon to Thouvend, No. 92, Dec. 28, 1860, Correspondance Politique, China, Vol. 32.

48. Bourboulon to Thouvenel, No. 94, Feb. 5, 1861, Correspondance Politique, China, Vol. 35; Kleczkowski to Bourboulon, Feb. 10, 1861, in Bourboulon to Thouvenel, No. 95, Feb. 20, 1861, *ibid.*

49. IWSM:HF, 65:10–13 (a memorial from Ch'ing-lien, governor of Honan); *ibid.,* 65:22–25 (from Yuan Chia-san, imperial commissioner and director-general of grain transport). See also a memorial received on November 15 from Weng T'ung-shu, governor of Anhwei (*ibid.,* 69:10–13).

Tu Ch'iao, former junior vice-president of the Board of Revenue, requested the emperor's return in a memorial received on October 8, 1860; his argument was that "the barbarian evils are no worse than the scabies; even if the barbarians behave furiously, their position does not tend to be incompatible with ours, their aim being profit making" (IWSM:HF, 64:24–26). On Tu Ch'iao's rather moderate attitude amidst the increasingly vocal war advocacy of 1858, see above Chap. II, note 60.

50. IWSM:HF, 68:12, 28–29.

51. *Ibid.,* 69:3–4; Tung Hsun, 1:31; Weng T'ung-ho, *chüan* 1, *keng-shen,* p. 52. In PLFC: Chung-wai hsiu-ping, the memorial appears under Nov. 11, 1860.

52. IWSM:HF, 69:4–5.

53. See Chap. V, note 153.

54. Shen Chao-lin, 1:16–19; *Ch'ing-shih lieh-chuan,* 47:5–6. Shen Chao-lin became a grand councillor in November 1861 (*ibid.,* 47:6).

55. A joint memorial of Sept. 12, 1860, from Ch'üan-ch'ing (president of the Board of Civil Appointments) and forty others, which opposed the emperor's flight, contains the following passage: " . . . the barbarians who have come far from across the ocean have hitherto shown that their object was only to trade. Their creeping into Kwan-tung, Fokien, Shanghae, and other places, was only to seize the ports, and not to take possession of the country; nor have they attempted any conquest of China . . . In all which is going

on, then, there is nothing to make one apprehend great misfortune" (*PP: Affairs in China*, pp. 261–262). This assertion, which contrasts with the generally warlike tone of the numerous memorials opposing the emperor's flight, may be taken as an indication of a subtle change in undercurrent.

56. IWSM:HF, 67:12, 69:35–41, 45.

57. *Ibid.*, 70:23–27, 30–33; Bruce to Russell, No. 199, Dec. 13, 1860, FO 17/339; Bourboulon to Thouvenel, No. 90, Dec. 13, 1860, Correspondance Politique, Chine, Vol. 32.

58. CSL:WT, 340:2–3; 342:22; 344:5; IWSM:HF, 74:11–12; Bruce to Russell, No. 14, Mar. 12, 1861, FO 17/350; Bruce to Russell, No. 25, Apr. 8, 1861, FO 17/351; Bourboulon to Thouvenel, No. 95, Feb. 20, 1861, Correspondance Politique, Chine, Vol. 35; Bourboulon to Thouvenel, No. 96, Mar. 12, 1861, *ibid.;* Bourboulon to Thouvenel, No. 98, Apr. 3, 1861, *ibid.;* Bourboulon to Thouvenel, No. 99, Apr. 5, 1861, *ibid.;* Kleczkowski to Benedetti, Feb. 22, 1861, *ibid.*

59. It was Su-shun in Jehol, it is said, who prevented the emperor's return to the capital, asserting that the enemy's movements were unfathomable. See CSK, *lieh-chuan*, No. 174. Cf. Hsueh Fu-ch'eng, "Hsien-feng chi-nien san-chien fu-chu," *Yung-an pi-chi, chüan* 1; CSL:MT, 5:26–27.

It is also asserted that Huang Tsung-han (then a junior vice-president of the Board of Civil Appointments), currying favor with Su-shun, went to Jehol in the spring of 1861 and strongly opposed the emperor's return (CSK, *lieh-chuan*, No. 181; CSL:MT, 6:24–26).

After peace had been made, it is said, Lin-k'uei went to Jehol to request the emperor to return, but was opposed by Prince I, Prince Cheng, and Su-shun (CSK, *lieh-chuan*, No. 176).

60. Colonel Foley to Russell, Nov. 17, 1860, *PP: Affairs in China*, p. 274; *North China Herald* (Nov. 10, 1860); Wolseley, p. 321; IWSM:HF, 69:18 (from Seng-ko-lin-ch'in); Bazancourt, II, 327. Prince Kung and his associates tended to minimize the strength of the force (IWSM:HF, 69:43, 70:25).

61. IWSM:HF, 67:6–7, 11, 39; 68:3, 10–12, 37; 69:6–7, 33, 43, 45. At one time in the course of his negotiations with Prince Kung's deputies in November 1860, Ignat'ev plainly hinted that he could easily recall the allied troops from Tientsin. This intimidation was effective. (Buksgevden, pp. 229–230).

62. Walrond, pp. 371–372. The *North China Herald* (Nov. 10 and Nov. 17, 1860) "deeply" regretted the withdrawal of the allied forces to Tientsin. In its opinion the step was fraught with evil and would prevent Bruce from re-entering Peking for permanent residence.

63. Bruce thought that while the emperor stayed away from the capital the troops should not be withdrawn from Tientsin (Bruce to Wade, Feb. 9, 1861, in Bruce to Russell, No. 14, Tientsin, Mar. 12, 1861, FO 17/350).

Notes to Chapter VII. The Tsungli Yamen

1. IWSM:HF, 71:17–29. Bruce's comment appears in Bruce to Russell, No. 51, May 23, 1861, FO 17/352. (The dispatch enclosed Wade's translation

of the memorandum which was printed in the *Peking Gazette*. Whereas the principal memorial was written in a conventional antiforeign style with abundant use of the term "barbarian," the term appears only once, perhaps "by mistake" as Wade noted, in the memorandum.) Bruce — and apparently Wade also — mistook the six-article memorandum for a minute submitted to the throne from the "High Committee" presided over by Prince Hui.

2. IWSM:HF, 71:17-19. See also Teng Ssu-yü and J. K. Fairbank, *China's Response to the West* (Cambridge, Mass., 1954), pp. 47-49.

3. Cf. Fan Wen-lan, *Chung-kuo chin-tai-shih*, rev. 8th ed. (Peking, 1953), Vol. 1, Part 1, pp. 208-209.

4. IWSM:HF, 71:28-29. At Wade's interview with Prince Kung and others on January 6, 1861, at the Chia-hsing Temple, "Wansiang [Wen-hsiang] volunteered the remark that the Emperor had resolved on establishing a Foreign Department. For economy's sake it is to be composed of members of other courts, or tribunals, now forming part of the civil establishment, and will sit in the office of the Board of Ceremonies [the Board of Rites]." On January 9, at his own private residence Wen-hsiang again told Wade about the plan in greater detail. (Wade to Bruce, private, Jan. 11, 1861, in Bruce to Russell, No. 14, Mar. 12, 1861, FO 17/350.)

Later Bruce gave the following summary: "[The dispatch of Wade to Peking] led to the withdrawal of the Prince's deputies from Tientsin, to the direct transaction of business with the Prince himself and with his associate Wen-siang; and to the formation of the Board of Foreign Affairs already reported" (Bruce to Russell, No. 25, Apr. 8, 1861, FO 17/351).

5. IWSM:HF, 71:19 (a vermilion endorsement on the principal memorial).

6. *Ibid.*, 72:1.

7. *Ibid.*, 72:1-3. The first edict was published on January 25 in the *Peking Gazette* (Wade to Bruce, private, Jan. 26, 1861, in Bruce to Russell, No. 14, Tientsin, Mar. 12, 1861, FO 17/350). It was apparently printed together with the six-article memorandum presented by Prince Kung and others. A translation by Wade of both documents is enclosed in Bruce to Russell, No. 51, May 23, 1861, FO 17/352. See above, note 1.

8. In retrospect Wen-hsiang told Wade on June 19, 1862, that there had been "fierce opposition" to [the establishment of] the Tsungli Yamen, which he and Heng-ch'i had maintained to be necessary "against all opponents" (Memorandum by Wade, June 20, 1862, in Bruce to Russell, No. 80, June 20, 1862, FO 17/372). Martin, p. 361, states that it was Wen-hsiang who "took the lead in the work of reorganization after the war of 1860, as well as in shaping the foreign policy of his government."

9. IWSM:HF, 71:26-27.

10. On the Ch'ing government organization, see *Shinkoku gyōseihō*, Vol. 1 (rev. ed., 1914). On the Council of Princes and High Officials, see Kanda Nobuo, "Shinsho no gisei daijin ni tsuite," *Wada Hakushi kanreki kinen Tōyōshi ronsō*, pp. 171-189 (Tokyo, 1951); and Kanda Nobuo, "Shinsho no

bairoku ni tsuite," *Tōyō gakuhō*, 40.4:349–371 (Mar. 1958). The decline in power and eventual disappearance of this Manchu institution is understandable in the context of the establishment of the despotic power of the throne, especially over the Manchu princes, which was finally achieved by the Yung-cheng emperor (r. 1723–36). On this background topic, see Meng Sen, "Pa-ch'i chih-tu k'ao-shih"; see also Miyazaki Ichisada, "Yōsei shuhi yushi kaidai," *Tōyōshi kenkyū*, 15.4:365–396 (Mar. 1957), esp. pp. 369–372. The Council of Princes in the Arrow War period (see Chap. II above), especially in its joint operation with the Grand Council, may be considered a sort of revival, in a different historical cotext and on a different power basis, of the Council of Princes and High Officials. On the Ch'ing Grand Secretariat, see Miyazaki Ichisada, "Shinchō ni okeru kokugo mondai no ichimen," *Tōhōshi ronsō*, 1:1–56 (July 1947).

11. For an excellent study of the Tsungli Yamen, see S. M. Meng; this was originally a Ph.D. thesis (Harvard, 1949) to which I am indebted in the writing of this chapter. Another useful study is Ch'en T'i-ch'iang, *Chung-kuo wai-chiao hsing-cheng* (Chungking, 1943).

12. IWSM:HF, 71:19, 21, 23. In a memorial that is assumed to have been presented in 1873, Prince Kung and his associates recalled that the Tsungli Yamen had originally been established as a temporary organ to function only until military operations against the insurgents were concluded and foreign affairs became less urgent. They pointed out, however, that although military operations were approaching a conclusion there still remained knotty diplomatic problems. They thus requested that abolition of the Tsungli Yamen be postponed for the moment (Chou Chia-mei, *cheng-shu*, Part 1, p. 12).

13. IWSM:HF, 72:1–2.

14. *Ibid.*, 72:19–22.

15. For instance, the term "trade" is dropped from the official title in the section on the Tsungli Yamen in *Kuang-hsü hui-tien, chüan* 99–100, and in *Kuang-hsü hui-tien shih-li, chüan* 1220, while it is retained in the section on "the casting of official seals, the Board of Rites" in *Kuang-hsü hui-tien, chüan* 34, and in *Kuang-hsü hui-tien shih-li, chüan* 223. The Tsungli Yamen was also sometimes referred to as the T'ung-shang Ya-men. For example, see a memorial from Wang Mao-yin criticizing the foreign policy conduct of the Tsungli Yamen (IWSM:TC, 5:14); and also *Kuang-hsü Shun-t'ien fu-chih*, 16:20.

Upon perusal of the edict announcing the establishment of the Tsungli Yamen (printed in the *Peking Gazette* on January 25), Wade reminded Wen-hsiang on the same day of "what [he] had said the other day on the inexpediency of inserting the words *t'ung shang*, commercial intercourse"; and Wen-hsiang told Wade that the edict would not be forwarded to the foreign ministers until the corrections were made (Wade to Bruce, private, Jan. 26, 1861, in Bruce to Russell, No. 14, Mar. 12, 1861, FO 17/350). As a matter of fact, the edict was officially forwarded to Bruce and to Bourboulon in a communication from Prince Kung dated as late as February 6, in which the term *t'ung-shang* was dropped from the title of the new office (Bruce to Russell, No. 7, Feb. 20, 1861, FO 17/350; Bourboulon to Thouvenel, No. 95 Feb. 20, 1861, Correspondance Politique, Chine, Vol. 35).

The French seem to have been less concerned about the insertion of *t'ung-shang,* probably because they got the impression that the Tsungli Yamen occupied "the first rank among the six Boards (now increased to seven)" (Bourboulon to Thouvenel, No. 94, Feb. 5, 1861, Correspondance Politique, Chine, Vol. 35).

16. IWSM:HF, 72:27. "I am happy to say that the Board of Ceremonies cannot find room for us in its Yamun [*sic*] and the Prince is looking out for some building to make an independent office of" (Wade to Bruce, private, Peking, Jan. 26, 1861, in Bruce to Russell, No. 14, Mar. 12, 1861, FO 17/350).

17. IWSM:HF, 72:32–35.

18. In making their original proposal (in the six-article memorandum) that provincial high officials report all foreign matters directly to the Tsungli Yamen as well as to the throne, Prince Kung and his associates had invoked "the established precedent for the provincial authorities of reporting to [the Board concerned] as well as to the throne" (*ko-sheng fen-pieh tsou-tzu chih li*) (IWSM:HF, 71:21). Referring to another established precedent, they now qualified the previous statement considerably and excluded reports on vital and confidential matters. (I have not been able to ascertain what the relevant precedents really were. See, however, *Shinkoku gyōseihō,* Vol. 1, Part 1, p. 189).

19. IWSM:HF, 72:35–36.

20. See S. M. Meng, pp. 24, 45. Meng asserts that actual cases indicate that this procedure "was strictly followed; indeed, practically all the information received by the Tsungli Yamen on important matters concerning foreign countries came through the Grand Council" (pp. 45, 122, note 53). On the other hand, there are certainly a great many instances (for example, see *Hai-fang tang* [Taipei, 1958], *passim*) in which the Tsungli Yamen seems to have received direct official reports from provincial high officials, including the Shanghai imperial commissioner and the Tientsin superintendent of trade. What the actual practice really was remains to be clarified.

An edict of June 1, 1861, gave the Tsungli Yamen the power to give orders (*ta-ch'ih*) to the provincial authorities. According to S. M. Meng, p. 40, however, that power was never exercised.

21. IWSM:HF, 73:10–12.

22. This description is based on actual conditions in 1861 as seen through the contemporary sources; it does not take into account the detailed regulations concerning the organization and functions of the Tsungli Yamen in *Kuang-hsü hui-tien* (compilation completed in 1899). Cf. S. M. Meng, pp. 26, 38.

In 1864 there was a great increase in personnel on the secretary level and below, as well as a radical change in the Yamen's organization (see IWSM: TC, 28:13–17).

On the expenditures of the Tsungli Yamen, see Ch'en Wen-chin, "Ch'ing-tai chih Tsung-li Ya-men chi ch'i ching-fei," *Chung-kuo chin-tai ching-chi-shih yen-chiu chi-k'an*. 1.1:49–58 (Nov. 1932).

23. IWSM:HF, 76:12–13.

24. In memorials and edicts of the period of the Yamen's inauguration the secretaries were referred to as *ssu-yuan*, a generic term for the secretaries of government offices in Peking. It seems, however, that they came to be called specifically *chang-ching*, probably because this was the designation for the secretaries of the Grand Council. Cf. *Kuang-hsü hui-tien, chüan* 99–100 (section on the Tsungli Yamen); Wu Ch'eng-chang, *Wai-chiao-pu yen-ko chi-lueh* (Peking, 1913), *chia-pien*, pp. 4ff.

25. IWSM:HF, 72:20, 28–29; 76:15.

26. *Ibid.*, 73:10–12.

27. *Ibid.*, 70:22; 76:16–19. En-ling, comp., *Cheng-hung-ch'i Man-chou Ha-ta Kua-erh-chia shi chia-p'u* (1849), 4:25. Prince Kung and others stated in retrospect in a memorial of 1864 that with the addition of four experienced men the fixed number of secretaries had been increased in 1861 from 16 to 20 (IWSM:TC, 28:13).

28. IWSM:HF, 76:17; CSK, *lieh-chuan*, No. 167. *Ta-Ch'ing chin-shen ch'üan-shu*, unidentified season of Hsien-feng 11, 1:52, 80.

29. IWSM:HF, 72:29, 31; 76:17. For a recent illuminating study of the yamen clerks of the Ch'ing period, see Miyazaki Ichisada, "Shindai no shori to bakuyū—tokuni Yōseichō o chūshin to shite," *Tōyōshi kenkyū*, 16.4:347–374 (Mar. 1958).

30. IWSM:HF, 72:29–30; 77:10–11.

31. *Ibid.*, 45:35; 71:32–34; 72:15–17. S. F. Wright, *Hart and the Chinese Customs* (Belfast, 1950), pp. 133–136, 146–151.

32. In the Chinese text, this clause also stated that the Chinese government would select students and let them study English, and when they had become proficient in that language, British communications would cease to be accompanied by a Chinese version.

33. IWSM, 71:24–25; see also *ibid.*, 72:2, 32. Kuo Sung-tao had urged in a supplementary memorial received on February 26, 1859, that some Mongols and Chinese who knew Russian or other Western languages be sent to Peking as language teachers (SKHT:YCLT, 16:60).

34. IWSM:TC, 8:29–35.

35. *Kuang-hsü Shun-t'ien fu-chih*, 7:28, 16:20. Rennie, *Peking and the Pekingese*, I, 39, 130, 243.

36. IWSM:HF, 72:28, 76:1–2. The building had once been a residence of Sai-shang-a, a grand secretary. See Chen-chün, 3:15.

37. IWSM:HF, 73:10.

38. *Ibid.*, 74:1–2. Ch'en T'i-ch'iang, p. 16; S. M. Meng, p. 42.

39. Rennie, *Peking and the Pekingese*, II, 164.

40. IWSM:HF, 71:20–21, 27–28.

41. *Ibid.*, 72:1-2.

42. The earliest memorial reproduced in IWSM from Ch'ung-hou as superintendent of trade is in IWSM:HF, 74:17-22.

43. *Ibid.*, 71:27.

44. As a matter of fact, when in the first half of the 1860's foreign powers other than Britain, France, Russia, and the United States wanted to enter into treaty relationships with China, the Peking government tried to avoid negotiating a treaty at all; whenever negotiations could not be avoided it sought to conduct them in Shanghai or at least in Tientsin and not to concede the right of diplomatic residence in the capital. Many cases of this kind are recorded in IWSM:HF and IWSM:TC. As the earliest indication of such an attitude we may cite a supplementary memorial received on January 24, 1861, from Prince Kung and his associates: fearing that minor nations trading at Shanghai might ask to conclude a treaty following the precedents of Britain, France, and the United States, the memorialists requested that Hsueh Huan be ordered to take precautionary measures against the coming to Tientsin of envoys of those small powers (IWSM:HF, 72:8-9).

45. Bruce to Russell, private, Feb. 5, 1861, P.R.O. 30/22/49. In the eyes of Lay, these two offices constituted "an insidious attempt to put us back into the old position we occupied before the treaty [of Tientsin]." In 1863(?) he insisted that they be discontinued (*Our Interests in China*, pp. 43, 45, 55, 58-59; S. F. Wright, p. 250).

46. See above, note 20, however.

47. CSL:MT, 23:38.

48. *Ibid.*, 72:34-35.

49. *Ibid.*, 188:3.

50. For example, it is stated in *Kuang-hsü hui-tien shih-li, chüan* 1220: "In Hsien-feng 10th year, . . . there was established a superintendent of trade affairs for Kiangsu, Chekiang, Kwangtung, Fukien, and the Great River (*pan-li Chiang Che Yueh Min nei-chiang ko-k'ou t'ung-shang shih-wu ta-ch'en*), a concurrent post of the governor of Kiangsu, which was called Nan-yang ta-ch'en, and a superintendent of trade affairs for the three ports of Newchwang, Tientsin, and Chefoo (*pan-li Niu-chuang T'ien-chin Teng-chou san-k'ou t'ung-shang shih-wu ta-ch'en*), which was called Pei-yang ta-ch'en." Here Nan-yang ta-ch'en and Pei-yang ta-ch'en are used as designations retroactively applicable to Hsien-feng 10th year. From earlier examples in IWSM we may cite a use in 1862 of the term Nan-pei t'ung-shang ta-ch'en and a use in 1862 of the designation Nan-yang t'ung-shang ta-ch'en, which was used as a comprehensive term retroactively covering the Canton imperial commissioner too (IWSM:TC, 5:20; 6:27).

51. IWSM:TC, 78:28-29, 42. For a recent study of the two superintendencies of trade, in the south and in the north, see Wang Erh-min, "Nan-pei-yang ta-ch'en chih chien-chih chi ch'i ch'üan-li chih k'uo-chang," *Ta-lu tsa-chih*, 20.5:152-159 (Mar. 1960).

52. IWSM:HF, 71:24; 72:2. Prince Kung and his associates had based their

proposal on a memorial from Ho Kuei-ch'ing presented "in the second month of Hsien-feng 9th year." This was Ho's memorial received on March 15, 1859 (see above, Chap. III), advocating a full-time commissionership at Shanghai and surveying critically the current machinery for foreign affairs (*ibid.*. 35:14–17).

Notes to Epilogue

1. Bruce to Russell, No. 25, Apr. 8, 1861, FO 17/351; Bourboulon to Thouvenel, No. 96, Mar. 12, No. 97, Mar. 26, and No. 98, Apr. 3, 1861, Correspondance Politique, Chine, Vol. 35; IWSM:HF, 74:12, 23–24, 29; 75:4–5.

2. In *Peking and the Pekingese,* D. F. Rennie, a medical doctor attached to the British legation in Peking, gives a detailed description in the form of a semiofficial diary covering one year beginning in the spring of 1861, of the way business was conducted by the ministers of the Tsungli Yamen and of the atmosphere surrounding intercourse between the Yamen and the British and other legations.

3. Bruce to Russell, No. 89, July 20, 1861, FO 17/353; IWSM:HF, 77:28, 79:12–13, 80:6–7, 18–19, 33–35.

4. *Papers Relating to Foreign Relations of the United States* (1862), p. 847; IWSM:TC, 7:51.

5. CSK, *chün-chi ta-ch'en nien-piao.* On the *coup d'état* of 1861, see Hummel, I, 295–296, 381–382; II, 668–669.

6. S. M. Meng, Appendix, "A Chronological Table of the Ministers of the Tsungli Yamen."

7. For instance, Shen Chao-lin, as mentioned in Chap. VI, pp. 215–216.

8. IWSM:HF, 28:45–49. See Chap. II, pp. 86–87. The case of Yin Chao-yung, a renowned war advocate in the Arrow War (see Chap. II. pp. 67, 84) may also be relevant. Yin Chao-yung lent his name, apparently very reluctantly, to the efforts of the local gentry to obtain foreign military assistance when the Taipings drew near Shanghai at the end of 1861 (Feng Kuei-fen, "Hu-ch'eng hui-fang chi," in *chüan* 4 of *Hsien-chih-t'ang kao* [preface dated 1877]; IWSM:TC, 6:31–33; Yin Chao-yung, pp. 41–42; Ono Shinji, p. 111). In 1862 he presented a memorial in which he advocated, on the basis of his observations at Shanghai, a policy of "self-strengthening": a proper conduct of diplomacy, a reorganization of military forces (an improvement in recruitment, discipline, training, and weapons), a supply of better ships and cannon (*ch'uan-chien p'ao-li*), and the study of foreign newspapers. He also suggested the necessity of again prohibiting by negotiation the importing of opium when the rebellions were suppressed and the import duties on opium were no longer needed as military funds (IWSM:TC, 6:31–33.)

9. Rennie, *Peking and the Pekingese,* pp. 166, 219.

10. Bruce to Russell, private, Nov. 12, 1861, P.R.O. 30/22/49.

11. Bruce to Russell, private, Mar. 12, 1862, P.R.O. 30/22/49.

12. Hansard, 165:1806–1815. Note also the debate on China in the House of Commons on July 8, 1862, *ibid.*, 168:29–81.

13. See Gregory.

14. For example, see Rennie, *Peking and the Pekingese*, II, 172–173, 176, 177, 178.

15. *Ibid.*, II, 166, 219; IWSM:TC, 2:47–48.

16. Rennie, *Peking and the Pekingese*, II, 297, 331–332; Gregory, p. 17.

17. Rennie, *Peking and the Pekingese*, II, 249, 271–274, 276–277, 283, 287, 290–291, 292; Bruce to Russell, Mar. 26, 1862, *PP: Further Papers Relating to the Rebellion in China* (1862), pp. 9–10; IWSM:TC, 3:44–45; 4:13–14, 36–38; 5:15–18.

18. Cordier, *Histoire des relations*, I, 257; IWSM:TC, 34:35–36.

19. Bruce to Russell, June 23, 1861, *PP: Papers Relating to the Rebellion in China and Trade in the Yang-tze-kiang River* (1862), p. 53.

20. Bruce to Russell, May 13, 1862, *PP: Further Papers Relating to the Rebellion in China, with an Appendix* (1863), pp. 9–10.

21. Bruce to Russell, No. 74, June 16, 1862, FO 17/372.

22. Bruce to Russell, July 24, 1862, *PP: Further Papers Relating to the Rebellion in China, with an Appendix* (1863), p. 70.

23. Bruce to Russell, Sept. 8, 1862, *ibid.*, pp. 82–83.

24. Bruce to Russell, Apr. 7, 1860, *PP: Affairs in China*, pp. 37–39. See Chap. I, p. 15. For a trenchant discussion of gunboat diplomacy, note J. K. Fairbank, "Patterns behind the Tientsin Massacre," *Harvard Journal of Asiatic Studies*, 20.3–4:482–490 (Dec. 1957).

25. On the Cooperative Policy, see Mary C. Wright, *The Last Stand of Chinese Conservatism*, Chap. III. On Britain's China policy of the day, see Pelcovits.

26. For a definitive study of Robert Hart, see S. F. Wright, *Hart and the Chinese Customs*. Morse, *International Relations*, Vols. 2 and 3, is also still useful.

Incidentally the affair of the Lay-Osborn Flotilla of 1863 is an illuminating example of the power struggle for military authority between the central government and such provincial high officials as Tseng Kuo-fan and Li Hung-chang, who had personally led regional forces at their command. It is also illustrative of the ambiguous involvements of the British authorities in that kind of dispute. Cf. J. L. Rawlinson, "The Lay-Osborn Flotilla: Its Development and Significance," *Papers on China* (Harvard University, East Asia Research Center), 4:58–93 (April 1950); S.F. Wright, pp. 225–257.

27. See Mary C. Wright, *The Last Stand of Chinese Conservatism*, Chaps. X and XI; Mary C. Wright, "The Adaptability of Ch'ing Diplomacy, the Case of Korea," *Journal of Asian Studies*, 18.3:363–381 (May 1958).

28. Hart to Hannen, Aug. 9, 1861, quoted in Morse, *International Relations*, II, 53, note 16.

29. For a neat selection of Western appraisals of Wen-hsiang, see Mary

Epilogue

C. Wright, *The Last Stand of Chinese Conservatism,* p. 71. See also, Rennie, *Peking and the Pekingese,* I, 182, 215, 248, 261, 333; II, 235.

The following is a rather unsympathetic observation by Sherard Osborn made in September 1863: "Wênseang is an intelligent, energetic-looking man, dark-skinned, with a sinister cast in his eyes, and a cruel mouth; richly clad, but without the slightest ostentation; had dirty nails, and was constantly using either a pipe or a snuff-bottle: he looked a refined Yeh [Ming-ch'en]" (Lay, *Our Interests in China,* p. 28).

30. Memorial of the Shanghae General Chamber of Commerce to Rutherford Alcock, undated, *PP: Memorials Addressed by Chambers of Commerce in China to the British Minister at Peking on the Subject of the Revision of the Treaty of Tientsin* (1868), pp. 1–2.

31. ". . . Wansiang, is a confirmed coward, and although at heart, the sincerest of the progressive party, so far as there is one, he is never game to follow up his first move if there is any clamour against it" (Wade to Hammond, private, Aug. 21, 1867, FO 391/19). Wade had recorded in 1866 the following observation: "As a politician he [Wen-hsiang] is at once timid and ambitious; hence eager to be *the* man in any scheme with which he is identified, and at the same time afraid of pushing it to the end" (Wade to Hammond, private, Mar. 6, 1866, FO 17/493). (Mr. Jack Gerson of the University of Toronto has kindly called my attention to these sources.)

Incidentally, when Thomas Wade negotiated in 1875 with the Tsungli Yamen to settle the Margary affair, he met with strong resistance, especially from Wen-hsiang. In Wade's opinion Wen-hsiang, Pao-yun, and Shen Kuei-fen betrayed "so obstinate a reactionary tendency" that their dismissal from the Yamen was the true means toward amelioration of the state of affairs. Wen-hsiang also impressed Hart, who joined the negotiations, as a thorough reactionary (S. T. Wang, *The Margary Affair and the Chefoo Agreement* [London and New York, 1940], pp. 78, 86, 87).

32. For instance, in a memorial presented in 1862, Wang Mao-yin criticized the Tsungli Yamen's handling of foreign affairs, basing his argument on the idea of "rationale of state" (*kuo-t'i*). Referring to Wang Mao-yin's criticism as "the doctrinaire reasoning of an outsider," Prince Kung and his associates launched a severe counterattack and explained in detail the compelling reasons for a conciliatory foreign policy (IWSM:TC, 5:42–43, 54–56).

33. Burlingame to Seward, Dec. 12, 1862, *Papers Relating to Foreign Relations of the United States* (1864) p. 837.

34. On the change of affairs in and out of the Tsungli Yamen after Wen-hsiang's death, see S. F. Wright, pp. 519–520. For an incisive analysis, based on Western sources, of the political conditions affecting the Tsungli Yamen, see E. V. G. Kiernan, *British Diplomacy in China, 1880 to 1885* (Cambridge, England, 1939), pp. 23–37, 47–48, 51, 52–53, 62, 134–135.

Index

Adjutants-general, 56, 76, 222, 266 n9, 269 n49; and Council of Princes, 63–64

Adkins, T., 212

Agreement Containing Rules of Trade, 27, 232, 286 n2

Ai-jen, 285 n190

Aigun, Treaty of, 127, 128, 148, 149 154, 159, 182

Alcock, Sir Rutherford: on British position in China, 10; memorandum on treaty revision, 14–15

An-ting Gate, surrender of, 186, 197–198, 199, 317 n44, 318 n58

Annam, as tributary state, 117, 249 n3, 258 n66

Anouilh, Father, 207

Antiforeign party, 103, 130, 238, 243, 245. See also Violent party; War party, or war advocates

Antiforeignism: throughout empire, 7, 67, 245; in and around Canton, 7, 72, 74, 91; in Peking, 7, 65, 198, 199–201; Alcock on, 15; in Kwangtung, 67, 68; leaders in Kwangtung, 67, 91, 98, 276 n102; incidents in Tientsin, 281 n151

Arrow incident, 10

Assembly of courtiers: (of June 23, 1858), 58, 62, 82–84, 130; (of September 9, 1860), 88–89, 282 n169; (of June 2, 1858), 282 n169

Audience question, 4, 5, 34–36, 39, 108, 215, 216, 217, 331 n23; dispute with Ward on, 31, 59, 116–118, 119, 120, 122, 123–125, 292 n63, 296 n131; Shen Chao-lin on, 216. See also Kowtow problem

Balance of domestic political forces, 1, 54, 55–56. See also Equilibrium, political, in Peking; Peking, power distribution in

Balliuzek, Captain (later Colonel) L., 142, 237, 320 n75

Banner forces, 55, 56, 131, 216

Banners, General Headquarters of, 132

Barbarians: China (Middle Kingdom) and, 2, 14, 124; management of, 7; as sinocentric expression, 9, 98, 335 n1. See also Equality or unequality; International order, modern; State system, modern Western; Sinocentrism; Tribute system

Board, president: stationed in provinces, 28, 93, 101; to confer with foreign diplomats, 39–40, 99, 101, 289 n39

Board of Punishments: and Council of Princes, 59; and trial of Ch'i-ying, 61

Board of Revenue: selection of Tsungli Yamen secretaries from, 230; and accommodation for Ward's mission, 293 n74

Board of Rites, 51, 185, 187, 202, 203, 206, 228; jurisdiction over tributary states, 2, 36, 37, 40, 224, 226–227, 249 n4; as medium of Russian correspondence, 41, 132, 133, 138–139, 146, 150, 153; and establishment of Tsungli Yamen, 226–227, 228, 336 n4; transmission of provincial reports to Tsungli Yamen, 226–227, 229, 235; selection of Tsungli Yamen secretaries from, 230; prepares official seal of Tsungli Yamen, 233

Board of War: selection of Tsungli Ya-

Index

skii, 129, 133–138, 139, 142, 155, 183; signs Supplementary Agreement, 134–135; and Commission of Defense, 174, 177, 182, 320 n74, 330 n2; negotiates with Ignat'ev, 181–182, 183, 188; negotiates with Gurii, 320 n75; and Balliuzek, 320 n75

Jui-ch'ang (Tartar general of Hangchow), 209

Jui-lien, 316 n40

Jui-lin, 185, 193, 314 n17, 326 n147

Junk trade, 71–72, 91–92

K'ang-hsi emperor, 265 n1

Karpov, Russian frontier commissar, 141

Khitrovo, adjutant of Murav'ev, 142

Kiying, see Ch'i-ying

Kleczkowski, Count, 214

Korea, as tributary state, 2, 23, 27, 117, 145

Kovalevskii, E. P., 144

Kowtow problem, 3–4, 19, 25, 35–36, 57, 125, 217, 249 n3, 258 n66, 261 n110; dispute with Ward on, 116–118, 122, 296 n131

Ku-ming, see "Testamentary decree"

K'u-lun pan-shih ta-ch'en, see Urga, imperial agents at

Kuan-wen, 265 n7

K'uan Yuan, 285 n190

Kuang-tung ch'in-ch'ai ta-ch'en, see Imperial commissioner at Canton

Kuei-liang (Guiliang, Kweiliang), 77, 99, 103, 107, 108, 132, 189, 277 n119, 282 n165, 288 n27, 290 n49, 308 n115, 309 n134; and Tientsin negotiations, 18–25 passim, 59, 69, 90, 141, 156, 157, 175, 268 n38, 281 n151, 286 n2; advocates peace, 22, 74, 175–176, 183, 188, 190; on diplomatic representation in Peking, 23–24; and Shanghai negotiations, 27–28, 52, 59, 85, 90–91, 93–98, 101–102, 130–131, 156, 157, 175; and ratification of French and British Tientsin Treaties, 29–30; and Ward's mission to Peking, 31, 59, 109, 111, 112, 113, 116–119, 120–121, 122, 123, 124, 156, 175, 180, 188, 293 n84; and Tientsin negotiations, 32–33, 79, 172, 175; Elgin sails up Great River, 45; and Council

of Princes, 59, 64–65, 124, 269 n53; as center of peace advocacy, 68–69, 101, 159, 176, 191; and treaty revision negotiations, 69; and Ho Kuei-ch'ing, 70, 273 n86; and Prince Hui, 75, 188; and Prince Kung, 75, 188; and Sengko-lin-ch'in, 79; flexibility as Manchu politician, 85, 245; Ignat'ev on, 87, 277 n112; and Peking negotiations, 89, 170, 173, 175–181, 183, 188, 190, 191, 192, 193–198, 200–201; proposal for imperial commissionership, 94, 96–98; and Bruce, in Shanghai, 104; requests retirement, 157, 159; as commissioner to conduct national affairs, 173–174; and release of Parkes, 193–197; and surrender of An-ting Gate, 197–198; and foreign military aid, 207–210; requests emperor's return, 211, 214; and imperial tour, 216; and establishment of Tsungli Yamen, 219–223, 225–229, 232–236 passim; as minister of Tsungli Yamen, 222, 230, 238; and Ch'ang-shan, 231; and coup d'état, 238–239; made grand councillor, 238–239; his death, 244; and Wang yu-ling, 273 n86

Kunshan, interview at, 289 n41, 292 n68

K'un-yü, 316 n40

Kuo Sung-tao: and Tseng Kuo-fan, 56–57; and Su-shun, 56–57; advocates peace, 280 nn137 and 139; and Sengko-lin-ch'in, 280 nn137 and 139; and Hsien-feng emperor, 280 n139; on language training, 339 n33

Kuo-t'i (rationale of state), 343 n32

Lan Wei-wen: and Shanghai, 71; career summarized, 172, 274 n90; and Peking negotiations, 171, 172–173, 175, 318 n59; and Ho Kuei-ch'ing, 172, 274 n90; and Huang Chung-yü, 172–173, 290 n49; and Tientsin negotiations (1860), 172, 173; and T'ungchou negotiations, 172; peace letter, intercepted by British, 172; Wade on, 274 n90; and Chang Chin-wen, 314 n16

Laos, as tributary state, 249 n3

Lay, Horatio Nelson: on imperial commissioner at treaty port, 6, 251 n17;

Reference Matter

BIBLIOGRAPHY
GLOSSARY

BIBLIOGRAPHY

Note on Archival Sources: The archival sources that I
used in writing the earlier Japanese articles from which this book
has been developed were such published diplomatic documents as
Ch'ou-pan i-wu shih-mo (IWSM), the Parliamentary Papers (Blue
Books), the Foreign Office's Confidential Prints, Henri Cordier's
two documentary works on the Arrow War, and the American diplomatic correspondence. In 1957 I spent two weeks consulting unpublished documents in the National Archives in Washington, D. C.,
two months at the Public Record Office in London, several days at
the British Museum, and two weeks at the Archives of the French
Foreign Office. Although I was not able to examine the Elgin
Archives, kept at the Elgin family estate in Scotland, I saw many
transcripts from the private correspondence of Lord Elgin and Sir
Frederick Bruce through the kindness of Mr. Jack Gerson of the
University of Toronto, who has spent considerable time perusing
the Elgin Archives. In November 1960 I had the opportunity to work
for three weeks at the Institute of Modern History, Academia Sinica,
Taipei, comparing IWSM with relevant unpublished documents deposited there.

Despite all these archival pilgrimages, the published documents still constitute the bulk of the primary sources used in this
book, although of course in many instances they are aptly supple-
mented by the unpublished materials, and a number of topics or
events are covered only in the unpublished documents. Incidentally,
in view of the fact that the Foreign Office's Confidential Prints are
probably not readily available in libraries, the original citations
from this source have been replaced insofar as possible by the
corresponding citations from the Public Record Office files.

The Archives of the Tsarist Foreign Office for the Arrow
War period are not accessible to outside researchers. Thus I have
had to rely for the Russian account upon secondary sources and a
very limited number of published documents. Perhaps this is a
primary reason for my Chapter IV (on Sino-Russian contact in
Peking) being rather long and inconclusive and somewhat inferential.

I have not been able to see Ignat'ev's report, submitted in 1861 to the Asiatic Department of the Russian Foreign Office, which is listed in **P. E.** Skachkov, Bibliografiia Kitaia, entry No. 5019.

The unpublished Chinese materials that I consulted in Taipei were Ssu-kuo hsin-tang 四國新檔 (New files concerning the four powers) and Pan-li fu-chü tang-an 辦理撫局檔案 (Documents on the management of peacemaking).

Ssu-kuo hsin-tang (SKHT) is divided into four parts: Ying-chi-li tang 英吉利檔 (British files), 20 chüan; Fo-lan-hsi tang 佛蘭西檔 (French files), 2 chüan (chüan 1 missing); Mi-li-chien tang 米利堅檔 (American files), 4 chüan; E-lo-ssu tang 俄羅斯檔 (Russian files), 20 chüan. Compiled for office reference by the Grand Council in 1859-1863 from its archives, as a continuation of the Tao-kuang series of IWSM, SKHT covers the years 1850-1859. Unlike IWSM, it is divided by countries, but it resembles IWSM in that it consists mainly of edicts, rescripts, memorials, and communications with Western officials, all arranged chronologically, and its four parts present a general picture of the foreign affairs of the period. As a matter of fact, it was probably used as an original draft for the Hsien-feng series of IWSM, which was completed in 1867. A close comparison would show, however, that twenty to twenty-five per cent of the documents in SKHT are not in IWSM. Probably all of the documents in IWSM are also in SKHT, and the same memorials in SKHT are usually longer or less abridged than those in IWSM. There are also certain kinds of information that are to be found only in SKHT. There you may learn, for instance, whether or not a certain edict was given orally to the grand councillors, whether a memorial was a supplementary one enclosed with a main memorial, or a separate memorial from the same official received on the same day; or whether the original of a certain memorial, edict, or letter was written in Manchu. You may also encounter joint memorials from the grand councillors, which appear in IWSM only very rarely and which sometimes throw light on the process of decision-making. Sometimes, though very rarely, you can trace the process of drafting or editing an edict, rescript, or letter. In some cases SKHT will tell you that a certain memorial to which an answering edict was issued has been lost from the archives. For further description of SKHT, see Banno Masataka, "Chuo Kenkyuin Kindaishi Kenkyujo no gaiko toan," pp. 560-568.

Pan-li fu-chü tang-an (PLFC) has no date of compilation and no pagination. It is one of the numerous series of "clean copies" (ch'ing-tang 清檔) compiled by the Tsungli Yamen, in which documents are selected by specific subjects (unlike IWSM) and arranged chronologically (as in IWSM). The collection has thirteen parts:

Chieh-kuan fu-chü an 接管撫局案 (Records on the taking-over of peace negotiations), 1 chüan. Covers Prince I's negotiations in T'ung-chou, but furnishes nothing directly relating to the rupture of September 18, 1860.

Pan-li fu-chü an 辦理撫局案 (Records on the management of peace negotiations), 7 chüan. Chüan 1-6 cover in considerable detail the activities at Prince Kung's headquarters from September 21 to November 2, 1860; chüan 7 consists mainly of documents concerning the visit to China in 1861 of the father of Captain Brabazon, who had been taken prisoner and presumably decapitated in September 1860.

Fu-chü ching-fei an 撫局經費案 (Records on the expenditures for the peace negotiations), 1 chüan. Contains particulars of the expenditures for feeding Parkes during his imprisonment, accommodating the British at Prince I's palace in 1860, and entertaining the British and French ministers in the spring of 1861.

Chung-wai hsiu-ping an 中外休兵案 (Records on the Sino-foreign cessation of hostilities), 1 chüan. Covers the period October 25-November 21, 1860.

Yueh-sheng yang-ping ch'e-t'ui 粵省洋兵撤退 (On the withdrawal [in 1861] of foreign troops from Kwangtung), 1 chüan.

Ying-Fa hui-Chin an 英法回津案 (Records on the return to Tientsin of the British and the French), 1 chüan. Mainly reports from Tientsin to Prince Kung's office between November 1860 and April 1861.

Chou-shan yang-ping ch'e-t'ui 舟山洋兵撤退 (On the withdrawal of foreign troops from the Chusan Islands), 1 ch''uan.

Ying-kuo sung-huan shang-ping an 英國送還傷兵案 (Records on the return of wounded soldiers by the British), 1 chüan.

T'ien-chin yang-ping ch'e-t'ui 天津洋兵撤退 (On the withdrawal of foreign troops from Tientsin), 3 chüan. Covers the periods March 1861-February 1862 and May-October 1865.

Yang-ping t'ui-huan p'ao-t'ai 洋兵退還砲臺 (On the rendition of the [Taku] forts by the foreign troops), 1 chüan.

T'ien-chin hsiu-cheng p'ao-t'ai 天津修整砲臺 (On the repairs to the Tientsin [i.e. Taku] forts [in 1865]), 4 chüan.

Huan-yueh chiang-li 換約獎勵 (On the bestowal of rewards for treaty-making), 1 chüan. Covers the period December 1860-November 1861.

Huan-yueh ch'ing-chiang 換約請獎 (On the proposal of rewards for treaty-making), 2 chüan. Reproduces documents relating to the bestowal of rewards for the conclusion of the Alcock Convention of 1869.

(Though not included in the check list of "clean copies" at the Institute of Modern History, the last two items, concerning the bestowal of rewards, apparently belong to the same series as the other eleven. They are kept in the same book cover [chih 帙].)

Of these thirteen items, the second, on the activities of Prince Kung's office, is the most important. In addition to a number of memorials not included in IWSM from princes and high officials remaining in Peking, it contains a great number of documents of a kind not to be found in IWSM--for instance, communications between Prince Kung's office and Seng-ko-lin-ch'in, Jui-lin, the Grand Secretariat, the Board of War, the Board of Punishments, the Board of Rites, the Court of Dependencies, the Office of the Gendarmerie, the police censors, the Commission of Defense and other temporary emergency commissions in the metropolis, the General Headquarters Office of the Banners, or the Grand Council in Jehol; semiofficial letters addressed to various persons including Princes Hui, I, and Cheng, and Chang Chin-wen, the Tientsin salt merchant; orders or summonses to officials, and reports from such subordinates as Heng-ch'i. For further description of PLFC, see Banno, "Chūo Kenkyuin Kindaishi Kenkyūjo no gaiko toan, " pp. 568-570.

Individual volumes cited below are those
that I have examined in whole or in part.

Ai-hsin chueh-lo tsung-p'u 愛新覺羅宗譜 (Genealogy of
the Aisin Gioro clan), comp. Man-chou Ai-hsin chueh-lo hsiu-
p'u-ch'u 滿洲愛新覺羅修譜處. 7 vols. and a
supplement; Mukden, 1938.

Allgood, G. China War 1860: Letters and Journal. London,
New York, and Bombay, 1901.

Banno Masataka 坂野正高. "Ahen sensō go ni okeru
saikeikoku taigū no mondai" 阿片戰爭後に於ける
最惠國待遇の問題 (The problem of the most-
favored-nation treatment after the Opium War); Tōyō bunka
kenkyū 東洋文化研究 (Oriental culture review),
6:19-41 (Oct. 1947).

------"Gaikō kōshō ni okeru Shimmatsu kanjin no kōdō yōshiki--
1845-nen no jōyaku kaisei kōshō o chūshin to suru ichikōsatsu"
外交交涉に於ける清末官人の行動樣式——
一八五四年の條約改正交涉を中心と

する 一考察 (Behavior of mandarins as diplomats in
the late Ch'ing period--with special reference to the treaty
revision negotiations in 1854); Kokusaihō gaikō zasshi 國際
法外交雜誌 (Journal of international law and diplomacy),
48.4:502-540 (Oct. 1949); ibid., 48.6:703-737 (Dec. 1949).

------"'Sōrigamon' setsuritsu no haikei" 總理衙門設立
の背景 (The background of the establishment of the
Tsungli Yamen); Kokusaihō gaikō zasshi, 51.4:360-402
(Aug. 1952); ibid., 51.5:506-541 (Oct. 1952); ibid., 52.3:89-
109 (June 1953).

------"Tenshin jōyaku (1858-nen) chōin go ni okeru Shinkoku gaisei kikō no dōyō--kinsa daijin no Shanhai ichū kara Beikoku kōshi Wōdō no nyūkyō made" 天津條約（一八五八年）調印後に於ける 清國外政機構の動搖 ——欽差大臣の上海移駐から米國公使ウォード의入京まで (Institutional development in the Chinese conduct of foreign affairs after the signing of the Tientsin Treaties in 1858--from the transfer of the imperial commissionership to Shanghai to the visit of the American minister, Ward, to Peking; Kokusaihō gaikō zasshi, 55. 6:595-616 (Mar. 1957); ibid. , 56. 1:35-69 (Apr. 1957).

------"Sorigamon no setsuritsu katei" 總理衙門の設立 過程 (The process of establishing the Tsungli Yamen); Kindai chūgoku kenkyū 近代中國研究 (Researches on Modern China), ed. Kindai Chūgoku Kenkyū Iinkai 近代中國 研究委員會 (The Seminar on Modern China), No. 1:1-105 (Tokyo, 1958).

------"Pekin ni okeru tai-Ro kōshō kikō no hembō--Tenshin jōyaku (1858-nen) chōin kara 1860-nen 5-gatsu made" 北京に 於ける對露交渉機構の變貌 ——天津 條約（一八五八年）調印から一八六〇年 五月まで (The institutional change in Sino-Russian contact in Peking--from the signing of the Tientsin Treaty of 1858 to May 1860); Kindai chūgoku kenkyū, No. 3:1-67 (Tokyo, 1959).

------"Chūō Kenkyūin Kindaishi Kenkyūjo no gaikō tōan" 中央 研究院近代史研究所の外交檔案 (On the diplomatic documents deposited at the Institute of

Modern History, Academia Sinica); Tōyō gakuhō 東洋學報 (Reports of the Oriental Society), 43.4:559-571 (Sept. 1961).

------"Kō Chūyo (Chō Tōun) to Arō sensō--Shin-Ei kōshō kikō no ichi sokumen" 黄仲畬（張彤雲）とアロー戦争 —— 清英交渉機構の一側面 (Huang Chung-yü [Chang T'ung-yün] and the Arrow War: an aspect of the machinery for Sino-British negotiations); in Hanabusa Nagamichi hakushi kanreki kinen ronbunshū, gaikōshi oyobi kokusai seiji no shomondai 英修道博士還曆記念論文集外交史及 國際政治の諸問題(Problems of diplomatic history and international politics: a collection of articles commemorating the sixtieth birthday of Dr. Hanabusa Nagamichi), ed. Hanabusa Nagamichi Hakushi Kanreki Kinen Ronbunshū Henshū Iinkai 英修道博士還曆記念論文集編集委員會, pp. 75-103. Tokyo, 1962.

------"Kō Keiren to Arō sensō--eigo no hanaseru ichi seinen no yakuwari" 黄惠廉とアロー戦争 —— 英語の話せる一青年の役割 (Huang Hui-lien and the Arrow War: the role played by a young person speaking English); Tōkyō Toritsu Daigaku hōgakukai zasshi 東京都立大学法学會雑誌 (Journal of law and politics, Tokyo Metropolitan University), 3.1-2:343-385 (Mar. 1963).

Barsukov, Ivan. Graf Nikolai Nikolaevich Murav'ev-Amurskii po ego pis'mam, offitsial'nym dokumentam, razskazam sovremennikov i pechatnym istochnikam (materialy dlia biografii) (Count Nikolai Nikolaevich Murav'ev-Amurski, as seen through his letters, official documents, contemporaries' accounts, and printed sources [materials for a biography]). 2 vols.; Moscow, 1891. Vol. II is a collection of Murav'ev's memoranda and official letters.

Bazancourt, César Lecat, Baron de. Les expéditions de Chine
et de Cochinchine d'après les documents officiels. 2 vols.;
Paris, 1861-1862.

Bland J. O. P. and E. Backhouse. China under the Empress Dowager.
Rev. ed.; Peking, 1939.

Bol'shaia Sovetskaia entsiklopediia (Great Soviet encyclopedia).
2nd ed.; Moscow, 1947-1957.

British Government Documents, published

Foreign Office Confidential Prints

Correspondence Relating to Affairs in China, March
to November 1859. Confidential; Printed for the
Use of the Foreign Office. Nov. 14, 1859.

Correspondence Respecting Affairs in China, 1859-61.
Confidential; Printed for the Use of the Foreign
Office. Jan. 18, 1861.

PP: Parliamentary Papers (Blue Books). Presented by
command either to the House of Commons or the House
of Lords, or to both houses.

1859, No. 33 (2571). Correspondence Relative to the
Earl of Elgin's Special Missions to China and
Japan, 1857-1859. HC.

1860, No. 69 (2587). Correspondence with Mr. Bruce,
Her Majesty's Envoy Extraordinary and Minister
Plenipotentiary in China. HC and HL.

1861, No. 66 (2754). Correspondence Respecting
Affairs in China, 1859-60. HC and HL.

1862, No. 63 (2976). Papers Relating to the Rebellion
in China, and Trade in the Yang-tze-kiang River. HL.

1862, No. 63 (3058). Further Papers Relating to the
Rebellion in China. HC and HL.

1863, No. 73 (3104). Further Papers Relating to the
Rebellion in China, with an Appendix. HC and HL.

1864, No. 63 (3295). Papers Relating to the Affairs
of China (In Continuation of Papers Presented to
Parliament in March 1863).

1868, No. 73 (3996). Memorials Addressed by Chambers
of Commerce in China to the British Minister at Peking
on the Subject of the Revision of the Treaty of Tientsin.
HC.

Hansard's Parliamentary Debates, Third Series, Commencing
with the Accession of William IV, vols. for 1858-1865.

British Government Documents, unpublished

Foreign Office, General Correspondence, China (key number FO 17).
Filed in the Public Record Office, London. Vols. 274-277
(to and from Elgin, Apr.-Dec. 1857); Vols. 284-291
(Elgin, 1858); Vols. 311-315 (Bruce, 1859); Vols. 328-
332 (Elgin, 1859 and 1860); Vols. 333-339 (Bruce, 1860);
Vols. 348-358 (Bruce, 1861); Vol. 359 (Elgin, 1861);
Vols. 368-375 (Bruce, 1862); Vol. 423 (from Wade, Jan.-
Feb. 1865); Vol. 493 (Anglo-Chinese Fleet, Vol. 2).

Foreign Office, General Correspondence, Russia (key number
FO 65).
Vol. 495 (from Wodehouse, May 4-June 10, 1857); Vol. 497
(from Wodehouse, Aug. 7-Sept. 10, 1857); Vol. 554 (from
Erskine, Aug. 9-Oct. 7, 1860).

Foreign Office, Private Collections, Hammond Papers (key
number FO 391), Vol. 19 (from Wade, 1866-1871).

Russell Papers (filed in the Public Record Office, London;
key number P.R.O. 30/22), Vols. 49-50 (Correspondence,
China and Japan, 1859-1865).

Brunnert H.S. and V.V. Hagelstrom. Present Day Political
Organization of China, tr. A. Beltchenko and E.E. Moran.
Shanghai, 1912.

Buksgevden, Baron A. Russkii Kitai: ocherki diplomaticheskikh
snoshenii Rossii s Kitaem, I--Pekinskii dogovor 1860 g.
(Russia's China: an account of the diplomatic relations
between Russia and China, Part I--the Treaty of Peking,
1860). Port Arthur, 1902.

Cady, John F. The Roots of French Imperialism in Eastern Asia.
Ithaca, 1954.

Chao Kuang 趙光. Chao Wen-k'o kung tzu-ting nien-p'u 趙文恪
公自訂年譜 (Chronological autobiography of Chao
Kuang). Postscript 1890.

Chen-chün 震鈞. T'ien-chih ou-wen 天咫偶聞 (Random notes
on the metropolis). 1907.

Ch'en Kung-lu 陳恭祿. "Ssu-kuo T'ien-chin t'iao-yueh ch'eng-li
chih ching-kuo" 四國天津條約成立之經過
(The course of events that led to the conclusion of the four
treaties of Tientsin); Chin-ling hsueh-pao 金陵學報
(Nanking journal), 1.2:407-422 (Nov. 1931).

Ch'en T'i-ch'iang 陳體強. Chung-kuo wai-chiao hsing-cheng 中國外交行政 (Administration of China's foreign affairs). Chungking, 1943.

Ch'en Wen-chin 陳文進 . "Ch'ing-tai chih Tsung-li ya-men chi ch'i ching-fei" 清代之總理衙門及其經費 (The Tsungli Yamen of the Ch'ing period and its expenditures); Chung-kuo chin-tai ching-chi-shih yen-chiu chi-k'an 中國近代經濟史研究集刊 (Studies in the modern economic history of China), 1.1:49-58 (Nov. 1932).

Cheng T'ien-t'ing 鄭天挺 . "Ch'ing-tai pao-i chih-tu yü huan-kuan" 清代包衣制度與宦官 (The bo-i system and the eunuchs in the Ch'ing period); in his Ch'ing-shih t'an-wei 清史探微 (An inquiry into some details of the history of the Ch'ing period), pp. 59-80. 1946.

Chi-p'u 基溥. Ssu-pu-kuo-chai chu-jen tzu-hsü nien-p'u 思補過齋主人自敘年譜 (Chronological autobiography of Chi-p'u). Undated.

Chia-ch'ing hui-tien: Ta-Ch'ing hui-tien 大清會典 (Collected statutes of the Ch'ing dynasty), Chia-ch'ing period. Completed 1818.

Chia-ch'ing hui-tien shih-li: Ta-Ch'ing hui-tien shih-li 大清會典事例 (Cases and precedents of the Collected Statutes of the Ch'ing Dynasty), Chia-ch'ing period. Completed 1818.

Chiang-shang-chien-sou 江上蹇叟 (Hsia Hsieh 夏燮). Chung-Hsi chi-shih 中西紀事 (A chronicle of Sino-Western relations). Postscript to table of contents 1865.

Chiang Siang-tse. The Nien Rebellion. Seattle, 1954.

Chiang T'ing-fu (T. F. Tsiang) 蔣廷黻 . "Tsui-chin san-pai-nien lai Tung-pei wai-huan-shih (shang), ts'ung Shun-chih tao Hsien-feng" 最近三百年来東北外患史（上）從順治到咸豐 (A history of foreign aggressions upon the northeastern area during the last 300 years, Part 1--from the Shun-chih period to the Hsien-feng period); Ch'ing-hua hsueh-pao 清華學報 (Tsing-hua journal), 8.1:1-70 (Dec. 1932).

Ch'iao Sung-nien 喬松年 . Ch'iao Ch'in-k'o-kung ch'üan-chi 喬勤恪公全集 (Collected writings of Ch'iao Sung-nien). 1877.

Ch'ing-shih kao, see CSK.

Ch'ing-shih lieh-chuan 清史列傳 (Historical biographies of the Ch'ing dynasty). Shanghai, 1928.

Ch'ing-shih-lu, see CSL.

Chou Chia-mei 周家楣 . Ch'i-pu-fu-chai ch'üan-chi 期不負齋全集 (Collected writings of Chou Chia-mei). 1895.

Ch'ou-pan i-wu shih-mo, see IWSM.

Chu Chih 朱智 et al., comps. Shu-yuan chi-lueh 樞垣記略 (A brief account of the Grand Council). Rev. ed.; preface 1875.

Chu Shih-chia 朱士嘉 , comp. Shih-chiu shih-chi Mei-kuo ch'in-Hua tang-an shih-liao hsuan-chi 十九世紀美國侵華档案史料选輯 (Selected archival sources concerning American aggression upon China). 2 vols.; Peking, 1959.

Ch'ung-hsiu Chia-shan hsien-chih 重修嘉善縣志 (A gazetteer of Chia-shan hsien). Rev. ed.; preface 1894.

Cordier, Henri. Histoire des relations de la Chine avec les puissances occidentales, 1860-1900. 3 vols.; Paris, 1901-1902.

------L'expédition de Chine de 1857-58: Histoire diplomatique, notes et documents. Paris, 1905.

------L'expédition de Chine de 1860: Histoire diplomatique, notes
et documents. Paris, 1906.

Correspondance Politique, Chine. Archives of the Ministère des
Affaires Etrangères, Paris. Vols. 32-37 cover Gros's
activities in 1860-1861 and Bourboulon's activities from September
1860 to April 1862.

Costin, W. C. Great Britain and China 1833-1860. Oxford, 1937.

CSK: Ch'ing-shih kao 清史稿 (Draft history of the Ch'ing dynasty),
comp. Chao Erh-hsun 趙爾巽 et al. Lien-ho shu-tien 聯合
書店 photolithographic ed., 1942.

CSL: Ta-Ch'ing li-ch'ao shih-lu 大清歷朝實錄 (or Ch'ing
shih-lu) (Veritable records of successive reigns of the Ch'ing
dynasty). Photo-offset; Tokyo, 1937-1938. Series for the
reigns of Hsuan-tsung 宣宗 (Tao-kuang emperor), Wen-tsung
文宗 (Hsien-feng emperor), Mu-tsung 穆宗 (T'ung-chih
emperor).

Dennett, Tyler. Americans in Eastern Asia. New York, 1922

Elgin Archives, Private Correspondence. Kept at the Elgin family
estate in Scotland.

En-ling 恩齡, comp. Cheng-hung-ch'i Man-chou Ha-ta Kua-erh-chia
shih chia-p'u 正紅旗滿洲哈達瓜爾佳氏家譜
(Genealogy of the Gualgiya clan). 1849.

Etō Shinkichi 衛藤瀋吉. "Mitcheru hōkoku ni tsuite" ミッチェル
報告書 (On the Mitchell report); Tōyō bunka 東洋文化
(Oriental culture), 20:25-40 (Jan. 1956).

Fairbank, John K.   "Tributary Trade and China's Relations with the

      West," Far Eastern Quarterly, 1.2:129-149 (Feb. 1942).

------Trade and Diplomacy on the China Coast: The Opening of the

      Treaty Ports 1842-1854.   2 vols.; Cambridge, Mass., 1953.

------"Patterns behind the Tientsin Massacre," Harvard Journal

      of Asiatic Studies, 20.3-4:480-511 (Dec. 1957).

Fairbank, John K. and S.Y. Teng. "On the Transmission of Ch'ing

      Documents," Harvard Journal of Asiatic Studies, 4.1:12-46

      (May 1939).   Reprinted in John K. Fairbank and Ssu-yu Teng,

      Ch'ing Administration: Three Studies (Cambridge, Mass.,1960).

------"On the Ch'ing Tributary System," Harvard Journal of Asiatic

      Studies, 6.2:135-246 (June 1941).   Reprinted in John K. Fairbank

      and Ssu-yu Teng, Ch'ing Administration: Three Studies.

Fan Wen-lan 范文瀾 . Chung-kuo chin-tai-shih 中國近代史

      (A history of modern China), Vol. I, Pt. 1.   Rev. 8th ed.;

      Peking, 1953.

Fang Chao-yin 房兆楹 and Tu Lien-che 杜連喆 , comps.

      Tseng-chiao Ch'ing-ch'ao chin-shih t'i-ming pei-lu 增校

      清朝進士題名碑錄 (A list of holders of the chin-shih

      degree in the Ch'ing dynasty, enlarged and re-edited).

      Peking, 1941.

Feng Kuei-fen 馮桂芬 . "Hu-ch'eng hui-fang chi" 滬城會防

      記 (An account of the joint defense of the city of Shanghai);

      in Hsien-chih-t'ang kao 顯志堂稿 (Literary works of Feng

      Kuei-fen), chüan 4.   Preface 1877.

------"Chieh-ping E-Fa i" 借兵俄法議(A proposal to get

      military assistance from Russia and France); in his Chiao-pin-

      lu k'ang-i 校邠廬抗議 (Personal protests from the study

      of Chiao-pin).   1885 ed.; also in 1897 ed.

Foster J. W. American Diplomacy in the Orient. Boston and New York, 1903.

Fu Yü-pu 福餘圃 . "Tu-ch'eng chieh-yen shih-chi" 都城戒嚴事記 (An account of the events in the capital under the siege). Handwritten copy in the Oriental Library, Tokyo.

Gregory, John S. "British Intervention against the Taiping Rebellion," Journal of Asian Studies, 19.1:11-24 (Nov. 1959).

Griffin, Eldon. Clippers and Consuls: American Consular and Commercial Relations with Eastern Asia 1845-1860. Ann Arbor, 1938.

Gros, Baron J. B. L. Négociations entre la France et la Chine en 1860: Livre jaune du Baron Gros, ambassadeur extraordinaire et haut commissaire de l'Empereur en Chine, en 1858 et en 1860--extrait de sa correspondance et de son journal, pendant la seconde mission qu'il a remplie dans l'extrême Orient. Paris, 1864.

Gutzlaff, Charles. The Life of Taou-Kwang, Late Emperor of China, with Memoirs of the Court of Peking: History of the Chinese Empire during the Last Fifty Years. London, 1852.

Hai-fang tang 海防檔 (Documents on maritime defense), ed. Institute of Modern History, Academia Sinica. Photo-offset; 9 vols. (cloth) or 17 vols. (paper); Taipei, 1958; 7,334 pp.

Hanawa Sakura 塙作樂 "Roshia teikoku no Kyokutō shinshutsu" 露西亞帝國の極東進出 (The advance into the Far East of the Russian empire); Rekishigaku kenkyū 歷史學研究 (Journal of historical studies), 10.9:894-923 (Sept. 1940);

ibid., 10.10:1025-65 (Oct. 1940).

Hérisson, Maurice, Comte de, ed. L'expédition de Chine d'après la correspondance confidentielle du Général Cousin de Montauban, Comte de Palikao. 1883.

Ho Ch'iu-t'ao 何秋濤. "E-lo-ssu kuan k'ao" 俄羅斯館考 (On the Russian Hostel); in his Shuo-fang pei-sheng 朔方備乘 (Historical source-book of the northern regions). Postscript 1881.

Hoo Chi-tsai. Les bases conventionelles des relations modernes entre la Chine et la Russie. Paris, 1918.

Hsien-feng t'iao-yueh 咸豐條約 (Treaties of the Hsien-feng period). Wai-chiao-pu T'u-shu-ch'u 外交部圖書處, no date.

Hsueh Fu-ch'eng 薛福成. Yung-an ch'uan-chi 庸盦全集 (Complete works of Hsueh Fu-ch'eng). 1884-1898; includes Yung-an wen-pien 庸盦文編 (Collected essays) and Yung-an-wen hsü-pien 庸盦文續編 (Supplementary collection of essays).

------Yung-an pi-chi 庸盦筆記 (Desultory notes of Hsueh Fu-ch'eng). Postscript 1898; lithographic ed., 1910.

------"Hsien-feng chi-nien san-chien fu-chu" 咸豐季年三奸伏誅 (On the execution of the three villains at the close of the Hsien-feng era); in Yung-an pi-chi.

------"Shu Ch'ang-pai Wen Wen-tuan kung hsiang-yeh" 書長白文文端公相業 (On Wen-ch'ing's achievements as a minister of state); in Yung-an-wen hsü-pien. 1887.

------"Shu Han-yang Yeh-hsiang Kuang-chou chih pien" 書漢陽葉相廣州之變 (On Yeh Ming-ch'en in the Canton incident); in Yung-an-wen hsü-pien. 1887.

------"Shu Ho-fei po-hsiang Li-kung yung Hu p'ing Wu" 書合肥
伯相李公用滬平吳 (On the pacification of Kiangsu by
Li Hung-chang, using the resources of Shanghai); in Yung-an-
wen hsü-pien. 1887.

------"Shu I-yang Hu Wen-chung kung yü Liao-yang Kuan Wen-kung
kung chiao-huan shih" 書益陽胡文忠公與遼陽官文
恭公交驩事 (On the cultivation of friendship between
Hu Lin-i and Kuan-wen); in Yung-an wen-pien. 1885.

------"Shu tsai-hsiang yu-hsueh wu-shih" 書宰相有學無識
(On the case of a prime minister being a man of learning but
not of real insight); in Yung-an-wen hsü-pien. 1887.

------"Su-shun t'ui-fu Ch'u-hsien" 肅順推服楚賢 (Su-shun
recommended and esteemed the worthies in Hunan and Hupei);
in Yung-an pi-chi.

Hsü, Immanuel C.Y.   China's Entrance into the Family of Nations:
The Diplomatic Phase, 1858-1880. Cambridge, Mass., 1960.

Hsü pei-chuan chi 續碑傳集 (Collection of tombstone biographies,
a second series), comp. Miao Ch'üan-sun 繆荃孫.
Preface 1910.

Hsü Tao-ling 許道齡. Pei-p'ing miao-yü t'ung-chien 北平廟
宇通檢 (Collected references concerning temples in
Peking). 2 vols.; Peking, 1936.

Hsü T'ien-chin hsien-chih 續天津縣志 (Gazetteer of Tientsin
district, supplementary compilation). Preface 1870.

Hummel, Arthur W., ed. Eminent Chinese of the Ch'ing Period.
2 vols.; Washington, D.C., 1943, 1944.

IWSM: Ch'ou-pan i-wu shih-mo 籌辦夷務始末 (A complete
account of the management of barbarian affairs). Photolithographic
reproduction; Peking, 1930. Tao-kuang period 1836-1850, 80
chüan, presented to the emperor 1856; Hsien-feng period 1851-1861,
80 chüan, presented 1867; T'ung-chih period. 1861-1874, 100 chüan,
presented 1880.

Kamenofuchi Ryūchō 龜淵龍長 , comp. Mō-chi 蒙地 (Lands
of Mongols). 1914; reprinted Sinkyō (Hsinking), 1935. A volume
in the series by Minami Manshū Tetsudō Kabushiki Kaisha 南滿
洲鐵道株式會社 , Manshū kyūkan chōsa hōkoku 滿
洲舊慣調查報告 (Reports on an investigation into the
old customs of Manchuria), 9 vols. (1913-1915).

Kanda Nobuo 神田信夫 . "Shinsho no gisei daijin ni tsuite" 清初
の議政大臣について (On the Council of Princes and
High Officials of the early Ch'ing period); Wada hakushi kanreki
kinen Tōyōshi ronsō 和田博士還曆記念東洋
史論叢 (Studies of Oriental history collected to commemorate
the sixtieth birthday of Dr. Wada), pp. 171-189. Tokyo, 1951.

------"Shinsho no bairoku ni tsuite" 清初の貝勒について
(On the beile of the early Ch'ing period); Tōyō gakuhō, 40.4:349-
371 (Mar. 1958).

Kiernan, E. V. G. British Diplomacy in China, 1880-1885.
Cambridge, England, 1939.

Knollys, Sir Henry. Incidents in the China War of 1860, Compiled
from the Private Journals of General Sir Hope Grant, G. C. B.,
Commander of the English Expedition. Edinburgh, 1875.

xviii

------, ed. Life of General Sir Hope Grant, with Selections from his
    Correspondence. 2 vols.; Edinburgh, 1894.

Kryzhanovskii, V. , comp. "Perepiska Nachal'nika Pekinskoi Dukhovnoi
    Missii Arkhimandrita Palladiia s General-Gubernatorom Vostochnoi
    Sibiri Gr. N. N. Murav'evym-Amurskim" (Letters from Archi-
    mandrite Palladius, head of the Ecclesiastical Mission in Peking,
    to Count N. N. Murav'ev-Amurskii, governor-general of Eastern
    Siberia); Russkii Arkhiv (1914), II, 482-512; III, 5-32, 155-206.

Kuang-hsü hui-tien: Ta-Ch'ing hui-tien (Collected statutes of the Ch'ing
    dynasty), Kuang-hsü period. Completed 1899.

Kuang-hsü hui-tien shih-li: Ta-Ch'ing hui-tien shih-li (Cases and pre-
    cedents of the Collected Statutes of the Ch'ing Dynasty), Kuang-
    hsü period. Completed 1899.

Kuang-hsü Shun-t'ien fu-chih 光緒順天府志 (Gazetteer of the
    metropolitan prefecture, Kuang-hsü ed.). Rev. ed.; postscript
    1889.

Kuo Sung-tao 郭嵩燾 . Yü-ch'ih lao-jen tzu-hsü 玉池老人
    自叙 (Autobiography of Kuo Sung-tao). 1893.

Kuo T'ing-i 郭廷以 . T'ai-p'ing T'ien-kuo shih-shih jih-chih 太平
    天國史事日誌 (History of the Taiping Kingdom, a
    daily record). 2 vols.; Shanghai, 1946.

La Servière, R. P. J. de, S. J. Histoire de la mission du Kiangnan.
    2 vols.; Shanghai, 1914.

Lay, Horatio N. Our Interests in China: A Letter to the Right
    Hon. Earl Russell, K. G. , Her Majesty's Principal Secretary
    of State for Foreign Affairs. London, 1864.

------Note on the Opium Question, and Brief Survey of Our Relations with China. London, 1893.

Legge, James. The Chinese Classics. 5 vols.; London and Hong Kong, 1861-1872.

Li Huan 李桓. Kuo-ch'ao ch'i-hsien lei-cheng ch'u-pien 國朝耆獻類徵初編 (Classified biographies of the worthies of our dynasty, first series). 1884-1890.

Li Tz'u-ming 李慈銘. Yueh-man-t'ang jih-chi pu 越縵堂日記補 (Diary of Li Tz'u-ming, a supplement). Photolithographic reproduction; 1936.

Liang Chia-pin 梁嘉彬. "Ying-Fa lien-chün chih i Kuang-tung chiu shih-san-hang hang-shang t'iao-t'ing chan-shih shih-liao" 英法聯軍之役廣東舊十三行行商調停戰事史料 (Some historical materials concerning the mediation for peace by merchants of the former thirteen hongs at Canton at the time of the Anglo-French war with China); Kuo-li Chung-shan ta-hsueh wen-shih-hsueh yen-chiu-so yueh-k'an 國立中山大學文史學研究所月刊 (National Sun Yat-sen University monthly of the Institute of History and Language), 1.1:77-82 (Jan. 1933). Reprinted in Liang Chia-pin, Kuang-tung shih-san-hang k'ao 廣東十三行考 (On the thirteen hongs at Canton; Shanghai, 1937).

Lo Erh-kang 羅爾綱. "Ch'ing-chi ping wei chiang-yu ti ch'i-yuan" 清季兵為將有的起源 (The origin of private armies in the late Ch'ing period); Chung-kuo she-hui ching-chi shih chi-k'an 中國社會經濟史集刊 (Chinese social and economic history review), 5.2:235-250 (June 1937).

------Hsiang-chün hsin-chih 湘軍新志 (A new gazetteer of the
Hunan Army). Changsha, 1939.

Lo Tun-jung 羅惇曧. "Hsiao-ch'üan Huang-hou tz'u-ssu, K'ang-
tz'u T'ai-hou tsun-hao" 孝全皇后賜死康慈太后
尊號 (Empress Hsiao-ch'üan ordered to commit suicide;
K'ang-tz'u given the rank of Empress Dowager), in his "Pin-t'ui
sui-pi" 賓退隨筆 (Random notes after the guests are gone);
Yung-yen 庸言 (Justice), 2.5:15-16 (May 1914).

Loch, Henry Brougham. Personal Narrative of Occurrences during
Lord Elgin's Second Embassy to China in 1860. 2nd ed.;
London, 1870.

M'Ghee, Rev. R.J.L. How We Got to Pekin: A Narrative of the
Campaign in China of 1860. London, 1862.

MacNair, Harley Farnsworth. China in Revolution: An Analysis of
Politics and Militarism under the Republic. Chicago, 1931.

Mancall, Mark. "Major-General Igantiev's Mission to Peking,
1859-1860," Papers on China, 10:55-96. Harvard University,
East Asian Research Center, 1956.

Martin, W.A.P. A Cycle of Cathay. 3rd ed.; New York, 1900.

Maybon, Ch.B. and Jean Fredet. Histoire de la concession française
de Changhai. Paris, 1929.

Mayers, W.F. The Chinese Government. 3rd ed., rev. by G.M.H.
Playfair; Shanghai, 1897.

Meng Sen 孟森. "Pa-ch'i chih-tu k'ao-shih" 八旗制度考實
(An historical study of the eight banner system); Li-shih yü-yen
yen-chiu-so chi-k'an 歷史語言研究所集刊　(Bulletin

of the Institute of History and Philology), 6.3:343-414 (July
1936). Reprinted in Meng Sen, Ming-Ch'ing-shih lun-chu chi-
k'an 明清史論著集刊　(Collected studies of Ming and
Ch'ing history; Peking, 1959), Vol. I.

------"Ch'ing Hsien-feng shih-nien yang-ping ju-Ching chih jih-chi
i-pien" 清咸豐十年洋兵入京之日記一篇
(A diary relating to the entry of foreign soldiers into Peking in
1860); Shih-hsueh chi-k'an 史學集刊　(Historical journal),
No. 2:179-193 (Oct. 1936). A diary of Liu Yü-nan 劉毓楠,
then an official of the Board of Rites, annotated by Meng Sen.
Reprinted in Meng Sen, Ming-Ch'ing shih lun-chu chi-k'an,
Vol. II.

Meng Ssu-ming, "The E-lo-ssu kuan (Russian Hostel) in Peking,"
Harvard Journal of Asiatic Studies, 23:19-46 (1961).

------The Tsungli Yamen: Its Organization and Functions.
Cambridge, Mass., 1962.

Michael, Franz. "Military Organization and Power Structure in
China during the Taiping Rebellion," Pacific Historical
Review, 18.4:469-483 (Nov. 1949).

Michie, Alexander. The Englishman in China during the Victorian
Era, As Illustrated in the Career of Sir Rutherford Alcock,
K.C.B., D.C.L., Many Years Consul and Minister in China
and Japan. 2 vols.; Edinburgh and London, 1900.

Min Erh-ch'ang 閔爾昌　, comp. Pei-chuan chi pu 碑傳集補
(Tombstone biographies, a supplementary collection).
Preface 1923.

Miyazaki Ichisada 宮崎市定　. "Shinagawa shiryō yori mitaru
Ei-Futsu rengōgun no Pekin shinnyū jiken, tokuni shusenron to

waheiron" 支那側史料より見たる英佛聯合軍 の北京侵入事件 —— 特に主戰論と 和平論 (The incident of the intrusion of the Anglo-French allied force into Peking, as viewed from the Chinese sources, with special reference to the counsels of war and peace); Tōa kenkyū shohō 東亞研究所報 (Reports of the East Asian Research Institute), No. 24:852-884 (Oct. 1943).

------"Shinchō ni okeru kokugo mondai no ichimen" 清朝に於ける 國語問題の一面 (An aspect of the problem of national languages in the Ch'ing dynasty); Tōhōshi ronsō 東亞 史論叢 (Studies of Oriental history), 1:1-56 (July 1947).

------"Yōsei shuhi yushi no kaidai" 雍正硃批諭旨の解題 (Explanatory comments on Yung-cheng chu-p'i yu-chih); Tōyōshi kenkyū 東洋史研究 (Journal of Oriental researches), 15.4:365-396 (Mar. 1957).

------"Shindai no shori to bakuyū--tokuni Yōseichō o chūshin to shite" 清代の胥吏と幕友 —— 特に雍正朝を中心として (The yamen clerks and the personal advisors of officials in the Ch'ing period--especially in the Yung-cheng era); Tōyōshi kenkyū, 16.4:347-374 (Mar. 1958).

Miyazaki Masayoshi 宮崎正義. Kindai Ro-Shi kankei no kenkyū, en Kokuryū chihō no bu 近代露支關係の研究, 沿黒龍 地方之部 (A study of modern Russo-Chinese relations, section on the region along the Amur). Dairen, 1922.

Moges, Marquis de. Souvenirs d'une Ambassade en Chine et au Japon en 1857 et 1858. Paris, 1860.

Montauban, Général Cousin de, Comte de Palikao. L'expedition de Chine de 1860: souvenirs du Général Cousin de Montauban,

Comte de Palikao. Published by his grandson le Comte de
Palikao; Paris, 1932.

Morse, H. B. The Chronicles of the East India Company Trading
to China 1633-1834. 5 vols.; Oxford, 1926-1929.

------The International Relations of the Chinese Empire. 3 vols.;
Shanghai, 1910, 1918.

Negishi Tadashi 根岸佶 . Shanhai no girudo 上海のギルド
(The guilds of Shanghai). Tokyo, 1951.

North China Herald, 1858-1861. Shanghai, weekly.

Oliphant, Laurence. Narrative of the Earl of Elgin's Mission to
China and Japan in the Years 1857, '58, '59. 2nd ed.; 2 vols.;
Edinburgh and London, 1860.

Ono Shinji 小野信爾 . "Ri Kō-shō no tōjō--Waigun no
seiritsu o megutte" 李鴻章の登場 ── 淮軍の成立
をめぐって (The advent of Li Hung-chang--with special
reference to the formation of the Anhwei Army); Tōyōshi
kenkyū, 16.2:107-134 (Sept. 1957).

Oriental Manuscripts, British Museum, London
A letter from Prince Kung to General Ko (i.e., Sir Hope Grant),
stating that he is returning twenty-nine persons and
promising compensation, Oct. 19, 1860 (call number:
Oriental 6597). A calling card of Huang Chung-yü is
in the same album.
Menu of a repast sent by Prince Kung to Sir Hope Grant,
Oct. 28, 1860 (call number: Oriental 6598).

Pan-li fu-chü tang-an, see PLFC.

Parry, Albert. "Russian (Greek Orthodox) Missionaries in China, 1689-1917: Their Cultural, Political, and Economic Role." Ph.D. thesis; University of Chicago, 1938.

Pelcovits, Nathan A. Old China Hands and the Foreign Office. New York, 1948.

PLFC: Pan-li fu-chü tang-an 辦理撫局檔案 (Documents on the management of peace-making). No date of compilation, no pagination. See Note on Archival Sources.

Popov, A. "Tsarskaia diplomatiia v epokhu Taipinskogo vosstaniia" (Tsarist diplomacy during the Taiping Rebellion); Krasnyi Arkhiv (Red archives), 21:182-199 (1927).

Powell, Ralph L. The Rise of Chinese Military Power 1895-1912. Princeton, 1955.

Pritchard, E.H. "The Kotow in the Macartney Embassy to China 1793," Far Eastern Quarterly, 2.2:163-203 (Feb. 1943).

Rantoul, Robert S. Frederick Townsend Ward (Historical Collection of the Essex Institute, Vol. 44). Salem, Mass., 1908.

Rawlinson, John L. "The Lay-Osborn Flotilla: Its Development and Significance," Papers on China, 4:58-93. Harvard University, East Asian Research Center, 1950.

Rennie, D.F. The British Arms in North China and Japan. London, 1864.

------Peking and the Pekingese. 2 vols.; London, 1865.

Sbornik dogovorov Rossii s Kitaem 1869-1881 gg. (Collection of treaties between Russia and China, 1869-1881). St. Petersburg: Ministerstvo innostrannykh del, 1889.

Shen Chao-lin 沈兆霖 . Shen Wen-chung kung chi 沈文忠
公集 (Collected writings of Shen Chao-lin). 1869; includes
Shen Wen-chung kung tzu-ting nien-p'u 沈文忠公自訂
年譜 (Chronological autobiography of Shen Chao-lin).

Shih-liao hsun-k'an 史料旬刊 (Historical materials published
every ten days). Peking: Palace Museum, 1930-1931.

Shinkoku gyōseihō 清國行政法 (Administrative laws of
the Ch'ing dynasty), comp. Rinji Taiwan Kyūkan Chōsakai
臨時臺灣舊慣調查會 . 6 vols.; Tokyo and
Kobe, 1910-1914. Vol. I revised and reissued in 1914 in
2 parts, and a further vol. issued as a general index.

Shumakher, Petr. "K istorii priobreteniia Amura, snosheniia
Kitaem s 1848 po 1860 god" (Toward a history of appropriating
the Amur--relations with China from 1848 to 1860); Russkii
Arkhiv (1878), III, 257-342.

Skachkov, P.E. Bibliografiia Kitaia (Bibliography of China).
Moscow, 1960.

SKHT: Ssu-kuo hsin-tang 四國新檔 (New files concerning
the four powers). Deposited at the Institute of Modern History,
Academia Sinica, Taipei, Taiwan. See Note on Archival Sources.

Ssu-kuo hsin-tang, see SKHT.

Stanmore, Arthur Hamilton Gordon. Sidney Herbert, Lord Herbert
of Lea. 2 vols.; New York, 1906.

Sullivan, Joseph Lewis. "Count N.N. Muraviev-Amursky."
Ph.D. thesis; Harvard University, 1955.

Swinhoe, Robert. Narrative of the North China Campaign of 1860.
London, 1861.

Swisher, Earl. China's Management of the American Barbarians:
A Study of Sino-American Relations, 1841-1861, with Documents.
New Haven, 1953.

Ta-Ch'ing chin-shen ch'üan-shu 大清搢紳全書 (A complete
list of government officials in the Ch'ing dynasty). The Red
Books, published four times a year. Series for the winter of
Hsien-feng 6 (1856), pub. Jung-chin-chai 榮晉齋 ; winter
of Hsien-feng 9 (1859), pub. Jung-chin-chai; spring of Hsien-
feng 10 (1860), pub. Jung-lu-t'ang 榮錄堂 ; unidentified
season of Hsien-feng 11 (1861), pub. Jung-lu-t'ang (the copy
at the Chinese-Japanese Library of Harvard-Yenching Institute lacks the cover on which the season is usually printed).

Ta-Ch'ing hui-tien, see Chia-ch'ing and Kuang-hsü for editions.

Ta-Ch'ing hui-tien shih-li, see Chia-ch'ing and Kuang-hsü for
editions.

Ta-Ch'ing li-ch'ao shih-lu, see CSL.

Te-hua hsien-chih 德化縣志 (A gazetteer of Te-hua hsien). 1872.

Teng Ssu-yü and J.K. Fairbank. China's Response to the West.
2 vols.; Cambridge, Mass., 1954.

Teng Tzu-ch'eng 鄧子誠. Ku-tung so-chi ch'üan-pien 骨董瑣
記全篇 (Complete collection of fragmentary notes).
Peking, 1957.

Thomas, A. Histoire de la mission de Pékin. Paris, 1923-1925.

T'ien-chin-hsien hsin-chih 天津縣新志 (A new gazetteer of
Tientsin hsien). An incomplete publication; 1931.

Timkovskii, Egor Fedorovich. Puteshestvie v Kitai chrez Mongoliiu
v 1820 i 1821 godakh (A journey to China via Mongolia in 1820-
1821). 3 vols.; St. Petersburg, 1824.

Ting-hai t'ing-chih 定海廳志 (Gazetteer of Tinghai subprefecture).
1885.

Ting Yun-shu 丁運樞, Ch'en Shih-hsun 陳世勳 and Ko Yü-ch'i
葛毓琦, comps. Chang-kung hsiang-li chün-wu chi-lueh
張公襄理軍務紀略 (A brief account of Chang Chin-
wen's contributions to military affairs). Preface 1862;
postscript 1910.

Toyama Gunji 外山軍治. "Shanhai no shinshō Yō Bō" 上海の
紳商楊坊 (The wealthy Shanghai merchant
Yang Fang); Tōyōshi kenkyū, new series, 1.4:17-34 (Nov. 1945).

------Taihei Tengoku to Shanhai 太平天國と上海 (The
Taiping Rebellion and Shanghai). Kyoto, 1947.

Treaties, Conventions, etc., between China and Foreign States.
2nd ed.; 2 vols.; Shanghai: Statistical Department of the
Inspectorate General of Customs, 1917.

Tsiang, T.F. (Chiang T'ing-fu). "Notes and Suggestions: 1. Origins
of the Tsungli Yamen; 2. Bismarck and the Introduction of
International Law into China," Chinese Social and Political
Science Review, 15.1:92-101 (Apr. 1931).

------"Notes and Suggestions: The Secret Plan of 1858," Chinese
Social and Political Science Review, 15.2:291-299 (July 1931).

T'ung-chih Shang-hai hsien-chih 同治上海縣志 (Gazetteer of
Shanghai district, T'ung-chih ed.). 1871.

Tung Hsun 董恂. Huan-tu-wo-shu-shih lao-jen shou-ting nien-p'u
還讀我書室老人手訂年譜 (Chronological auto-
biography of Tung Hsun). 1892.

Ueda Toshio 植田捷雄. "Taiheiran to gaikoku" 太平亂
と外國 (The Taiping Rebellion and the foreign powers);

Kokka gakkai zasshi 國家學會雜誌 , 62.9:464-
494 (Sept. 1948); ibid. , 62.12:669-687 (Dec. 1948); ibid. ,
63.1-3:31-78 (Mar. 1949).

------"The International Relations of the T'ai P'ing Rebellion, "
Japan Annual of Law and Politics, No. 2:119-148 (1953).
A condensed English translation of the preceding article.

United States Government Documents, published

Papers Relating to Foreign Relations of the United States.
Washington, D.C. , 1862 and 1864.

Senate Executive Documents, 36th Congress, 1st Session, No. 30.
Includes official correspondence with Reed, Williams,
and Ward.

United States Government Documents, unpublished

Department of State Archives (at National Archives, Washington,
D.C.)

Diplomatic Dispatches, China. Vols. 17-19 (from Reed,
Williams, and Ward).

Diplomatic Instructions, China. Vol. 1 includes instructions in the Arrow War.

Records of Foreign Service Posts of the State Department,
Consulate, Shanghai, Miscellaneous. Vol. for Aug. 7,
1856 to Dec. 31, 1961.

Vladimir (Zenone Volpicelli). Russia on the Pacific and the Siberian
Railway. London, 1899.

Walrond, Theodore, ed. Letters and Journals of James, Eighth
Earl of Elgin. London, 1872.

Wang Erh-min 王爾敏 . "Nan-pei-yang ta-ch'en chih chien-chih chi ch'i ch'üan-li chih k'uo-chang" 南北洋大臣之建置及其權力之擴張 (The superintendent of trade for the southern ports and the superintendent of trade for the northern ports: their establishment and expansion of their power); Ta-lu tsa-chih 大陸雜誌 (Continental review), 20.5:152-159 (Mar. 1960).

Wang K'ai-yun 王闓運 . "Wang Hsiang-ch'i hsien-sheng lu Ch'i-hsiang ku-shih" 王湘綺先生錄祺祥故事 (Historical events relating to the era named Ch'i-hsiang, as recorded by Wang K'ai-yun); Tung-fang tsa-chih 東方雜誌 (Eastern miscellany), 14.12:93-96 (Dec. 1917).

Wang Mao-yin 王茂蔭 . Wang-shih-lang tsou-i 王侍郎奏議 (Memorials of Wang Mao-yin). Editor's preface dated eleventh month of Kuang-hsü 13 (Dec. 1887 or Jan. 1888).

Wang, S.T. The Margary Affair and the Chefoo Agreement. London and New York, 1940.

Wen-hsiang 文祥 . Wen Wen-chung kung tzu-ting nien-p'u 文文忠公自訂年譜 (Chronological autobiography of Wen-hsiang); in his collectanea, Wen Wen-chung kung shih-lueh 文文忠公事略 (A brief account of the deeds of Wen-hsiang). 1882.

Weng T'ung-ho 翁同龢 . Weng Wen-kung kung jih-chi 翁文恭公日記 (Diary of Weng T'ung-ho). Photolithographic reproduction; 1925.

Williams, F.W., ed. "The Journal of S. Wells Williams, LL.D...," Journal of the North-China Branch of the Royal Asiatic Society, 42:1-232 (1911).

------The Life and Letters of S. Wells Williams. New York and
    London, 1889.

Williams, S.W. "Narrative of the American Embassy to Peking,"
    Journal of the North-China Branch of the Royal Asiatic Society
    (old series, Vol. 1), No. 3:315-349 (Dec. 1859).

Wolseley, Garnet Joseph. Narrative of the War with China in 1860.
    London, 1862.

Wright, Mary C. The Last Stand of Chinese Conservatism: The
    T'ung-chih Restoration, 1862-1874. Stanford, 1957.

------"The Adaptability of Ch'ing Diplomacy, the Case of Korea,"
    Journal of Asian Studies, 18.3:363-381 (May 1958).

Wright, S.F. Hart and the Chinese Customs. Belfast, 1950.

Wrong, G.M. The Earl of Elgin. London, 1905.

Wu Ch'eng-chang 吳成章 . Wai-chiao-pu yen-ko chi-lueh 外交
    部沿革紀略 (A short history of the Ministry of
    Foreign Affairs). Peking, 1913.

Wu Han 吳唅 . "Wang Mao-yin yü Hsien-feng shih-tai ti hsin
    pi-chih" 王茂蔭與咸豐時代的新幣制
    (Wang Mao-yin and the new monetary system of the Hsien-feng
    era); Chung-kuo she-hui ching-chi shih chi-k'an, 6.1:113-146
    (June 1939). Reprinted with slightly changed title in Wu Han,
    Tu-shih cha-chi 讀史劄記 (Critical essays on history;
    Peking, 1957).

Wu Hsiang-hsiang 吳相湘 . Wan-Ch'ing kung-t'ing shih-chi 晚
    清宮廷實紀 (A veritable history of the late Ch'ing
    court). 2nd ed.; Taipei, 1953.

Wu K'o-tu 吳可讀 . "Wang-chi p'ien" 罔極篇 (In memory
    of my deceased mother who had unlimited love and kindness);

in Hsi-hsüeh t'ang ch'üan-chi 攜雪堂全集 (Complete
works of Wu K'o-tu). Printed in or after 1893.

Yamaguchi Michiko 山口迪子 . "Shindai no sōun to senshō"
清代の漕運と船商 (The grain tribute transport
and the shipping merchants in the Ch'ing period); Tōyōshi
kenkyū, 17.2:180-196 (Sept. 1958).

Yano Jin'ichi 矢野仁一 . "Pekin no Rokoku kōshikan ni tsuite"
北京の露國公使館 について (On the Russian
legation in Peking); Geimon 藝文 (Art and literature),
6.9:884-897 (Sept. 1915); ibid. , 6.10:1065-91 (Oct. 1915).

------Kindai Shina ron 近代支那論 (Essays on modern China).
Tokyo and Kyoto, 1923.

------Kindai Mōkōshi kenkyū 近代蒙古史研究 (Researches
in modern Mongolian history). Kyoto, 1925.

------Shina kindai gaikoku kankei kenkyū 支那近代外國關係
研究 (A study of modern Chinese foreign relations).
Kyoto, 1928.

Yin Chao-yung 殷兆鏞 . Yin P'u-ching shih-lang tzu-ting
nien-p'u 殷譜經侍郎自訂年譜 (Chronological
autobiography of Ying Chao-yung). Printed after 1900.

Yin-hsien chih 鄞縣志 (Gazetteer of Yin-hsien). 1877.

Yin Keng-yun 尹耕雲 . Hsin-pai-jih-chai chi 心白日齋集
(Collected writings of Yin Keng-yun). Original ed. , 1884;
slightly enlarged ed. with preface by Wang K'ai-yun 王闓運
dated fifteenth day of twelfth month of Kuang-hsü 21 (Jan. 29,
1896).

Yuan Chia-san 袁甲三 . Yuan Tuan-min kung chi 袁立端敏
公集 (Collected writings of Yuan Chia-san); in Ting Chen-to
丁振鐸, comp., Hsiang-ch'eng Yuan-shih chia-chi 項城
袁氏家集 (Collections of writings of the Yuan family of
Hsiang-ch'eng). 1911.

Ai-jen 愛仁

Aigun (Ai-hun) 愛琿

an-chao ch'ing-li 按照情理

An-ting Gate 安定門

Borjigit 博爾濟吉特

Canton (Kuang-chou) 廣州

chang-ch'eng liu-t'iao 章程六條

chang-ch'eng shih-t'iao 章程十條

Chang-chia-wan 張家灣

Chang Chih-wan 張之萬

Chang Chin-wen 張錦文

chang-ching 章京

Chang Ping-to 張秉鐸

Chang T'ing-hsueh 張廷學

Chang T'ung-yun 張彤雲

Ch'ang-ch'i 長啟

Ch'ang-chou 常州

Ch'ang-lu yen-cheng 長蘆鹽政

Ch'ang-shan 長善

Changsintien 長新店

chao-hui 照會

Chao Kuang 趙光

chao shang-shu li tz'u-hsü 照尚書例賜卹

Chao Te-ch'e 趙德轍

ch'ao-kung-kuo 朝貢國

Ch'ao-yang Gate 朝陽門

Ch'en Fu-en 陳孚恩

Cheng, Prince 鄭親王 (Chi-erh-ha-lang 濟爾哈朗)

Cheng, Prince 鄭親王 (Tuan-hua 端華)

cheng-shu 政書

Cheng Tun-chin 鄭敦謹

Cheng-yang Gate 正陽門

ch'eng 呈

Ch'eng-ch'i 成琦

ch'eng-huang-miao kung-so 城隍廟公所

Ch'eng-lin 成林

ch'eng-shou wang ta-ch'en 城守王大臣

Chi Chih-ch'ang 季芝昌

Chi-erh-ha-lang (Jirgalang), see Prince Cheng

Chi-erh-hang-a 吉爾杭阿
chi-hsin shang-yü 寄信上諭
Chi-la-ming-a 吉拉明阿
chi-pu chu-shih 即補主事
Chi-p'u 基溥
Ch'i Chün-tsao 祁寯藻
Ch'i Kung 祁墳
Ch'i-ying (Kiying) 耆英
Chia Chen 賈楨
Chia-ch'ing 嘉慶
Chia-hsing-ssu, or Chia-hsing
   Temple 嘉興寺
chia-pien 甲編
chia-ts'e 甲冊
Chiang-ning pu-cheng-shih
   江寧布政史
Chiao Yu-ying 焦祐瀛
Ch'iao Sung-nien 喬松年
chieh-yen 戒嚴
"Chien hsun-hsing Mu-lan su"
   諫巡幸木蘭疏
Ch'ien Hsin-ho 錢忻和
Ch'ien Pao-ch'ing 錢寶青
Ch'ien Ying-p'u 錢應溥
chih-cheng 執政
chih-ch'i t'ung-suan
   制器通算
chih-kuan-piao 職官表
Chin An-ch'ing 金安清

Chin kuei-ch'u shih yen pu-chun
   今貴處始言不准
chin-shih 進士
ch'in-ch'ai ta-ch'en 欽差
   大臣
ch'in-ch'ai ta-ch'en tsung-li ko-k'ou
   t'ung-shang shih-wu 欽差
   大臣總理各口通商
   事務
ch'in-ming tsung-kuan chiu-ch'eng
   hsun-shou ta-ch'en 欽命總
   管九城巡守大臣
ch'in-p'ai ta-ch'en 欽派大臣
ch'in-p'ai wang ta-ch'en 欽派
   王大臣
ch'in-wang 親王
Ching-ch'ung 景崇
Ch'ing 清
Ch'ing-ho-tao 清河道
Ch'ing-hui 慶惠 (Prince K'o-
   ch'in 克勤郡王)
Ch'ing-lien 慶廉
Ch'ing-ying 慶英
Chiu-ch'ing 九卿
"Chiu-ch'ing k'o-tao chien hsing
   Mu-lan su" 九卿科道諫
   幸木蘭疏
chiu-men tsung-t'ung 九門
   總統
Chou Chia-hsun 周家勳

Chou Tsu-p'ei 周祖培

"Ch'ou-i su" 籌夷疏

"Ch'ou-i su ch'i" 籌夷疏七

"Ch'ou-i su erh" 籌夷疏二

"Ch'ou-i su pa" 籌夷疏八

"Ch'ou-i su san" 籌夷疏三

"Ch'ou-i su wu" 籌夷疏五

ch'ou-pan fu-chü 籌辦撫局

"Ch'ou-yang su" 籌洋疏

Chu Hsueh-ch'in 朱學勤

Chu Tsun 朱嶟

Chu Wen-chiang 朱文江

chuan-pan t'ung-shang shih-wu 專辦通商事務

chuan-tzu 轉咨

chuan-yuan 專員

ch'uan-chien p'ao-li 船堅礮利

Ch'un, Prince 醇親王
(I-huan 奕譞)

Chung-hua 中華

Chung-kuo pan-li wai-kuo shih-wu chih ch'in-ch'ai ta-ch'en 中國辦理外國事務之欽差大臣

Chung-wai chih fen 中外之分

Ch'ung-hou 崇厚

Ch'ung-lun 崇綸

Ch'ung-wen Gate 崇文門

Chunliangcheng 軍糧城

chü-jen 舉人

Ch'üan-ch'ing 全慶

chün-chi ta-ch'en nien-piao 軍機大臣年表

chün-wang 郡王

E-lo-ssu-kuan 俄囉斯館

E-lo-ssu nan-kuan 俄囉斯南館

e-wai hsing-tsou 額外行走

Fa-hua Temple 法華寺

Fa-yuan Temple 法源寺

Fan Ch'eng-tien 范承典

fan-fu 藩服

Fang Ting-jui 方鼎銳

feng-ming ta-chiang-chün 奉命大將軍

fu-chü 撫局

fu-chü nan-ch'eng 撫局難成

fu-chü yu-lieh 撫局又裂

Fu-i-chü 撫夷局

fu-yü 撫馭

Gualgiya 瓜爾佳

Hai-kuo t'u-chih 海國圖志

hai-wai fan-feng 海外藩封

Hei-lung-chiang chiao-chieh
黑龍江交界

Heilungkiang 黑龍江

Heng-ch'i (Hangki) 恆祺

Heng-ch'i Lan Wei-wen teng
恆祺藍蔚文等

Heng-fu 恆福

Ho-ch'un 和春

Ho Ju-lin 何如霖

Ho Kuei-ch'ing 何桂清

Hong Kong 香港

Hsi-ling-a 西淩阿

Hsi pien-men, or Western Side
    Gate 西便門

Hsi-yang 西洋

Hsiao-chen 孝貞

Hsiao-ch'in 孝欽

Hsien-feng 咸豐

"Hsien-feng wu-wu wu-yueh
    shih-san-jih t'ing-ch'en hui-i
    lueh" 咸豐戊午五月十三
    日廷臣會議略

Hsien-liang Temple 賢良寺

hsin-chi shang 辛集上

Hsing-wen 興文

Hsiu-wen 秀雯

Hsueh Huan 薛煥

hsun-ch'ang kuan-wu 尋常館務

Hsun-fang-ch'u 巡防處

Hsun-fang wang ta-ch'en
巡防王大臣

hsun-shou ta-ch'en 巡守
大臣

Hsü Kuang-chin 徐廣縉

hsü-li 胥吏

Hsü Nai-p'u 許乃普

Hsü P'eng-shou 許彭壽

Hsü Yu-jen 徐有壬

Hu Lin-i 胡林翼

hu-shih chu-kuo 互市諸國

hu-sung 護送

Hua-sha-na (Hwashana)
花沙納

Hua-yen Temple 華嚴寺

Huang Chung-yü 黃仲畬

Huang Hui-lien 黃惠廉

Huang Tsung-han 黃宗漢

Hui, Prince 惠親王 (Mien-yü
)
綿愉

Hui-ch'in-wang teng 惠親
王等

hui-kuan 會館

Hui-lin 惠麟

Huo Heng-ch'i huo Lan Wei-wen
    teng 或恆祺或藍蔚
    文等

i 夷

i 役

I, Prince 怡親王 (Tsai-yuan
載垣)

I, Prince 怡親王 (Yun-hsiang
允祥)

i-cheng-wang 議政王

i-cheng wang ta-ch'en 議政王
大臣

I-chou 易州

i-chu 移駐

i-fen 夷氛

I-hsin, see Prince Kung

I-huan, see Prince Ch'un

i-kuan 驛館

I-li-pu 伊里布

I-liang (governor-general of
Kiangnan and Kiangsi) 怡良

I-liang, palace of 奕樑府

I-shan 奕山

I-tao, see Prince Yü

i-ti 夷狄

i-tse 乙卅

I-tsung, see Prince Tun

Jehol 熱河

Jen-ho 仁和

Jen Lien-sheng 任連升

jen-wu 人物

Jirgalang, see Chi-erh-ha-lang

ju hai-k'ou wu-shih 如海口
無事

Ju-i Gate 如意門

Jui-ch'ang (president of the
Court of Dependencies) 瑞常

Jui-ch'ang (Tartar general of
Hangchow) 瑞昌

Jui-lien 瑞廉

Jui-lin 瑞麟

Jui-ying Temple 瑞應寺

kai-chu 改駐

K'ang-hsi 康熙

K'ang-hsi san-shih-erh-nien
fu-chun 康熙三十二年
覆准

Kao-miao 高廟

keng-shen 庚申

Kiangnan 江南

Kirin 吉林

ko-kuo shih-wu 各國事務

ko-sheng fen-pieh tsou-tzu
chih li 各省分別奏咨
之例

ko-sheng t'ung-shang shan-hou
shih-i 各省通商善後
事宜

K'o-ch'in, Prince, see Ch'ing-hui

k'o-tao 科道

k'ou-t'ou (kowtow) 叩頭

Korchin 科爾沁

ku-ming 顧命

K'u-lun pan-shih ta-ch'en
庫倫辦事大臣

kuan 官

kuan-li 管理

kuan-mien chin-kao i-chien
官面謹告一件

Kuan-wen 官文

Kuang-hsü 光緒

Kuang-hua Temple 廣化寺

Kuang-tung ch'in-ch'ai ta-ch'en
廣東欽差大臣

K'uang Yuan 匡源

Kuei-liang (Kweiliang) 桂良

kuei-pai 跪拜

K'un-ming 昆明

K'un-yü 崑玉

Kung, Prince 恭親王 (I-hsin
奕訢)

kung-shih 供事

kung-shih 公使

Kunshan 崑山

kuo-chia ta-shih 國家大事

"Kuo-shih hsun-li chuan" 國史
循吏傳

kuo-shu 國書

Kuo Sung-tao 郭嵩燾

kuo-t'i 國體

kuo-wang 國王

K'uo-t'un-t'un 闊呑屯

Lan Wei-wen 藍蔚雯

Lan Wei-wen Huang Chung-yü
teng 藍蔚雯黃仲畬等

Lao-chün-t'ang 老君堂

Lao-chün-t'ang fang-wu 老君
堂房屋

Lao-chün-t'ang kuan 老君
堂館

Lao-chün-t'ang Mi-li-chien
shih-kuan 老君堂咪唎
喽使館

Lao-chün-t'ang ti-fang fang-wu
老君堂地方房屋

Lao-chün-t'ang ti-fang kuang-fang
老君堂地方官房

li 吏

li 理

li 禮

Li-fan-yuan 理藩院

Li Hsing-yuan 李星沅

Li Huan-wen 李煥文

Li Hung-chang 李鴻章

Li T'ung-wen 李同文
Lianghuai 兩淮
Liaoyang 遼陽
lieh-chuan 列傳
Lien Chao-lun 廉兆綸
Lien-ch'eng 連成
Lin-k'uei 麟魁
Lin Shou-t'u 林壽圖
liu-Ching hsun-fang wang ta-
    ch'en teng 留京巡防
    王大臣等
liu-Ching pan-shih wang ta-ch'en
    留京辦事王大臣
Liu-pu 六部
Lo-pin 樂斌
Lo Ping-chang 駱秉章
Lo Tun-yen 羅淳衍
Lu Chien-ying 陸建瀛
Lu-kou-ch'iao 蘆溝橋
Lu Ping-shu 陸秉樞
Lung Yuan-hsi 龍元僖

Macao 澳門
men-sheng 門生
Mi-kuo shih-ch'en 咪國使臣
Mi-yün 密雲
Miao-tao 廟島
Mien-sen 綿森
Mien-yü, see Prince Hui

ming-fa shang yü 明發上諭
Ming-shan 明善
Mu-chang-a 穆彰阿
Mu-yin 穆蔭

Nanking 南京
Nan-kuan 南館
nan-pei t'ung-shang ta-ch'en
    南北通商大臣
nan-yang ta-ch'en 南洋大臣
nan-yang t'ung-shang ta-ch'en
    南洋通商大臣
Ningpo 寧波
Nurhaci 努爾哈赤

Palikiao (Pa-li-ch'iao)
    八里橋
pan-fang wang ta-ch'en
    辦防王大臣
pan-li Chiang Che Yueh Min nei-
    chiang ko-k'ou t'ung-shang
    shih-wu ta-ch'en 辦理江
    浙粵閩內江各口通
    商事務大臣
pan-li chih ch'ang-jen 辦理
    之常人
pan-li fu-chü 辦理撫局
pan-li hai-k'ou t'ung-shang
    shih-i 辦理海口通商
    事宜

xl

pan-li ko-kuo shih-wu 辦理 各國事務

pan-li Niu-chuang T'ien-chin Teng-chou san-k'ou t'ung-shang shih-wu ta-ch'en 辦理牛莊天津登州三口通商事務大臣

pan-li t'ung-shang shih-wu ta-ch'en 辦理通商事務大臣

pan-li wu-k'ou chi wai-kuo shih-wu ta-ch'en 辦理五口及外國事務大臣

P'an Shih-ch'eng 潘仕成

P'an Tseng-ying 潘曾瑩

P'an Tsu-yin 潘祖蔭

pang-pan ta-ch'en 幫辦大臣

pao-chü 保舉

pao-ch'üan hsiang-li 保全鄉里

Pao-fang Lane 報房胡同

pao-i 保衣

Pao-yun 寶鋆

Paoting 保定

Pehtang 北塘

Pei-kuan 北館

Pei-ts'ang 北倉

pei-yang ta-ch'en 北洋大臣

pei-yang t'ung-shang ta-ch'en 北洋通商大臣

Peichihli (Pe-chi-li) 北直隸

Peiho 北河

Peking 北京

pen-chi 本紀

P'eng Yun-chang 彭蘊章

Pi Shu-t'ang 薛書堂

pi-t'ieh-shih 筆帖式

piao 表

Pien Pao-shu 卞寶書

pin-fu 賓服

ping 稟

P'ing 平

Po-chūn 柏葰

pu-yuan ta-ch'en nien-piao 部院大臣年表

Sai-shang-a 賽尚阿

San-hsing 三姓

san-kuei chiu-k'ou-li 三跪九叩禮

san-ssu-p'in Ching-t'ang hou-pu 三四品京堂候補

Seng-ko-lin-ch'in (Sang-ko-lin-sin) 僧格林沁

Shan-yuan Temple 善緣庵

shang 上

shang-shu 尚書

Shang-shu-fang 上書房

Shanghai 上海

Shektsing 石井
Shen Chao-lin 沈兆霖
Shen-chi-ying 神機營
Shen Kuei-fen 沈桂芬
shen-shih chung chih hsien-che
紳士中之賢者
Sheng-pao 勝保
Shih-ch'un 史醇
shih-hsueh 實學
Shih-mi Wei-liang (W. L. G. Smith)
士覓威良
Shih-san-t'iao 十三條
shou-ch'eng wang ta-ch'en
守城王大臣
shou-ch'eng wang ta-ch'en teng
守城王大臣等
Shu-ching 書經
shu-li 書吏
shu-yuan 書院
Shun-t'ien 順天
So-t'e na-mu to-pu-chi
索特納木多布濟
Soochow 蘇州
ssu-yuan 司員
Su, Prince 蕭親王
su-la 蘇拉
Su-shun 蕭順
Su T'ing-k'uei 蘇廷魁

sui 歲
Sun Chih 孫治
Sung Chin 宋晉
Süanhwa 宣化
ta-ch'ih 劄飭
ta-hsueh-shih nien-piao
大學士年表
Taku 大沽
T'an T'ing-hsiang 譚廷襄
t'ang-kuan 堂官
Tanyang 丹陽
Tao-kuang 道光
Te-ch'un 德椿
Te-hsiang 德祥
Te-sheng Gate 德勝門
teng 等
Ti-an Gate 地安門
t'i-chih 體制
T'ieh-ch'ien-chü 鐵錢局
T'ieh Ying-p'u 鐵應溥
T'ien-an Gate 天安門
t'ien-ch'ao ting-chih
天朝定制
T'ien-ning Temple 天寧寺
Tientsin 天津
Ting, Prince 定郡王 (Tsai-ch'üan 載銓)
t'ing-chi 廷寄

Tinghai 定海

tsa-chi 雜記

"Tsai-chien hsun-hsing Mu-lan su"

再諫巡幸木蘭疏

Tsai-ch'üan, see Prince Ting

"Tsai-lun i-wu su" 再論夷

務疏

Tsai-yuan, see Prince I

Ts'ai Hsieh 蔡燮

tsan-hsiang cheng-wu ta-ch'en

贊襄政務大臣

Ts'ang-chou 滄州

Ts'ao Yü-ying 曹疏英

Tseng Hsieh-chün 曾協均

Tseng Kuo-fan 曾國藩

Tso Tsung-t'ang 左宗棠

tso-yu ch'in-wang ju Tuan-hua

teng 左右親王如端

華等

tsou erh pu-tzu 奏而不咨

tsou-i 奏議

Tsung-li ko-kuo shih-wu ya-men

總理各國事務衙門

tsung-li ko-kuo shih-wu ya-men

pang-pan ta-ch'en 總理各

國事務衙門幫辦大臣

Tsung-li ko-kuo t'ung-shang shih-

wu ya-men 總理各國通

商事務衙門

tsung-li wai-kuo t'ung-shang

shih-i ta-ch'en 總理外國

通商事宜大臣

tsung-li wu-k'ou ta-ch'en

總理五口大臣

Tsungli Yamen 總理衙門

"Tsung-li ya-men hui-tien ti-kao"

總理衙門會典底稿

tsung-pan 總辦

Tsung-shu 總署

tsung-shui-wu-ssu 總稅

務司

tsung-t'ung hsun-shou chiu-men

總統巡守九門

tsung-t'ung hsun-shou ta-ch'en

總統巡守大臣

Tu Ch'iao 杜翻

Tu Han 杜翰

Tu Lai-hsi 杜來錫

Tu Shou-t'ien 杜受田

Tuan Ch'eng-shih 段承實

Tuan-hua, see Prince Cheng

t'uan-fang 團防

T'uan-fang-ch'u 團防處

t'uan-lien 團練

Tun, Prince 憻郡王，憻親王
(I-tsung 奕誴)

Tung-ch'ang-an Gate 東長
安門

Tung-ch'eng 東城

Tung-chih Gate 東直門

Tung Hsun 董恂

Tung-t'ang-tzu Lane 東堂
子胡同

T'ung-chih 同治

T'ung-chou 通州

t'ung-shang 通商

t'ung-shang shih-wu 通商
事務

T'ung-shang ya-men 通商
衙門

T'ung-wen-kuan 同文館

tzu-t'u chen-hsing 自圖振興

Wai-ch'eng 外土城

wai-kuo shih-wu 外國事務

Wai-wu-pu 外務部

Wan Ch'ing-li 萬青黎

Wan-shou Temple 萬壽寺

Wang Cheng 王拯

Wang Chin-jung 王金鎔

Wang-hea (Wang-hsia, Wanghia)
望厦

wang i-hsia chih k'o-tao
王以下之科道

Wang K'ai-yun 王闓運

Wang Mao-yin 王茂蔭

wang ta-ch'en 王大臣

wang ta-ch'en teng 王大臣等

wang teng 王等

Wang Yu-ling 王有齡

wei-shu chu-shih 委署主事

wei-yuan 委員

Wei Yuan 魏源

Wen-an 文安

Wen-ch'ien 文謙

Wen-ch'ing 文慶

Wen-hsiang 文祥

Wen-lien 文廉

Wen-tsung 文宗

Wen-yü 文煜

Weng T'ung-shu 翁同書

Whampoa (Huang-pu) 黃埔

wo-hsuan ch'i-yun chih kung
斡旋氣運之功

Wo-jen 倭仁

Wu Chien-chang 吳健彰

Wu Ch'ung-yueh 伍崇曜

Wu-erh-kun-t'ai 烏爾棍泰

Wu Hsü 吳煦

wu-k'ou ch'in-ch'ai ta-ch'en
五口欽差大臣

Wusih 無錫

Yang Fang 楊坊
Yang-ts'un 楊村
yang-wu 洋務
yeh-lang tzu-ta 夜郎自大
Yeh Ming-ch'en 葉名琛
Yen Ching-ming 閻敬銘
Yen-shu 延煦
Yin Chao-yung 殷兆鏞
"Yin Chao-yung ch'ing pa T'ien-
  chin fu-i yuan-tsou" 殷兆鏞
  請罷天津撫議原奏
Yin Keng-yun 尹耕雲
yin-yang chan-hou 陰陽占候
Yin Yen-ho 尹彥錄
Ying-hsiang 英祥

Ying-hsiu 英秀
Ying-kuei 英桂
Yuan Chia-san 袁甲三
yuan-pan chih jen 原辦之人
Yuan-p'ing 宛平
Yun-hsiang, see Prince I
Yung-cheng 雍正
Yü, Prince 豫親王 (I-tao 義
  道)
Yü chün-chi ta-ch'en teng
  諭軍機大臣等
yü Hui-ch'in-wang teng t'ung-k'an
  與惠親王等同看
Yü Nei-ko 諭內閣
"Yü ta-ch'en Su-shun shu"
  與大臣肅順書